The Making of an Economic Vision

John Paul II's
On Social Concern

Oliver F. Williams, C.S.C.
and John W. Houck
Editors

UNIVERSITY
PRESS OF
AMERICA

Lanham • New York • London

Copyright © 1991 by

University Press of America®, Inc.
4720 Boston Way
Lanham, Maryland 20706

3 Henrietta Street
London WC2E 8LU England

Co-published by arrangement with the
Notre Dame Center for Ethics and Religious Values in Business

Library of Congress Cataloging-in-Publication Data

Williams, Oliver F.
The making of an economic vision : John Paul II's On social
concern / Oliver F. Williams and John W. Houck, editors.
p.   cm.
"Co-published by arrangement with the Notre Dame Center
for Ethics and Religious Values in Business"—T.p. verso.
Includes bibliographical references.
1. Economics—Religious aspects—Catholic
Church—Congresses.
2. Catholic Church. Pope (1978- : John Paul II).—Sollicitudo rei
socialis—Congresses.   3. Sociology, Christian (Catholic)—
Congresses.   4. Church and social problems—Catholic
Church—Congresses.   5. Catholic Church—Doctrines—
Congresses.   I. Houck, John W.   II. Notre Dame Center
for Ethics and Religious Values in Business.   III. Title.
BX1795.E27W54   1991   261.8'5—dc20   91-477 CIP

ISBN 0–8191–8252–4 (cloth : alk. paper)
ISBN 0–8191–8253–2 (pbk. : alk. paper)

The paper used in this publication meets the minimum requirements of
American National Standard for Information Sciences—Permanence
of Paper for Printed Library Materials, ANSI Z39.48–1984.

To our students—
over several decades.

Solidarity helps us to see the "other"—whether a *person, people or nation*—not just as some kind of instrument, with a work capacity and physical strength to be exploited at low cost and then discarded when no longer useful, but as our "neighbour", a "helper" (cf. *Gen.* 2:18-20), to be made a sharer, on a par with ourselves, in the banquet of life to which all are equally invited by God.

John Paul II

Contents

Preface

John Paul takes a grim view of the last two decades, noting a widening gap between rich and poor nations and concluding that "hopes for development," which in the 1960s seemed "so lively, today appear very far from being realized." He does not see some positive developments, including greater concern for the environment and human rights.

The New York Times, February 20, 1988.

Preferential protection must go to the point of greatest vulnerability—to the poor whose dignity is most under assault in the absence of these protective measures. This "love of preference for the poor" will, in John Paul II's view, save the industrialized "North" from a "superdevelopment" taken at the expense of the "underdevelopment" that characterizes the poverty-burdened "South." A preference for the poor will not only rescue the poor from poverty, it will save the "first" and "second" worlds from themselves.

America, April 30, 1988.

The encyclical elaborated on themes that the American bishops have raised in their pastoral letters, condemning nuclear warfare and calling for a more equitable distribution of U.S. economic resources. The pope urged all people, not just Christians, to work for reforms that would seriously tackle the plight of the under-privileged.

The Washington Post, February 20, 1988.

A close reading of *The Social Concern of the Church* turns up criticisms of single-party states, of bureaucratic control of economies, and of the stultifying effects of illiteracy, discrimination, and exploitation—in other words, descriptions of Eastern Europe and a host of developing nations in Africa, Latin America, and Central America. In the pope's analysis the brightest future of the third world lies in building institutions and practices analogous to those of liberal democracy, including limited government, individual rights, participatory political processes, and systems that foster individual economic initiatives.

Commonweal, March 11, 1988.

How do we realize economic justice in our global society? What is economic justice? Are materialism, consumerism, and capitalism a threat or a promise to a peaceful earth? Commentators offer various interpretations of the hallmarks of our time: the Japanese phenomenon, Thatcherism, the European Economic Community, Perestroika, Reaganomics, and the Third World debt watch.

There is one voice that continues to offer a prophetic challenge both to Marxist collectivism and capitalism. Decribed by one noted Protestant theologian as ''the most powerful leader in the world,'' Pope John Paul II has authored two documents that may have much to say to our times: *On Human Work (Laborem Exercens)* and *On Social Concern (Sollicitudo Rei Socialis)*. Is the religious social teaching in these documents in such contrast to the prevailing wisdom of political economy that it might properly be called countercultural? Does this teaching offer a new vision, a strikingly different way of interpreting economic events?

Is it possible to advocate successfully an alternate vision that challenges unexamined consumerism? How realistic are the Church documents on economics and business, particularly the recent teaching of the Catholic Church?

To address these and many other issues, the Notre Dame Center for Ethics and Religious Values in Business convened a symposium in April 1989 on the recent teaching of the Catholic Church on economic ethics, assembling business executives, labor leaders and scholars at the University of Notre Dame. They included:

Ernest J. Bartell, C.S.C., executive director, Helen Kellogg Institute for International Studies, University of Notre Dame; Robert Benne, professor of philosophy and religion, Roanoke College, Virginia; Richard T. De George, professor of philosophy, University of Kansas; Teresa Ghilarducci, professor of economics, University of Notre Dame; Denis Goulet, O'Neill professor of education for justice, University of Notre Dame; Leslie Griffin, professor of theology, University of Notre Dame; J. Bryan Hehir, counselor for social policy, U.S. Catholic Conference, Washington, D.C.; John Langan, S.J., professor of Christian ethics, Woodstock Theological Center, Georgetown University; Dennis P. McCann, professor of religious studies, DePaul University; Michael Novak, senior scholar, American Enterprise Institute, Washington, D.C.; James E. Post, professor of management and public policy, Boston University; Ricardo

Ramirez, C.S.B., bishop of Las Cruces, New Mexico; S. Prakash Sethi, professor of business policy, Baruch College, New York; Paul Steidlmeier, professor of management, State University of New York; Lee A. Tavis, C.R. Smith professor of finance, University of Notre Dame; Theodore R. Weber, professor of theology, Emory University; Preston Williams, professor of theology and contemporary change, Harvard Divinity School; J. Philip Wogaman, professor of Christian social ethics, Wesley Theological Seminary, Washington, D.C.; and John Howard Yoder, professor of theology, University of Notre Dame.

. . . . .

The Center for Ethics and Religious Values in Business seeks to build bridges among business, business studies and the humanities. Its programs are designed to strengthen the Judeo-Christian ethical foundations in business and public policy decisions by fostering dialogue between academic and corporate leaders, and by research and publications. The Center is under the co-directorship of Oliver F. Williams, C.S.C. (theology), associate provost, and John W. Houck (business), professor of management, College of Business Administration.

In 1978 the Center published *Full Value: Cases in Christian Business Ethics,* which was the inaugural volume of Harper & Row's Experience and Reflection Series. Michael Novak commented that the book ". . . quite successfully juxtaposes the power of the Christian story, in its biblical immediacy, to concrete problems Christians in the world of business are likely to meet." James M. Gustafson wrote about *Full Value:* "Religious traditions provide, as these writers observe, a story, for example the Christian story, which informs our moral outlook, creates our moral vision, sustains our moral loyalties, and nurtures our moral character."

In 1980 the Center hosted a national symposium, *The Judeo-Christian Vision and the Modern Business Corporation. The Los Angeles Times* contrasted ". . . the competitive success-oriented style necessary for corporate promotion with the traditional Christian view of the virtuous person." *The New York* Times reported ". . . there would be no facile resolution to the conflict between the values of a just society and the sharply opposing values of successful corporations." Speakers at the symposium were:

John C. Bennett, Claremont School of Theology, and former president, Union Theological Seminary, New York; Catherine B. Cleary, director, AT&T, General Motors Corporation, Kraft Inc. and Northwestern Mutual Life Insurance, and former chair and chief executive officer, First Wisconsin Trust Company, Milwaukee; Richard Eells, director, Center for the Study of the Corporation, Columbia University; Denis Goulet, O'Neill professor of education for justice, University of Notre Dame; James M. Gustafson, university professor, University of Chicago Divinity School; Kenneth P. Jameson, professor of economics, University of Notre Dame; Elmer Johnson, senior partner, Kirkland and Ellis, Chicago; Burton M. Leiser, professor of philosophy, Drake University; Enda McDonagh, Huisking professor in theological ethics, University of Notre Dame; Michael Novak, resident scholar, American Enterprise Institute, Washington, D.C.; James M. Schall, S.J., Department of Government, Georgetown University, and the Gregorian, Rome; S. Prakash Sethi, director, Center for Research in Business and Social Policy, University of Texas-Dallas; William P. Sexton, chair, Department of Management, University of Notre Dame; Edward R. Trubac, professor of finance and business economics, University of Notre Dame; Thomas Werge, chair, Department of English, University of Notre Dame; Charles Wilber, chair, Department of Economics, University of Notre Dame; and John Howard Yoder, professor of theology, University of Notre Dame.

A second symposium, *Co-creation: A Religious Vision of Corporate Power*, followed in 1982, focusing on Pope John Paul II's encyclical letter, *Laborem Exercens. Newsweek* characterized the conference as a ''free marketplace of ideas,'' exploring a religious vision of corporate power. Contributors to this conference included:

Ernest J. Bartell, C.S.C., executive director, Helen Kellogg Institute for International Studies, University of Notre Dame; Thomas P. Carney, president, Metatech Corporation; John B. Caron, president, Caron International; Mary Cunningham, vice president, Joseph E. Seagram & Sons; Thomas R. Donahue, secretary-treasurer, AFL-CIO; Mark J. Fitzgerald, C.S.C., professor of economics, University of Notre Dame; Denis Goulet, O'Neill professor of education for justice, University of Notre Dame; Stanley Hauerwas, Department of Theology, University of Notre Dame; J. Bryan Hehir, director, Social Development and World Peace, U.S. Catholic Conference, Washington, D.C.; David Hollenbach, S.J., Weston School of Theology; Elmer W. Johnson, senior partner, Kirkland and Ellis, Chicago; Barry P. Keating, professor of finance and business economics, University of Notre Dame; Andrea Lea, I.H.M., dean, Continuing Education, Marygrove College, Detroit; George C. Lodge, Harvard Business School; Bernard Marchland, Department of Philosophy, Ohio Wesleyan University; Amata Miller, I.H.M., financial vice president, I.H.M. Sisters of Monroe, Michigan; Michael Novak, resident scholar, American Enterprise Institute, Washington, D.C.; and Joseph A. Pichler, executive vice president, Dillon Companies, Inc.

In 1983 the Center assisted the U.S. Bishops' Committee charged to write a pastoral letter on the economy by convening a three-day symposium, *Catholic Social Teaching and the American Economy*. *The Los Angeles Times* observed: "About one-third of the major speakers represented conservative viewpoints, the remainder voiced moderate-to-liberal positions." *The New York Times* reported that ". . . contentiousness is commonplace here at Notre Dame. . . . And when dozens of business leaders, theologians and academics lined up against each other at the university this week, the debate over the economy was fought as hard as any gridiron encounter." More than 250 people attended the meeting, including the five bishops who were to draft the letter. Joining in the drafting of the working papers, and providing a religious commentary and perspectives on the theme of the symposium, were:

Gar Alperovitz, co-director, National Center for Economic Alternatives; Ernest J. Bartell, C.S.C., executive director, Helen Kellogg Institute for International Studies, University of Notre Dame; C. Fred Bergsten, director, Institute for International Economics; Daniel Rush Finn, Department of Theology and Department of Economics and Business Administration, St. John's University, Collegeville, Minnesota; Joe Holland, co-director, Center for Concern; David Hollenbach, S.J., Weston School of Theology; Elmer W. Johnson, chief counsel and group executive-public affairs, General Motors Corporation; F. Ray Marshall, Lyndon B. Johnson School of Public Affairs, University of Texas at Austin; Dennis P. McCann, professor of religious studies, DePaul University; Michael Novak, resident scholar, American Enterprise Institute; Graciela Olivarez, attorney-at-law, Albuquerque, New Mexico; Rudy Oswald, research director,

AFL-CIO; Peter G. Peterson, chair, Lehman Brothers Kuhn Loeb Inc.; Joseph A. Pichler, president, Dillon Companies, Inc.; Marina von Neumann Whitman, vice president and chief economist, General Motors Corporation; and Oliver F. Williams, C.S.C., University of Notre Dame.

The Common Good and U.S. Capitalism was the theme of a 1986 symposium to explore the possible retrieval of the notion of "the common good" in philosophical-economic discourse. Ralph McInerny saw the concept of the common good as needed "to draw attention to flaws in our economic thinking and policies as well as to make positive suggestions that will be manifestly in line with our tradition." *New Catholic World* wrote: ". . . a collection of eighteen essays . . . by social scientists, theologians, philosophers, business faculty, and television producers. The essays represent different points of view from both theoretical and practical perspectives. . . . It would be a valuable contribution to Catholic social teaching if all it did was to make people aware that a concept of the common good once was alive and well. It does much more than that." Contributors to the conference included:

Gar Alperovitz, co-director, National Center for Economic Alternatives; Ernest J. Bartell, C.S.C., executive director, Helen Kellogg Institute for International Studies, University of Notre Dame; Bette Jean Bullert, independent television producer; Gerald F. Cavanagh, S.J., Department of Management, University of Detroit; John J. Collins, professor of theology, University of Notre Dame; John W. Cooper, dean, Academic Affairs, Bridgewater College, Virginia; William J. Cunningham, research economist, AFL-CIO; Charles E. Curran, Department of Theological Ethics, Catholic University of America; Richard T. De George, university distinguished professor of philosophy, University of Kansas; Peter Mann, producer of television programs for the Diocese of Rockville Center, New York; Dennis P. McCann, professor of religious studies, DePaul University; Ralph McInerny, Grace professor of medieval studies, and director, Jacques Maritain Center, University of Notre Dame; Richard J. Neuhaus, director, The Center on Religion and Society, New York City; Michael Novak, resident scholar, American Enterprise Institute; David Vogel, Department of Business Administration, University of California–Berkeley; Charles C. West, Stephen Colwell professor of Christian ethics, Princeton Theological Seminary; Charles K. Wilber, professor of economics, University of Notre

Dame; and J. Philip Wogaman, professor of Christian social ethics, Wesley Theological Seminary, Washington, D.C.

The 1987 symposium focused on ethics and the investment industry. Much has been written in the eighties about the misdeeds of actors in the investment community; suggestions for legislative reform abound. Very little has been said about the ethical vision and institutional bonding that form the context for a humane capitalism. It is these themes, as well as the appropriate market and legal aspects, that were explored at Notre Dame. *America* said of *Ethics and the Investment Industry* that it ". . . will be an important reference for future participants in the international business community." The speakers and panelists were:

G. Robert Blakey, O'Neill professor, University of Notre Dame Law School; George P. Brockway, former chair, W.W. Norton and Company; Gerald F. Cavanagh, S.J., professor of management, University of Detroit; Richard T. De George, university distinguished professor of philosophy, University of Kansas; Edward J. Epstein, contributing editor, Manhattan, Inc.; Kirk O. Hanson, Stanford Graduate School of Business; Gregg Jarrell, former chief economist of the Securities and Exchange Commission; Burton M. Leiser, Edward J. Mortola professor of philosophy, Pace University; Dennis P. McCann, professor of religious studies, DePaul University; Patricia A. O'Hara, professor of law, University of Notre Dame Law School; John J. Phelan, Jr., chair of the boards of the New York Stock Exchange and the New York Futures Exchange; Frank K. Reilly, Bernard J. Hank professor of business administration, University of Notre Dame; Donald W. Shriver, Jr., president, New York Union Theology Seminary; Paul E. Tierney, Jr., partner, Gollust, Tierney and Oliver; Alfred C. Morley, president and chief executive officer, The Institute of Chartered Financial Analysts, and president, Financial Analysts Federation; Clarence C. Walton, Charles Lamont Post distinguished professor of ethics and professions, American College, and former president, Catholic University; John G. Weithers, chair of the board, Midwest Stock Exchange; Robert Wilmouth, president and chief executive officer, National Futures Association, and chair, LaSalle National Bank, Chicago.

. . . . .

Publications by the Center include:

The Making of an Economic Vision
Full Value: Cases in Christian Business Ethics
Matter of Dignity: Inquiries into the Humanization of Work
The Judeo-Christian Vision and the Modern Corporation
Co-Creation and Capitalism: John Paul II's "Laborem Exercens"
Catholic Social Teaching and the U.S. Economy
The Common Good and U.S. Capitalism
The Apartheid Crisis
Ethics and the Investment Industry

Articles have appeared in *California Management Review, Business Horizons, Theology Today, Business and Society Review, Horizons, Journal of Business Ethics* and *The Harvard Business Review.*

For the conference, *The Recent Social Teachings of the Catholic Church: the Making of an Economic Counterculture?* and the publication of this volume, we are most grateful for the encouragement and financial support provided by the John M. Olin Foundation, the General Electric Foundation and the Hershey Foods Corporation.

We wish to recognize the competence and enthusiasm of our executive coordinator, Madeline Day—an editor's editor—for preparing this volume for publication as well as for the planning of the symposium.

Oliver F. Williams, C.S.C.
John W. Houck
Co-directors
Center for Ethics and Religious Values in Business
University of Notre Dame
Notre Dame, IN 46556.

Part I

The Economic Vision— The Global Perspective

. . . to lead people to respond, with the support also of rational reflection and of the human sciences, to their vocation as responsible builders of earthly society.

On Social Concern, Par. 1

The twin elements of a comprehensive development ethic, namely a regard for social justice and a call for ecological responsibility are evoked . . .

Denis Goulet

. . . the stronger and richer nations must have a sense of moral *responsibility* for the other nations, so that a *real international system* may be established which will rest on the foundation of the *equality* of all peoples and on the necessary respect for their legitimate differences. The economically weaker countries, or those still at subsistence level, must be enabled, with the assistance of other peoples and of the international community, to make a contribution of their own to the common good with their treasures of *humanity* and *culture*, which otherwise would be lost for ever.

On Social Concern, Par. 39

The Pope's aim is not only to seize the moral initiative on labor and economic issues from Marx, but also to replace the Marxist perspective with a Christian one.

Richard T. De George

1

. . . I must repeat that whatever affects the dignity of individuals and peoples, such as authentic development, cannot be reduced to a "technical" problem. If reduced in this way, development would be emptied of its true content, and this would be an act of *betrayal* of the individuals and peoples whom development is meant to serve.

On Social Concern, Par. 41

A "problem" always presents us with both *facts* and *values*. If factual expertise is required to deal with the factual side, a corresponding clarity about values is needed to define what is ultimately at stake. Religious bodies, when true to their own nature, have much to say about values. They are vocationally committed to clarifying the relationship between the particular values of human existence and what they consider to be the source of all good.

J. Philip Wogaman

Surmounting every type of imperialism and determination to preserve their own hegemony, the stronger and richer nations must have a sense of moral responsibility for other nations, so that a real international system may be established which will rest on the foundation of the equality of all peoples and on the necessary respect for their legitimate differences.

On Social Concern, Par. 39

The reach of the papal proposal is often beyond what those who work with the details of world politics feel is possible in the short to middle range. The papal role, however, may be precisely to maintain this tension: providing a vision which is empirically relevant, but ethically stretching for those seeking to shape the system.

J. Bryan Hehir

One

On Authentic Social Development: Concepts, Content, and Criteria

Denis Goulet

Development has served as the governing myth of the post-World War II age. In the postwar years development emerged as a national goal, both as a vision of a better life and as a process of deliberate political and economic change to attain it. Initially, it was generally assumed that rapid national development could be made self-sustaining through a massive infusion of financial and technological resources, allied to rational planning of targeted investments, and the transfer of specialized institutional models from rich to poor countries. Experience quickly revealed, however, that development also depends critically on a society's own efforts to change its policies, social structure, institutions, and values. External resource inputs might help to bring about change but it was soon recognized that developmental assistance follows its own dynamics and is far more related to the interests of the countries extending aid than it is to the objective development needs of the beneficiary nations.

Not surprisingly, therefore, the meanings of "development" remain as diverse today as the political, economic, and social conditions of life found in different urban and rural settings around the world. To people whose physical circumstances are vastly more comfortable than those of their families a generation or two ago, development may stand for access to a more diversified basket of consumer goods. But to those who live in extreme poverty very much like that of their forebears at the turn of the century—and over two billion people continue to live such lives—development is still the hope of obtaining a secure supply of food and drinking water, adequate shelter, and access to rudimentary health services. Yet even very poor people also

3

desire the varied consumer goods that have become everyday expectations elsewhere.

Nevertheless, some people, whether extremely poor or relatively well off, do not define development primarily in material terms. Brazil's revolutionary educator Paulo Freire considers development to be the ability of powerless masses to shape their own destiny as active subjects, and not merely as passive objects. Particularly in Latin America, theorists of social change speak less of development than of liberation, arguing that political power must first be transferred from the landowning elites to the poor masses before meaningful change can take place.

Most technical problem-solvers, in turn, view development as the "modern" way of doing things. Modern settlement patterns have concentrated people, jobs, services, and amenities in cities—thereby linking development to urbanization in the perceptions of countless millions of people. And because the modern mode of creating wealth requires the use of technology to raise productivity, industrialization has become synonymous with development. Moreover, since the West industrialized first, industrialization is often assumed to entail the Westernization of attitudes and values.

Many observers in developing countries, however, now consider such notions as insulting to their civilizations. In the words of one South African poet, European man "walked into Africa like a one-eyed giant"—with science, but without wisdom and certainly without sensitivity to the cultures that earlier flourished there. Most developing countries today place great value on the preservation of national cultural identity in the face of imported values and practices, and on the pursuit of development in a self-reliant manner. Self-reliance does not necessarily mean self-sufficiency, nor does it rule out cooperation with outsiders. It does mean, however, that basic decisions about the speed and direction of change must come from within poor nations and in accord with their traditions—not in blind imitation of the practices and policies of Western or Eastern industrial nations.

Consequently, a growing chorus of voices now condemns development as the instrument used by rapacious industrialized Western nations to destroy the cultures and the autonomy of societies throughout Africa, Asia and Latin America. For many, development has become a pejorative word.

According to the noted French agronomist, René Dumont, the performance of the last forty years has been a dangerous epidemic of mis-development.[1] In Africa, he argues, development has simply not oc-curred. And in Latin America much new wealth has been created, ranging from sophisticated nuclear and electronic industries to vast skyscraper cities, but growth has been won at the price of massive pol-lution, urban congestion, and monumental resource waste. What is worse, the majority of the continent's population has not benefited from this new wealth. Dumont[2] concludes that misdevelopment, or the mismanagement of resources in the socialist and capitalist worlds, is the main cause of world hunger. And it afflicts ''developed'' coun-tries as severely as it does Third World nations.

Other writers strike the same theme, *viz.,* that economic growth is often inequitable, destructive, and worsens the lot of poor people. Among these are the late Swiss anthropologist Roy Preiswerk, the Afri-can civil servant Albert Tévoèdjré and the Haitian geographer George Anglade.[3] The most categorical attack, however, comes from the pen of those who totally repudiate development, both as concept and as project. Prominent among these are the French economist Serge La-touche[4] and the Montreal-based Monchanin Intercultural Centre; both promote the thesis that development must be rejected because it de-stroys native political, judicial, and economic institutions, while de-molishing precious symbolic meaning systems.[5] Similarly, the Cultural Survival Movement, headquartered at Harvard University, has strug-gled since its creation in 1972 to prevent ''development'' from de-stroying indigenous peoples and their cultures. Its founder, anthropol-ogist David Maybury-Lewis, considers that ''violence done to indigenous peoples is largely based on prejudices and discrimination that must be exposed and combated. These prejudices are backed up by widely held misconceptions, which presume that traditional soci-eties are inherently obstacles to development or that the recognition of their rights would subvert the nation state. Our research shows that this is untrue.''[6]

Notwithstanding the attacks made upon it, however, development continues to be the dominant concept shaping social policy through-out the world. Indeed, most national governments and international financial agencies still take development to mean maximum economic growth and a concerted drive toward industrialization and mass con-sumption. The success stories praised worldwide are Korea and Tai-wan, twin paragons of capital-intensive and high-technology economic growth, allied to competitive international trading.[7] Development reports remain discreetly silent, however, as to the costs in political repression attendant upon these economic successes![8]

Conventional growth models still enjoy a practical hegemony in macro arenas of policy-setting. Nevertheless, a new development paradigm is now in gestation in micro, or small-scale, arenas of strategy innovation. A two-fold search—conceptual and practical—is on for what John Paul II, in his encyclical letter *On Social Concern*, calls "an authentic development of man and society which would respect and promote all the dimensions of the human person."[9]

This encyclical takes its place in a growing normative stream of development writings which center attention on ethical value questions posed by development decisions and actions.[10] Until recent years such normative writings were dismissed as the work of a minority of writers who remained largely "outsiders" to the self-confident universe of development experts. Certain dissident authors, notably Mahatma Gandhi,[11] worked as utopian social activists, preaching and experimenting the merits of small-scale village development, the slow progression from artisanal to technological skills, and simple modes of living so that people might free themselves from the thraldom of escalating desires for more material goods. Other critics such as L.J. Lebret and Erich Fromm,[12] after systematically evaluating competing visions of the good life and the just society, opted for a model of development which promotes community, spiritual fulfillment, and the enhancement of creative freedom over mere material abundance, technological prowess, or functionally efficient institutions. Others still, notably E.F. Schumacher,[13] pleaded for an economics which gives primacy to people, and for soft technologies that protect local cultures and environments. Finally, alternative paradigm-setters like Ivan Illich and J. P. Naik[14] called for the recapture by ordinary people of the monopoly on problem-solving appropriated, under the banner of modernization, by professional specialists of all kinds: educational, medical, and economic.

The value themes and action priorities advocated by these dissident strategists have now made their way into the general lexicon of mainstream development planners and policy-makers. Participation of non-elites, self-reliant local initiatives, the primacy of basic needs, a regard for ecological sanity, equity in the distribution of the fruits of economic growth, and respect for traditional cultures—these now have become indispensable agenda items in all development debates. Even large impersonal financial organizations which promote structural adjustment—the "rationalization" of finances around market forces, the orientation of production toward export trade, and the privatization of enterprises—look for ways to put what they call a "human face" onto their policy.[15] Although development thinking and action is dominated still by a concern with the adjustment crisis in the Third World,[16] macroplanners and policy analysts nonetheless search for means of strengthening the poor[17] and for social policies which work in the fight against poverty.[18] In typical fashion, a recent World Bank technical report on public finance expresses its concern lest "careless fiscal austerity . . . lead to prolonged recession . . . and can place a disproportionately heavy burden on the poor. For this reason the structural aspects of public finance policy—how spending is allocated and revenue raised—matters as much as the overall macroeconomic balance."[19]

The Papal Experience

John Paul's encyclical takes its place in the body of normative writings on development but the methodology it employs differs sharply from that found in other works located in this stream. *On Social Concern* is evidently not an exercise in social analysis but a sermon, an "*appeal to conscience*."[20] The Catholic Church aims at promoting the moral and spiritual welfare of humankind; consequently, when it speaks of development, it does so "to lead people to respond, with the support also of rational reflection and of the human sciences, to their vocation as responsible builders of earthly society."[21] The papal document, accordingly, draws the value content it places on "authentic development" from the religious doctrine of the Church on the purposes of human life and history as revealed in its scriptures and traditions.

Quite apart from its purely spiritual functions, the Church plays four distinct, albeit interrelated, roles in society. Its first role consists of raising high certain banners: truth, justice, solidarity, human rights, and peace. The Church keeps reminding humanity that these values are more important than economic efficiency, political realism, or technical virtuosity. A second task consists of contributing its own distinctive analysis and prescriptions to the larger process of policy formation in a pluralistic society. Like other voluntary associations, the Church speaks as a body of citizens with a special view of what social policy ought to be. This it does in domains as diverse as tax policy (to plead for equity therein) or investment and housing policy. The third "secular" function of churches is to engage in local problem-solving actions. Over centuries, the Church has engaged in works which institutionalize what it terms "corporal works of mercy"—feeding the hungry, healing the sick, consoling prisoners, educating the ignorant, and so on. The fourth and final function of religious organizations in society consists of practicing solidarity with those who are persecuted or victimized by natural or humanly caused disasters. Early Christian churches in scattered points of the Roman Empire took up collections to aid the impoverished local church in Jerusalem. Similarly, in our day, churches operate relief and developmental aid programs to assist groups in need throughout the world.

It is in the context of such a self-definition of its role in global and national societies that the Catholic Church deems itself as authorized to speak of development. This it does primarily in normative and prescriptive terms.

Nevertheless, the approach adopted by papal encyclicals, and particularly John Paul's document *On Social Concern*, differentiates it from other advocates of normative development, who derive their conclusions from quite different sources. Thus, Gandhi gets his theory and vision of a developed society from his experiments with truth, endless trial-and-error probes into new patterns of work, social organization, and living styles. Lebret, the national planner and strategist, derives his norms from a pluridisciplinary scientific study of economic and social reality, of resources and needs, of benefits and costs attaching to alternative policies. Dumont, Latouche and other radical critics of development obtain their values from a critique of mainstream development and its disastrous effects. All critical strategists have this trait in common; however, they search for ways to broaden a purely economic or technical analysis of development to make economics serve larger human needs. Alternatively, they draw out in explicit terms the ethical requirements of conducting economic analysis and prescription in a realistic and socially responsible mode.[22]

Beyond the criticism of mainstream paradigms of development and the advocacy of humane alternative models, however, one needs to ask what precise *value content* is to be given to authentic development? Representative answers given to this question comprise the burden of the pages which follow.

Components of Authentic Development

A week-long seminar on "Ethical Issues in Development," held in September 1986 at the Marga Institute in Colombo, Sri Lanka,[23] reached consensus that any adequate definition of development must include five dimensions:

- an economic component dealing with the creation of wealth and improved conditions of material life;
- a social ingredient measured as well-being in health, education, housing, and employment;
- a political dimension pointing to such values as human rights, political freedom, enfranchisement, and some form of democracy;
- a cultural element in recognition of the fact that cultures confer identity and self-worth to people; and
- a fifth register called the full-life paradigm, encompassing symbols and beliefs as to the ultimate meaning of life and of history.

Integral human development is all of these things, according to Marga.

An almost identical definition of authentic development had emerged some years earlier from a Latin American seminar held in Ottawa, Canada. For participants in that seminar, the definition of authentic development embraces four pairs of words: economic growth, distributional equity, participation/vulnerability, and transcendental values.[24] The two final sets of words require explanation. Participation is a decisive voice exercised by people directly affected by policy decisions, whereas vulnerability is the obverse side of the participation coin: poor people, regions, and nations must be rendered less vulnerable to decisions which produce external shocks upon them.[25] The reference to "transcendental values" raises a vital question: "Does man live by GNP alone?" As David Pollock explains:

Let us assume that a country's economic pie increases. Let us further assume that there is a heightened degree of equity in the way the fruits of that economic pie are distributed. Let us, finally, assume that decisions affecting production and consumption of the economic pie—internationally and nationally—involve the full participation of all affected parties. Is that the end of the matter? Does man live by GNP alone? Perhaps the latter has been the prevailing line of thought throughout the post-war period since, in the short-run, policy-makers must focus primarily upon the pressing issue of increased incomes for the masses; particularly for those below the poverty line. But, despite the obvious importance of such short-run objectives, we should also be asking ourselves other, more uplifting, questions. Should we not take advantage of our longer-term vision and ask what kind of person Latin America may wish to evolve by the end of this century. What are the transcendental values—cultural, ethical, artistic, religious, moral—that extend beyond the current workings of the purely economic and social system? How to appeal to youth, who so often seek nourishment in dreams, as well as in bread? What, in short should be the new face of the Latin American society in the future, and what human values should lie behind the new countenance.[26]

Human progress is not the fruit of some inevitable historical necessity: it is always the achievement of human wills struggling to overcome the determinisms they face from nature, from the social systems they have forged, and from their own technological and cultural artifacts. Progress or "development" takes place, therefore, when expanding freedoms find their expression in institutions, norms of exchange, patterns of social organization, educational efforts, relations of production, and political choices which enhance the human potential.

Because the human potential thrusts the human species forward into transcendence, no truncated model of humanism which neglects spiritual fulfillment or imprisons human destiny within the confines of an immanentist view of history is acceptable. Such a form of humanism closes the door to genuine transcendence and diminishes the stature of human beings.[27]

In the setting of development efforts, transcendence refers to the ability of all human beings to go beyond their own limitations and reach levels of achievement higher than those presently enjoyed. Champions of transcendence reject any mass-consumer model of development or any form of social utopia which unilaterally defines egalitarianism in reductionist terms of mere consumption or production.

On the contrary, the opening toward metahistorical transcendence is a requisite of the full blooming of developmental potentialities.

An explicit and detailed formulation of the requirements of authentic development has been made by Lebret. He is that rare development expert cited by name in the 1967 encyclical *On the Development of Peoples,* the text which is commemorated and amplified in the 1987 papal document *On Social Concern.* In the 1967 encyclical, Paul VI recalls what "an eminent specialist has very rightly and emphatically declared: 'We do not believe in separating the economic from the human, nor development from the civilizations in which it exists. What we hold important is man, each man and each group of men, and we even include the whole of humanity.' "[28] Lebret served as the major expert advisor to Paul VI in drafting *On the Development of Peoples.* Accordingly, to analyze the formal requirements of authentic development as he defines them is to find the key to understanding the normative vision put forth by the two papal authors, Paul VI and John Paul II.

Lebret defines development as "the series of transitions, for a given population and all the sub-population units which comprise it, from a less human to a more human phase of existence, at the speediest rhythm possible, at the lowest possible cost, while taking into account all the bonds of solidarity which exist (or ought to exist) amongst these populations and sub-population groups."[29]

It follows logically from this definition that the discipline of development is the study of how to achieve a more human economy.[30] The normative expressions "more human" and "less human" need to be understood in the light of a distinction Lebret considered vital: the difference between *plus avoir* ("to have more") and *plus être* ("to be more"). Any society, Lebret contends, is more human or developed not when men and women "have more," but when all its citizens are enabled to be more."[31] The main criterion of value is not the production or possession of goods, but the totality of qualitative human enrichment. Some material growth and quantitative increases doubtless are needed for genuine development, but not any kind of growth or increase at any price. The world as a whole will remain underdeveloped or will fall prey to an illusory antidevelopment so long as a small number of nations or privileged groups remain alienated in an abundance of luxury (facility) goods at the expense of the many who are deprived thereby of their essential (subsistence) goods. When such situations prevail, both rich and poor suffer from insufficient satisfaction of their "enhancement" needs.

The scope of Lebret's concept of integral development can be grasped by examining the attributes he attaches to it. If development is to be genuine, he asserts, it must be:

1) *Finalized.* It must serve the basic ends, that is, to build a human economy and to satisfy all human needs in an equitable order of urgency and importance.

2) *Coherent.* All major problem sectors must be attacked in coordinated fashion. Agriculture must not be sacrificed to industry, nor one segment of the population to another. (This injunction does not, however, rule out a strategy of deliberately unbalanced growth, provided it is pursued judiciously and constantly rectified.)

3) *Homogeneous.* Even when revolutionary innovations are introduced, these must respect the people's past history and their present capacities. No elitist imposition from above, in total rupture with a people's cultural heritage and absorptive capacity, is justified.

4) *Self-propelling.* Unless development heightens a society's capacity to direct itself autonomously, it is invalid. This demands a battle against dependency, parasitism, passivity, and inertia.

5) *Indivisible.* There is no genuine development unless all the people benefit from it, unless the common good is achieved. Privilege systems, excessive gaps between the city and the countryside, alienating divisions of labor, are all ruled out.

The policy implications of these attributes are as far-reaching as Lebret's analysis of development.[32]

Sound development policies ought to adopt as their first priority the production of essential necessities for all. A second priority is to produce goods and services which enhance the quality of life: amenities and comforts as well as esthetically, culturally and spiritually ennobling goods. Only in the final instance can one justify devoting any significant resources to the production of luxury goods. Luxuries undoubtedly have some value and contribute to civilization, if only because they reveal the glittering esthetic possibilities latent in human imagination and creativity. To allocate significant resources to the production of luxuries for a few beneficiaries, however, while the more fundamental needs of the masses remain unmet, represents a gross structural distortion which is at once irrational and immoral.[33]

The key moral element in Lebret's concept of development is solidarity, that perceptual and behavioral disposition which binds together the destinies of all persons, societies, and nations. Solidarity places on the "haves" a moral claim, a veritable duty in justice, to assure that the "have nots" of the world come to *have* that minimum supply of essential goods without which they cannot *be* fully human. If there exists some threshold point *below which* human beings cannot be integrally human or live a truly human life, there also exists a ceiling *above which* the pursuit of further possessions one desires to *have* interferes with the quality of one's *being*. In the words of the psychologist Erich Fromm, "affluent alienation" is no less dehumanizing than "impoverished alienation."[34] According to Lebret, it is the selfishness, avarice, and fear of the rich and powerful which undermine solidarity.[35] Many contemporary development writers blame the persistence of poverty on "a failure of political will" on the part of human societies to endow themselves with economic systems, social structures, and political institutions which could abolish massive underdevelopment. All acknowledge that sufficient material and technological resources to eliminate misery exist in the world. For Lebret, however, the major obstacle lies not in deficient *political* will, but in the *moral* blindness of the rich and the selfish defense of their privileges.[36] The Independent Commission on International Development Issues, chaired by Willy-Brandt, likewise bases its appeals to solidarity on an ethical, or moral, value. In its report on *North-South, a Program for Survival,* the Commissioners write that:

History has taught us that wars produce hunger, but we are less aware that mass poverty can lead to war or end in chaos. While hunger rules peace cannot prevail. He who wants to ban war must also ban mass poverty. Morally it makes no difference whether a human being is killed in war or is condemned to starve to death because of the indifference of others.

Mankind has never before had such ample technical and financial resources for coping with hunger and poverty. The immense task can be tackled once the necessary collective will is mobilized. What is necessary can be done, and must be done, in order to provide the conditions by which the poor can be saved from starvation as well as destructive confrontation.

Solidarity among men must go beyond national boundaries: we cannot allow it to be reduced to a meaningless phrase. International solidarity must stem both from strong mutual interests in cooperation *and* from compassion for the hungry."[37]

In no domain is solidarity more urgently needed than in ecology. Unless the human race extends its effective solidarity to the biosphere and to all life within it, it will itself perish. The ecological imperative is at once clear and cruel: nature must be saved or we humans will die. And the single greatest threat to nature—menacing irreversible destruction of its regenerative powers—comes from "development." This same "development" is also the culprit which perpetuates the underdevelopment of hundreds of millions of people. Therefore, the task of eliminating dehumanizing underdevelopment imposes upon itself the same urgency as the safeguard of nature. A comprehensive ethic of authentic development will, of necessity, look to the sustainability of economic growth and resource use as well as to the equitable distribution of its fruits. What Ignacy Sachs calls "eco-development" relies on an anthropological economics that simultaneously serve human needs and manage nature with wisdom.[38]

Ecology: On Seeing the Whole Picture

Ecology has become a household word now. There is illuminating symbolism here for, in its Greek etymology, "ecology" designates the science of the larger household, the total environment in which living organisms exist. Indeed, whenever it is faithful to its origins and inner spirit, ecology is holistic: it looks to the whole picture, the totality of relations. As a recently certified pluridisciplinary field of study, ecology embraces four distinct, interrelated subjects: environment, demography, resource systems, and technology. Its special contribution to human knowledge is to draw a coherent portrait of how these four realms interact in patterns of vital interdependence.

Ecological wisdom is the search for optimal modes and scales in which human populations may apply technology to resource use within their environments. Both as an intellectual discipline and as a practical concern, ecology *presupposes some philosophy of nature*. Traditional human wisdoms long ago parted ways, however, in their fundamental conceptions of nature and their views as to how human beings should relate to it. All wisdoms acknowledge humans to be part of nature and subject to its laws and constraints. The common destiny of all natural beings, humans included, is generation and corruption: they are born, grow, get old, and die. But certain world views, more than others, have elevated humans above their encompassing nature and assigned them a cosmic role of domination over that very nature of which they are a part. In the interrogatory words that aptly serve as the title of a recent publication in Sri Lanka, *Man in Nature, Guest or Engineer?*[39]

Nature and human liberty have, therefore, come to be perceived as opposing poles in a dichotomy. Are human animals *free* to treat nature as they would? Or must humans, like all other animals, submit to nature's laws or at least to its penalties? The paradox lies in this: that human beings are not physically compelled to respect nature but they need to do so if they are to survive and preserve the very existential ground they require to assert their freedom. Since this is so, there can be no ultimate or radical incompatibility between the demands of nature and the exigencies of human freedom, those of environmental sanity, of wise resource stewardship, and of technology. Theoretical and practical problems arise because ecologists, betraying their very identity, have not looked at the whole picture. Looking at the whole picture also enables one to transcend numerous other apparent antinomies, chief among them being the alleged contradiction between anthropocentric and cosmocentric views of the universe.

Robert Vachon, a philosopher of intercultural dialogue, believes that "Orientals, unlike Westerners, do not think of man, nature, and the divine primarily as realities or dimensions which are distinct and autonomous, co-existing face to face with each other. Rather, their vision is non-dualistic, situated between monism and dualism. The Oriental is more concerned with the union, harmony, inter-connection, inter-relation and non-duality existing among all dimensions [of being] than with the affirmation of their distinction, inasmuch as for him, life resides rather in the harmony of the whole than in the difference of its parts."[40] According to Vachon, any holistic vision of reality must grant priority to totality over polarity.[41]

Viewed in this light, the opposition between human freedom and nature can be subsumed under a larger whole, namely, integral authentic, sustainable development, a normative concept embracing three elements: the good life, the optimal foundations of life in society, and the proper stance toward nature and man-made environments. As the French ecologist Bernard Charbonneau insists, freedom itself is nature and both form part of a larger whole.[42]

In a similar vein, Raimundo Panikkar pleads for a radical change in our understanding of relationships between man and nature. He calls for "a thoroughgoing conversion which recognizes and appropriates their common destiny. As long as man and world remain estranged, as long as we insist on relating them only as master to slave—following the metaphor used by Hegel and Marx—as long as their relation is not seen to constitute both world and man, no lasting remedy will ever be found. For this reason, I submit that no dualistic solution can endure."[43] He divides human history into three epochs or "kairological moments" of human consciousness: pre-historical, historical, and trans-historical.[44] These "moments" are not chronologically separate but define qualitatively different attitudes prevailing at given periods. In the epoch of historical consciousness, "Man lives mainly in *space*. . . . The World of pre-historical Man, his environment, is the *theocosmos* or theocosm, the divinised universe. It is not a World of Man, but it is also not the world of the Gods as a separate and superior realm hovering over the humans. . . . In the pre-historical mentality, it is the World that is divinised (to use historical language). The divine permeates the cosmos. The forces of nature are all divine. Nature is supernatural. Or rather, nature is that which is 'natured,' born, from the divine. Pre-historical Man's milieu is a cosmotheological one. *Harmony* is the supreme principle—which does not mean that it has been achieved."[45] The second "kairological moment" is marked by historical consciousness, in which "Historical time is under the spell of the future and the guidance of reason. Only the historical is real."[46] Panikkar explains that "The world of historical Man, his environment, is the *anthropocosmos* or anthropocosm, the human world, the universe of Man. He is not inserted in the evolution of the cosmos; his destiny has little to do with the fate of the stars or the phases of the moon, or even the seasons and the rivers. . . . Nature has been tamed and subjugated. It has been demythicized and there is nothing 'mysterious' about it. Historical Man has overcome the fear of nature. His backdrop is *cosmosociological*. The meaning of his life is not to be found in the cosmic cycles, but in the human sphere, the society. Justice is the supreme principle—which does not mean that it has been achieved."[47]

These two degrees of consciousness, pre-historical and historical, have not disappeared from the face of the earth but, says Panikkar, "A third degree of consciousness is coming more and more to the fore."[48] This is trans-historical consciousness, in the form of metaphysical insights and mystical experiences which have always been in the air but which nowadays gain momentum and change their character. "There really is no issue of 'development' for the famine-plagued masses— over half the world's population. . . . What is worse, people have also lost any vestige of hope that the lot of their children is somehow going to be better. . . . Today the heavenly paradise, or the collective Utopia, or the glittering 'good life,' have all lost their grip on the people. A life of privation here, a vale of tears now, a bad karma in this life so that I may be rewarded later on with a heavenly Garden, a city of Brahman, a vision of God or a more comfortable rebirth—all these are rapidly receding myths. . . . The goods have to be delivered *now*, and not when God or the party is going to win. And despair is not limited to the poor. There is equally disenchantment among the rich. The poor of the world still retain a certain pre-historical religiosity that gives them something to hold on to. Those who live in scientific and technological comfort have discarded the Gods and now find that their practical supreme value shows signs of radical impotence. But no solution is at hand, and we have lost innocence."[49]

A new myth is in the process of emerging, which situates transhistorical Man in what Panikkar calls the theanthropocosmos. "Prehistorical Man has *fate*. He is part and parcel of the universe. Historical Man has *destiny*. He predestines where he stands. He arranges his own life. Trans-historical Man has his lot. He is involved in the total adventure of reality, by participating freely in the portions alloted to him. . . . The World of trans-historical Man, his environment or ecosystem, is the cosmotheandric universe. . . . The destiny of Man is not just an historical existence. It is linked with the life of the Earth and with the entire fate of reality, the divine not excluded. God or the gods are again incarnated and share in the destiny of the universe at large. We are all in the same boat, which is not just this planet Earth, but the whole mystery of Life, Consciousness, Existence. *Love* is the supreme principle—which, again, does not mean that it has been achieved."[50] The "new innocence" of which Panikkar speaks is neither cosmocentric nor anthropocentric, but brings all together in a "consciousness lived neither naively nor by rational projection into the future."[51] The center is "neither in God, nor in the cosmos, nor even in man. It is a moving center which is only to be found in the intersection of the three."[52]

Ethicists who stress the integrity of nature take as their highest values conservation of resources, the preservation of species, and the need to protect nature from human depradations. Those who stress human freedom, in contrast, follow an ethic whose primary values are justice (which takes the form of an active assault upon human poverty, branded as the worst form of pollution) and the need to "develop" or actualize potential resources into their actualized state. Both ethical orientations adhere to all five values listed here, but they rank them differently. A "nature" emphasis locates development and the elimination of human misery below biological conservation and resource replenishment in its hierarchy of values. Conversely, a "freedom" orientation places development and the active conquest of justice in resource allocations above environmental protection or the preservation of endangered species in the scale of values it pursues. In truth, however, all these values should enjoy parity of moral status and stand on an equal footing. The reason is that any long-term, sustainable, equity enhancing combat against poverty requires wisdom in the exploitation of resources. On the other hand, the preservation of other living species cannot be persuasively held out as a priority goal if the human species is threatened with degrading poverty or extinction. Nature itself is diminished or wounded when its human members are kept "underdeveloped." Reciprocally, those human members cannot become truly "developed" if they violate their supportive nature.

It may well be that no world view can integrate successfully the requirements of nature and freedom except around some higher *telos*, or end-value, to which both nature and human freedom are subordinate. Because neither nature nor freedom can be taken as absolute values, diverse philosophies and religions assign different value weights to each. But different religions and meaning systems possess varying "coefficients of insertion in history."[53] They are more or less compatible with positive valuations placed on time, history, and human efforts. To illustrate, Christianity has, throughout its history, harbored tendencies toward exaggerated supernaturalism (in which the realms of nature and human activity are treated merely as arenas where human beings test their virtue or save their souls) and, conversely, toward excessive naturalism (in which God's transcendent and mysterious salvation are reduced merely to a better way of organizing human society). Similarly, there have flourished, within Christianity, schools of interpretation favoring either an exaggerated God-centered (or theocentric) kind of humanism in which it was assumed that anything given to humankind was stolen away from God, or, conversely, an imbalanced anthropocentric (or human-centered) theism in which God became nothing but a glorified magnification or projection of whatever human values enjoyed popularity at a particular time.

Conclusion

The encyclical *On Social Concern* endorses the multidimensional, humanistic, ecologically wise and culturally nurturing view of development advocated by alternative development strategists. John Paul II considers that "modern underdevelopment is not only economic but also cultural, political and simply human. . . . We have to ask ourselves if the sad reality of today might not be, at least in part, the result of a too narrow idea of development, that is, a mainly economic one."[54] The encyclical issues its summons to solidarity in universal terms: "It should be obvious that development either becomes shared in *common* by every part of the world or it undergoes a *process of regression* even in zones marked by constant progress. This tells us a great deal about the nature of *authentic* development: either *all* the nations of the world participate, or it will not be true "development.""[55] *On Social Concern* denounces the selfishness of both blocs—the capitalist West and the Socialist East alike. Both are guilty of "a betrayal of humanity's legitimate expectations—a betrayal that is a harbinger of unforeseeable consequences—but also a real desertion of a moral obligation."[56] The twin elements of a comprehensive development ethic, namely, a regard for social justice and a call for ecological responsibility are evoked by the encyclical which calls for "an ever greater degree of rigorous respect for *justice* and consequently a fair distribution of the results of true development" along with "the need to respect the integrity and the cycles of nature and to take them into account when planning for development, rather than sacrificing them to certain demagogic ideas about the latter."[57]

For John Paul, the struggle to achieve authentic development is "an essential dimension of man's vocation."[58] The human race, he adds, is called by God to be co-creator and co-manager of the whole creation. "When man disobeys God and refuses to submit to his rule, nature rebels against him and no longer recognizes him as its 'master.' "[59]

Development in the mode of solidarity, binding all persons and communities to each other and to the planet they inhabit, is the only authentic form. If humans persist in promoting antidevelopment, they will perish. In Barbara Ward's cryptic phrase: "We are either going to become a community, or we are going to die."[60]

Notes

1. René Dumont and M.F. Mottin, *Le mal-développement en Amérique latine*, Paris: Les Editions du Seuil, 1981.

2. See Bob Bergmann, "René Dumont on Misdevelopment in the Third World: A 42 Year Perspective," in *Camel Breeders News*, Ithaca, NY: Cornell University, Spring 1987, p. 19.

3. See Albert Tévoèdjré, *La pauvreté, richesse des peuples*, Paris: Economie et Humanisme, 1978; and Georges Anglade, *Eloge de la pauvreté*, Montréal: ERCE, 1983.

4. Serge Latouche, *Faut-il refuser le développement?*, Paris: Presses Universitaires de France, 1986.

5. "No to Development?" *Inter-Culture*, Spring-Fall 1987, p. 95.

6. David Maybury-Lewis, Editorial letter "Dear Reader" in *Cultural Survival Quarterly*, Vol. 11, No. 1, 1987, p. 1.

7. Cf., *e.g.*, Lawrence J. Lau, ed., *Models of Development, A Comparative Study of Economic Growth in South Korea and Taiwan*, San Francisco: Institute for Contemporary Studies, 1986; Arnold C. Harberger, ed., *World Economic Growth, Case Studies of Developed and Developing Nations*, San Francisco: Institute for Contemporary Studies, 1984.

8. Selig S. Harrison, "Dateline South Korea: A Divided Seoul," *Foreign Policy*, No. 67 (Summer 1987), pp. 154–175. Yu-ming Shaw and Guo-cang Huan, "The Future of Taiwan," *Foreign Affairs*, Summer 1985, Vol. 63, No. 5, pp. 1050–1080.

9. John Paul II, *On Social Concern*, Washington, DC: United States Catholic Conference, 1987, p. 3.

10. On this see Denis Goulet, "An Ethical Model for the Study of Values," *Harvard Educational Review*, Vol. 41, No. 2, May 1971, pp. 205–227.

11. On this see J. P. Naik, "Gandhi and Development Theory," *The Review of Politics*, Vol. 45, No. 3, July 1983, pp. 345–365.

12. L.J. Lebret, *Montée Humaine*, Paris: Les Editions Ouvrières, 1958; Erich Fromm, *To Have or to Be?*, New York: Harper & Row, 1976.

13. E.F. Schumacher, *Small is Beautiful*, London: Blond & Briggs, 1973.

14. Ivan D. Illich, *Toward a History of Needs*, New York: Pantheon, 1977; and J.P. Naik, *An Alternative System of Health Care Services in India—Some Proposals* and *Some Perspectives on Non-Formal Education*, New Delhi, India: Allied Publishers Private Limited, 1977.

15. G.A. Cornia, R. Jolly, and F. Stewart, *Adjustment with a Human Face*, Oxford: Clarendon Press, 1987; cf. Lionel Demery and Tony Addison, *The Alleviation of Poverty Under Structural Adjustment*, Washington, D.C.: World Bank, 1987.

16. See R. Feinberg and V. Kallab, editors, *Adjustment Crisis in the Third World*, New Brunswick, N.J.: Transaction Books, 1984.

17. John P. Lewis, *et al.*, *Strengthening the Poor: What Have We Learned?* New Brunswick, N.J.: Transaction Books, 1988.

18. S. Danzinger and D. Weinberg, *Fighting Poverty, What Works and What Doesn't*, Cambridge, MA: Harvard University Press, 1986.

19. *World Development Report 1988*, Washington, DC: World Bank, 1988, p. 1.

20. John Paul II, *op. cit.*, p. 6.

21. *Ibidem*, p. 4.

22. On this see Amartya Sen, *On Ethics and Economics*, London: Basil Blackwell, 1987; Mark A. Lutz and Kenneth Lux, *Humanistic Economics*, New York: The Bootstrap Press, 1988; and Thomas Michael Power, *The Economic Pursuit of Quality*, Aremonk, N.Y.: M. E. Sharpe, Inc., 1988; Paul Ekins, ed., *The Living Economy, A New Economics in the Making*, London: Routledge & Kegan Paul, 1986.

23. No documents have yet been issued from the seminar. The author participated in it and here reports from notes taken at the time.

24. David H. Pollock, "A Latin American Strategy to the Year 2000: Can the Past Serve as a Guide to the Future?" *Latin American Prospects for the 80's: What Kinds of Development?* Ottawa: Norman Patterson School of International Affairs, Carleton University, Conference Proceedings, Vol. I, November 1980, pp. 1–37.

25. Denis Goulet, "Participation in Development: New Avenues," *World Development*, Vol. 17, No. 2, February 1989, pp. 165–178.

26. David Pollock, *op. cit.*, p. 9.

27. On this see Denis Goulet, "Development Experts: The One-Eyed Giants," *World Development*, Vol. 8, No. 7/8, July/August 1980, pp.

481–489. Cf. H. W. Richardson and D. R. Cutter, *Transcendence,* Boston, MA: Beacon Press, 1969.

28. Pope Paul VI, *Populorum Progressio,* March 26, 1967, #14, citing L. J. Lebret, *Dynamique Concrète du Développement,* Paris: Les Editions Ouvrières, 1961, p. 28.

29. L.J. Lebret, "Editorial," *Développement et Civilisations,* No. 1 (March 1960), p. 3. Cf. also Lebret, *Développement = Révolution Solidaire,* Paris: Les Editions Ouvrières, 1967, p. 82.

30. See Denis A. Goulet, "Secular History and Teleology," *World Justice,* Vol. 8, No. 1, September 1966, pp. 5–18.

31. For more on this distinction, see Erich Fromm, *To Have or To Be?,* New York: Harper and Row, 1976.

32. Cited in Madeleine Barthelemy Madaule, "La Personne dans la Perspective Teilhardienne," *Essais sur Teilhard de Chardin,* Paris: Editions Fayard, 1962, p. 76.

33. The hierarchy of needs—life-sustenance needs, enhancement needs, and luxury needs—as well as the policy measures which flow from them, are examined in detail in Denis Goulet, *The Cruel Choice,* New York: Atheneum, 1971, pp. 236–249.

34. "Introduction" to Erich Fromm, ed., *Socialist Humanism: An International Symposium,* New York: Anchor Books, p.ix.

35. L.J. Lebret, *Développement = Révolution Solidaire,* op. cit., p. 49.

36. For more on obstacles to development see Denis Goulet, "Obstacles to Development: An Ethical Reflection," *World Development,* Vol. 11, No. 7, July 1983, pp. 609–624.

37. Willy Brandt, *North-South: A Programme for Survival,* Cambridge, MA: MIT Press, 1980, p. 16.

38. Ignacy Sachs, *Développer, les Champs de Planification,* Paris: Université Coopérative Internationale, 1984.

39. S.J. Samartha and Lynn de Silva, editors, *Man in Nature, Guest or Engineer?* Columbo, Sri Lanka: The Ecumenical Institute for Study and Dialogue, 1979.

40. Robert Vachon, "Relations de l'homme à la Nature dans les Sagesses Orientales Traditionnelles," in *Ecologie et Environnement* (Cahiers de Recherche Ethique), Montreal, Vol. 9, 1983, p. 157, translation mine.

41. *Ibidem,* p. 160.

42. Bernard Charbonneau, *Je Fus, essai sur la Liberté,* Pau, France: Imprimerie Marrimpouey Jeune, 1980, pp. 149–156. Cf. also the same author's *Le Feu Vert: Auto-critique du Mouvement Ecologique,* Paris: Editions Karthala, 1980.

43. Raimundo Panikkar, "The New Innocence," *Cross Currents,* Spring 1977, p. 7.

44. Raimundo Panikkar, "Is History the Measure of Man? Three Kairological Moments of Human Consciousness," *The Teilhard Review*, Vol. 16, Nos. 1 and 2, 1981, pp. 39–45.

45. *Ibidem*, p. 40.

46. *Ibidem*, p. 40.

47. *Ibidem*, p. 41.

48. *Ibidem*, p. 42.

49. *Ibidem*, p. 42.

50. *Ibidem*, p. 45.

51. Panikkar, "The New Innocence," *op. cit.*, p. 13.

52. *Ibid*, p. 14.

53. Denis A. Goulet, "Secular History and Teleology," *op. cit.*, pp. 5–18.

54. John Paul II, *op. cit.*, #15.

55. *Ibidem*, #17.

56. *Ibidem*, #23.

57. *Ibidem*, #26.

58. *Ibidem*, #30.

59. *Ibidem*, #30.

60. This phrase served as the theme of the 25th Anniversary World Conference of the Society for International Development on "The Emerging Global Village," held in Baltimore, Maryland, July 18–22, 1982.

Two

Decoding the Pope's Social Encyclicals

Richard T. De George

Pope John Paul II's social encyclicals, *On Human Work* and *On Social Concern*[1] have not caught the conscience of the American people despite the fact that they enunciate sound moral principles and challenge fundamental aspects of the U.S. economy and of U.S. international relations. The encyclicals contain more than enough to think about, fight over, and learn from, yet they have not received much attention in either the popular press or the scholarly community, especially when compared with the pastoral letter of the American Catholic bishops on the economy. Why not? Some American commentators who have paid attention to the encyclicals have even seen in them the making of a counterculture. This reaction, as well as the absence of much other reaction, is all part of a piece. The reasons the encyclicals have not caught on here also explain in a paradoxical way the countercultural interpretation of the encyclicals.

First and most important, the two encyclicals were not written primarily for or aimed at a U.S. audience. Some Americans might take this as an affront, even though there is little reason for such a reaction. Even though encyclicals are in a certain sense universal and addressed to all Catholics, they address particular issues and are written with a certain aim. The Pope's major concern in both encyclicals is not with the U.S. and what it should do, but with the Church's need to counter the appeal and continuing threat of Marxism. The Pope's Polish heritage makes him understandably sensitive to and aware of this appeal and this threat. For the Church, the main ideological struggle is not between Communism and Capitalism—a struggle toward which it can be neutral, if not indifferent—it is between Marxism and Catholicism. The encyclicals, I shall argue, attempt to seize the global moral initiative from Marx. The Pope's primary target audience, thus, is people in areas where Marx's writings are well known and influential—Eastern Europe (including Poland), much of Western Europe, and Latin America. In his social encyclicals the Pope seizes Marxist themes and Christianizes them. Here, perhaps, lies their appeal as a countercul-ture.

Second, the encyclicals fail to speak to Americans because the style, the diction, and the rhetoric are not American; they are at best Euro-pean. The encyclicals are rife with subtle and not so subtle allusions to Marx and are filled with Marxist diction, vocabulary, and jargon. Al-though most Americans miss these references, they help explain what some perceive as the countercultural tone of the encyclicals. Of course, Pope John Paul II is not a Marxist. He is anything but a Marxist. Yet Marx is his antagonist on social issues in the world. No revolutions are fought currently in the name of free enterprise. They are fought in the name of Marxism in Latin America, in Africa and in Europe. That is the ideology that opposes Catholicism and that threatens it. In a style familiar to those who live in a repressed society, the words of the encyc-licals are not always the message. One must read between the lines. This style is well known in Poland. References rarely are direct. The thesis is not stated openly; the reader must divine it. Pope John Paul II was raised on that style and knows it well. The style is lost on most Americans who are not used to it, trained in it, or taught to read that way.

Third, the two encyclicals, but especially the second, have a strong anti-U.S. flavor. They show little awareness of, much less appreciation for, anything American—a point not lost on Americans. The encycli-cals are more negative about the wealthy than about any other group, including those in the Second World or the Eastern Bloc. The target of Marxism is capitalism and, in struggling against Marxism, Pope John Paul II's strategy is to seize Marx's moral critiques of capitalism, and revise them just enough to capture the high moral ground of human rights and concern for the poor. Although he acknowledges the right to private property, he joins with it the obligation to share the wealth to such a degree that he breaks with the traditional natural law defense of private property, say, of John Locke.[2] He attacks wealth as strenu-ously as does Marx, and for somewhat the same reasons. This is the third reason why some read his encyclicals as a call for a counterculture in the U.S.

No one can call Pope John Paul II soft on Soviet communism. Yet he is clearly not a fan of capitalism. He allows for some private property, yet calls for centralized control and "rational" government planning. Both of these resonate with Marx's claims. Marx contrasts rational planning to what he sees in capitalism, namely, the anarchy of the marketplace, which is guided not by reason but by self-interest, and which is wasteful—another theme the Pope adopts. His heart lies with socialism of some sort, although exactly of what variety he never says. If one pieces together what Pope John Paul II does not attack, what he allows, and what he calls for, the result is probably something like self-management socialism of the mixed Yugoslavian type which permits some small private ownership as well as state and worker ownership. The fact that no such economic structure has been successful—Yugoslavia comes closest to having tried, with less than impressive results—seems to him beside the point.

The two encyclicals are not letters on economics but on theology and morality. Yet the attacks on wealth show little understanding of production and what makes countries wealthy. The belief that wealth must come from exploitation is a disputed Marxist claim, which John Paul II implicitly accepts. The Pope, like Marx, emphasizes distribution. What there is to distribute, how it was created, and how it can continue to develop so that people may benefit are not beside the point—either economically or morally. That has been the concern of Americans. Because the encyclicals ignore that dimension and underline only the obligation to distribute what one has, it is little wonder they have not moved the American people.

My claim that the encyclicals were not primarily addressed to Americans, even though they were, in fact, addressed to all people, in no way implies that Americans were singled out. For instance, the Pope did not have the Japanese or the Koreans or the Australians in mind any more than he did the Americans. The moral principles he enunciates apply to all, because they are universal. But the rhetoric he uses is no more Japanese than it is American. The emphasis is not on excluding any group, but on purposely addressing a specific audience. The fact that the encyclicals may have less to say to some other parts of the universal Church is a price that anyone who writes for a particular audience must pay. To expect any encyclical to be addressed to all equally and to be written in a style and diction that will appeal to all equally is either to expect the impossible or to be content with vacuous prose that in effect appeals to no one.

John Paul claims that his encyclical *On Social Concern* is not ideological. To Americans, this is a strange claim to find in an encyclical. But the Pope knows full well that the Marxist-Leninist tradition sees Christianity as the most dangerous counterideology to Marxism. He knows that in adapting Marx's critique of capitalism he runs the risk of being charged with adopting an ideological perspective. He claims not to present an ideology to replace liberal capitalism or collectivist Marxism, but he knows that in attacking them both he is open to the charge. He speaks the language of morality, conscious of the fact that, for Marx, morality was as ideological as religion or philosophy or politics. Denying that one's position is ideological does not automatically make it so.

Challenging the Young Marx

The actual target of the encyclicals' attack, I claim, is Marxism, and the primary audience is those for whom Marxism might be an option, namely, the people of Eastern and Western Europe and of Latin America. A remarkable fact about the encyclical *On Human Work* is that, with the exception of the citations from religious sources, the last chapter, and a brief critique of Soviet communism, it could have been written by the young Karl Marx. In fact, much of it was. A brief comparison between the Pope's text and those of the young Marx shows this to be the case. From this we should not conclude that Marx and the Pope think alike, or that each has more going for him than his followers respectively acknowledge about the other, or that they both misunderstand the phenomenon they both call capitalism. The point, if you see the closeness of language and hence the unattributed allusions, is that the Pope is challenging Marx on his own ground.

Marx is the defender of labor; the leader of the labor union movement; the originator of the call for all working men of the world to unite (read: "solidarity"); the defender of human liberation; the champion of the oppressed, the poor, the downtrodden; the attacker of alienation and exploitation. Pope John Paul II knows this all too well. He knows the moral power of that message. By making many of the same claims about labor that Marx does, the Pope attempts to show that the Catholic message contains all that and more; that Christianity, not Marxism, is the real humanism; that Christ was the friend of the poor before Marx. In Christianizing Marx's analysis, the Pope emphasizes that justice and morality must infuse the critique of labor. In this encyclical the Pope fights to reappropriate the doctrine that Marx, through Ludwig Feuerbach, wrested from the Church in the nineteenth century. Feurbach, in his influential work *The Essence of Christianity*,[3] said theology must be replaced by anthropology, and religion by humanism. Following him, Marx claimed that the critique of religion was over, and that religion, the opium of the people, the sigh of the oppressed masses, would wither away when their ills were remedied. Feuerbach secularized Christianity; Marx was his heir.

Critics have commented on the originality of the encyclicals. They are original because they are the first attempt by a Pope to get back what Marx took from Christianity. Instead of attacking Marxism directly, as did his predecessors, John Paul II usurps Marx's ground, just as Marx usurped Christianity's. That is the battle raging in the encyclical, a battle all but lost to the bulk of American readers who neither know, nor really care much about, Marx or Marxism. In the United States, Marxism and socialism are no threat and have little popular appeal. In Western Europe and Latin America they are alive. In Eastern Europe they are in power.

In writing *On Human Work* the Pope left the theological development for the end. In the earlier chapters he relies on just a few biblical quotations, mostly from *Genesis*. This structure underlies the claim that John Paul is taking on Marx on Marx's own ground. The moral tone throughout is Christian, yet the audience the Pope wants to reach, and the minds for which he is fighting, are not likely to be moved by theology. They will be moved by moral ideals, and it is the Pope's aim to win the battle for those minds. The last chapter, which seems almost an afterthought with citations piled one on another, bows to the fact that *In Human Work* is not only a work inspired by theology, but that there are actually theological references one could make all along the line, if one were so inclined. For those who want them, they are there. But those who want them really do not need them, and any who really need them would not be convinced by them anyway. The Pope knows what he is doing.

The last chapter cites the spirituality of work and gives a Christian interpretation to work based on the *New Testament*. The rest of the encyclical relies on *Genesis,* especially on the command to subdue the earth, a text which the Pope makes bear more weight than it can withstand, and which becomes a device for making the points he wishes to make. He takes a great deal of Marx's analysis of work and *a posteriori* derives it from *Genesis*. Nonetheless, he persuasively and skillfully weaves it into a Christian perspective, relying heavily as well on his own predilection toward personalism.

In arguing for my claims I shall draw first a comparison between the language of the encyclicals and that of Marx. I have no quarrel with the Pope's principles. I applaud and agree with them. I shall ask whether the description the Pope gives of the current state of affairs is accurate, or whether it is slanted through its language. The way one describes the world is vital to how one evaluates it; and how one evaluates it is vital to how one might act to remedy its perceived defects. My aim primarily is to explain why the encyclicals have fallen mainly on deaf ears in the United States and why the ears that have heard it have been led to the idea of a counterculture.

The Priority of Labor over Capital

Let us look a little more closely at the text, rather than just at the spirit of the encyclicals, which is what most Americans who have reacted to it have tended to do.

From the very start, in the first paragraph of *On Human Work*,[4] Pope John Paul II says, "Work is one of the characteristics that distinguish man from the rest of creatures" (p. 1). The claim is remarkable in an encyclical. Traditionally, the notion of humankind as rational animals with divinely created souls has been the Christian distinguishing characteristic of parenthood. The opening shot invites comparison with Marx's statement in *The German Ideology* that "Men . . . begin to distinguish themselves from animals as soon as they begin to *produce* their means of subsistence, a step which is conditioned by their physical organization."[5] Work as a distinguishing characteristic of human beings is Marx's insight, and one that is traditionally linked to him. In the Christian tradition the interpretation of *Genesis* has not focused on work as a distinguishing characteristic of people, but as a punishment for sin. Pope John Paul II knows all of this. He clearly and at the outset adopts Marx's characterization of humankind and incorporates it into the Christian position. He refuses to yield to Marx the moral high ground on labor, and the only way to seize that ground is to claim it as one's own and to incorporate it into an overall view where it fits more or less comfortably.

Talk about humankind as rational beings, with emphasis on the immortal soul, will not fill the bill when it comes to labor—at least that is the clear signal we get in the opening paragraph of the encyclical. Of course, the Pope does not mention Marx. He assumes the statement is clear enough and shocking enough in the opening paragraph of an encyclical to alert the reader to what he is doing. Those who miss the allusion to Marx will read the rest of the text without the central connection the Pope makes here. Since most Americans will miss it, the encyclical on this level is not written with them in mind.

The opening salvo is just the first of many appropriations of famous passages in Marx. Two paragraphs later, in the encyclical's "Introduction," the Pope writes: "Man's life is built up every day from work, from work it derives its specific dignity" (p. 3). Once again, the Christian tradition has been that people derive their dignity from their immortal souls, made in the image of God. That people derive their dignity from work is not part of the Christian tradition. It is part of Marx's claim, and it forms the basis of his celebrated 1844 Paris manuscript on alienated labor. Marx claims there that people are made by work; that in work they fulfil and realize their capacities; and, that to the extent they are not able to do this, they are alienated from and by their work. The Pope quietly slips from the claim that people's lives derive their dignity from work to the more traditional Christian claim of the dignity and rights of those who work (p. 4). But in the Christian tradition the dignity of the worker does not rest on the claim that a person's life *derives* its dignity from work. The Pope has assimilated a piece of Marx, and linked it to traditional doctrine.

The Pope concludes the Introduction by highlighting the point that "human work is a key, probably the essential key, to the whole social question" and that the solution "must be sought in the direction of 'making life more human' " (p. 7). That human work is the key to the social problem is once again the basic claim of Marx in his analysis of politics, law, and all other social problems. Pope John Paul II takes the phrase "making life more human" from *Gaudium et Spes*; but the phrase "more human" fits Marx's notion of humankind and human conditions better than it does the view in which an individual's essence, and so humanity, comes from God. From the latter perspective, how human life can be "more human" is puzzling. The conditions of life can be better and more appropriate to the dignity of a person, but human life cannot be more human.

The development of humankind in relation to nature, another new ecological theme in an encyclical (p. 13), parallels Marx's statement that "The universality of man appears in practice in the universality which makes all nature his *inorganic* body."[6] The biblical injunction to "subdue the earth" has been given as a justification for what some have called the rape of nature. Marx's view of nature as an extension of humankind, on the other hand, has been used in defense of the protection of nature. Here, the Pope attempts to seize the moral initiative on ecology from Marx.

On page 14 the Pope says "in the first place work is 'for man' and not man 'for work.' " Compare Marx: "the worker . . . in his work . . . does not affirm himself but denies himself. . . . His labor is . . . not the satisfaction of a need; it is merely a *means* to satisfy needs external to it"[7] and "My work would be a *free manifestation of life,* hence an *enjoyment of life.* . . . [Because] I work *in order to live.* . . . [m]y work *is not* my life."[8] The theme that work is for people and not people for work is at the heart of Marx's critique of alienated labor. On page 16 the Pope says: "Man is treated as an instrument of production, whereas he—he alone, independent of the work he does—ought to be treated as the effective subject of work and its true maker and creator." Once again, Marx's theme of alienation is borrowed and placed in *Genesis.* Listen to Marx: "The *alienation* of the worker in his product means not only that his labor becomes an object, . . . but that it exists *outside him,* . . . as something alien to him, and that it becomes a power on its own confronting him."[9]

Marx critiques three aspects of alienated labor under capitalism: first, the alienation of the worker from the product of his or her labor; second, the alienation of the worker from the labor process; and third, the alienation of the worker from other people. The Pope addresses the first aspect in section 6 of Chapter II of the encyclical, "Work in a Subjective Sense"; the second in section 7, "A Threat to the Right Order of Values"; and, not surprisingly, the third in section 8. Marx finds the solution to this third aspect of alienation, that of the worker from other people, in species-being, a Feuerbachian notion in which people are related to other people. The Pope proposes a similar theme "Worker

Solidarity.'' The parallel development is not a coincidence. This is Pope John Paul II's answer to Marx's critique of labor under capitalism. He appropriates the critique, and places it in a personalist context. The citations from *Genesis* cannot support the doctrine he builds and, wisely, he does not place undue emphasis on those quotations.

In further defense of the claim that the encyclical does not have Americans as its primary audience, note the Pope's choice of words for section 8: ''Worker Solidarity.'' ''Solidarity'' to the American ear calls up—if one is of the older generation—the labor union movement, and the song ''Solidarity Forever.'' It has the ring of the 1930s to it; it is a little passé and archaic. The only other connotation it has for an American is the Solidarity movement in Poland. The Pope's choice of the word resonates with Poland and with the labor union movement there. Americans do not use the term in the same way, and would tend to speak of communion or community instead.

As the Pope develops the theme of solidarity, he refers to ''the proletariat question'' (p. 17). There is no proletariat question in the United States. Americans do not describe workers or union members as the proletariat. ''Proletariat'' is a Marxist term used to describe workers, and ''the proletariat question'' is framed in Marxist terms. This becomes even clearer a few lines later in the encyclical when the Pope links that issue with ''exploitation.'' The Pope openly borrows the terminology of Marx to describe work and working conditions. He is appropriating the Marxist terms and using them for his own purposes, his own solution. But he clearly speaks the language of Marx. He does so knowingly to assimilate and Christianize Marx's critique in the struggle for people's hearts, minds and souls. But the language and the analysis leave most Americans cold. Americans do not think in rigid class terms, in terms of bourgeoisie and proletariat, and in terms of the exploitation of all workers by capitalists; Europeans and Latin Americans do.

The Pope's discussion of the proletariat question recapitulates Marx's analysis of alienated labor and, again, we can match the one to the other. The Pope's statements that ''through work man not only transforms nature, adapting it to his own needs, but he also achieves fulfillment as a human being'' (pp. 20–21); that ''in work, whereby matter gains in nobility, man himself should not experience a lowering of his own dignity''; that ''work can be made into a means for oppressing man, and that in various ways it is possible to exploit human labor, that is to say, workers'' (p. 21); and so on, all have direct correlations Marx's writings.

The parallels continue in Chapter III, ''Conflict between Labor and Capital in the Present Phase of History.'' The very title of the chapter is Marxist. Americans speak of the conflict between labor and management. In appropriating Marx's use of the term ''capital,'' the Pope not only appropriates Marx's term but assimilates his analysis, and his critique of capitalism. This is tactically and rhetorically an effective device if one's audience is those for whom Marxism has an appeal. It is not effective tactically or rhetorically for most Americans who will either not catch the references or who will not recognize the descriptions as a reflection of their experience.

The Pope points to the conflict between ''capital'' and ''labor,'' ''that is to say between the small but highly influential group of entrepreneurs, owners or holders of the means of production, and the broader multitude of people who lacked these means and who shared in the process of production solely by their labor'' (p. 24). The terms and their definitions are direct paraphrases of Engels' definitions in a footnote to the 1888 English edition of *The Communist Manifesto*. Engels there defines the bourgeoisie as ''the class of modern Capitalists, owners of the means of social production and employers of wage-labour'' and the proletariat as ''the class of modern wage-labourers who, having no means of production of their own, are reduced to selling their labour-power in order to live.''[10]

In describing the conflict between capital and labor the Pope says, ''This conflict . . . found expression in the ideological conflict between liberalism, understood as the ideology of capitalism, and Marxism, understood as the ideology of scientific socialism and communism. . . . The real conflict between labor and capital was transformed into a systematic class struggle'' (p. 24). To see the relation of management and labor in this way is to see it precisely as Marx describes it in the *Communist Manifesto*. That the conflict between management and labor in the United States is a conflict between liberalism and Marxism would come as news to both management and labor. The Pope then equates Marxism with its Soviet version—thereby robbing it of its original legitimacy—saying that the Marxist program ''presupposes the collectivization of the means of production'' (p. 24), whereas for Marx it involves the socialization of the means of production.

The Pope then notes "... we cannot go into the details [of Marxism], nor is this necessary, for they are known both from the vast literature on the subject and by experience" (p. 25). Clearly, he assumes his audience is familiar with Marxism and the debates surrounding it, an assumption that is false with respect to most Americans. The Pope's confrontation with Marxism is clear, and the alternative that the Pope proposes is based on "the principle of the priority of labor over capital" which "has always been taught by the church" (p. 25). But that principle is one that we find also in Marx. The Pope says "capital cannot be separated from labor" (p. 27). Marx said "Capital is *stored-up labor*"[11]—a claim that follows more obviously from his labor theory of value than the Pope's statement follows from Christian doctrine.

The Pope's aim is not only to seize the moral initiative on labor and economic issues from Marx, but also to replace the Marxist perspective with a Christian one. Thus far in the encyclical he has adapted only Marx. Finally, after describing the relation between labor and capital in Marxist terms, the Pope suddenly and abruptly attacks economism. An American reader may well be lost here. The Pope's attack on what he calls "economism" is his attack on the economic determinism attributed to the later Marx. Here the Pope makes the crucial equation of Marxism and philosophical materialism. He says that the error of economism is the error of materialism which includes "the primacy and superiority of the material, and directly or indirectly places the spiritual and personal (man's individual activity, moral values and such matters) in a position of subordination to material reality" (p. 29). He continues, stating that "In dialectical materialism too man is not first and foremost the subject of work . . . but continues to be understood and treated, in dependence on what is material, as a kind of 'resultant' of the economic or production relations prevailing at a given period" (p. 30). This is true of Soviet dialectical materialism—the Pope's real target—even if not of the early Marx.

What initially is puzzling is that after this diversion, the Pope continues discussing work and ownership in Marxist terms: "On the one side are those who do the work without being the owners of the means of production, and on the other side those who act as entrepreneurs and who own these means or represent the owners" (p. 31). The description was accurate in Marx's time, and still may be accurate of some places. It does not capture accurately the fact that in the United States, through pension funds, workers are in fact owners of a significant portion of the means of production.

We have here the crux of the Pope's strategy. The target is materialistic Soviet Marxism-Leninism and its offshoots. All the allusions to Marxism and the continued use of Marx's analysis of work and of capitalism are a concerted effort to assimilate them into the Christian view and message, to seize the initiative with respect to workers and the poor, and to separate them from metaphysical materialism. The condemnation of materialism and of dialectical materialism—a term coined by Plekhanov and never used by Marx—comes abruptly, and forces us to see that simply assimilating Marx is not enough. One must see that, despite the use of similar language, only a Christian, personalist base, and not a materialist base, can do justice to the message the Pope has been developing.

The Pope attacks "rigid" capitalism and argues for "joint ownership of the means of work, sharing by the workers in the management and/or profits of business, so-called shareholding by labor" (p. 32). He says "merely taking these means of production (capital) out of the hands of their private owners is not enough to ensure their satisfactory socialization" (p. 33). Having attacked both capitalism and Soviet collectivism, he suggests a number of intermediary bodies that resemble most of all the structures of Yugoslav self-management socialism.

Chapter IV also is strongly reminiscent of Marxism. It starts with the duty to work—a duty not recognized as such in the United States, but one enforced by law in the Soviet Union which outlaws parasitism. The discussion of direct and indirect employers brings in the exploitation of the less developed by the more developed countries, and the dependency thesis—two doctrines developed by Lenin and taken over whole in the Pope's analysis of international relations of rich and poor countries.

Pope John Paul II says the state "must make provision for overall planning with regard to the different kinds of work by which not only the economic life, but also the cultural life of a given society is shaped; . . . they must also give attention to organizing that work in a correct and rational way" (p. 41). That these are proper tasks of the state are views compatible with Marxism but not with the notion of a free economy. The "rational planning" (p. 42) he refers to is a Marxist ideal (as I have noted already) in which the anarchy of the marketplace is rationalized. The U.S. view is that such planning does not work; and if it does not work, it cannot be a moral imperative to be followed.

In speaking of wages, the Pope departs from the Marxist position to some extent. Wages, for Marx, necessarily involve exploitation, whereas the Pope calls for a just wage in the tradition of the social encyclicals of his predecessors.

The Pope defends unions and the right to strike, the rights of the disabled, the right of emigration. The final chapter on "Element for a Spirituality of Work" presents the theological basis for the Christian assessment of work.

The Pope's opponent throughout is Marx whom, as I have claimed, he fights on his own ground. Unless one sees this, one misses a major point of the encyclical. The Pope appropriates what he sees as correct in Marx's position, without attributing it to Marx. Implicitly, the Pope suggests that Christianity held those positions before Marx, even if it were Marx who brought them to the fore. The Church, it can be noted, did not institute the workers' movement or attack alienation or economic exploitation until after Marx had done so. The social encyclicals were responses to Marxist initiatives as well as to existing conditions, and the two social encyclicals from the hands of Pope John Paul II continue to be so.

Capitalism is the name the Pope uses for free enterprise of whatever kind. There is no nuanced examination of the present-day structures of free enterprise. All existing forms of free enterprise are indiscriminately attacked in the same language that Marx, and later Lenin, used in attacking capitalism. This is an important reason why the encyclical fell on predominantly deaf ears in the United States. The Pope was not speaking directly to Americans but to those for whom Marxism has an appeal, and he was presenting an alternative to them that built on the strength of Marx's critique, while adding a spiritual and religious dimension lacking in Marx. To say this is not to criticize the encyclical but to understand it. Those who read the encyclical as countercultural should consider carefully the extent to which they may be misreading it.

A Tendency toward Imperialism

The encyclical *On Social Concern* also is not addressed, except indirectly, to Americans, even though they may seem to be the villains and those called upon to do the most. Marxism is present in three ways. The first is in the Pope's analysis of what he refers to as the "capitalist" countries and the doctrine of "liberal capitalism." The second is in his adoption of the Leninist claims of imperialism and of the dependency of the less developed countries on the more developed ones. The third is in the use of dialectics and dialectical language. All three are once again acceptable to the European and Latin American audiences who are familiar with Marxism, but these references are alien to Americans.

I shall comment briefly on these three Marxist ingredients by turning to a more extended analysis of the Pope's so-called "East-West Battlefield Thesis."

In Chapter III, "Survey of the Contemporary World," the Pope notes the poverty in the world and "the widening of the gap between the areas of the so-called developed North and the developing South" (p. 21). The gap is, in fact, between the rich nations of the North—the United States and Canada, most of Western Europe, and Japan—on the one hand, and most of the rest of the world on the other. South America and Africa are in the Southern hemisphere. India, Pakistan, Bangladesh and other poor countries are in the North, but are also less developed. The Soviet Union, Eastern Europe, and perhaps China are the Second World, even though China ranks among the less developed countries. The Pope's critique in any case is primarily of the rich countries. He notes as well the housing crisis, unemployment, illiteracy, and the international debt.

If my thesis about *On Human Work* is correct, we should not be surprised to find that the Pope, in the encyclical *On Social Concern*, again assimilates the Marxist critique of capitalism. The Pope seizes the moral appeal of the Marxists and addresses an audience to which Marxism is a live option. Marxism remains the major threat to Christianity, even if it is not the major target of this encyclical. The point continues to be to seize the initiative from those Marxists who appeal to the poor, the down-trodden, the oppressed, the exploited, and to develop the message that Christianity is their original and true champion. Not only are Americans not the target audience, but the U.S. can be read as the dominant unnamed object of attack.

The Pope states that the central reason for the ills he identifies is the "*existence of two opposing blocs,* commonly known as the East and the West" (p. 33). His analysis is strongly reminiscent of Mao Tse-tung's. Mao, in his work *On Contradictions,* claimed that in any analysis one should look for the principal contradiction. Within the principal contradiction, one should look for the principal aspect of the contradiction; and within the framework of the principal contradiction, or opposition, one can look for secondary and other contradictions.[12]

Somewhat disconcertingly for the American reader, Pope John Paul II follows this methodology in his analysis of world conditions. In the spirit of dialectics he searches for, and finds, polar oppositions—political opposition, ideological opposition, and military opposition. He distinguishes contradictions in social life—not in the sense of logical inconsistencies—but in the Hegelian-Marxist dialectical sense of opposing forces. There is nothing wrong with using the dialectical method, either for description or for analysis. Yet it is not used frequently in U.S. analyses and the terminology is foreign to American ears, which helps explain why the analysis is somewhat strange to Americans.

The Pope claims "Each of the two blocs tends to assimilate or gather around it other countries or groups of countries, to different degrees of adherence or participation" (p. 33). This may seem like a neutral statement, but it is far from such. It implicitly equates the relation of Poland to the Soviet Union and of England to the United States. It is certainly the case that each smaller country is allied with one of the blocs. But Poland in a very real sense is an occupied country. The Soviet Union did not simply "gather around it other countries." It did "assimilate" the Baltic states. To equate the situation of Czechoslovakia vis-à-vis the Soviet Union to the situation of France vis-à-vis the United States is scarcely accurate. Hence, to equate the blocs as similar—for example, from a moral point of view—will seem to Americans simply not to be the case. It is difficult to believe that it seems to be the case for the Poles, and for the Polish Pope. Or is it? It is not difficult to imagine the description as appealing to many people in Europe and Latin America, despite its inaccuracies.

The Pope describes the ideological level of oppositions as one between liberal capitalism and Marxist collectivism. Liberal capitalism, we are told, "developed with industrialization during the last century" (p. 33). What that doctrine or ideology is at the present time is far from clear. Whatever it is, it is surely not what it was in the nineteenth century. The welfare state has made an important difference, a difference which the pat opposition of liberal capitalism to Marxist collectivism ignores. Once again, it is not surprising that most Americans have not resonated to the description of their country in terms they do not accept and scarcely recognize.

The third tension, the military one, characterized by cold war, wars of proxy, and the threat of an open and total war (p. 34) is all too well known.

The Pope continues in the same apparently evenhanded manner to say that the "two *concepts* of the development of individuals and peoples" are both "imperfect and in need of radical correction" (p. 35). Is it really evenhanded to say both concepts are in need of radical correction? From an American perspective, the United States does not occupy any country, while the Soviet Union does. The United States has given and continues to give a great deal of aid to less developed nations, while the Soviet Union gives very little. Americans have championed freedom and human rights while the Soviet Union has restricted freedom and ignored human rights.

The Pope goes on in this supposedly evenhanded manner saying, "Each of the two *blocs* harbors in its own way a tendency toward *imperialism,* as it is usually called, or toward forms of neo-colonialism" (p. 37). Here the Marxist bias and analysis are again clear. Lenin, in his widely known book *Imperialism: The Highest Stage of Capitalism,*[13] defended the thesis that through colonialism the European nations were able to transfer the worst exploitation to their colonies. The European nations thus were able to exploit their own workers less, allow them higher standards of living and, by doing so, fend off a proletarian revolution. The analysis does not fit the United States well. The United States itself was once a British colony. It has no colonies and has never had any. It has not conquered and subjugated any foreign peoples. To accuse it of imperialism or of colonialism or of neo-colonialism, as if those charges were self-evidently true, is not something most Americans are willing to accept. In some senses of imperialism a case might be made. But the case has to be made. With respect to the Eastern bloc, since the Soviet Union brought communism into the countries of Eastern Europe with its troops, which have remained, the claim of imperialism makes more sense.

The Pope's claim that "the West gives the impression of abandoning itself to forms of growing and selfish isolation" (p. 39) is puzzling in the light of the earlier claims about imperialism and neo-colonialism, which seem antithetical to isolationism. Americans may well wonder, especially since no countries are named, to what countries the Pope is referring.

In Chapter V the Pope returns once again to the two blocs analysis, and says, ". . . a world which is divided into blocs, sustained by rigid ideologies, and in which instead of interdependence and solidarity different forms of imperialism hold sway, can only be a world subject to structures of sin" (p. 68). Two typical ones are "on the one hand, the *all-consuming desire for profit,* and on the other, *the thirst for power,* with the intention of imposing one's will upon others"(p. 71). Will Americans see themselves in the description of having an all-consuming desire for profit "at any price" (p. 71)? Some people may have such a desire. But it is not accurate to characterize all Americans in this way, nor is it accurate to characterize the government in this way. The characterization is typically Marxist, and perhaps widely believed of America in many parts of the world. It can be rightly rejected by Americans as an overgeneralization.

Nor will Americans understand the "principle that the goods of creation *are meant for all.* That which human industry produces through the processing of raw materials, with the contribution of work, must serve equally for the good of all" (p. 76). What does that principle mean? It seems to be addressed to the West and to the rich. Does it truly mean that all manufactured goods must be distributed to all who want or need them, regardless of who makes the product or of anyone's ability to pay? The principle deals with distribution and ignores production and, in this way, follows the Marxist critique of capitalism. The Pope once again seizes the initiative from the Marxists and assimilates and Christianizes their critique. This may play well in Europe and Latin America. It has not played well in the United States.

The Pope tells us in Chapter VI that "The Church's social doctrine is *not* a 'third way' between *liberal capitalism* and *Marxist collectivism,* nor even a possible alternative to other solutions less radically opposed to one another: rather, it constitutes a *category of its own,*" which aims "to *guide* human behavior" (p. 83). The guidance it provides is clearer for those to whom the encyclical is primarily addressed, namely, to Europeans and Latin Americans, than it is for those in the United States.

A Supreme Irony

I have claimed that Americans have not responded to the Pope's social encyclicals because they are written in a style and diction foreign to

Americans and because, in a real sense, they seem not to be written for Americans. Yet, surely, it will be argued, the Pope clearly wants the rich countries—especially the United States—to help the poor countries. He also wants the United States to change its liberal capitalist ideology and the system built on it, as well as to stop the production and sale of arms, and to help the less developed countries develop. This is true; and it is on this aspect of the encyclicals that those who argue for a counterculture may seize. But this is compatible with my thesis that the Pope, primarily or directly, does not address America because that is not where his major concern lies. His major concern lies with Eastern and Western Europe and with Latin America.

The Catholic Church in the United States, despite its vocal dissent on some issues, is the strongest in the world. The Catholic churches in the United States are filled. Americans do not suffer the anti-clericalism of Europe; nor do we find in the United States the liberation theology movement which causes the Pope so much concern, in part because of the Marxist doctrines with which it is mixed. For the Pope the major threat is Marxism, and the major opponent is the Soviet Union. The United States is not really a problem for him; rather it is a possible solution. It is the possible solution to poverty, among other things.

I do not wish to claim that the Pope's social encyclicals have nothing to say to Americans or that Americans have nothing to learn from them. I do not think that either claim is true. There is much worthy of note and study in the two encyclicals. Whether or not the Pope understands the U.S. or speaks directly to Americans in his social encyclicals is of little importance in the last analysis. If the Pope has something to say from which Americans can learn—and he surely does—then our aim should be to learn from him what we can. Because of the reasons I have given, for the larger U.S. audience this will mean that intermediaries will have to translate the positions the Pope espouses into the American idiom and develop independent arguments for them. They must develop the moral principles and make relevant what often seems extremely abstract, unclear, and sometimes contradictory to U.S. readers. The American bishops have given us an example of how to do that.

The American bishops address many of the same themes and come to many of the same conclusions as do the Pope. They do so in the American idiom. They do not take as their target Marx or Marxism, nor do they try to assimilate the moral ground to which Marxism laid claim. They do not do so because Marxism is in no way a threat or challenge to the Church in the U.S.

It is difficult to imagine Pope John Paul II offering a first draft of his encyclical for criticism and reaction—even to the bishops, much less to the general public, as the American bishops did—before issuing the final version. Therein may lie part of the Pope's failure to understand the American mind. Democracy, participation, and freedom are at least as essential to it as is profit. The Pope's failure to appreciate this, and his description of America in Marxist terms might lead one to believe that the rigid ideology of which he speaks is not America's but the Pope's view of America.

If my analysis has been persuasive, Americans should not be surprised that the Pope had a special interest in addressing the problems he did in the way he did. It would be naive to think the Pope wrote his social encyclicals with no agenda in mind or to consider them a-temporal or a-historical. It is naive to think that they are universal in the sense of being addressed to all equally. To the extent that they are universal in the moral principles they articulate, they are necessarily vague, general, invite interpretation, and require concrete development. We should not be disappointed to find little in the way of clear policy guidelines. Providing these was not its aim. Following the bishops' lead, a U.S. response can take the development of appropriate, morally based, policy guidelines as its aim, developing them from the encyclicals but with an appreciation of the strengths of the U.S. system which the Pope, for strategic, tactical, or for other reasons, ignores.

In his two encyclicals Pope John Paul II has sought to take the moral initiative away from the Marxists in Europe and the liberation theologians in Latin America. To the extent that the Pope has succeeded in Christianizing the Marxist approach to labor and social issues, he has accomplished no mean feat. In the process he has adopted too uncritically the Marxist critique of capitalism and used it as a device for analyzing the world situation. The appeal to those who accept that point of view is understandable. Although Americans, among others, are justified in not accepting his analysis uncritically, we can well be tolerant of the Pope's description of capitalism and of the West in Marxist terms if we keep in mind his aim.

In the long run, the success of John Paul's social encyclicals will depend on whether they are successful in allowing the Church to seize the moral initiative from Marxism on oppression, alienation, exploitation, and the poor. To those who find in the encyclicals a call to create an American counterculture, they should be careful of the Marxist presuppositions and critiques of free enterprise they may unconsciously and uncritically assimilate from the encyclicals. It would be a supreme irony if Pope John Paul II's encyclicals led critics in America unwittingly and uncritically to adopt the very Marxist positions he wishes to replace.

Notes

1. John Paul II, *On Human Work*, Washington, D.C.: Office of Publishing and Promotion Services, United States Catholic Conference, 1981; *On Social Concern*, Washington, D.C.: Office of Publishing and Promotion Services, United States Catholic Conference, 1988. All page references in the text are to these editions.

2. John Locke, *The Second Treatise of Government*, Indianapolis: The Bobbs-Merrill Company, Inc., 1975, Chapter V, "Of Property."

3. Ludwig Feuerbach, *The Essence of Christianity*, trans. by George Eliot, New York: Harper Torchbooks, 1957.

4. *On Human Work*, p. 1.

5. *The German Ideology*, in *Karl Marx and Frederick Engels: Collected Works*, New York: International Publishers, Vol. 5, p. 31.

6. *Economic and Philosophic Manuscripts of 1844*, in *Collected Works*, Vol. 3, p. 275.

7. *Ibid.* p. 274.

8. *Comments on James Mill, Elemens d'economie politique*, in *Collected Works*, Vol. 3, p. 228.

9. *Economic and Philosophic Manuscripts*, *Collected Works*, Vol. 3, p. 272.

10. *Manifesto of the Communist Party*, *Collected Works*, Vol. 6, p. 482.

11. *Economic and Philosophic Manuscripts*, *Collected Works*, Vol. 3, p. 247.

12. *On Contradiction, Selected Works of Mao Tse-tung*, Peking: Foreign Language Press, 1975, Vol. 1, pp. 331–337.

13. *Imperialism: The Highest Stage of Capitalism. V. I. Lenin Selected Works*, London: Lawrence & Wishart Ltd., 1936, Vol. 5.

Three

The Economic Encyclicals of Pope John Paul II

Theological and Economic Perspectives

J. Philip Wogaman

Not everybody appreciates the intervention of churches into the great economic debates of our time. Economic questions are largely technical, and churches, as such, can claim no expertise on factual problems unless they have specifically earned it. Even the members of churches can be critical of what they take to be a lack of expertise in the social pronouncements issued by their own leaders.[1] Still, if ecclesial social teachings are never purely theological, neither are they wholly technical. A "problem" always presents us with both *facts* and *values*. If factual expertise is required to deal with the factual side, a corresponding clarity about values is needed to define what is ultimately at stake. Religious bodies, when true to their own nature, have much to say about values. They are vocationally committed to clarifying the relationship between the particular values of human existence and what they consider to be the source of all good.

From at least the time of the great prophets, the biblical religions have understood that ordinary life is not neutral to good and evil. Evil often comes masked as normal occurrence, and goodness is likewise taken for granted. The prophetic role is to expose the connections to view; the teaching role is to help people recognize those connections.

Twentieth century Christian leadership has been enormously active at both points but, even so, it has been difficult for the churches to keep pace with the complex changes of social life. Economics, which touches virtually all of human existence, has posed particularly difficult challenges. The great social encyclicals since Pope Leo XIII's *Rerum Novarum* (1891) have devoted much attention and no little competence to the analysis of economic questions, as have the Assemblies of the World Council of Churches and predecessor conferences and the statements and messages of other denominations and ecclesial communities. Final closure cannot be expected from such a body of ecclesial social teaching, since economic history will not stand still. But a symposium, such as the one in which we are engaged, does well to ask whether the fundamental directions are sound and, if so, where they might lead us.

Pope John Paul II's encyclical letters *Laborem Exercens* (hereafter, *LE*)[2] and *Sollicitudo Rei Socialis* (hereafter, *SRS*)[3] are useful points of departure, partly because they touch upon so many of the key economic issues of late twentieth-century life and partly because they have been viewed by many as marking important new departures in Catholic social thinking.

The Making of a Counterculture?

The symposium wishes to examine in particular whether such documents represent movement toward the "making of an economic counterculture." Obviously, one's answer depends partly on what is meant by "counterculture." If one defines the term to mean a sectarian or separatist withdrawal from modern life—in the manner of an Amish community, for instance—then the encyclicals clearly have little to do with that. The encyclicals are addressed to people in the mainstream of contemporary life, worldwide, and those people are not asked to withdraw from the mainstream so much as to seek to change its direction.

Nor, indeed, are the encyclicals fundamentally hostile to technological change—in the manner, say, of a Jacques Ellul.[4] The encyclicals plainly are relevant to technological questions, and there is much criticism of technology for its own sake or technology undisciplined by humane values. But these encyclicals are not unappreciative of the contributions technology makes to precisely those values. Thus, "technology is undoubtedly man's ally. It facilitates his work, perfects, accelerates and augments it. It leads to an increase in the quantity of things produced by work and in many cases improves their quality."[5] But at the same time, "it is also a fact that in some instances technology can cease to be man's ally and become almost his enemy."[6] We are left with a recognition that some aspects of technical culture are to be affirmed, others resisted; but we are not invited to be in a fundamentally adversarial or ''counter'' stance toward technology as such.

Nor can the encyclicals be described as revolutionary, at least not in the ideological sense. As we will note below, a ground is laid out for criticism of the ideological tendencies of both left and right. In economic terms, the result looks more like the ideology of a ''mixed economy'' or the welfare state than any of the more radical possibilities. So, in these senses of the term ''countercultural,'' it would be difficult to characterize Pope John Paul II in that way.

There is a looser sense in which the encyclicals could warrant that description, however. There is a persistent theme of criticism of idolatry, as manifested in contemporary culture. For instance, in the condemnation of ''the all-consuming desire for profit'' and ''the thirst for power,''[7] Christians are challenged to live out the Gospel, i.e., not to succumb to such idolatries in their own existence. But whether or not *that* is to be characterized as ''countercultural'' depends upon whether one considers culture to be utterly captive to such desires. Clearly, there are theologians and ecclesial bodies in the contemporary world who take such a pessimistic view of culture as it exists beyond the Christian community,[8] but that is hardly the attitude conveyed by these encyclicals. Indeed, the encyclicals do not give enough attention to ecclesiology to warrant that kind of characterization of the Christian community as ''countercultural.'' There is a challenge to the Church, to be sure; but it is of a much more modest sort than one finds among more radical Christian sectarians—or even among such Roman Catholic groups as the Center of Concern and the various Catholic-base communities.

Still, the encyclicals are far from being a simple accommodation to the contemporary world. They do not represent an expression of H. R. Niebuhr's ''Christ of culture'' type.[9] Their theological grounding and economic applications are worth exploring as a significant challenge to economic life in our time.

Theological Groundings

Early in *LE* the point is registered that it is a reversal of ''the right order of values'' to treat human beings as mere instruments of production.[10] This makes explicit what is implicit in both encyclicals: economics must always be understood to be instrumental to deeper human values, not the other way around. Those deeper human values are finally theological in character, for they relate humanity to the fundamental purposes of creation. Human beings are created by God. They are accountable to God, and they are given by God the inestimable opportunity to participate in the ongoing divine work of creation.[11] Human dignity consists in our being subjects, not objects only—a gift we have from the Creator.

Nor is human dignity an altogether individual attribute. We are also social by nature—a point underscored theologically by reference to the social character of the divine Trinity.[12] Distinguishing between the natural bonds of human relationships and the specifically Christian understandings of community, he writes that

> Awareness of the common fatherhood of God, of the brotherhood of all in Christ—"children in the Son"—and of the presence and life-giving action of the Holy Spirit will bring to our vision of the world *a new criterion* for interpreting it. Beyond human and natural bonds, already so close and strong, there is discerned in the light of faith a new *model* of the *unity* of the human race, which must ultimately inspire our *solidarity*. This supreme *model of unity,* which is a reflection of the intimate life of God, one God in three Persons, is what we Christians mean by the word "communion."[13]

The import of this theological perspective is to save us from excessive individualism in the way we conceive of human dignity. We are individual in the fullest, deepest sense; but we are also social; we belong to one another as we belong to God. It follows that the effects of economic institutions, policies, and practices upon human solidarity must be weighed seriously, along with their effects upon persons as individuals.

The point is developed also in relationship to sin, although here John Paul emphasizes that social or "structural" sin is "the result of the accumulation and concentration of many *personal sins.*"[14] Sin is understood by him as specific acts for which persons are specifically responsible, although obstacles are created to the realization of the common good through actions introducing and consolidating "structures of sin." It is not proper, he feels, to refer to institutions or structures or society itself as the "subject of moral acts," for "the real responsibility . . . lies with individuals."[15] Hence, he continues, "a situation cannot in itself be good or bad."

That, of course, is also partly a matter of definition. In context the Pope seems to be saying that structures and "situations" are not themselves moral actors. He does not, in context, appear to be saying that structures and situations do not have good or evil *effects*—for the identification of good and evil effects at work in the structures of human society is the main point of both these encyclicals.

I suspect that the Pope's reason for emphasizing individual responsibility for sin may be related to his somewhat guarded references to liberation theology. Acknowledging that there are "positive values" in the latter, he cites as well "the deviations and risks of deviation, which are damaging to the faith and are connected with this form of theological reflection and method."[16] Liberation that touches only the economic sphere is incomplete; authentic liberation requires the overcoming of the obstacles presented by sin. Thus, he has implicitly rejected the notion that evil is wholly structural in its nature. And to the extent that liberation theology implies that it is, the Pope points to deeper theological ground. Thus also, he insists that

> Development that does not include the *cultural, transcendent and religious dimensions* of man and society . . . is *even less* conducive to authentic liberation. Human beings are totally free only when they are completely *themselves,* in the fullness of their rights and duties. The same can be said about society as a whole.[17]

The message is not simply one of individualistic moralism, although the Pope has an almost Kantian tendency to focus moral responsibility at the personal level—a point to which we shall return below. He recognizes that there can be a left- as well as right-wing reduction of our humanity to economic instrumentality. If our humanity does not in some fundamental way transcend the circumstances of our existence—even those that enslave us, then we are truly objects only and not subjects. To concede that we are altogether made what we are by the structures of society is already to invite the conclusion that our humanity is simply to be "used" by whatever powers, of left or right, happen to be in control. Whether the implied criticism here of liberation theology is on target is a question largely beyond the purview of this paper,[18] although there are certain insights typical of liberation theology to which the Pope may not have attended sufficiently in his encyclicals.

He clearly has not overlooked one theme of importance to the liberation theologians: the "preferential option for the poor." Referring to the treatment accorded this theme by the Magisterium in recent years, the Pope speaks of this as a "*love of preference* for the poor." It is to be understood as "a *special form* of primacy in the exercise of Christian charity, to which the whole tradition of the Church bears witness. It affects the life of each Christian inasmuch as he or she seeks to imitate the life of Christ."[19] Applying this insight to the contemporary world, he remarks that "this love of preference for the poor, and the decisions which it inspires in us, cannot but embrace the immense multitudes of the hungry, the needy, the homeless, those without medical care and, above all, those without hope of a better future." If we ignore these realities, he continues, we are "like the 'rich man' who pretended not to know the beggar Lazarus lying at his gate."[20]

There is some ambiguity about the structural implications of this (a matter to which we shall return), and much of the language Pope John Paul II uses would be consistent with a rather paternalistic response to poverty. Nevertheless, he has marked poverty as a theological concern of fundamental importance.

That is underscored further by his recognition of the moral importance of equality. The means of subsistence were intended for all; therefore, inequality of distribution constitutes a "serious problem."[21] "Both peoples and individuals," he writes, "must enjoy the *fundamental equality* which is the basis, for example, of the Charter of the United Nations Organization: the equality which is the basis of the right of all to share in the process of full development."[22] The foundational principle of equality is not developed theologically in these encyclicals, but it flows easily from his understanding of the doctrine of creation.

Theological Assessments

One does not expect fully elaborated theological treatises in papal encyclicals, though some address the theological task with greater clarity and sophistication than others. These two, LE and SRS, in my judgment, are not bad. As a Protestant Christian, I note (with appreciation) the continued movement of twentieth century encyclicals away from an almost exclusive reliance on fairly sterile Thomism to a more richly grounded theological argumentation. The doctrine of creation, in which these documents are largely grounded, can incorporate the basic insights of the natural law tradition while acknowledging that that tradition finally rests on faith claims about the source of all being. The work of Christ through redemption is incorporated also in these texts, though not with the richness of insight of a Karl Barth. The great biblical themes of covenant and grace might have added enormous theological weight to the points Pope John Paul II was seeking to make. Those themes could have saved the encyclicals from the hint of prescriptive moralism we have already noted. The doctrine of creation could be seen as the intersection between the grace-filled covenant and the structures and possibilities of human existence. Our action, our "work," could then been seen more clearly as a response to the grace we have as a free gift from God.

The encyclical on work does go some distance in this direction, and one notes (again with appreciation) that papal teaching on vocation is broadening out to include secular work as a sphere for divine calling. That encyclical contains eloquent witness to the importance of the creative work of all people as a part of God's own creative purposes. Obviously, that broader theological appreciation for secular work has enormous implications for the legitimization of economic activity, just as it places much contemporary economic activity under judgment for its destructiveness.

But what about the Pope's handling of the doctrine of sin?

I remarked earlier that I suspect his treatment of the subject was influenced by his response to liberation theology. If so, it is a response with which I am partly in agreement. At least I agree that sin is present in individuals, and not only in structures, and that we cannot expect to cure the roots of human evil and injustice by addressing only structures. But has the Pope's brief treatment of this quite come to grips with the realities of corporate or systemic evil?

It may be true that institutions are not, in the moral sense, responsible actors. An Adolf Eichmann or Klaus Barbie, caught up as they were in massive institutional evil, still retained personal moral responsibility. They could not claim, ultimately, that they were literally *forced* to do the evil deeds they were later convicted of doing. On one level, to be a human being is to acknowledge personal accountability before God, before one's fellows, and before the bar of history. The anti-war slogan of the Viet Nam War era made the point: "What if they threw a war and nobody came?" If people refuse to participate in evil, it dies then and there. Institutions, structures and systems do not function of their own accord. It takes *people,* individual people, to make them function.

But to leave the question on that ground is largely to miss the point: Those same moral beings are affected and influenced by the social structures of which they are a part. Setting aside the question of personal accountability for the moment, is it not a matter of grave moral consequence whether the structures and institutions and systems tend toward evil or toward good? Surely the Pope would be the first to say yes, it does matter very much—so much so that one must (as a pope) write encyclicals to expose and denounce social evil and its attendant human suffering! But to acknowledge that is to concede that what is at stake in social evil is not just the question of correctly assigning guilt but the further—ofttimes more important question of dealing with the problem. A recognition that we are all sinners, while it can sometimes lead to complacency, at least helps us recognize that we all depend upon God's grace to get out of the messes we have created.

While liberation theology, in its various forms, has sometimes been overly moralistic in presentation, it does at least grasp the systemic character of evil and the systemic roots of much concrete human suffering. One of its central points was particularly well stated by Walter Rauschenbusch, principal theological spokesperson of the forerunner "Social Gospel" movement. In a book analyzing the task of transforming human society in accordance with the will of Christ, Rauschenbusch remarked that an unchristian social order can be known by the fact that it *makes good people do bad things.*[23]

Now there is an insight worthy of papal examination! It may be that nobody is literally *forced* to do either good or bad things. But an unjust social order can force agonizing dilemmas upon good people, and a just social order can force unjust people to think twice. The former is illustrated by the dilemma of those who must choose between doing corrupt or unethical things and depriving the loved ones who are dependent upon them. There are numerous situations in the world today where the basic structures are so dominated by corruption that one must act corruptly to get by. Then should one try to "get by"? One may have to in order to act lovingly. The real world of harsh, unjust institutions often enough confronts moral people with alternatives that are *all* morally unacceptable in the pure sense. Christabel Bielenberg describes the horror she and her husband faced as morally sensitive citizens of Germany in the 1930s:

> They were the years when Peter and I, ordinary young citizens, willing and probably capable of making some useful contribution to the society in which we lived, were being forced to face the stark reality that, although our circumstances appeared outwardly to be ordinary, in truth they were not; for, if we valued our integrity, no normal or natural ambition could find any outlet whatsoever under a regime such as Hitler's. We could evade making major concessions . . . , but it became increasingly difficult to escape the occasional compromise. By compromising we could learn how each small demand for our outward acquiescence could lead to the next, and with the gentle persistence of an incoming tide could lap at the walls of just that integrity we were so anxious to preserve.[24]

In our preoccupation with individual moral responsibility we must not forget just how tightly the world is wired together. An important part of the Christian vocation in a fallen world is to help create institutions and systems in which normal activity yields moral results, replacing or reforming institutions and systems in which ordinary behavior yields evil.

No Christian should expect perfection in this. Surely the Pope is right in reminding us that the Kingdom of God will not finally be realized until the end of history.[25] We must not expect to achieve a perfect society; by the same token, even in this fallen world human society is not totally evil. The truly significant moral questions respecting social institutions and systems are the relative ones. But that does not mean that such questions *are* unimportant; to the contrary, it means that such questions are the ones that really are important. Indeed, whether we choose the relatively good over the relatively evil is important enough to be termed an absolute choice. Confronted by a choice between "better" or "worse," it is absolutely wrong to choose "worse"—it being acknowledged that our knowledge of the relative good of human culture is itself limited.[26]

Problems in Contemporary Economic Culture

The papal encyclicals we have been considering take up a variety of economic problems in the contemporary world, subjecting them to analysis in light of the theological perspective. The listing is somewhat predictable, both in light of that perspective and the issues being debated in the world of the 1980s. On the whole, I do not find the Pope's diagnosis to be radical enough to warrant the term "countercultural," although his judgments are often searching ones. I wish here to comment on eight of the problems upon which he has touched.

1. The Role of Ideology in Economic Debate

We might note first the Pope's attitude toward economic ideology. As we have suggested in relation to his theological views, John Paul II wishes to avoid ideologies of both left and right. Seeking to situate the Church above both tendencies, he insists that "the Church's social doctrine *is not* a 'third way' between *liberal capitalism* and *Marxist collectivism,* nor even a possible alternative to other solutions less radically opposed to one another; rather, it constitutes a *category of its own.*"[27] This "category" is not "an *ideology,* but rather the *accurate formulation* of the results of a careful reflection on the complex realities of human existence" with an aim toward interpreting those realities."[28] The Church's social doctrine is not ideology, he concludes, but theology.

The Pope here adds his voice to a procession of other Christian thinkers who have asserted the priority of theology to ideology. If one thinks of "ideology" as "a pattern of beliefs and concepts (both factual and normative) which purport to explain complex social phenomena with a view to directing and simplifying sociopolitical choices facing individuals and groups,"[29] then it should be clear that the sources of the norms or values are prior to ideologies themselves. But then, when one spells out a "pattern of beliefs and concepts" to explain and deal with social reality, surely one is engaging in ideological thinking. Perhaps it would be better to acknowledge forthrightly that Christians do engage in such thinking.

But some ideologies are more adequate than others, seen in light of Christian faith. Pope John Paul II does well to criticize ideological extremes of capitalism and Marxism, as he does in both encyclicals.[30] His brief discussions at this point remind one of the critiques of capitalism and communism in the 1930s and 1940s by the Life and Work Movement and World Council of Churches,[31] and he might have improved the encyclicals by tapping into some of that literature. It seems clear to me that his own ideological dispositions are those of the ''mixed-economy'' welfare state—or ''social market capitalism'' as some have termed it.[32] He defends the rights of property and freedom of economic initiative, while clearly calling for substantial public involvement meeting the needs of poor people and providing for the common good. He specifically doubts that laissez faire will automatically care for such needs, but the Marxist alternative appears to him to err at the other end by choking off freedom and recognition of the broader cultural life of human society. In these judgments he is in the company of much Western political-economic thought.

2. Work and the Problem of Unemployment

The Pope has, of course, devoted an entire encyclical to the subject of work. He regards work as fundamental to human existence, not only because it is generally a requisite for livelihood but also because it is necessary to human fulfillment. It is through work that we become ''more a human being.''[33] That means fulfillment in the social context and not simply as an individual alone.[34]

Accordingly, unemployment can be a very great tragedy. In *LE,* the Pope cites ''a disconcerting fact of immense proportions: the fact that while conspicuous natural resources remain unused there are huge numbers of people who are unemployed or underemployed and countless multitudes of people suffering from hunger.''[35] While wishing to avoid a ''one-sided centralization by the public authorities,'' he clearly regards employment to be ''in the final analysis'' a concern for the state. Repeating his words in the later encyclical, he notes grimly that unemployment and underemployment are growing in the industrialized countries and that in the developing countries ''the *sources of work* seem to be shrinking, and thus the opportunities for employment are decreasing rather than increasing."[36]

The fact of unemployment is obvious to everybody, and the Pope's words on the subject are no less welcome for being somewhat predictable. In current debates, his call for greater state involvement (and greater involvement by the international organizations) is modestly controversial, at least among people who think the free market mechanism will automatically provide enough jobs at home and abroad if we just leave it alone. Even a Peter Berger, impressed by the economic take-off of such countries as South Korea and Taiwan through reliance on market principles, could question whether the Pope has emphasized enough the possibilities of private investment and capitalism.[37] The Pope does observe that when the "right of economic initiative" is suppressed there are negative results. But the Pope, who thus cannot be accused of being anti-capitalist, is also clear that capitalism alone is not enough.

One might wish that he had also addressed the trade-offs represented by the "Phillips Curve" and the increasing mobility of capital in the contemporary world. The Phillips Curve alleges a more or less necessary trade-off between full employment and high rates of inflation: the fuller the employment rate, the more likely an economy is to have higher inflation; the more unemployment, on the other hand, the less likelihood of inflation. Full employment in a market economy means that employers must bid higher wages to attract workers, with the consequence of increased costs, prices, etc., in an upward spiral. Unemployment, on the other hand, means that workers who are competing for the available jobs are more likely to accept lower wages, thus decreasing costs, prices, etc., in a downward spiral. The Phillips Curve does not work exactly in the real world. But insofar as it does, it is a nice question whether some unemployment is worth the resulting price stability or, for that matter, whether some other alternative—such as wage- and price-fixing—may be desirable. Certainly, the Pope's moral conception of the importance of work opportunity would not be consistent with economic policies deliberately maintaining unemployment for the sake of price stability—with the unemployed alone having to bear the social cost of this aspect of the common good. It does no good to invoke the cliché that "inflation hurts poor people the most." That may or may not be the case in general; but inflation with income is likely to be better than price stability without income!

The other question is particularly poignant in industrialized countries such as the United States in which large numbers of industrial jobs have been lost through the export of productive operations to Third World settings. It is increasingly possible for companies to save on labor costs by moving operations from high labor cost, unionized settings in North America to developing countries where adequate labor can be had for a fraction of the cost. No doubt this does, to some extent, benefit workers in the developing countries, though at the cost of considerable social dislocation in the previous setting. There may be no easy moral answer to this dilemma, since a strong moral case can be made both for the job security of the original workers (and their communities) and for the employment and economic development of people in the new setting. Nevertheless, some moral criteria and legal principles may need to be established to cope with this dilemma.

3. Economic Inequality

Absolute economic inequality is an impossibility in the real world but, as we have seen, Pope John Paul II strongly affirms equality as a governing moral principle to the extent of its possibility.[38] In these encyclicals, he confronts the great social and economic inequalities in the contemporary world, noting that gaps exist within both rich and poor nations as well as between them. "The abundance of goods and services available in some parts of the world," he writes, "is matched in the South by an unacceptable delay." He notes:

> Looking at all the various sectors—the production and distribution of foodstuffs, hygiene, health and housing, availability of drinking water, working conditions (especially for women), life expectancy and other economic and social indicators—the general picture is a disappointing one, both considered in itself and in relation to the corresponding data of the more developed countries. The word "gap" returns spontaneously to mind.[39]

He concludes that "*the unity of the world,* that is, *the unity of the human race,* is seriously compromised."

The point could have been stated with even greater emphasis for a world culture in which the proposition has been accepted too readily that the only thing at stake in economic life is whether people have enough goods and services to protect their *physical* well-being. Important as that is, the relational consequences of economics are also fundamental, and the effects of inequalities—particularly great ones—upon social unity can be serious.

Within the United States, a recent study by the Ways and Means Committee of the U.S. House of Representatives suggests that economic disparities have widened enormously in the past fifteen years. The lowest quintile of the population has dropped nearly 11 percent in average income during that period, while the average income of the highest fifth has *increased* by 24 percent.[40] The social pathologies plainly evident in the country at the present time no doubt have multiple causes. But one cannot suppress the thought that the widening social gaps are important contributing factors, making it more difficult for people to identify with the society as mutual participants working together for the common good. Many of the poorer Third and Fourth World countries are plagued by even wider gaps of wealth and income, as the Pope notes, and these gaps may not be unrelated to other kinds of social pathology.

4. Materialism

The Pope, in both encyclicals, strongly condemns the increases of materialism to be observed worldwide. The value of work, he writes in his labor encyclical, is distorted by a "onesidedly materialistic civilization," and "man is treated as an instrument of production."[41] In even stronger language, the second encyclical notes the emptiness of the materialism of this civilization:

> This superdevelopment, which consists of an *excessive* availability of every kind of material goods for the benefit of certain social groups, easily makes people slaves of "possession" and of immediate gratification. All of us experience firsthand the sad effects of this blind submission to pure consumerism: in the first place a crass materialism, and at the same time a *radical dissatisfaction,* because one quickly learns—unless one is

shielded from the flood of publicity and the ceaseless and tempting offers of products—that the more one possesses the more one wants, while
deeper aspirations remain unsatisfied and perhaps even stifled.[42]

The point is obviously related to the theological criticism of idolatry;
for the materialistic consumerism truly is a worshipping of false gods,
with the concomitant effect of falsifying our humanity as well.

The cultural criticism is easier to register than an appropriate economic prescription. Indeed, there may be no economic prescription.
Consumerism is expressed in forms that are specific to different environments, but it is present everywhere in the modern world—not ex-
cepting the socialist countries where it is sometimes heightened by
scarcity. A truly countercultural prescription—which we do not encounter in these encyclicals—might call for withdrawal into enclaves of
self-sufficient simplicity. But that would not easily be accomplished in
an increasingly interdependent economic world supporting now a
greatly enlarged population whose needs must be supplied by large-
scale production.

I suspect that economic idolatries, like other false gods, can only be
made to yield to the positive claims of more authentic forms of human
fulfillment. Materialism, at best, is really only the consolation prize
compensating for a greater loss. What may be needed is a clearer creative vocation and a deeper sense of the common good. Economic policy may have some contribution to make to this insofar as it summons
us to common purpose and to address the needs of others. But the essentially religious and cultural dimension is equally important, for materialism is essentially a cultural and religious question.

5. The Economic Role of Women

The importance of family life is emphasized by the Pope at various
points, such as in his reiteration of the now classic family criterion of the
just wage articulated by Pope Leo XIII in *Rerum Novarum*.[43] But his conception of the economic role of women remains substantially bounded by
their traditional place in family life. Thus he writes that "it will redound
to the credit of society to make it possible for a mother—without inhibiting her freedom, without psychological or practical discrimination, and

without penalizing her as compared with other women—to devote herself to taking care of her children and educating them in accordance with their needs, which vary with age.''[44] It is wrong for a mother to have ''to abandon these tasks in order to take up paid work outside the home.'' While noting that ''in many societies women work in nearly every sector of life,'' the Pope remarks that ''they should be able to fulfill their tasks *in accordance with their own nature,* without being discriminated against and without being excluded from jobs for which they are capable, but also without lack of respect for their family aspirations and for their specific role in contributing, together with men, to the good of society.''[45] So women should not ''have to pay for their advancement by abandoning *what is specific to them* and at the expense of the family, in which women as mothers have an irreplaceable role.''[46]

The underlined phrases in these quotations suggest that the Pope considers the role differentiations between women and men to be fixed by nature—a viewpoint which complicates the Church's ecclesiology as well as its social teaching in the contemporary world. Whether one regards such a viewpoint as countercultural or not depends upon whether one regards the traditional role differentiations as the dominant norm or the more recent entry of millions of women into previously male-dominated jobs and professions. The question remains whether these differentiations are grounded in nature.

While writing this paper, I chanced again upon a fascinating passage in a 1944 writing of Reinhold Niebuhr which might usefully supplement the Pope's judgments on this matter:

> The mother is biologically more intimately related to the child than the father. This fact limits the vocational freedom of women; for it makes motherhood a more exclusive vocation than fatherhood, which is indeed no more than an avocation. The wider rights of women have been achieved in the modern period, partly by defying this limitation which nature places upon womanhood. But it is also a fact that human personality rises in indeterminate freedom over biological function. The right of women to explore and develop their capacities beyond their family function, was unduly restricted in all previous societies.[47]

Niebuhr concluded that ''the wisdom of the past which recognized the hazard to family life in the freedom of women, was not devoid of the

taint of male ideology,' " with a male oligarchy using "fixed principles of natural law to preserve its privileges and powers against a new
emergent in history."[48]

Clearly, women have been endowed by their Creator with all the
gifts of intelligence and creativity accorded men. Even the differentials
in physical strength are relatively modest and, in an age of technological sophistication, increasingly unimportant. Moreover, men are discovering that their participation in the parenting role is more important than they had supposed; fatherhood need not be as
"avocational" as even Niebuhr supposed.

In any event, the changing role of women in economic life can be
affirmed more generously than the Pope has done, and the issues for
family life can be addressed more creatively in an age where the equality of women and men can be respected more fully.

6. The Population Problem

The population problem, which has been vexatious for Catholic social teaching at various points, is touched upon by Pope John Paul II in
SRS. Acknowledging that "one cannot deny the existence, especially
in the southern hemisphere, of a demographic problem which creates
difficulties for development," the Pope adds that many of the countries of the northern hemisphere are suffering from a birthrate lower
than needed to replace an aging population.[49] He also expresses concern over the coercive campaigns being launched "against birth" in
many countries and the "*absolute lack of respect* for the freedom of
choice of the parties involved."[50]

In respect to this, I am not sure the Pope has fully comprehended the
enormity of the twentieth century population explosion and how des-
perately important it has been for many countries to get a "handle" on
it. His concern about draconian population measures may well have
had China in mind. Reports on China need to be interpreted cautiously. Possibly population planning there has been too coercive. But
clearly something had to be done to bring population growth into a
more sustainable balance with limited resources. If the "invisible
hand" of the laissez faire economists is not to be trusted, can we be so

certain that the individual decisions made by individual couples will inevitably add up to the common good for society as a whole.

The concern for human life and respect for the dignity of family life that probably underlie the Pope's concerns on this point are altogether laudable. But the Christian doctrine of creation is a reminder of our finitude; we are created on a finite planet with limited dimensions and resources. Response to God in this setting must include coming to terms with our limitations as well as our possibilities.

7. Environmental Problems

The ecological problem is one of the few points where one can discern some real movement between the two encyclicals. The encyclical on work gives great emphasis to the theme of "dominion" in creation. The human mandate is to "subdue," to "dominate" the earth. "As man, through his work, becomes more and more the master of the earth, and as he confirms his dominion over the visible world, again through his work, he nevertheless remains in every case and at every phase of this process within the creator's original ordering." All human beings take part "in the giant process whereby man 'subdues the earth' through his work."[51]

That emphasis, combined with a fundamentally affirmative attitude toward technology, could suggest a corresponding insensitivity toward the limits, balances, and vulnerabilities of nature. In the other encyclical, however, as if to correct for a certain one-sidedness, the Pope writes of the realization that *natural resources* are limited; some are not, as it is said, *renewable*. Using them as if they were inexhaustible, with *absolute dominion,* seriously endangers their availability not only for the present generation but above all for generations to come."[52]

The point is well taken. It is reminiscent of the prophetic call of the World Council of Churches for a society that is just, participatory, and *sustainable.*[53] The point also has important implications for the relationship between the developed and developing countries. For numbers of the latter situations are confronted with the dilemma that rapid development will inevitably increase environmental problems unless the cost of development is shared by others. The great rain forests of the Amazon, for instance, are an economic resource that are there to be exploited by a Brazil that feels severe pressures for ways to eradicate an enormous international debt. The question is whether the wealthier countries, which have a great, long-term stake in the preservation of those same rain forests, will be willing to help pay the cost.

8. The International Economic Order

Much of the encyclical *SRS* is concerned with these and other aspects of global economic interconnectedness. Its major themes are somewhat reminiscent of the North/South report of the Brandt Commission, although the Pope may be more realistic about the extent of the justice questions at work *within* the poorer countries and not just in the relationship between those societies and the wealthier lands of the north.

The analysis is not deeply technical, nor is it strikingly radical. It does convey recognition that the whole world is a single moral community and, echoing Pope John XXIII, that there is need for a better crafting of international institutions. Humanity today "needs a *greater degree of international ordering,* at the service of the societies, economies and cultures of the whole world."[54] Because that truth is not spelled out in great detail is a reminder that an encyclical letter can only tackle so much!

The Agenda for Christians

Both encyclicals seek to challenge the Christian conscience of this age and to appeal to Christians and to the Church to act with new sensitivity and moral intelligence in the economic sphere. Action is both civic and personal, both ecclesial and vocational. Christians are not summoned here to a new sectarianism in their gathered life as a community of faith, nor are they urged to adopt an ascetic lifestyle. They are asked to live in real tension with the excessive materialism of the age and to seek, through their economic activity, to work for genuine community.

Returning again to the question with which we began, whether this agenda is "countercultural" is a matter for definition. I should say it is not, at least in the accepted sense of the term. But the tension which must be accepted by faithful Christians between the implications of the gospel they profess and the realities of the world does at least entail dimensions of the countercultural. No Christian can be comfortable with an economic order consigning hundreds of millions of people to severe deprivation, for those multitudes are sisters and brothers in a sense that is deeper than the biological. Nor can a Christian be complacent with the pressures we all feel to accept materialistic values threatening our essential humanity.

The Pope's encyclicals are a call to live in that kind of tension. But they are also a reminder that we are not alone. Christians—Catholics, Protestant, Orthodox alike—are legion in number, and they are joined also by non-Christians whom the Pope addresses as other persons "of good will." The test of our good faith and our good will is our readiness to work with others in addressing these economic problems.

Notes

1. Such criticism is illustrated by Paul Ramsey's polemic against the United Methodist bishops' pastoral letter "In Defense of Creation" and the Roman Catholic Lay Commission's ongoing debate with the U.S. Catholic bishops' pastoral letter on the U.S. economy. See Ramsey, *Speak up for Just War or Pacifism* (University Park and London: Penn State Univ. Press, 1988), and Lay Commission, *Toward the Future: Catholic Social Thought and the U.S. Economy* (N.Y.: American Catholic Committee, 1984) and "Liberty and Justice for All" (1986).

2. Pope John Paul II, *On Human Work: Laborem Exercens* (Washington, D.C.: U.S. Catholic Conference, 1981), henceforth cited as *LE*.

3. Pope John Paul II, *On Social Concern: Sollicitudo Rei Socialis* (Washington, D.C.: U.S. Catholic Conference, 1987), henceforth cited as *SRS*.

4. See Jacques Ellul, *The Technological Society* (N.Y.: Alfred A. Knopf, 1964) or his *The Meaning of the City* (Grand Rapids: Wm. B. Eerdmans, 1970).

5. *LE*, II-5.

6. *Ibid.*

7. *SRS*, V-37.

8. The Amish, many Mennonite communities, and the Sojourners community illustrate the point among communities of faith; the writings of Jacques Ellul, John Howard Yoder and, to some extent, Stanley Hauerwas and James Wm. McClendon illustrate it among theologians.

9. H. Richard Niebuhr, *Christ and Culture* (N.Y.: Harper and Brothers, 1951). Typologies are not instruments of precision, and it is not clear exactly where the encyclicals of Pope John Paul II should be classified in Niebuhr's. If pressed, I would locate his views somewhere between the "Christ above culture" and "Christ transforming" types. There is too little revelational content in the encyclicals to locate them without qualification in the latter, but the agenda is too oriented toward change to make the former entirely appropriate.

10. *LE*, 11-7.

11. *LE*, V-25 cites the words of Vatican II's *Guadium et Spes* in noting that when "men and women are performing their activities in a way which appropriately benefits society" "they can justly consider that by their labor they are unfolding the Creator's work, consulting the advantages of their brothers and sisters, and contributing by their personal industry to the realization in history of the divine plan."

12. *SRS*, V-40.

13. *Ibid*.

14. *SRS*, V-37. John Paul here is quoting from his Apostolic Exhortation *Reconciliatio et Paenitentia* (2 December, 1984), 16.

15. *Ibid*.

16. *SRS*, VII-46. Here he affirms the critique of liberation theology published in 1984 by the Congregation for the Doctrine of the Faith.

17. *Ibid*. Emphasis in the original text in this and another papal quotations unless otherwise indicated.

18. Elsewhere, in a discussion of liberation theology, I have noted the radical importance of the theological question of original sin. Where that doctrine is neglected there is a corresponding tendency to fail to anticipate abuses of power in the post-revolutionary liberated society. See J. Philip Wogaman, *Christian Perspectives on Politics* (Philadelphia: Fortress Press, 1988), esp. chapter 4. Of course, liberationists themselves quite properly criticize Christian complacency about *present* abuses of power.

19. *SRS*, VI-42.

20. *Ibid*.

21. *SRS*, II-9.

22. *SRS*, IV-33.

23. Walter Rauschenbusch, *Christianizing the Social Order* (N.Y.: Macmillan, 1912), p. 127.

24. Christabel Bielenberg, *Christabel* (N.Y. and London: Penguin Books, 1989 [1968]), pp. 25–26.

25. *SRS*, VII-48.

26. I have explored such issues at greater length in *Christian Moral Judgment* (Louisville: Westminster/John Knox Press, 1989).

27. *SRS*, VI-41.

28. *Ibid.*

29. The definition, which I find felicitous, is from Julius Gould, as quoted by Harry M. Johnson, "Ideology and the Social System," *Encyclopedia of the Social Sciences* (N.Y.: Macmillan, 1968), p. 76.

30. See *LE*, III-14 and *SRS*, III-20.

31. See especially, World Council of Churches, *The Church and the Disorder of Society*, Report of Section III of the First Assembly of the World Council of Churches (N.Y. Harper and Brothers, 1948), pp. 193–195). The incisive analysis on those pages leads to the conclusion that both communism and laissez-faire capitalism have made promises they could not redeem and that Christians should "seek new, creative solutions which never allow either justice or freedom to destroy the other." (p. 195).

32. I have explored this and other ideological tendencies more fully in J. Philip Wogaman, *The Great Economic Debate: An Ethical Analysis* (Philadelphia: Westminster Press, 1977).

33. *LE*, II-9. The Pope's point is developed with even greater richness by the U.S. Catholic bishops in their community participation criterion of economic good. See *Economic Justice for All: Pastoral Letter on Catholic Social Teaching and the U.S. Economy* (Washington, D.C.: National Conference of Catholic Bishops, 1986); see especially paragraphs 77, 97, and 141.

34. "Work" is defined very broadly by the Pope as "any activity by man, whether manual or intellectual, whatever its nature or circumstances . . ." *LE*, Introduction. Accordingly, work is not limited to the things people are compensated for doing. The Pope specifically includes the work of a mother in the home in his definition.

35. *LE*, IV-18.

36. *SRS*, III-18.

37. Peter Berger, *The Capitalist Revolution: Fifty Propositions about Prosperity, Equality, and Liberty* (N.Y. Basic Books, 1986). Berger's fifty propositions suggest the broad superiority of capitalist development over socialist development on the basis of recent economic experience with both models, especially in Asia. Such an analysis, into which we cannot enter in this paper, leaves open the question of the necessity or wisdom of government interventions into an economy that is still conducted basically on free market principles—that is, the question of a "mixed economy."

38. I have dealt with the equality as a moral presumption, with inequalities having to face the burden of proof, in J. Philip Wogaman, *Christian Moral Judgment* (Louisville: Westminster/John Knox Press, 1989), pp. 89–96.

39. *SRS*, III-14.

40. Spencer Rich, "The Rich Get Richer and . . . ," in *The Washington Post* (March 28, 1989). The study indicates that the bulk of this increased gap opened up during the 1980s, paralleling severe cutbacks in social welfare programs and heightened reliance on free market principles.

41. *LE*, II-16.

42. *SRS*, IV-28.

43. *LE*, IV-18.

44. *Ibid.*

45. *Ibid.* Emphasis supplied.

46. *Ibid.* Emphasis supplied.

47. Reinhold Niebuhr, *The Children of Light and the Children of Darkness* (N.Y.: Scribner's, 1944), pp. 76–77.

48. *Ibid.*, p. 77.

49. *SRS*, III-25.

50. *Ibid.*

51. *LE*, II-4.51.

52. *SRS*, IV-34.

53. See David Gill, ed., *Gathered for Life: Official Report, VI Assembly of the World Council of Churches* (Geneva: World Council of Churches, 1983), pp. 30, 78, 84, 90.

54. *SRS*, VI-43.

Four

John Paul II and the International System

J. Bryan Hehir

The purpose of this paper is to examine the position of Pope John Paul II on the contemporary international system. It is written at the end of the first decade of John Paul II's ministry and on the threshold of the final decade of the twentieth century. In his first ten years the Pope, by word and action, demonstrated his major interest in international affairs. He is also likely to lead the Catholic Church through this next decade into the twenty-first century, a decade promising major changes in international relations. From his record of international engagement, it is possible to extract a conception of John Paul II's view of how the world is and how it ought to be. The position is not systematically set forth in the style of a scholar's monograph, although the Pope has demonstrated his scholarly capacities earlier in his career. Now, the demands and opportunities of his office both require and allow him to use a variety of forums to comment on the empirical and normative aspects of world politics. The literary forms he uses run from encyclicals, through addresses, to the homilies and lectures he gives on his trips to local churches throughout the world. The style and purpose of these statements vary greatly, and the assessment of how the Pope influences the direction of international events must consider both the range of his interests and the mixture of diplomacy and teaching which he employs.

In assessing his role and views on the international system, this paper will look at the Pope as both a diplomatic actor and a religious-moral teacher. I look first at the Pope as a pastor and diplomat; secondly, I will examine central themes of his teaching on the international system. Although the principal focus of this volume is on the Pope's economic vision, I am not equipped by training or background to make this theme the major concern of a paper. Hence I will concentrate on other aspects of the papal teaching which relate to and set the context for the economic ideas.

Style: The Pope as Pastor and Diplomatic Actor

To examine John Paul II's views on international relations requires that he be watched and read. For the Pope, in the style of deGaulle, engages the political order by actions and by words. The office he occupies allows him to function as both religious teacher and head of state. In his mind the religious office is the controlling element of his activity, but he clearly intends to make use of both the religious and diplomatic capacities of his role.

From the outset of his ministry, the Polish Pope raised international expectations. The fact of electing a non-Italian would have been noteworthy in any event, but the reaction of the secular press and of experienced analysts of world affairs about *this* non-Italian involved more than simply surprise that a traditional institution had again (after Vatican II) broken the expected pattern of its activity. The comments of journalist Tad Szulc communicate the kind of interest evoked by John Paul II's election:

> By electing Poland's Karol Cardinal Woytyla to the papacy, the Roman Catholic church has thrust world politics into a wholly new dimension with extraordinary and far reaching consequences that can be measured only with the passage of time. . . . The elevation of the 58 year old Polish prelate to the Holy See as Pope John Paul II constitutes a global political event of vast proportions.[1]

At the outset the expectations reflected in Szulc's statement were primarily due to the fact that a "Second World" personality would now have the world's most visible pulpit. Within months, however, this initial geopolitical interest had become more complex and its salience enhanced by John Paul's conception of how he would use the papal pulpit. The most perceptive biographer of the Pope has compared him with Gregory I (590–604),[2] the pope who helped lay the intellectual and political foundations of Europe after the fall of the Roman Empire. Gregory led the Church through the transition of two centuries and this pope likely will do the same. Indeed, as he defines his ministry he uses the approaching Third Millenium as a horizon for proposing what should be changed in the personal, political and international levels of life.[3] Moreover, the approach of a new century is not purely of chronological significance; the Pope returns regularly to the theme that profound and far-reaching political, economic and social changes are both necessary and possible as humanity approaches the year 2000.

His conception of the papacy, and more deeply of the role of religion in the world, produces an activist view of the life and ministry of the Church. Precisely because of his Second World origins, and because the Church in Poland has been involved in a classical conflict of resistance to a Marxist state, the early commentary of John Paul II was cast in terms of political expectations. His activism meets the prediction of Szulc that this papacy has global political implications, but the Pope refuses a definition of his ministry as political in content or intention. He is conscious that he holds diplomatic status and acts in a diplomatic arena, but he expends significant effort to resist a politicization of his papacy or the ministry of the Church as a whole.

The themes of an activist papacy, a socially engaged Church and the religious roots of both are particularly on display in the papal trips which have characterized his tenure. The Pope has made fifty trips in ten years, visiting the local church in every significant political and ideological setting in the world, save the Soviet Union and China. The range of his visits, criss-crossing capitalist and socialist societies, engaging the East-West and North-South dimensions of world politics, set him apart from any other world leader. The trips are treated by political observers and the diplomatic community as political events. The Pope tenaciously holds to defining them as pastoral events, designed to strengthen the local church and acquaint him with the specific problems and possibilities facing the Catholic community in each place.

As one tries to sort out this dispute certain things are clear. First, the *political significance* of the trips cannot be disputed or discounted. In spite of how the Pope defines his intent, his two visits to Poland (confronting the state and opening the way for Solidarity), his complex and conflicted trip through Central America, his determination to visit England and Argentina when they were at war, his open challenge to Mr. Marcos at the start of his Philippine visit, and the catalytic effect his words in Haiti had in moving the Church to open opposition to the Duvalier regime, all these interventions have carried political weight and consequence. Second, it is not difficult to understand why the Pope resists a political definition of his activity; not only might it restrict his future access to countries, but it would, in fact, reduce his capacity to address issues of human rights, social justice and peace from a position defined as nonpartisan and transcendent of normal political divisions. Third, there is little doubt that when the Pope visits a country, he seeks to set a style and direction for the local church. Hence, the definition of his activity carries implications over the long-term for the local church.

What then does he want to say to the local church? What view of his undoubtedly political action does he hold for himself and for the bishops, priests and nuns whom he warns not to be "political," but to leave the political arena to the laity?

The answer seems to lie in his understanding of the teaching of *Gaudium et Spes* of Vatican II. The Pope wants a socially engaged Church at every level—local, national and international—but he does not want a Church *politically identified* with particular interests at any of those levels. Hence, his determined effort, as a Second World Pope, not to be captured by one side of the East-West argument—much to the chagrin of some commentators in the West. His equally determined view that within countries the Church can make "an option for the poor," but it cannot use this in the model of class conflict—this to the chagrin of some church members in Third World settings.

In his explanation of the social ministry of the Church, the Pope reverts often to *Gaudium et Spes*. The conciliar text fits his model of a socially activist, but religiously rooted ministry.[4] In the Council's view the Church is directed to the service of the Kingdom of God; this ministry will find its completion only in the eschaton. Yet the Church fulfills this service of the Kingdom in history. Hence, the Church should pursue its *religious* ministry in a fashion which serves four historically significant objectives: promoting human dignity, protecting human rights, fostering unity in society and providing a sense of meaning to human activity. To pursue these objectives in the diverse political, economic, ideological and social settings in which the Catholic Church lives is to be engaged in ways that are politically significant. But to affirm and accept the religious basis, motivation and intention of the social ministry is to accept restraints on methods and means which other institutions do not accept. It also means acknowledging that not all socially useful tasks should be the Church's work to fulfill. Some roles, e.g., the use of force, may be necessary, but could compromise the Church's ministry.

This conception of ministry does not keep John Paul II aloof from the political process or the diplomatic arena. He supports actions governments take (like the INF Treaty or the Camp David Accords); he criticizes the policies of governments (on human rights) and groups (opposing terrorist tactics); he intervenes to provide social legitimation (the recent Polish accords) and he calls key actors to go beyond their normal patterns of activity when human needs remain unfulfilled (the debt problem).

But the diplomatic actor believes all this flows from and is shaped by a religious ministry. *The pastor controls the diplomat.* The Church at every level must be identifiably related to its religious roots and purpose. In his teaching on the international system the Pope locates what he says and does in this broader conception of ministry.

Substance: The Pope as Teacher

The pastoral and diplomatic activism of John Paul II should not distract observers from the fact that he has an abiding faith in the power of words and ideas. He stresses the role of a bishop as a teacher, and his own ministry is a continuation of his earlier role as a teacher. Like Leo XIII (1878–1903) and Pius XII (1939–1957) this pope as destined to have an enormous corpus of encyclicals, addresses, and apostolic letters as his legacy. Precisely because every trip adds about fifty new addresses, John Paul probably will surpass his predecessors in the amount of teaching he will leave to the Church.

In the realm of international affairs, precisely because the Pope does not have the normal resources of other heads of state (military or economic capacities), the role of words and ideas takes on even greater significance. The Pope can act in well-defined circumstances, but he has many more possibilities to speak, to seek to influence the actions of others, in the Church and in the international community, by the way he defines reality, evaluates policies, encourages lay choices and calls attention to groups or issues being ignored in the daily flow of world events.

In the first decade of his ministry the Pope has addressed every major area of international relations. In international forums, on his visits to fifty nations and to the constant stream of public figures whom he receives at the Vatican, he has spoken on war and peace, wealth and poverty, human rights and needs in an interdependent world, the value and limits of sovereignty and the role of international organizations and international law in a still decentralized, "anarchic" international order. These statements are usually made in response to specific events or on key anniversaries of other papal texts; the Pope has not set forth a systematic treatment of international relations in the style of Raymond Aron or Kenneth Waltz, yet it is possible to derive from his texts a systematic vision of the world. In this section I will use three topics to illustrate the position of John Paul II on the contemporary international system. To summarize the case, I contend that he is a revisionist voice on the role of the superpowers; he is a nuclear abolitionist; and he combines revolutionary objectives and nonviolent methods to respond to regional conflicts in the developing world. In each instance I will characterize the papal position and comment on its relationship to other views of the international system.

The System and the Superpowers: A Revisionist View

From the beginning of his papacy John Paul II has had what secular analysts would call a "systemic" view of international politics. His addresses to specific issues in the world are situated in the framework of an ongoing assessment and critique of the dynamics of international politics. Two documents, spanning the first ten years of this papacy, illustrate the Pope's proclivity to see world affairs in terms of the international system as a whole. The first was his address to the United Nations in 1979; the second, his most recent encyclical, *On Social Concern*. The texts have different purposes and use quite different styles, but both address the structure and dynamics of international politics as a whole. The U.N. address is a diplomatic text which examines the international system through the prism of human rights; it is a philosophical assessment cast in normative terms with little or no commentary on specific situations. The encyclical is addressed first to the Church and, through this community, to the world; it is fundamentally a normative critique of international affairs but its style is quite explicitly geopolitical in the tone and analysis of patterns of international politics at the end of the 1980s.

Both texts were building on the thought of Pope Paul VI who declared in his 1967 encyclical, *The Progress of Peoples,* that the social question was now worldwide, touching not simply certain nations but the international system as a whole.[5] The specific purpose of *On Social Concern* was to commemorate *The Progress of Peoples,* and to analyze the systemic social question twenty years later. Paul VI had addressed the new dimensions of the social question in terms of its North-South axis; his letter had been a call to the industrialized nations of the North to respond to the needs of developing countries in terms of trade, aid and foreign investment. John Paul II changed the dimensions of the question by making the theme of his encyclical the linkage of the North-South economic agenda with the East-West security agenda. Previous papal teaching had addressed these two questions in separate documents (e.g., John XXIII's *Peace on Earth* and Paul VI's *Progress of Peoples*). Moreover, in the academic study of international relations the same division of labor was usually present; some scholars focused on the security dilemma of political-strategic issues, others probed the interdependence agenda of political-economic questions.[6] There were few attempts to integrate the two tracks on which international relations moved in the 1970s and 1980s.

In the world of practical politics two very different U.S. administrations had failed in their attempts to define the relationship of the East-West to the North-South issues. President Carter's effort, his address at the University of Notre Dame in 1977, sought to displace the East-West axis of the Cold War with a new North-South agenda. The proposal overstated the case; in trying to lift the importance of the economic-human-rights-environmental issues, Carter left himself vulnerable to the charge that he underestimated continuing Soviet efforts to shift the global balance of forces against the West. Soviet increases in military spending in the 1970s plus Soviet activism in the Third World doomed Carter's effort to transform the logic of superpower relations. In reaction to Soviet policies of the 1970s and in accord with the basic vision he brought to the presidency, Ronald Reagan's administration moved to subordinate the North-South issues to the East-West competition. The prism of superpower competition was the lens used to interpret Central America, Southern Africa and the Middle

East. This dramatic reversal of the Carter position also failed to grasp the world as it is. The plan for a strategic consensus in the Middle East was discarded by 1983; constructive engagement in South Africa was dead by 1986 and the Contras were marginalized by 1988. Moreover, mounting Third World debt demonstrated the truth of the argument about interdependence: a Third World default would be also a First World disaster.

Simply the fact of joining the security and interdependence themes in a single encyclical earned *On Social Concern* a worldwide hearing in 1988. The way in which the Pope interpreted the dynamics of international politics guaranteed his letter not only attention but vigorous response. The Pope's letter was an unyielding critique of the role of the superpowers in world affairs. Commentators in the unlikely alliance of *The New York Times* and *The National Review* thought the Pope had succumbed to "moral equivalence."[7] The notion had been spawned in the 1980s to criticize anyone who failed to affirm that U.S. and Soviet actions could not be compared because the nature of their domestic systems is so different. To fail to acknowledge this was to be led down the slippery slope of equating U.S. and Soviet policies. John Paul II did not enter the intricacies of the moral equivalence argument other than to say that both major social systems were in need of urgent and essential changes.[8] But his concern was not to focus on the nature of the superpowers as social systems, but to evaluate the consequences of their competition on others. In contrast to the moral equivalence perspective, the Pope was saying that, in spite of their differences, the superpowers produced similar effects in the lives of smaller and weaker nations. The key line of the indictment was this: "Each of the two blocs harbours in its own way a tendency toward imperialism, as it is usually called, or toward forms of neocolonialism: an easy temptation to which they frequently succumb as history, including recent history, teaches."[9]

This is the "logic of the blocs"—the most celebrated phrase of the encyclical. The logic is rooted in ideological competition; each superpower, as Stanley Hoffmann has observed, "represents a principle of international order and legitimacy as well as a principle of domestic political and social organization which is opposed to the principles of the other side and incapable of worldwide success short of the elimination of the rival."[10] The ideological conflict takes a political shape in terms of the East-West alliances which form the blocs. And the political competition is played out in the race for military preparedness. The consequence of this ideological, political and military competition of the last twenty years is that it has been "an important cause of the retardation or stagnation of the South."[11] The East-West dominance of world affairs has been "a direct obstacle to the real transformation of the conditions of underdevelopment in the developing and less advanced countries."[12]

This theme of the logic of the blocs is the Pope's shorthand version of the consequences of the Cold War. In 1989 we were awash with declarations that the Cold War was passing into history; *what makes the Pope's view distinctive is that he reads the record of the Cold War through that lens of the developing world.* For a Polish Pope, himself a product of the Cold War, its full meaning is not captured by the effects on development, but the emphasis he gives this dimension of the superpower conflict highlights his moral interests.

It also points toward his larger purpose in the encyclical. He goes far beyond the categories of the moral equivalence debate—to confine the Pope in those terms is a diversion and a distortion. The Pope is pressing, instead, a revisionist position regarding the role of the superpowers in the international system. Revisionist powers are usually disruptive and prone to use force to accomplish their objectives. The papal case is moral revisionism: it does seek to disrupt patterns of the last forty years, but to do it in the name of justice and to achieve it through the instruments of peaceful change.

In opposition to the logic of the blocs, the Pope is pursuing a devolution of power, a movement away from the bipolar structure of the Cold War. The call to end the Cold War today does not necessarily imply a change of superpower status. The emphasis of most proposals envisions a situation in which the scope and intensity of the superpower competition is moderated, and the dangers of nuclear war occurring are significantly reduced. These objectives are clearly of great importance to the Pope, but the revisionism of John Paul is particularly focused on a change in the structure of power in the world. He seeks not only to reduce superpower tensions, but to create space which middle powers and small nations can use to expand their choices and take hold of their destiny.

The logic of the papal critique of "the blocs" points toward a more pluralistic international system, a world marked by diffusion of power from the superpowers and toward new patterns of political, economic and strategic relationships.

It is precisely in this explicitly "geopolitical" call that John Paul II goes beyond the style and substance of his predecessors. At one level *On Social Concern* is a reiteration of Paul VI's call to the industrial West to deal more justly with the developing world; John Paul repeats the injunction and extends it to the industrialized East (a point the moral equivalence critics seldom note). But this pope reaches beyond the economics of development and addresses the structure of the international system. The Pope's call to the superpowers is about "high politics."

> Surmounting every type of imperalism and determination to preserve their own hegemony, the stronger and richer nations must have a sense of moral responsibility for other nations, so that a real international system may be established which will rest on the foundation of the equality of all peoples and on the necessary respect for their legitimate differences.[13]

The passage distinguishes between a "real" international system and the existing one. The steps needed to move beyond a system marked by "imperalism and hegemony" involve economic measures, but ultimately they must be political in character. Even in a "real system" the superpowers will not be simply two nations among others; they will have unique status and they will have special responsibilities. But the logic of the blocs prevents them from fulfilling these roles. The Pope does not set forth a systematic vision of his revisionist proposal, but two examples illustrate the kinds of change his view of the world would require.

First, the Pope has persistently criticized the role of outside powers in regional conflicts. In his pastoral visits to the war zones of the globe, he has developed a position which is expressed in *On Social Concern*. The encyclical does not hold that the superpowers cause the regional conflicts, but that they qualitatively increase the complexity, danger and human suffering in regions like Central America, Southern Africa and the Middle East. The Pope does not engage in analysis of a specific region nor does he offer a detailed critique of the policy of either superpower. He singles out the arms trade (not an exclusively superpower phenomenon) and proxy wars, along with the general criticism that the big power competition diverts resources from funding "authentic development" as examples of how the logic of the blocs runs counter to the welfare of the developing countries.

The Pope's aim is to insulate regional conflict from the escalatory effect which superpower involvement brings in its train. While such a measure is a standard objective of many analysts and governments, John Paul II presses the degree of restriction he wants to impose beyond the usual limits. He is critical of spheres of influence in principle, refusing to acknowledge any moral legitimacy for them. Undoubtedly, the Pope's experience of Eastern Europe as well as his moral principles combine to shape his views on spheres of influence, but his opposition in this encyclical clearly is not confined to one region. He wants superpower restraint throughout the system.

Second, the revisionist position has implications for Europe as a whole. In a series of statements over the last decade the Pope has pressed the possibility and desirability of a "European Europe" of Gaullist proportions. George Williams sums up the direction and content of John Paul II's hopes for Europe: "It's evident from a close reading of all the pope's messages. . . that John Paul II has woven a rather tight tapestry of religio-political policy with respect to Europe, despite the fact that Christianity in many parts of NATO and the Iron Curtain countries is either in retreat or under oppression. He looks for the possible military neutralization of several Central European countries, an act that would allow the reunification of the two Germanies and the withdrawal of Soviet and NATO forces to the margin of the two blocs. . . ."[14]

The Pope has sustained this notion of an independent, united Europe in spite of the stress it can cause in East and West. In the West, overcoming Yalta is a popular policy objective, but there are great differences over method, timetable and the shape of the outcome. In the East, already in ferment, the Pope's call can serve to raise expectations well beyond standard views of *glasnost*.

While undoubtedly aware of these concerns, the Pope's conviction about a European Europe is grounded in different soil from that of the standard policy debate. He is convinced the shared religious and cultural heritage of Europe can be the foundation of a renewed political reality, in Williams's words, "a third force between the Soviet Union and North America—economic, cultural, spiritual and necessarily military."[15] While not tying the Pope to Williams's specific position on a "third force," it is possible to say that what the Pope has already set forth goes substantially beyond the standard Western debate. Neither the next step in European economic integration of 1992, nor the post

INF proposals for a European defense pillar approach the scope of John Paul's conception.[16]

In fact, it is the case that each aspect of the Pope's revisionist vision is both reflective of the wider policy debate and yet different from it. Drawing some points of comparison will highlight the Pope's distinctive—some would say problematical—vision. John Paul II has been developing his revisionist position for over a decade. But it stands out more clearly today because of the way the U.S.-Soviet relationship is developing. The dominant aspect of the international system which the Pope has criticized (and proposes to change) is the role of the superpowers. Today, the superpower relationship stands at a unique moment. From George Kennan to Henry Kissinger, the U.S. policy debate reflects a conviction that deep, pervasive and probably irreversible changes are under way in the Soviet Union. The policy analysts agree on the significance of the changes, but divide over the implications for U.S.-Soviet relations. The papal proposal for devolution of power puts the Pope into the center of the policy argument. How does he relate?

First, the secular policy discussion focuses upon the bilateral U.S.-Soviet relationship as its first priority, then upon the European theatre and, finally, on its implications for other regions and states. The papal analysis is different on two counts. On the one hand, the Pope, as noted above, accords priority to relaxing superpower influence over others in the international system. This means placing at the center of the superpower agenda a topic which seldom receives such attention. The standard assessments of superpower relations give priority to enhancing stability, reducing risks and maintaining a general equilibrium of power. The papal emphasis on reshaping the distribution of power in the world, of reducing the qualitative gap between the superpowers and others can threaten the stability which others prize so highly. Whereas the Pope resists hegemony as an ordering principle, Robert Tucker reflects the view of many analysts when he judges the "inequality of nations" as a favorable characteristic of world politics. In Tucker's view—and this is hardly idiosyncratic—the normal state of international politics is one in which "those states possessing the elements of great power once again play the role their power entitles them to play."[17] Revisionist proposals, stressing interdependence of all states, a multipolar structure of power and space for middle and smaller actors to move on the political stage are seen as a threat to order, stability and stable expectations in world affairs. Revisionism—

even if termed moral revisionism—seems to many more dangerous than promising.

Similar differences between the papal perspective and the policy community in the United States are found in the discussion of Europe. When the Pope has pressed the case for a political-cultural unity of Europe and the possibilities open to a "European actor" on the global stage, he has not spelled out at all what role—if any—he sees for the military alliances which have sustained the logic of the blocs. Nor has he addressed the question of the status and role of a united Germany. To some degree these are not papal questions; but the papal proposal makes an answer to these questions necessary, precisely because the weight of history reminds us of past unsuccessful answers to these questions. The need to address both the German and the alliance questions becomes even clearer when the Pope's desire for a united Europe is joined to his position of nuclear abolitionism (cf. below). To revive a united Germany and to return to conventional defense in the European theater is to open two very large historical debates.

The point here is not to say that wisdom lies with trying simply to project the last forty years indefinitely into the future. On both political and strategic grounds, there are strong reasons to resist such a complacent assessment. But the papal willingness to think afresh about Europe is both a valuable and a perplexing voice in the policy debate. This is particularly the case when the Pope in question has unique capabilities to address hearts and minds in Eastern Europe.

Third, it is clear that a summary statement of John Paul's position, as expressed between the U.N. Address and *On Social Concern,* involves both *less hegemony* in the system and *greater solidarity* between North and South. The Pope is arguing for restraint and disengagement on security issues (arms trade, intervention, military assistance) and for a more expansive big-power role on interdependence issues (trade, aid, debt relief). There is a case to be made for both objectives; moreover, the case is both normatively and empirically defensible. But there is also a tension between the goals. What is being called for is less political control, less influence, yet greater engagement of resources. In the end the papal proposal is not simply providing space for others; it is also a call for enhancing the ability of others to refashion patterns of internal and international order through a restructuring of trade and financial relations as well as a recasting of political relations.

Here again, there are signs that some of this will occur on the basis of the evolution already taking place in international affairs. But the papal proposal is that this natural diffusion of power should be consciously fostered and designed to benefit those least likely to be empowered by the normal dynamic of world politics.

Nuclear Weapons: Papal Abolitionist

Since the apostolic age, the moral argument about the use of force has run through the Christian tradition. Since the rise of the nation state, the ethic of war has been an essential theme in international relations. In assessing the position of John Paul II on the international system, it is necessary to review his arguments about war and peace at two levels of the system. First, he has engaged the question in principle of whether any resort to force can be justified. Second, he has entered the ongoing ecclesial and secular debate about the meaning of traditional Catholic teaching as applied to nuclear weapons and nuclear strategy. I will examine the nuclear question in this section of the paper, and treat the Pope's basic position on force and violence in the context of regional and local conflicts in the next section.

When John Paul II was elected to the papacy in 1978, the secular and ecclesial interest in the nuclear question was just beginning to surface after a period of neglect. The spate of analysis and activity of the period 1958–1972, which produced the basic strategic literature, the arms control philosophy and the international agreements on the Limited Test Ban (1963), the Nonproliferation Treaty (1968) and the SALT I Agreements (1972), had given way, in both church and state, to interest in other questions. The ethical arguments about war and peace in the period (1968–1978) had been about Vietnam; the empirical and ethical literature of international relations in the same period was focused less on security issues and more on the transnational interdependence issues of political economy, human rights, and population and the environment. These were the issues one found in *The Progress of Peoples*, in papal messages to the spate of U.N. conferences held in the 1970s and in the document of the 1971 synod, *Justice in the World*.

But the years 1978–1982 saw a return to the nuclear question in both its empirical and normative dimensions. There were several forces driving the issue: the failure to achieve the SALT II agreements, the Soviet strategic build-up of the 1970s, the NATO "two-track" decision of 1979, and the U.S. policy of the early 1980s, which seemed uninterested in arms control of any kind and committed to a major escalation of the strategic competition. Suddenly the nuclear question became a public issue again—a public policy concern for governments (now with renewed intensity about both building and controlling nuclear weapons) and a public interest issue of unique intensity. One characteristic of the renewed nuclear debate was the saliency of the moral questions; they were examined in both church and state with much greater attention and detail than they were in the 1950s and 1960s.

The Pope entered the nuclear debate in 1981 and has remained in it. A review of his position leads, I believe, to the conclusion that he is a nuclear abolitionist. This puts him in the company of Mr. Ghorbachev, Mr. Reagan and Jonathan Schell, but he gets there by his own route. The key texts of the Pope's first decade on the nuclear question are his addresses in Japan (1981), his message to the U.N. Second Special Session on Disarmament (1982), and his address to the Diplomatic Corps at the Vatican (1987). From these texts it is possible to outline the Pope's definition of the nuclear question, his judgment on the strategy of deterrence and his abolitionist position on nuclear weapons.

The Pope consistently locates the issue of nuclear weapons in the broader context of the relationship between ethics and technology. This theme is a pervasive concern of his pontificate, cutting across his teaching on medical issues, economic progress and military strategy. In his first encyclical he described "the main drama" of contemporary life this way: "The man of today seems ever to be under threat from what he produces, that is to say from the result of the work of his hands and, even more so, of the work of his intellect and the tendencies of his will."[18] Nuclear weapons embody this threat, in the Pope's mind, in a unique fashion.

He specified their role in this drama in his *Address to Scientists and Scholars* at Hiroshima in 1981. While defending both scientific research and technological development against any sweeping condemnation, the Pope argued that the threat of nuclear war, "should finally compel everyone to face a basic moral consideration: From now on, it is only through a conscious choice and through a deliberate policy that humanity can survive."[19] While choice and policy inevitably mean addressing the specifics of nuclear strategy and arms control, the Pope used his Hiroshima address to focus on the thematic moral question of political and moral control over technology.

A year later, however, the nuclear debate has assumed center stage in Western Europe, the United States and at the United Nations. The Pope used the Special Session on Disarmament to send a lengthy message through Cardinal Casaroli, Vatican Secretary of State. Here he entered the thicket of specific issues, providing the most detailed commentary from the Vatican since *Peace on Earth* (1963) and *Gaudium et Spes* of Vatican II (1965). While stressing the continuity of his message with previous Church teaching, the Pope made a distinctive addition with judgment about the strategy of deterrence: "In current conditions 'deterrence' based on balance, certainly not as an end in itself but as a step on the way to disarmament, may still be judged morally acceptable."[20]

The passage had an immediate purpose and a long-term role in the nuclear argument. Its immediate impact in 1982 was to signal that the Church's teaching authority had grave difficulties with deterrence, but was not prepared to condemn it in principle. The message of 1982 was both more critical of deterrence than Vatican II had been, and more flexible in its moral judgment than other voices in the Catholic debate of the 1980s.

In a larger sense the papal message of 1982 *both* legitimated deterrence and placed a moral mortgage on the deterrence relationship. Deterrence has, at best, an instrumental value; its role, as Cardinal Casaroli later described it, was "to give time for seeking agreement and understanding" which can both reduce the nuclear arsenals and build the structure of peace.[21] The moral mortgage on deterrence is grounded in the risk posed by the failure of the strategy, the quantitative and qualitative competition it generates and the resources it consumes.

John Paul II has not addressed deterrence directly since 1982, but he has increased the price of the mortgage. The occasion was his commentary on the INF Treaty signed by the United States and the Soviet Union in 1987. In his address to the Diplomatic Corps at the Vatican, the Pope both acknowledged the significance of the treaty and reiterated his doubts about deterrence. The treaty was a significant political initiative, the first agreement consummated since 1972. It both eliminated a class of weapons and opened the door for further efforts of arms control. It was based on the underlying superpower relationship of deterrence; at this point the Pope stressed again that this strategy should be transitional:

> Such a strategy, applied within the context of detente and cooperation, should lead to a progressive search for a new balance at the lowest arms level in order to reach, at a further stage, a complete elimination of nuclear weapons, for in this respect we must aim at total disarmament.[22]

It is this text which makes clear the abolitionist logic of the Pope's position. In one sense, he is simply reflecting hopes his predecessors had expressed. But precisely his legitimation of deterrence and his abolitionist stand limiting the moral status of deterrence put him in a distinct position in the wider nuclear debate.

On one hand, the Pope cannot simply be described as an advocate of arms control. It, too, has only instrumental value; he can support it (like deterrence) but he has the intent to transcend arms control. In taking this position—absolutist and abolitionist on nuclear weapons—the Pope separates himself from the dominant consensus in the secular strategic literature. In different ways he opposes those who want more nuclear weapons and those who want to maintain some. In the last thirty years, the strategic consensus distinguished sharply the goals of arms control and disarmament. The latter objective is how to live without nuclear weapons; the former is how to live with (some of) them. The arms control perspective stresses the irreversability of the nuclear discovery. Nuclear innocence is impossible even if nuclear abolitionism were successful. Standard arms control wisdom sees a world without nuclear arms, but with the knowledge of how to make them, as a potentially dangerous world—more dangerous than a stable deterrence regime. Arms control seeks reductions of nuclear arsenals as an instrumental value—it must serve stability.[23] Abolitionism sees reductions to zero as an imperative; it equates zero with stability.

The Pope must inevitably worry committed arms controllers. But no less than Ghorbachev and Reagan at Reykjavik; the response of three veterans of arms control in *The New York Times Magazine* shortly after

Reykjavik was illustrative: "A Way Out of Reykjavik: Three Strategic Arms Experts Say Reagan Enthusiasms Must Be Curbed." In their view: "The Reykjavik proposals may well have set back the cause of responsible arms control by many years."[24]

Admittedly, not all arms control advocates would agree with this assessment, but in a period where deep cuts in arsenals may be possible, the questions of how deep and why not elimination will be much more a part of the nuclear discussion than in the 1980s. The Pope, in an interesting ways, may come to be seen as a friend of those seeking stable reductions of weapons, but a threatening friend. Nothing short of zero would seem to qualify for his total support.

On the other hand, the abolitionist Pope is willing to await moderate tactics. He does not seem inclined to translate his abolitionist goal into an immediate imperative to withdraw from deterrence. In this posture he resists, as Catholic teaching has for over twenty years, a coherent and in many ways very traditional critique of the nuclear age. From Walter Stein and Gordon Zahn in the 1960s to Finnis, Grisez and Boyle in the 1980s,[25] some have drawn an unbreakable moral line between nuclear abolitionism and nuclear abstention. The argument asserts an insoluble conflict between the requirements of credible deterrence and the prohibition against intending to kill the innocent. In the Pope's view, abolition is the goal and deterrence is an imperfect but permissible—perhaps even unavoidable—means. For the nuclear abstention position, the goal is to disengage immediately from an untenable moral position. Abolition may or may not follow; it is a secondary consideration. Thus far the Pope has been more taken by the goal to be achieved than by the means being used.

In summary, the papal position on the nuclear question is abolitionist in its objective, gradualist in its methods, supportive of arms control but unconvinced by its conservative philosophical premise that living with nuclear weapons is the best resolution of the ethics, politics and technology problem for which we can hope.

Regional Conflict: Revolutionary Goals and Moderate Means

During the first decade of his pontificate, John Paul II has used two basic themes in addressing local and regional conflicts. As we have seen, at the systemic level he has openly resisted intervention by the superpowers or other major actors. He has refused to allow arguments appealing to "security and stability" or "spheres of influence" claims to go unchallenged. They fall under his indictment of "hegemony and imperialism." In his view the outside powers intensify local conflicts and expand the capacity of local actors to escalate the level of violence. To be fair, it should be noted he has never dealt with the claim that outside actors can also moderate conflicts and—through pressure, persuasion and rewards—enhance the possibilities for diplomatic settlement in some cases. It has been primarily in his role as teacher and diplomat that the Pope has tried to reduce the pattern of intervention which marks so many regional conflicts.

It should be noted here also that another dimension of the Pope's systemic approach to local and regional conflict in the Third World is to press for the reshaping of international economic relations to provide developing countries with resources to meet the urgent social demands the Pope sees as major sources of local and regional conflict.

As a pastor the Pope has injected himself directly into the settings of local and regional conflicts. His trips have not avoided any major area of conflict save the Middle East (where security considerations make a papal trip a nightmare). Going as a pastor and teacher to Latin America, Southern Africa and Eastern Europe, John Paul has pursued a definite policy comprised of two elements: a call for radical social change and unyielding commitment to nonviolent methods.[26] While reflections of both ideas can be found in Paul VI, John Paul II has joined them in a new synthesis.

From his first papal trip—to open the Puebla Meeting of Latin American Bishops in 1979—through his trip to Southern Africa in 1988, he has set forth an argument for deep and extensive structural change in developing countries. He joins this consistently with his larger case for economic change in the international system. The record of ten years shows a Pope who cannot be enlisted in the argument that the Third World's condition is solely its problem; nor does he stay only at the level of systemic change in the style of some versions of the New International Economic Order. Across the spectrum of his visits, the calls for socioeconomic change remain constant, although different applications are needed. He draws upon the universal teaching of the Church—from *Mater et Magistra* (1961) through *On Social Concern*—and he picks up and endorses themes from the local church as he calls for land reform, supports the economic and cultural claims of peasants, endorses the rights of workers and constantly asserts the right of religious liberty.

He has espoused the ''preferential option for the poor'' as it emerged from Latin America; he universalizes the call, applying it to other countries, and he amends the call lest it be interpreted as narrowing the Church's concern for all in society.

At both the systemic and local levels he returns to the question of human rights, using it as he did in *On Social Concern* to join his call for systemic and internal economic change: ''The intrinsic comment between authentic development and respect for human rights once again reveals the moral character of development.''[27]

These calls for structural change are often made in the face of social systems which have been long resistant to peaceful protest for change. The papal message is heard by peasants in El Salvador who remember the *Matanza* of the 1930s, and by blacks in South Africa who remember history in terms of Sharpesville and Soweto. Inevitably the question arises about means: If all else fails, does the papal call imply a right to arms for the dispossessed? The logic of the question arises not only from the dispossessed, but from the tradition the Pope represents. In *Progress of Peoples,* Paul VI alluded to the possibility of using force in the face of long-standing injustice, and the brief reference became a focal point of the post-encyclical debate. The Pope himself drew back from the statement, but the question remained.

John Paul II has been categorical about the need to rule out violence as a means of social change. He has resisted both resort to force in practice and appeals to the principle of class conflict in Catholic teaching. It has been in the context of his visits to local churches that he has pressed the nonviolent theme, but a full understanding of his position on the use of force in principle must balance the local statements with his *World Day of Peace Message* of 1982.

First, the local texts: In a string of statements from Drogheda, Ireland, in 1979 to Lesotho in 1988, the Pope has opposed the use of force in principle and in practice. The significance of these statements is that they are made in the face of articulated arguments that all else has failed, and in the face of groups which are already using force and put their cause (implicitly) before the Pope for judgment. At Drogheda, at the outset of his ministry, John Paul II stated his case in personal, emotional terms:

I join my voice today to the voice of Paul VI and my other predecessors, to the voices of your religious leaders, to the voices of all men and women of reason, and I proclaim, with the conviction of my faith in Christ and with an awareness of my mission, that violence is evil, that violence is unacceptable as a solution to problems, that violence is unworthy of man. Violence is a lie, for it goes against the truth of our faith, the truth of our humanity. Violence destroys what it claims to defend: the dignity, the life, the freedom of human beings.[28]

A decade later in Southern Africa, on the border of South Africa, and in a highly politicized setting, the Pope reaffirmed his conviction: "Above all . . . you must renounce every form of violence and hatred. Violence only begets further violence . . . . The increase of violence in the world can never be halted by responding with more of the same."[29]

At the local level the very consistency of the papal texts over ten years raises the question of whether he is *de facto* reversing a stand in the Catholic tradition which said that, in the face of injustice, force could be used morally as a last resort. The only evidence in the decade which runs counter to the nonviolent philosophy (understood not as a tactic, but as a philosophical position) is the Pope's *World Day of Peace Message* for 1982. The context of the statement is significant; the nuclear debate was in full view in the Atlantic nations. The Pope used the timing of his annual message to set forth the basic elements of a Christian view of the ethic of force.

In Augustinian fashion, he rooted his ethic reflection in a theological anthropology. The pursuit of peace must be grounded in a correct understanding of human nature; such a view rules out facile assumptions about the possibilities of permanent peace among nations. Consequently, there must be room, in principle, for resort to force to defend basic values: "That is why Christians have no hesitation in recalling that, in the name of an elementary requirement of justice, peoples have a right and even a duty to protect their existence and freedom by proportionate means against an unjust aggressor."[30]

Both the context and content of this quotation points to an affirmation of the right of a legitimate government to use force against an external threat. What then of the applicability of the principle when the legitimacy of a government is in question in situations of domestic conflict? John Paul II has not been reluctant to set forth principles of human rights and social justice which can provide the basis for questioning the legitimacy of a given political system. But in diverse settings—Eastern Europe, Central America, the Philippines under Marcos, he has stopped short of justifying any resort to force.

In traditional Catholic teaching, the ethic which justified the use of force by the state contained the same principles that sustained "the right of revolution." While the resort to force was always severely constrained in both cases, the Pope's disjunction of the two constitutes a distinctive interpretation of the tradition. He appears to have raised Pius XII's practical judgment in 1956, when he ruled out justification for revolt in Eastern Europe, to the level of a principle. Pius XII's statement, made after the Hungarian revolution was crushed, did not dispute a *jus ad bellum* in Eastern Europe, but it did conclude that the possibilities of success were so slim that resort to force was imprudent. John Paul seems to have concluded that even necessary social change, to relieve oppression and/or to meet human needs, cannot justify the inevitable suffering which accompanies civil war today. This position has met with mixed response.

On one hand, the Pope's message of pursuing social change through nonviolence has met with agreement in theory and practice. In a time of the most significant ferment in Eastern Europe in thirty years, there is resistance to existing regimes, but no hint that this generation of dissidents—whether moved by religious or secular reasons—considers the use of force possible or desirable. In the Third World in the 1970s, key leaders were espousing the papal position before he became Pope. Archbishop Camara, Cardinal Arns in Brazil, and Bishop Claver in the Philippines took enormous personal risks by challenging the power of authoritarian regimes, but they tied their critiques to a commitment of nonviolence. The test case in practice was the revolution in the Philippines in 1986: a major change with a minimum of violence.

On the other hand, the applicability of the papal position is questioned or contested in other settings. When the Pope arrived in Zimbabwe last September to congratulate the government and its people on their independence, President Mugabe pointedly told the Pope that the change to majority rule would not have occurred without some resort to force.[31] Mugabe's comments, of course, have a contemporary reference. In spite of the ecumenical nonviolent positions of the Pope and Archbishop Tutu in South Africa, other leaders of the resistance refuse to rule out the possibility that all other means may fall short in their struggle to overturn apartheid. In an ecumenical manifesto,

''Challenge To The Church'' a group of leading South African theologians used Aquinas's argument against tyrants to justify action to overthrow the South African regime.[32] The document does not openly espouse the use of force, but it does not rule it out either.

The papal position on the use of force is a tenable argument, but one with severe internal tensions. It is hardly a passive posture in the face of injustice; it presents a narrow option for the state to use force to protect its people, but it offers only an heroic ethic for people who find themselves not protected but oppressed by their own state. The logic of the position is understandable but open to criticism. The Pope's design is to avoid the use of force at all levels of the system—nuclear, conventional war between states and domestic social violence. At every level he can invoke Pius XII's practical criterion of the disproportionality of the violence of modern warfare: What we know of nuclear war, what we have seen in the Iran-Iraq slaughter and what we have been part of in Vietnam and Central America all point to the wisdom of stressing the disproportionate damage of war today. Yet the Pope at the extreme does not rule out deterrence or the traditional threat states make to defend their nations against attack.

By closing off the possibility of force within domestic political conflict in a time when states already possess overwhelming power, he can be charged with having weighted the deck against those in whose name he speaks on the grounds of social justice and human rights. One suspects that he believes that in the end they suffer most when the war begins. This practical judgment is reason enough to draw the line as he has. But it may not be persuasive to all those he seeks to shield.

Conclusion

At the end of a paper already too long, it should be acknowledged that the categories used do not exhaust John Paul II's view of international relations. To fill out the papal conception would require a more systematic study of his hundreds of addresses made during the fifty trips he has taken.

Even within these limits, however, it is possible to ask about the prospects of realizing in this decade the vision of the international system he has developed over the past ten years. To ask the question is to be faced with the reality that the Pope has valuable, but limited, resources in the field of international politics. He may have more divisions in Eastern Europe than Stalin could have imagined, but the fact remains that John Paul's primary influence as pastor, diplomat and teacher is his ability to move others to share his vision. Crucial to an understanding of the limits and possibilities is a recognition that others who can be touched and moved by the Pope include not only those with the material elements of power, but those in whose name power is exercised. While the Pope's military resources are non-existent and his economic resources negligible, his access to peasants and policymakers, workers and world institutions is his unique possession. He works with words and ideas, symbols and a sense of meaning about life, but these have their place and role in the shaping of domestic and international politics. Few doubt the catalytic role the Pope had in Poland, Haiti and the Philippines. Solidarity and People's Power were home-grown revolutionary products, but John Paul provided a stimulus and a source of external support for both movements (even when there was not always agreement on tactics). The possibility of papal influence will remain at this level; even specific interventions by the Pope personally depend for their viability on his leadership of and links with a transnational community.

Substantively, one can assess the revisionist, abolitionist and nonviolent social vision of John Paul II in light of other forces moving international politics. The point here is to identify elements of convergence with other assessments of world politics, and to see where the papal conception either stands alone or at the margin of what others believe will happen in international affairs.

Most analysts identify the nuclear danger and the fact of interdependence as the dominant characteristics of world politics today. The Pope agrees; his writings and statements seek to place both of these dimensions of world affairs into a framework of moral restraint and direction. He seeks to contain, reduce and eliminate the nuclear dimension of world politics. And he argues that the fact of political and economic interdependence must be given moral content by the vision and principles of solidarity. The Pope's design for addressing the nuclear danger goes beyond what many analysts believe is possible; hence, some are convinced his ultimate goal (abolition) is not desirable.

His conception of what justice requires in reshaping North-South relations cuts across the political and economic fabric of global politics.

To implement the papal program involves structural change of an order comparable in political and economic terms to the emergence of the Westphalia order of the seventeenth-century. Other analysts deal with pieces of the papal program (debt or trade or nonintervention in the security sphere). On specific items the Pope and at least some empirical analysts converge. For the entire papal program of political economy, there are few others who play the theme out so specifically.

The Pope's revisionism is proposed as a desirable goal to be pursued. While some analysts join him in advocating devolution of power as an empirically wise and normatively valuable goal, the larger area of convergence is with those who see superpower "decline," or at least "relative decline," as a fact of life in this decade.

On all three fronts—revisionism, abolitionism and the goals and methods of social change in the North-South equation—the Pope finds support in the wider policy argument, but not identity with his position. The reach of the papal proposal is often beyond what those who work with the details of world politics feel is possible in the short to middle range. The papal role, however, may be precisely to maintain this tension: providing a vision which is empirically relevant, but ethically stretching for those seeking to shape the system.

Notes

1. T. Szulc, "Politics and the Polish Pope," *The New Republic* (Oct. 28, 1978) p. 29.

2. G. H. Williams, "An Intellectual Portrait of Pope John Paul II," *Worldview* (Jan.-Feb. 1979) p. 21; cf. also *The Mind of John Paul II: The Origins of His Thought and Action* (N.Y: The Seabury Press, 1981).

3. John Paul II, *The Redeemer of Man* (Washington: U.S. Catholic Conference, 1979) #1; *On Social Concern* (Washington: U.S. Catholic Conference, 1988) #4.

4. Vatican II, *Gaudium et Spes* (*The Pastoral Constitution on the Church in the Modern World* (1965), cf. #40-42; cf. also John C. Murray, "The Problem of Church and State at Vatican II," *Theological Studies* 27 (1966) pp. 580-606.

5. Paul VI, *The Progress of Peoples* (Boston: St. Paul's Press, 1967) #3.

6. For a commentary on the relationship of the security and interdependence perspectives cf. R. O. Keohane and J. S. Nye, *Power and Interde-*

pendence: World Politics in Transition (Boston: Little, Brown and Co., 1977); "Power and Interdependence Revisited," *International Organization* 41 (1987) pp. 725–753; J. S. Nye, "Neorealism and Neoliberalism," *World Politics* 40 (1988) pp. 235–251.

7. T. Bethell, "Mea Maxima Culpa?" *The National Review* (April 15, 1988) pp. 34–36; M. Novak, "Beyond Populorum Progressio," *Crisis* (March 1988) pp. 8–9.

8. *On Social Concern,* cited, #21.

9. *Ibid.,* #22.

10. S. Hoffmann, "The Rules of the Game," *Ethics and International Affairs,* 1 (1987) p. 39.

11. *On Social Concern,* cited, #22.

12. *Ibid.,* #22.

13. *Ibid.,* #39.

14. G. H. Williams, *The Contours of Church and State in the Thought of John Paul II* (Waco, Texas: Institute of Church-State Studies, 1983) p. 52; cf. also, *The Law of Nations and the Book of Nature* (Collegeville, MN: The Christian Humanism Project, 1984) pp. 1–18.

15. *Ibid.,* p. 52.

16. The political and academic commentary goes beyond the present proposals of government. In this literature contending ideas about the future shape of Europe approach the topic in the long-term view used by the Pope, although not necessarily coming to his conclusions: e.g., H. A. Kissinger, "Reversing Yalta," *Washington Post* (April 16, 1988); S. Rosenfeld, "Kissinger's Path or Brzezinski's," *Washington Post* (April 21, 1988).

17. R. Tucker, "The Purposes of American Power," *Foreign Affairs* 59 (1980–81) p. 273.

18. *The Redeemer of Man,* cited, #15.

19. John Paul II, Address to Scientists and Scholars, *Origins* 10 (1981) p. 621.

20. John Paul II, *Message to U.N. Special Session on Disarmament 1982,* #3.

21. Cardinal Casaroli, "The Vatican's Position on Issues of War and Peace, *Origins* 13 (1983) p. 439.

22. John Paul II, Address to the Diplomatic Corps, *L'Osservatore Romano* (Eng. Edit) (Jan. 25, 1988) #5.

23. Cf. The standard literature on arms control, e.g., T. Schelling and M. Halperin, *Strategy and Arms Control* (N.Y: Pergamon-Brassey, 1985—2nd edition); T. Schelling, "What Went Wrong with Arms Control?" *Foreign Affairs* 64 (1985–86) pp. 219–233; cf. also, J. S. Nye, G. T. Allison and A. Carnesale, eds., *Fateful Visions: Avoiding Nuclear Catastrophe* (Cambridge: Ballinger Publishing Co., 1988) pp. 1–10.

24. B. Scowcroft, J. Deutch, J. Woolsey, "A Way Out of Reykjavik," *New York Times Magazine* (Jan. 25, 1987) p. 40 ff.

25. Cf. J. Finnis, "Nuclear Deterrence, Christian Conscience and the End of Christendom," *New Oxford Review* 55 (1988) pp. 6–16. The full argument is to be found in J. Finnis, J. Boyle, G. Grisez, *Nuclear Deterrence, Morality and Realism* (N.Y: Clarendon Press, 1987).

26. Narrative and documentation on the Pope's visits to local churches can be found in E. Hansen, *The Catholic Church in World Politics* (Princeton, N.J.: Princeton University Press, 1987).

27. *On Social Concern* #33.

28. John Paul II, Address in Drogheda, Ireland, *Origins* 9 (1979) p. 274.

29. John Paul II, "Message to Youth on Nonviolence," *Origins* 18 (1988) p. 253.

30. John Paul II, World Day of Peace Message 1982, *Origins* 11 (1982) p. 477.

31. A. Meldrum, "The Pope's Message," *Africa Report* (Nov.-Dec. 1988) p. 46.

32. The Kairos Document, *Challenge to the Church: A Theological Comment on the Political Crisis in South Africa* (London: CIIR, 1985) pp. 20–23.

Part II

On the Proper Role
for the Church in Social Matters

. . . I wish *to appeal* with simplicity and humility to *everyone,* to all men and women without exception. I wish to ask them to be convinced of the seriousness of the present moment and of each one's individual responsibility, and to implement—by the way they live as individuals and as families, by the use of their resources, by their civic activity, by contributing to economic and political decisions and by personal commitment to national and international undertakings—the *measures* inspired by solidarity and love of preference for the poor. This is what is demanded by the present moment and above all by the very dignity of the human person, the indestructible image of God the Creator, which is *indentical* in each one of us.

On Social Concern, Par. 47

Both the political institutions and the economic institutions of the free society implicitly contain hidden references to the specific new virtues required to make these institutions function according to their own inner rules. Too seldom do we make these underlying virtues explicit in our thinking. They are quite different from the virtues of traditional societies. They include such virtues as civic responsibility, self-reliance, cooperativeness, openness, and personal economic enterprise. They are acquired during that long process of learning the habits of democratic living.

Michael Novak

The Church's social doctrine *is not* a "third way" between *liberal capitalism* and *Marxist collectivism* nor even a possible alternative to other solutions less radically opposed to one another: rather, it constitutes a *category of its own*. Nor is it an *ideology*, but rather the *accurate formulation* of the results of a careful reflection on the complex realities of human existence, in society and in the international order, in the light of faith and of the Church's tradition.

On Social Concern, Par. 41

There is a rich potential in the Catholic tradition for helping moderns achieve an *ordered* liberty. And that is one of the most important needs of contemporary society. In a context of liberty and affluence, our people are sorely tempted to pursue the chaotic, short-term impulses of desire. There are serious signs that the capacities for self-government are eroding.

Robert Benne

. . . when the scientific and technical resources are available which, with the necessary concrete political decisions, ought to help lead peoples to true development, the main obstacles to development will be overcome only by means of *essentially moral decisions.*

On Social Concern, Par. 35

The problem is that in virtually all the concrete problems the Pope cites as indications of failure, namely, the alleged "widening of the gap between the area of the so-called developed North and the developing South" (Par. 14), including, besides a poverty gap, a gap in the recognition and implementation of human rights (Par. 15), the chronically high levels of unemployment and underemployment (Par. 18), and the international debt crisis (Par. 19)—in virtually all of these—the Pope tends to overestimate the moral or political nature of the problem and to discount radically the economic constraints upon any significant progress toward a solution, constraints which are usually denounced as inhibiting and occasionally sinful "mechanisms."

Dennis P. McCann

This superdevelopment, which consists of an *excessive* availability of every kind of material goods for the benefit of certain social groups, easily makes people slaves of "possession" and of immediate gratification. All of us experience firsthand the sad effects of this blind submission to pure consumerism: in the first place a crass materialism, and at the same time a *radical dissatisfaction,* because one quickly learns— unless one is shielded from the flood of publicity and the ceaseless and tempting offers of products—that the more one possesses the more one wants, while deeper aspirations remain unsatisfied and perhaps even stifled.

On Social Concern, Par. 28

Consumerism is a system of greed. Greed is a drive for the attainment not only of basic human needs but for status, power and material goods in excess of what we actually need. When we succumb to the enticement of greed, we lose our perspective as citizens of the world with the responsibilities that this entails.

Ricardo Ramirez, C.S.B.

It is important to note therefore that a world which is divided into blocs, sustained by rigid ideologies, and in which instead of interdependence and solidarity different forms of imperialism hold sway, can only be a world subject to structures of sin. The sum total of the negative factors working against a true awareness of the universal *common good,* and the need to further it, gives the impression of creating, in persons and institutions, an obstacle which is difficult to overcome.

On Social Concern, Par. 36

A little more than twenty years ago African Americans had called for a weak form of solidarity: integration. Their demands were rejected. The dominant white majority and liberal white capitalists placed upon the oppressed blacks the responsibility for evil and injustice in society as well as the discovery of a remedy for it. The nation turned away from interdependence and solidarity, and increased the gaps between white and black, white and white, and black and black. The people elected leaders who sought not solidarity but the triumph of the strong over the weak and the destruction of the communal aid provided to the weak. Moreover, the policies and programs of many religious bodies and persons who professed to be motivated by the religious values held by the Pope took the lead in forwarding alienation and discrimination among persons and groups. African Americans see the path to interdependence and solidarity to be even longer and more complex than does the Pope.

Preston Williams

Five

Countering the Adversary Culture

Michael Novak

In considering a nation's common good, it is not sufficient to be critical of its political structure and economic system. One must also be vigilant concerning its culture, and especially the cultural elites who create the stories, images and symbols of the nation's self-understanding and moral direction. After a long period of political criticism and a more recent period of economic criticism, the new critical frontier is likely to be a sustained critique of U. S. culture. Indeed, Pope John Paul II and Cardinal Joseph Ratzinger already have called for such criticism, both for its own sake and because U. S. culture now exercises massive moral influence around the world.

Meanwhile, U. S. culture after the 1950s has fallen under the dominance of a new and now larger cultural elite, whose power base lies in the universities, the media of communications, governmental bureaucracies, public relations experts, and a growing "therapeutic" industry ("the life-style engineers"). And this new class of cultural specialists holds ideas adversarial to America's traditional values and institutions. Thus, the extent to which basic U. S. institutions—the democratic republic matched to an innovative capitalist economy—represent still today a unique "counterculture" with respect to communist, socialist, and Third World institutions frequently has been lost to view. Therefore, I begin by discussing the U. S. political economy as a revolutionary and dynamic counterculture in the institutional order, whose example is widely imitated around the world.

The U. S. Political Economy as Counterculture

Most of the world still neglects the American Revolution, while seizing upon the failed French Revolution of 1789 as the great symbolic center of the modern era of liberty. Even Cardinal Ratzinger, whose sympathies are plainly with the former and not the latter, cited the French Revolution in his second "Instruction on Christian Freedom and Liberation," and ignored the American Revolution.[1] "The sad truth of the matter," Hannah Arendt has written, "is that the French Revolution, which ended in disaster, has made world history, while the American Revolution, so triumphantly successful, has remained an event of little more than local importance."[2] How sad this really is becomes clear from Professor Arendt's earlier line: "The colonization of North America and the republican government of the United States constitute perhaps the greatest, certainly the boldest, enterprises of European mankind"—and yet it still lives in "isolation from the mother continent."

Intellectually isolated from Europe, and separated by hundreds of tacit understandings, customs, habits, laws, and institutions from Latin America, Asia, Africa, and Eastern Europe, the United States is still the world's most original and most profound counterculture. Its underlying presuppositions are unknown to, or left inarticulate by, even the larger part of its own intellectual elite—that "adversary culture" that Lionel Trilling was the first, although not the last, brilliantly to analyze.[3] "It is odd indeed," Arendt writes, "to see that twentieth-century *American* even more than European learned opinion is often inclined to interpret the American Revolution in the light of the French Revolution, or to criticize it because it so obviously did not conform to the lessons learned from the latter."[4]

The U. S. system was in its beginnings unlike the European, and the Framers were quite aware of their originality.[5] Do not deny to us, James Madison in effect said in *Federalist* 14, the originality of our *novus ordo seclorum*, through which the American people "accomplished a revolution which has no parallel in the annals of human society. They reared the fabrics of governments which have no model on the face of the globe."[6] One of the original features of the new system erected by the people of the United States was the primacy it afforded to the institutions of conscience, information, and ideas—precisely to its moral culture—over the realms of politics (limited government) and economics (the least statist in history).

Another, and at first more striking novelty, Professor Arendt writes, is that the American experiment drew Europe's long slumbering attention to "the social question." "America," she wrote, "had become the symbol of a society without poverty. . . . And only after this had happened and had become known to European mankind could *the social question* and the rebellion of the poor come to play a truly revolutionary role."[7] The American experiment embarrassed the sluggish conscience of Europe.

Indeed, long after one Frenchman, Crevecoeur, had reported back to Europe the amazing prosperity of those Americans who had not long since departed from Europe bitterly poor,[8] and about the same time as another, Alexis de Tocqueville, was describing the systemic prosperity and ordered liberty that "the hand of Providence"[9] had launched in the world through the American experiment, Victor Hugo was still able to describe the dejection and virtual hopelessness of *Les Miserables* in the France of 1832. The poverty of the poor in France already had shocked Jefferson some forty years earlier; and the French Revolution—and, in general, the political economies of Europe—had done little to mitigate that poverty. Only gradually did the example of the United States in moving so many millions of the poor out of poverty awaken Europe to the social condition of its poor, whom it had consigned to a relatively fixed status for centuries. Thus did the U. S. call into being the "social question." Poverty no longer being inevitable or irreparable, its continued existence became for the first time in history a problem for human conscience.

In 1886, the Liberal Party of France (the Party of Tocqueville), seeking to awaken the world again to the difference that the United States made to the history of liberty, commissioned and executed a magnificent gift to the United States: the Statue of Liberty. Imagine the work of its planning committee. "How shall we symbolize the specifically American idea of liberty?" they must have asked themselves. Being French, they decided the symbol would be in the shape of a woman, not a warrior. In this, they followed a tradition as old as the image of Lady Philosophy in Boethius' *The Consolations of Philosophy*: Woman as wisdom, bearing aloft in one hand the torch of understanding against the swirling mists of passion and the darkness of ignorance. In her other hand, they placed a book of the laws, inscribed "1776" to signify the truths Americans hold, the inalienable rights their experiment began by declaring. Her face would not be that of a libertine (as today on 42nd Street), but on the contrary: resolute, serious, purposive. In other words, not precisely the French *Liberté* (the prostitute on the altar of the black Mass) but, rather, that "ordered liberty" to which Pope John Paul II was to call attention in Miami, just 101 years later.[10] A new idea of liberty, later sung of in the classic American hymn: "Confirm thy soul in self-control/thy liberty in law." The liberty of virtue, not solely of freedom for restraint. Thus, the primacy of morals in the American idea was grasped by the Liberal Party of France, heirs of Tocqueville.

Virtue is the pivotal and deepest American idea. Indeed, "Virtue" was the inscription, later supplanted by *Novus ordo Seclorum*, at first inserted as the *leitmotif* on the Great Seal of the United States. To imagine an experiment in republican, self-governing government without virtue, Madison had told the Virginia Assembly, is "chimerical."[11] For how could a people, unable severally to govern their own passions, combine to govern their own body politic?

In fact, tied together in the then novel conception of "political economy," neither a free polity nor a free economy could long survive an incapacity among the people for the virtues that make liberty possible. According to the American idea, learned from Jerusalem, Athens, Rome, Paris and London, liberty springs from the human capacities for *reflection* and *choice* (just as *Light* and *Love* are the very names of God, in whose image humans are made, and by whom they are endowed with "inalienable rights"). It is the role of virtues such as temperance, fortitude, justice, prudence, and others to keep the paths of *reflection* and *choice* readily available. And it was exactly to these capacities, *reflection* and *choice*, that from its first paragraph the authors of *The Federalist* addressed their reflections to the American people,[12] as the latter were making the precedent-shattering decision whether to constitute the new American republic or no.

The framers appealed again and again to the primacy of morals, and indeed to God and to Providence, in whose image they believed the human capacities of reflection and choice were created. "The God who made us made us free," Jefferson said, proud most of all in his life for having authored the Declaration of Independence and for having founded the University of Virginia (dedicated to the education of "good character"). Hannah Arendt quotes John Adams (and could as well have quoted George Washington, Benjamin Franklin, James Madison, Alexis de Tocqueville, Abraham Lincoln, and others): "I always consider the settlement of America as the opening of a grand scheme and design in Providence for the illumination of the ignorant and the emancipation of the slavish part of mankind all over the earth."[13]

It is important to underline such a powerful stream of thought as this, and its embodiment in a thousand institutional and ritual ways, for it helps to understand how, to Americans, it is somehow fundamental to stand under the judgment of God. Like the ancient Israelites (to whom, John Adams said, Americans owe more than to any other people),[14] they know that no achievement of material prosperity or of military might would spare them a yet more demanding judgment. And this judgment would be rendered by a transcendent, almighty, and unswervingly *just* God, whose judgment was to be dreaded as "a terrible swift sword." The primacy of morals is written into the American soul.

So also have Americans given primacy of place to the institutions of morals and culture: to churches preaching to the faithful, to universities (in whose support, more than any other peoples before or since, they have invested so many of their private and public energies) learning, and to the press. Had he to choose between having a free government or a free press—and God forbid the choice, Jefferson said—he would prefer a free press.[15] If these moral and cultural institutions go sour, if that salt loses its savor, all the rest of ordered liberty is lost: the polity is doomed to division and self-destruction, the economy to hedonism and raw self-interest.

It is absolutely critical to the American experiment, therefore, that the institutions of conscience, information, culture, and ideas retain this primacy. Should there ever be a "treason of the clergy," all is lost.

Indeed, such redoubtable and magisterial social thinkers as Joseph Schumpeter and Daniel Bell have discerned that its moral and cultural system is the weakest link in the threefold political economy of the democratic republic and the capitalist economy. In *Capitalism, Socialism and Democracy* and in *The Cultural Contradictions of Capitalism*, both Schumpeter and Bell argue that, in the long run, the American experiment is doomed.[16] They argue also that this self-destruction will begin, first of all, in the place of primacy, among the spiritual and intellectual elites. Both give long and vivid descriptions of the special vulnerabilities of station and of occupation that favor this self-

destruction among spiritual and intellectual elites. Both fear this betrayal will spread outwards rapidly, through the cinema and music,
through magazines and newspapers, and through other fibers of the
nation's spiritual and intellectual nervous system.

Nonetheless, however accurate and penetrating so many of
Schumpeter and Bell's concrete discernments undoubtedly are, there
is no need to find their pessimism paralyzing. For if the primary flaw in
our political economy lies, not so much in our political system (democracy being a flawed and poor type of governance, until compared to the
alternatives), and not so much in our economic system (capitalism being a flawed and poor organization of economy, except compared to
the alternatives), *but in our moral-cultural system*, then we may well
find this prognosis more hopeful than it first appears. For if the fatal
flaw lies most of all in our ideas and in our morals, then its source lies
not in our stars but in ourselves, where by the grace of God we have a
chance to mend our ways. Good ideas can (and often do) drive out bad
ideas. And even as vice wreaks its social and personal destruction,
sound morals work creatively. If the flaw lies in ourselves—especially in
our moral, intellectual, and cultural elites—then we ourselves have a
magnificent opportunity to do something about it. That is all that free
women and men can ask. A chance. No guarantee, but a chance.

Pope John Paul II's Challenge to the U. S.

If I am not mistaken, this is precisely the diagnosis that Joseph Cardinal Ratzinger and Pope John Paul II have for several years now been
applying to the United States. They appeal to our elites, most of all, on
the plane of ideas and on the terrain of morals and of faith. They call us
to step back from ourselves and to look at ourselves as others abroad see
us. They ask us to look at the moral decadence obvious in the American
films, videotapes, music, television shows, magazines, newspapers,
novels and books that our culture sends as emissaries across the world.
Are we not embarrassed by *Dallas*, spoof though it may be, a series (at
last count) being shown in seventy-seven different nations of the
earth? Just recently, a young Korean-American attorney in Washington, D.C., wrote that the young people of his nation of origin, just two

decades ago wildly pro-American, have come to hold our nation in contempt for three reasons, of which I mean to stress the last: (1) its military impotence; (2) its inconstancy and changeability; and (3) its immorality. He begged the proper authorities to take American Armed Forces television off the airwaves where it is shocking and disgusting to ordinary South Koreans, and if we mean to keep it, to keep it at least on restricted cable lines which only Americans can watch, to their quarantined corruption.[17]

In a word then, the weakest of the three American systems—political, economic, and moral-cultural—is the moral-cultural system. Whatever the weaknesses of the American political system, it is far from being the weakest in the world, and it may be one of the strongest; it is certainly the most long lasting. Whatever may be the weaknesses of the U.S. economy, it is still experiencing the longest period of steady growth with low inflation in its history, and its techniques for producing growth are now being imitated throughout Europe, most remarkably in socialist countries. It has proven over the years to be far more successful in raising the poor and in elevating standards of living than either socialist or traditional societies around the world.

In many ways, of course, U.S. culture is also a pacesetter in the modern world. Our films, our music, and even many of our books are appreciated and imitated in every corner of the world. Nonetheless, it is also widely recognized that the public exploits of our culture tend to generate a loosening of morals. Moreover, America's pre-eminent critic of culture, Lionel Trilling, noted the adversary intention now deeply embedded in our cultural elites:

> . . . we readily see the extent to which the art and thought of the modern period assume that it is possible for at least some persons to extricate themselves from the culture into which they were born. Any historian of the literature of the modern age will take virtually for granted the adversary intention, the actually subversive intention, that characterizes modern writing—he will perceive its clear purpose of detaching the reader from the habits of thought and feeling that the larger culture imposes, of giving him a ground and a vantage point from which to judge and condemn, and perhaps revise, the culture that produced him.

This adversary intention in modern art is more than a century old, Trilling continues, but

> . . . the circumstances in which it has its existence have changed materially. . . . The difference can be expressed quite simply, in numerical terms—there are a great many more people who adopt the adversary program than there formerly were. Between the end of the first quarter of the century in the present time there has grown up a populous group whose members take for granted the idea of the adversary culture. This group is to be described not only by its increasing size but by its increasing coherence. It is possible to think of it as a class. As such, it of course has its internal conflicts and contradictions but also its common interests and presuppositions and a considerable efficiency of organization, even of an institutional kind.

Trilling notes that "three or four decades ago, the university figured as the citadel of conservatism, even of reaction." The very phrase "ivory tower" suggested its removal from reality. Taste, however, "has increasingly come under the control of criticism, which has made art out of what is not art and the other way around," and now this "making and unmaking of art is in the hands of university art departments and the agencies which derive from them, museums and professional publications."[20]

This is the classic text identifying a specific "adversary culture" within U. S. culture, a culture that now governs the mainstream in the universities, the magazines, movies, and television. Coincident with its rise is the gradual collapse of the prestige of scientific, technical elites, and even of the idea of progress. This adversary culture celebrates the anti-bourgeois virtues. By its own innermost intention, it defines itself against the common culture. It has, increasingly, lost its connection with ordinary people whom it is inclined to scorn.

Here is not the place to launch into a fuller discussion of this "new adversary class." The literature concerning its existence is already vast.[21] Indeed, critics have long since linked Eastern European discussions of "the new class" in socialist societies, such as are found in the work of Milovan Djilas,[22] with the "adversary culture" in Western societies.

The point, rather, is as follows. To the extent that the Catholic Church is and must be countercultural, will it wish to link its criticism of U.S. culture with the criticism of that culture made by the new adversary class? This is certainly a temptation. It has even tempted many socialists, particularly those in Latin cultures such as in southern Europe and in Latin America, who have become enamored of the project launched by the Italian communist Antonio Gramsci (1891-1937).[23] According to Gramsci, it is a mistake to understand socialism as an economic doctrine, that is, to tie socialism to the outmoded economic theories of the Marxists of the 19th century. On the contrary, democratic and capitalist societies have proven that they can raise up the proletariat into the middle class rather quickly. Therefore, Gramsci argued, the true socialist project lies not in the realm of economics, but in the realm of culture. The true socialist is an adversary of Western culture, both in its Christian and in its bourgeois aspects. A "long march through the institutions" is necessary to subvert this culture and its fundamental values.

Is this the counterculture that the Catholic Church ought to join? It is true that the Gramsci project is aimed specifically at intellectual elites not only in the universities but also in the organs of mass culture and in the governmental bureaucracies that have administrative powers over the works of culture, especially where radio, television, and the arts are supported by the state. In this respect, the term "intellectuals" is to be understood in a very broad sense; it signifies the whole range of intellectual workers in the realm of symbol-making and the propagation of values. Both politically and intellectually, therefore, the central debate of our time has switched from matters of politics and economics to matters of culture. Catholic intellectuals will need to be very careful in choosing where and how to direct their efforts in this more general debate. In a sense, we are arriving on the field a little late, the battles already having been joined.

Once having identified the proper battleground, what should we do?

Tasks for a New Counterculture

In the Jewish community, Irving Kristol has pointed out,[24] there has long been a division of labor. Receiving most notice in recent years have been the Jewish prophets of the Old Testament. But the prophets were relatively few in number and of considerably less than immediate relevance to the daily lives of most ordinary people. To meet these ordinary needs, the rabbinic tradition has nurtured the custom of practical commentary, carried through in the Talmud and in associated practical writings. The rabbis greatly outnumber the prophets, not only in raw numbers but also in the magnitude of their daily influence.

In the Catholic tradition, by analogy, there have also been two major lines of development: one, incarnational; the other, eschatological. On the one hand, more than typical Protestant communities, the Catholic community has tried to emphasize the presence of Christ in daily physical life, the incarnation of Christ in culture. It has blessed harvests, tools, and objects of daily living. It has tried to awaken the baptized to the reality that the Kingdom of God has already begun in them and among them. Catholic faith welcomes ordinary life, even blesses it; this is, so to speak, its priestly or rabbinic work.

On the other hand, especially (but not only) through its tradition of celibacy and the "setting aside" of a special way of life for nuns, priests and brothers, the Catholic tradition has also tried to maintain an eschatological witness, a sense of rupture with this world and its ordinary demands, a foretaste of the Kingdom to come. This witness is seen to be akin to the witness of the prophets of old.

In one moment, then, the Catholic tendency is to affirm every culture in which it finds itself. In another moment, it has always called every culture beyond itself and toward the Kingdom yet to come and, thus, has set itself up as a counterculture. For the Catholic community to be truly Catholic, both moments are always indispensable.

Furthermore, the Catholic Church is not a gnostic church. Consistently, it has set its face against the "spiritualizers" and the "enthusiasts,"[25] that is, against those who would interpret Christianity as a project for fleeing from the world, for rejecting the world, or for merely condemning the world. It has preferred to see that "God so loved the world that He gave His only son" (John 3:16), and in this respect it has always tried to affirm the goodness of each being and every event within the providential order. In every aspect of being, it has seen mystery, fruitfulness, and the presence of God. Nonetheless, it has also been careful to observe that the Kingdom of God is not yet here; that history is an ongoing pilgrimage; and that everything within history is under the judgment of an undeceivable God.

In a certain sense, then, every Christian should represent in his or her own project in life both of these emphases. Each should be at home in the world, and work within it with affirmation and love; simultaneously, each should be in the world as a stranger.

It seems to me that at the present time "the new adversary class" has more than fulfilled its adversary intention. Hardly any aspect of the U.S. systems—political, economic, and moral-cultural—now escapes withering criticism, often even unfair and inaccurate criticism. Much of this criticism serves the self-interest of the adversarial class whose bottom line often consists in expanding the powers and offices of the state, thereby creating yet more jobs for its members. There is profit in the prophet motive. That such criticism is self-interested would matter little if it were accurate and fair but most often, one finds, it is not. Ambition and desire outweigh calm reflection and judicious assessment; the desire to be adversarial overpowers a willingness to see the other side (and, sometimes, even to concede that there is one). The appetite for prosecution outweighs the appetite for giving a fair hearing to the defense. The sense of possessing a superior moral standing breeds impatience and contempt. Consequently, the truly prophetic task, these days, is to give fair and accurate affirmation where affirmation is due.

Nonetheless, no democratic capitalist regime pretends to be the Kingdom of God. The U.S. regime, in particular, has been deliberately contrived to operate within a world of sin and fallibility, supplying to every ambition a counterambition; it does not permit the perfect to become an enemy of the good. Such a political economy is self-consciously imperfect, flawed, and resolved to make the best out of the weak materials of human nature. "If men were angels, government would not be necessary," Madison wrote in *Federalist* 10. But men are not angels, and democratic capitalist regimes are not made of celestial airs. Their aim is to get us through this veil of tears with a maximum possible degree of "liberty and justice for all," in the firm hope that good fruits will outweigh those of any previous or existing regime. They do not ask to be compared to utopias, but to be compared to other realistic alternatives. And they are open to reform and development, for their starting place is in the drive to raise questions, to inquire, and to invent.

One of the achievements of democratic capitalist regimes, in fact, is to have cleared a wide path for social criticism and prophecy. Even when these are misused, as they are being misused by the adversary class, both are necessary and both are creative. Unlike fascism and communism (its two chief twentieth-century rivals), the democratic capitalist philosophy is not a pseudo-religion. It does not pretend to offer a way of salvation, natural or supernatural. It offers no more than limited government and an effective economy. The limits on the one and the effectiveness of the other create unprecedented space for its moral-cultural system which is open and pluralistic, and for vigorous moral and religious development. In such a regime, no one is coerced into being religious or even moral, but everyone is allowed the space and the freedom in which to become so. Moreover, the political system and the economic system depend upon the creative use of moral and religious freedom.[26]

Criticism and prophecy do not of themselves injure a democratic capitalist regime. Even false prophecy and misplaced criticism may be put to creative use. Still, criticism and prophetic claims are to be assessed according to how accurately and creatively they are launched. Critics—and, in particular, the adversary culture—must carry the burden of being self-critical. They must, if they are to be taken seriously, make sure that the interests they are serving are truly creative and truly just.

Pope John Paul II particularly has called upon U. S. Catholics to question our nation's widely diffused public morality, as this is witnessed in the international media of communication, which have so dramatic an effect upon the rest of the world. In raising this challenge, Pope John Paul II goes to the heart of our system's most glaring weakness. And he does so just when, ironically, many "progressive" Catholic theologians have been complaining recently that Rome does not understand U. S. culture, while at the same time the Pope has been raising the complementary question: Do American Catholic theologians themselves understand American culture? He has thus opened a debate about the true moral standing of U. S. culture. Is it really something that the rest of the world—including Rome—should emulate?

A distinction may be useful here. There are certain virtues inherent in the successful practice of democratic politics and capitalist economies. These may be thought of as those parts of public morality that are embodied in *institutional* practices, and are accordingly thought of as the specifically "democratic" and "capitalist" virtues. But there are other virtues—equally necessary for the successful practice of democracy and capitalism—proper to the moral-cultural sphere itself. Let us consider each in turn.

When "progressive" Catholic theologians speak admiringly of the high moral standards of the U.S. experience, often they have in mind the panoply of virtues associated with democratic *institutions*: open inquiry, due process, judgment by a jury of one's peers, and the like. This, too, is a form of public morality. Both the political institutions and the economic institutions of the free society implicitly contain hidden references to the specific new virtues required to make these institutions function according to their own inner rules. Too seldom do we make these underlying virtues explicit in our thinking. They are quite different from the virtues of traditional societies. They include such virtues as civic responsibility, self-reliance, cooperativeness, openness, and personal economic enterprise. They are acquired during that long process of learning the habits of democratic living to which Tocqueville often refers.[27] Living on the boundary between the traditional society and the democratic society, Tocqueville himself saw more clearly than most the differences in the virtues required in democratic, as opposed to aristocratic societies.[28] (Actually, he saw them more clearly with respect to political institutions than he did with respect to economic institutions.)

By comparison, the virtues proper to the moral-cultural system are distinct, but not separate, from the virtues proper to the political system. The founders of the U.S. order, such as Thomas Jefferson and James Madison, understood quite clearly the connection between the virtues of the moral order and the virtues of the political order. Next to the writing of the Declaration of Independence, the achievement for which Jefferson most wanted to be known was his charter for the University of Virginia, in which he assigned primacy to training in "character." And Madison observed that it would be "chimerical" to imagine that republican institutions could be made to work apart from the practice of republican moral virtues.

Thus, when Pope John Paul II suggests that the U.S. media of communication may be undercutting the practice of the moral virtues, he is suggesting also that this may be a threat to the survival of democratic capitalist institutions. If true, this is a devastating criticism. It suggests that the very qualities of U. S. institutions that the "progressive"

Catholic theologians profess to admire are being undermined by the widely broadcast public morality of our country's major media of communication. This would suggest a form of environmental pollution in the moral order even more destructive than pollution of the physical environment. There is, so to speak, an ecology in morals as well as in the biosphere.

From a theoretical point of view, the analysis offered by Pope John Paul II seems to be well aimed. Many important moral virtues are required to make a free and democratic society function according to its own inner logic; there is a set of moral virtues without which democratic institutions cannot be made to work. How, for example, can citizens who cannot govern their own passions and appetites succeed in governing a well-ordered republic? Without a considerable degree of self-government in private life, self-government as a public project would appear to be chimerical. I am no doubt too fond of quoting the lines of the famous American hymn, "Confirm thy soul in self-control/they liberty in law." Yet few lines capture so well the fundamental premise of republican life; namely, the concept of *ordered* liberty.[29]

Ordered liberty is quite different from libertinism. It is constituted, as Lord Acton suggests, not by doing what we wish, but by doing what we ought. The phrase "ordered liberty" no doubt follows the classical definition of practical wisdom, *recta ratio agendi* (that is, ordered reason in acting). Practical reason, to hit the mark exactly, must be governed by (corrected by, *rectified* by) a good will. To do the truth, we must first love the truth—and love it well and accurately. In a similar way, to be truly free, our passions and appetites must be governed by a well-ordered love of the inner law of our humanity. (It is perhaps less Greek to place the emphasis upon self-*mastery* and self-*discipline* than upon the *attraction* that the good exerts upon the will, the true upon the intellect. In the moral life, the Greeks thought less about obligation than about attraction. They stressed the right order that follows from being *drawn* by love to the good for which one's heart longs. To speak of self-*discipline* and self-*mastery* seems somehow a little more Kantian than Aristotelian. Still, the point is not dissimilar.)

In this respect, I see two tasks for a new counterculture; the first is a moral task, the second an institutional task.

1. The Moral Task

Since the present practices of our public media seem to be deleterious to the moral life of the republic, it appears to be quite necessary for critical and prophetic witnesses to launch a major effort to assess the vision of public morality to which our people are daily subjected. In this connection, one might examine the moral teachings being propounded in our various university departments, not only in philosophy, but also in such fields as psychology, literature, and the like. Here Alasdair MacIntyre and Allan Bloom have raised significant questions.[30] One might also examine the field of education and its new enthusiasms for "values clarification," sex education, global education, and the like. Still a third line of inquiry might be to study the moral content of the narratives, symbols, and ways of living celebrated—or denounced—in major films of our time. Another might be to evaluate the morals taught by rock videos and the recording industry. The tasks are many. And it may well be found, as Charles Krauthammer once wrote, that the moral teachings of priests, rabbis, and even parents count as very little in young minds that have listened admiringly to the moral solicitations of Madonna.

In beginning to think about the moral witness presented to our people (and to the world) by our public media of communication, theologians and other scholars may well conclude that much that is not consonant with Christian visions of virtue is being presented, and even a great deal that is not consonant with natural virtue. We human beings are very weak, and much more commonly than we would normally like to admit we are seduced rather easily by the three classic enemies of the human soul: the world, the flesh, and the devil. To resist these was hard enough when mass media of communication were absent from the world. It is much more difficult today.

During the last sixty years, in interpreting the social doctrine of the Church, a great deal has been written about politics and, more recently, economics. No doubt this work has been necessary and valuable. It is surprising, however, to note the lack of sustained criticism regarding the cultural system in which we live and move and have our being. Neither a sound economy nor sound politics can be maintained for long in an atmosphere of moral decadence.

I do not think that our mass media are quite as decadent as some in our midst often say. Any well-told story requires the dramatization of the essential components of human moral action. Drama and narrative, even in the most attenuated forms, necessarily pay testimony to the basic capacities of the human soul for reflection and choice, and for the courage necessary to sustain both. Nonetheless, it can hardly be said that ours is an age of moral toughness, or that our public media of communication typically (or even often) present a full Christian vision of the moral life. Such a vision would have a great deal to say about the fall into temptation, about human sinfulness, and about the human weakness to which all of us are prey. It is not the portrayal of weakness and sinfulness that constitutes decadence; it is, rather, giving in to weakness and calling it virtue. It is not weakness that makes for decadence, but moral dishonesty. A fully Christian vision certainly would be much less likely than much of what we see today to call sin virtue, and virtue sin.

Indeed, the hardest part of the moral task we face is the immense power of the adversary culture. To oppose that power is to risk excommunication from the "mainstream." Nonetheless, the intention of the modernist project is (as Trilling, who loved modernist works, was compelled by intellectual honesty to state) to subvert the classic Jewish, Christian and natural virtues. It is to perform a massive transvaluation of values, to turn the moral world upside down. It is to substitute the new, modernist virtues for ancient Jewish and Christian virtues, to suggest that what Jews and Christians have for centuries called sin is actually a high form of liberation, and that what for centuries Jews and Christians have thought to be virtuous is actually vicious. It is to hate what Jews and Christians love, and to love what Jews and Christians hate.

Ironically, the very virtue of progressivism that is its most endearing quality—namely, its openmindedness—stands here defenseless. In trying to be broadminded about the modernist subversion, even many Christians give it the best possible interpretation, and ascribe to the traditional Jewish and Christian agenda the most negative and hostile associations. Thus it happens that, in the name of launching a counterculture, some progressives baptize the worst features of the contemporary modernist project. In the name of openness, they try to shock the bourgeois middle-class by collaborating in this deliberate transvaluation of values.

The truth is, is it not, that there is all too little resistance to the modernist project and to the adversary culture. To oppose these would cause one to seem to be unsophisticated, backward, and unwashed. Thus does the treason of the intellectuals proceed, silently, as if under a cloud of invisible but deadly gas.

2. The Institutional Task

Since I have written about this task more frequently in other places, here I will be brief. All around the world there are stirrings among people suffering under socialist and traditionalist institutions, but longing for a freer life. They dream of living under institutions that would liberate their human capacities for reflection and for choice. There is, it seems, a longing in the human heart to live under a system of natural liberty, that is, under those sorts of institutions that allow the human soul to express itself naturally in all three major fields of life: political, economic, and moral-cultural. The vast majority of peoples on this planet, in the past and still today, have not lived under such institutions. But the broad outlines of these institutions are now fairly well known to more and more peoples of the world. They have glimpsed these outlines through their own harsh experiences under mean alternatives.

Thus, with Pope John Paul II, more and more of the world's peoples seem to understand that their best protection from torture, tyranny and other forms of political oppression derives from living under institutions that are (a) subject to the consent of the governed, (b) protective of minority rights, and (c) designed around internal sets of checks and balances. We are quite likely to hear a great deal more about "democracy," even in cultures in which the very word has long been spoken of (as in "bourgeois democracy") with much disdain.

Similarly, since neither communist nor traditionalist societies seem to be capable of producing the goods which the poor of the world need and desire, the reputation of the hitherto much scorned system, capitalism, is growing. In an ever-increasing number of countries one hears the demand for freer markets, for private property, and for incentives that reward greater labor and superior skills. One hears expressed the longing for institutions that sustain personal economic enterprise and economic creativity.

Finally, in such places as the Soviet Union and the Peoples' Republic of China, in South Africa and throughout Black Africa, in Latin America and elsewhere, the demand is increasingly expressed for institutions that allow liberty of conscience, inquiry, and expression.

In sum, more and more citizens of the world are still seeking the three basic institutional liberations of human life: a free polity, a free economy, and a free moral-cultural system. This is seldom today a matter of ideology; it has arisen from harsh lessons of trial and error. One cannot speak of these three liberations without also speaking of *institutions*. And, as we have seen above, one can hardly speak of institutions without speaking of the *moral virtues* that sustain them. Political and economic liberation, then, focus new attention on moral matters.

For human rights are not protected by words on parchment. They are protected by habits, free associations and institutions. Moreover, the institutions that protect human rights do not coerce conscience, demand virtue, or force citizens to develop their individual moral and spiritual capacities. Those institutions create space for those achievements, but do not automatically produce them. Thus, the mere achievement of the basic institutions of political and economic liberty will not itself fulfill human moral and spiritual longing. Politics and economics are not enough. That is why I would like to end these remarks by stressing, once again, that the next frontier for those who think counterculturally concerns the moral and spiritual dimension of our culture. We come around then to the theme that Pope John Paul II set forth in the beginning as the *leitmotif* of his pontificate: the primacy of morals. Here is where the next and most important battles lie.

Notes

1. Congregation for the Doctrine of the Faith, "Instruction on Christian Freedom and Liberation" (Vatican City: Vatican Polyglot Press, 1986), p. 7.
2. Hannah Arendt, *On Revolution* (New York: The Viking Press, 1965), p. 49.
3. Lionel Trilling, *Beyond Culture: Essays on Literature and Learning* (New York: The Viking Press, 1968).
4. Arendt, *Ibid.*, p. 49 (italics added).

5. At a critical point in the Constitutional Convention on June 28, 1787, Franklin suggested the depths of the Framers' struggle to concur on a new order: "We indeed seem to feel our own want of political wisdom, since we have been running about in search of it. We have gone back to ancient history for models of Government, and examined the different forms of those Republics which having been formed with the seeds of their own dissolution now no longer exist. And we have viewed Modern States all round Europe, but find none of their Constitutions suitable to our circumstances." Speech of Benjamin Franklin to the Federal Convention, June 28, 1787, cited in James Madison, *Notes of Debates in the Federal Convention of 1787*, with an introduction by Adrienne Koch (New York: W. W. Norton & Company, 1987), p. 209.

6. Alexander Hamilton, James Madison, John Jay, *The Federalist Papers*, introduced by Clinton Rossiter (New York: Mentor, 1961), No. 14 (pp. 104-105).

7. Arendt, *Ibid.*, p. 15.

8. "The American ought therefore to love this country much better than that wherein either he or his forefathers were born. Here the rewards of his industry follow with equal steps the progress of his labour; his labour is founded on the basis of nature, *self-interest*; can it want a stronger allurement? Wives and children, who before in vain demanded of him a morsel of bread, now, fat and frolicsome, gladly help their father to clear those fields whence exuberant crops are to arise to feed and to clothe them all; without any part being claimed, either by a despotic prince, a rich abbot, or a mighty lord." Hector St. John Crevecoeur, *Letter from an American Farmer* (1782; reprint ed., New York: Fox, Duffield & Co., 1904), p. 55.

9. "If patient observation and sincere meditation have led men of the present day to recognize that both the past and the future of their history consist in the gradual and measured advance of equality, that discovery in itself gives this progress the sacred character of the will of the Sovereign Master. In that case effort to halt democracy appears as a fight against God Himself, and nations have no alternative but to acquiesce in the social state imposed by Providence." Alexis de Tocqueville, *Democracy in America*, trans. by George Lawrence, ed. by J. P. Mayer (Garden City: Anchor Books, 1969), p. 12.

10. "The Miami Meeting with President Reagan," *Origins*, Vol. 17, No. 15 (September 24, 1987), p. 238.

11. "Is there no virtue among us?" asked Madison defiantly. "If there be not, we are in a wretched situation. No theoretical checks, no form of government, can render us secure. To suppose any form of government will secure liberty or happiness without any virtue in the people, is a chimerical idea." Jonathan Elliot, ed., *Debates in the Several State Conventions on the Adop-*

tion of the Federal Constitution (Philadelphia: Lippincott, 1907), Virginia, June 20, 1788.

12. "You are called upon," Hamilton writes to the people of the United States in *Federalist* 1, "to deliberate on a new Constitution for the United States of America. . . . It has frequently been remarked," he continues, "that it seems to have been reserved to the people of this country, by their conduct and example, to decide the important question, whether societies of men are really capable or not of establishing good government from *reflection* and *choice*, or whether they are forever destined to depend for their political constitutions on accident and force." (Italics added).

13. Arendt, *Ibid.*, p. 15.

14. "I will insist," wrote John Adams in 1809, "that the Hebrews have done more to civilize men than any other nation. If I were an atheist, and believed in blind eternal fate, I should still believe that fate had ordained the Jews to be the most essential instrument for civilizing the nations. If I were an atheist of the other sect, who believe or pretend to believe that all is ordered by chance, I should believe that chance had ordered the Jews to preserve and propagate to all mankind the doctrine of a supreme, intelligent, wise, almighty sovereign of the universe, which I believe to be the great essential principle of all morality, and consequently of all civilization." John Adams to F. A. Vanderkemp, February 16, 1809, in C. F. Adams (ed.), *The Works of John Adams* (Boston: Little, Brown, 1854), Vol. IX, pp. 609–10.

15. "The basis of our governments being the opinion of the people, the very first object should be to keep that right [a free press]; and were it left to me to decide whether we should have a government, I should not hesitate a moment to prefer the latter." Letter to Edward Carrington, January 16, 1787, in *Thomas Jefferson* (New York: Literary Classics of the United States, Inc., 1984), p. 880.

16. Joseph A. Schumpeter, *Capitalism, Socialism and Democracy*, Third Edition (New York: Harper & Row, 1975), and Daniel Bell, *The Cultural Contradictions of Capitalism* (New York: Basic Books, Inc., 1976).

17. Sung-Chull Junn, "Why Koreans Think We're Jerks," *Washington Post*, "Outlook," April 9, 1989.

18. Trilling, *Beyond Culture*, p. xii. Irving Kristol adds an important clarification; the new class is adversarial not just to the practices of the nation but to its ideals: "We are so used to this fact of our lives, we take it so for granted, that we fail to realize how extraordinary it is. Has there ever been in all of recorded history, a civilization whose culture was at odds with the values and ideals of that civilization itself? It is not uncommon that a culture will be critical of the civilization that sustains it—and always critical of the failure of this civilization to realize perfectly the ideals that it claims as inspiration. Such

criticism is implicit or explicit in Aristophanes and Euripides, Dante and Shakespeare. But to take an adversary posture toward the ideals themselves? That is unprecedented. . . . The more 'cultivated' a person is in our society, the more disaffected and malcontent he is likely to be—a disaffection, moreover, directed not only at the actuality of our society but at the ideality as well. Indeed, the ideality may be more strenuously opposed than the actuality." Irving Kristol, *Reflections of a Neoconservative: Looking Back, Looking Ahead*, (New York: Basic Books, Inc., 1983), pp. 27–28.

19. *Ibid.*, p. xii.

20. *Ibid.*, p. xiv-xv.

21. A useful introduction to the "new class" may be found in B. Bruce-Briggs, *The New Class?* (New Brunswick, New Jersey: Transaction Books, 1979). In *Beyond Culture*, Lionel Trilling showed the influence of the "new class" in literature; to see the influence of the "new class" on politics and economics see, respectively, Jeane J. Kirkpatrick, "Politics and the 'New Class,' " *Dictatorships and Double Standards: Rationalism and Reason in Politics* (New York: American Enterprise Institute and Simon and Schuster, 1982), and Irving Kristol, *Two Cheers for Capitalism* (New York: Basic Books, 1978), Chapter 2, "Business and the 'New Class.' "

In Marxist countries, the danger of a "new class" was discerned as early as 1939 by Bruno Rizzi; see his *The Bureaucratization of the World*, trans., with an Introduction by Adam Westoby (New York: The Free Press, 1986). Almost simultaneously, James Burnham discerned an equivalent to the "new class" in *The Managerial Revolution* (New York: John Day Co., 1941). The concept became prominent on the left with the publication of Milovan Djilas's *The New Class* (New York: Praeger, 1957). In the United States, writers on the left, such as John Kenneth Galbraith, David T. Bazelon, Michael Harrington and others, began to point to the "new class" as a potential ally of, if not a replacement for, the proletariat. See Galbraith, *The Affluent Society* (Boston: Houghton Mifflin, 1958); Bazelon, *Power in America* (New York: New American Library, 1967); Harrington, *Toward a Democratic Left* (New York: Macmillan, 1968), ch. 10.

22. See Milovan Djilas, *The New Class*.

23. See *Antonio Gramsci: Selections from Political Writings, 1910–1920*, John Mathews, trans. (Ann Arbor: Books on Demand, UMI, 1976). See also Jaime Antunex, "Socialism Chic," *Crisis*, (April 1989), pp. 38–40.

24. "The terms 'prophetic' and 'rabbinic' which come, of course, from the Jewish tradition, indicate the two poles within which the Jewish tradition operates. They are not two equal poles: The rabbinic is the stronger pole, always. In an Orthodox Hebrew school, the prophets are read only by those who are far advanced. The rest of the students read the first five books of the Bible,

and no more. They learn the Law. The prophets are only for people who are advanced in their learning and not likely to be misled by prophetic fever." Irving Kristol, *Reflections of a Neoconservative*, pp. 316–317.

25. See Ronald A. Knox, *Enthusiasm* (Westminster, Maryland: Christian Classics, 1983).

26. For further elaboration see Michael Novak, "Boredom, Virtue, and Democratic Capitalism," *Commentary* (September 1989), pp. 109–116.

27. "It cannot be repeated too often that nothing is more fertile in prodigies than the art of being free; but there is nothing more arduous than the apprenticeship of liberty. . . . Liberty . . . is perfected by civil discord; and its benefits cannot be appreciated until it is already old." Alexis de Tocqueville, *Democracy in America*, 2 vols., the Henry Reeve Text as revised by Francis Bowen, further corrected and edited with an historical essay, editorial notes, and bibliographies by Phillips Bradley (New York: Vintage Books, 1945), p. 256.

28. "When the world was under the control of a few rich and powerful men, they liked to entertain a sublime conception of the duties of man. It gratified them to make out that it is a glorious thing to forget oneself and that one should do good without self-interest, as God himself does. That was the official doctrine of morality at that time.

"I doubt whether men were better in times of aristocracy than at other times, but certainly they talked continually about the beauties of virtue. Only in secret did they study its utility. But since imagination has been taking less lofty flights, and every man's thoughts are centered on himself, moralists take fright at this idea of sacrifice and no longer venture to suggest it for consideration. So they are reduced to inquiring whether it is not to the individual advantage of each to work for the good of all. . . ." Tocqueville, *Ibid.*, p. 525.

29. "There is," writes Cotton Mather, "a *liberty* of corrupt nature, which is affected by *men* and *beasts* to do what they list; and this *liberty* is inconsistent with *authority*, impatient of all restraint; by this *liberty*, *Summus Omnes Deteriores*, 'tis the grand enemy of *truth* and *peace*, and all the *ordinances* of God are bent against it.' But there is a civil, a moral, a federal *liberty* for that only which is *just* and *good*; for this *liberty* you are to stand with the hazard of your very *lives*." Cited by Tocqueville, *Democracy*, p. 46 (emphasis in the original).

30. See Allan Bloom, *The Closing of the American Mind* (New York: Simon and Schuster, 1987), and Alasdair MacIntyre, *After Virtue* (Notre Dame: University of Notre Dame Press, 1981).

Six

John Paul II's Challenge to Democratic Capitalism or Be Still and Know That I Am the Pope

Robert Benne

If I were asked to make a judgment on the Pope's two encyclicals, *On Human Work* and *On Social Concern*, as to their economic and political insight, I would be hard pressed to place them on the credit or debit side. They seem to contain an equal number of pluses and minuses. It is a stalemate.

True enough, there are significant concessions. The Pope affirms the right to economic initiative and criticizes "levelling down" as an approach to equality. (*OSC*, 56,24) He rejects statist conceptions of development and connects authentic development to democratic rights and processes. He states that his social teaching is not a third way between liberal capitalism and Marxist socialism. (*OSC*, 83) He argues that laity must take their proper role in the practical world of economics and politics and thus he avoids any hint of clericalism. He asserts that the poor must also take the responsibility for improving their situation and that poor countries should discover their economic advantage. (*OSC*, 66) He remarks that culture and value systems are relevant for development. (*OSC*, 22) He observes that "having" in itself is not bad. (*OSC*, 50) He is repeatedly critical of collectivism and its denial of human rights. Finally, he dashes any unqualified utopian impulses by denying that any earthly political or economic accomplishment can be identified with the Kingdom of God. (*OSC*, 98)

These themes warm the hearts of those who defend democratic capitalism. Indeed, commentators such as Michael Novak see strong convergences between Catholic social teaching and the liberalism of the American tradition (Novak, *Free Persons and the Common Good*). Richard

Neuhaus, George Weigle and John Cooper also celebrate this rapprochement between the Pope and the Capitalist. John Cooper entitles his commentary on *On Social Concern*, "Pope's Economics Lean Toward Reformed Capitalism." Even Catholics further left on the spectrum concede that Catholic social teaching is in the process of coming to terms with Western liberalism. (Hollenbach, "Liberalism, Communitarianism, and the Bishops' Pastoral Letter on the Economy.")

However, it is unwise and inaccurate to see only the convergences. There are as many, if not more, themes in the Pope's encyclicals that are dear to the enemies of democratic capitalism. I will enumerate only those in *On Social Concern*. He repeats the nostrums of the New International Economic order. (87) He retains the medieval notion of the just wage. (43) He has little appreciation for the role of profit and competition in a market system. (39) He makes dubious empirical judgments about the shrinking sources of work, a widening gap between developed and developing nations and about the likelihood of military cuts releasing money for development aid. He talks about the "traditional dependence of the worker-proletarian in capitalism." (24) He makes blanket assertions about the earth and its wealth belonging to all without regard for differences in peoples' capacities to become economically productive. He proposes work as a positive right. (41) He gives a strong push for planning and asserts the priority of labor over capital (whatever that might mean). Perhaps most galling for U. S. conservatives, he wheels out the moral equivalency theory concerning the two blocs of "imperialist" powers. (33–35)

These ideas give a great deal of ammunition to those on the left who want to delegitimate liberal capitalism's role in the world. The Catholic Bishops of Canada and Gregory Baum will use these themes in strengthening their left wing point of view, as they did earlier with the Pope's *On Human Work*.

Given this rough balance between those who claim the Pope for their side, it was tempting to try to nudge the scales to one side or the other. But such an exercise would seem also a bit juvenile on my part: strike a blow for your side by putting the Pope in the proper column.

I was saved from such a fate by the conference organizers. They suggested a topic for me which is reflected in the title of the paper. As I see it, I do not need to assess the Pope's total message from my point of view, but rather to allow major motifs in the Pope's reflections to address U. S. democratic capitalism. Hence, the subtitle, which suggests that we drop our defenses and let the Pope's concerns hit home. So the question becomes: What unique insights does the Pope bring to U. S. democratic capitalism that might guide it in a more fulfilling direction?

This less defensive way of proceeding may open the way to fruitful dialogue, and such dialogue is very important to the evolution and reform of democratic capitalism. It is important because it seems clear that the democratic capitalist model has won decisively its contest with directed socialism in the West and in the world. Even democratic socialism is on the wane as a viable vision for shaping real-life political economies.

In the West the great debate is now over who can best manage democratic capitalism. Few social democratic parties are calling for a more "full-blooded socialism." Privatization is much more dominant than nationalization. There is a continuing debate in all democratic capitalist countries about the extent and mode of democratic interventions and about the scope of the welfare state, but almost everyone affirms the wealth-producing capacities of competitive market systems. Few want to submit them to the direct political control of the state. Everyone seems to want enterprises to behave efficiently in competitive markets.

The East, in fact, now has admitted the economic benefits of private enterprise in a competitive context. Experimentation with various forms of enterprise is widespread. Though this will certainly not lead to dominantly free economies soon, it reveals a strong disillusionment with directed economies. Perhaps even more interesting, and threatening to their respective governments, are the pressures for democratization that are emerging in many eastern lands. This "triumph" of democratic capitalism has been noted not only by its ideological proponents who would be expected to make such a judgment, but by persons such as Robert Heilbroner who has made virtually a career out of pronouncing doom on capitalism. "Less than seventy-five years after it officially began, the contest between capitalism and socialism is over: Capitalism has won. The Soviet Union, China, and Eastern Europe have given us the clearest possible proof that capitalism organizes the material affairs of humankind more satisfactorily than socialism." (*New Yorker*)

Besides material prosperity, which Heilbroner duly notes, there are many other strengths accruing to the combination of political democracy, market economic arrangements, and pluralist society. I have tried to make a full accounting of those strengths in an earlier book, *The Ethic of Democratic Capitalism—A Moral Reassessment*. In addition to the capacity of capitalism to raise the living standards of the masses, a not insignificant practical and moral achievement, its wealth-producing capacities sustain enough people at a high enough level that democracy becomes possible, sustainable and eminently desirable. Capitalism and democracy are historically linked in the sense that capitalism is most likely a necessary, but not a sufficient, condition for democracy. (Berger, *The Capitalist Revolution*)

Further, the mostly self-coordinating character of market systems allows a healthy division of labor and power between the polity and economy. In democratic capitalism the state need not be omnicompetent, an impossible standard that is fatefully presupposed in state socialism. Therefore, it is less likely to accrue oppressive power—the economy and society provide significant counterbalance.

Market systems also support the values of individual and social freedom, opportunity, and reward for contribution. The economic freedom in democratic capitalism is part and parcel of personal liberty itself. As important as individual freedom is, the social freedom and pluralism supported by free economies are even more significant. In such contexts persons have discretionary money and the necessary freedom to spend it in support of private institutions and associations that bear their cherished values. This is immensely important, as anyone who teaches in a private institution will affirm. Only democratic capitalist lands have the profusion of private institutions and associations that we enjoy.

Market economies are generally dynamic and creative enough to spew out all sorts of opportunities for employment. People have enhanced chances to better themselves and their families. Finally, competitive systems constitute roughly democratic ways of rewarding persons for their productive contributions to the formal economy. Again, the state need not get into the business of setting most wages and prices.

This catalogue of strengths certainly does not mean that democratic capitalism is without problems. In fact, Heilbroner believes that socialism will retain its inspirational potential among small groups of people who will then challenge democratic capitalism to become more humane. But the question, he says, is not "Can capitalism work?" It has proven it can. The question has now become: "Will capitalism work well enough?" (Heilbroner, *New Yorker*)

That, it seems to me, is where the Pope's encyclicals come in. They bear religious and humane concerns that need to be addressed to the "victor," lest he and she in some fit of hubris come to believe in his or her own invulnerability. These concerns are more likely to be entertained seriously because they are spoken from a not unfriendly perspective. That is the significance of the many concessions to liberal theory and practice the Pope has made, even though they are balanced by as many concessions to the "other side." The balance prevents his encyclicals from falling into the "economic counterculture" syndrome.

There are four themes strongly present in the Pope's letters that are crucial for guiding U. S. democratic capitalism toward higher ends. They are: (1) the closely related themes of solidarity and the common good; (2) the richly textured and expanded notion of development; (3) the ethical duty toward the development of others; and (4) the moral dimension of economic interdependence.

Each of these themes has a domestic and an international dimension. Each has a connection with earlier Western thought and each is partially realized in present worldly arrangements. But each is threatened by trends in the current unfolding of democratic capitalism on the domestic and world scenes.

Solidarity and the Common Good

Certainly a major theme is struck by the Pope's repeated use of these two related concepts. Solidarity is based on the fundamental connectedness of all beings in God and provides the basis for a moral commitment to the common good. There are certain qualities, needs and aspirations that we, as humans and creatures of God, share and they provide a basis for a common good—the publicly constructed arena of shared values that lead to mutual rights and responsibilities for all participants.

The Pope begins his reflections on solidarity by pointing out the empirical facts of interdependence. "It (our growing awareness) is above all a question of interdependence, sensed as a system determining relationships in the contemporary world, in its economic, cultural, political and religious elements . . ." (OSC, 74) This interdependence is not only international and national, but also characterizes the structure and activities of all enterprises, whether they be social, economic or political. Human creative activity is essentially an exercise in interdependence.

However, merely recognizing this as an empirical fact is not enough. The Pope insists that interdependence "be accepted as a moral category." (OSC, 74) Solidarity is "a firm and persevering determination to commit oneself to the common good; that is to say, to the good of all and each individual, because we are all really responsible for all. (OSC, 74) It is a recognition of each other as persons, as neighbors, in whatever common endeavor we find ourselves.

The practical offshoot of this moral virtue of solidarity is *collaboration*. "This is precisely the act proper to solidarity among individuals and nations." (OSC, 77) This notion is clearly echoed in the American Catholic Bishops' letter where "participation" is such an important principle. It is also evident that collaboration does not mean a functional equality in which everyone has equal authority or power or, for that matter, reward. But it does mean that the interconnectedness involved in all endeavors be accepted as a moral reality. There are moral bonds involved, not only economic or political.

The Pope uses this solidarity principle to emphasize the fair treatment of labor in On Human Work and to call for inclusion of the poor and weak in national and international development in On Social Concern, about which we shall speak later. But it has a much wider and deeper application. *Indeed, if taken seriously, it challenges the tendency in capitalism to understand—or misunderstand—and thereby reduce an increasing number of areas of human endeavor to economic rationality and exchange.* The principle of solidarity resists the reduction of democratic capitalist civilization to a chilly economism.

Tendencies in this direction are obvious. We are finding out that treating firms or corporations as purely economic entities that can be disassembled at will and that are held together solely by the economic self-interest of participating parties leads to a decline in morale and productivity. We are discovering that the moral principle of solidarity has much to say about morale. This is true not only in business, but in education, sport and political life.

As education is viewed increasingly as a commodity to be bought and sold, the interactions of faculty, students and administrators is viewed along the contractual lines of economic bargaining. The organic connections accepted as morally relevant are diminished and the sense of collaboration toward common ends is thwarted, if indeed any common ends can be found. The same is true in sports. As they have come to resemble large business enterprises, professional teams lose their sense of local rootedness, player loyalty, and their cohesiveness in the face of either victory or defeat. In short, their *Cubness* disintegrates and winning becomes everything. Politics also become the function of economic interest. Even more seriously, we cannot decide whether babies should be bought and sold in the market.

These tendencies are furthered by intellectual efforts to understand all human activities through the prism of economic rationality. Gary Becker attempts to understand marriage and family life in this way. (Becker, *The Economic Approach to Human Behavior*) Richard Posner views the law through the lens of economic rationality. (Posner, *The Economic Analysis of Law*) The "public choice" school interprets politics as a species of economic interaction. Indeed, the neoclassical model of economics strips away all motivational considerations except rational self-interest in the marketplace.

It is certainly not the case that economic elements are absent from those areas; however, reducing them to economic rationality does gross injustice to how, in fact, they do, but also should, work. Economists like Joseph Schumpeter are far wiser. He argued long ago that bourgeois rationality must be complemented and sometimes checked by "extra-rational determinants of conduct" if capitalist societies are to function adequately. (Schumpeter, *Capitalism, Socialism and Democracy*, p. 144)

Capitalist practice, if not theory, assumes the presence of these "extra-rational determinants" for motivation (the Protestant Ethic), for guidance about what should be produced and consumed, for the moral capacities for promise-making and keeping, and for direction for the uses of profit and wealth. And those instances of solidarity are taken only from business. The solidarity principle was and is present in democratic political practice, in family, associational and, above all, religious life.

But the imperialism of economic rationality threatens to eat away at the organic moral interconnectedness that supports a tolerable life together. Fortunately, there are some strong countercurrents. Business ethics is a growing concern among us. Economic theory is being pressed to include social and moral dimensions. We worry about economic influence in politics. There may be enough health in us to resist this fateful reduction of Western life.

If solidarity as a moral theme reminds us that life together cannot be reduced to economic exchange and rationality, it also insists on the inclusion of all persons into what is commonly good—shelter, health, food, education and basic security. We certainly agree these are goods and that for most of us they are assured through our own efforts. The principle of solidarity, however, insists that all persons ought to have access to these goods. Everyone's access is part and parcel of the common good. Thus, the principle of solidarity brings a distributive thrust to the goods that are generally available to most citizens.

It is not the job of the economy to provide everyone with the wherewithal to purchase these goods for it is clear that many persons will not be able to contribute enough to the economy to receive rewards adequate for the purchase of them. However, it is the mark of a good economy to be able to recompense the vast majority of participants at a high enough level so that they can provide these goods for themselves, their families and sometimes for others in need. Nevertheless, all are not covered and the state must provide access for those who cannot provide for themselves, assuring that all participate in the common good.

Some goods, such as elementary and secondary education, are guaranteed positive rights. We might quarrel with the proviso that they can be claimed only within the public system, but most would agree that the access to free education should be part of the common good. Education is crucially important for adequate employment, enlightened citizenship and the enjoyment of higher culture. Therefore, we remove it from the vagaries of the market; we do not demand that persons pay directly for the good.

There is continued debate over whether other goods should be considered universal positive rights—entitlements—guaranteed by the government. I maintain that our present system of regarding shelter, health and food as conditional positive rights is morally defensible. Indeed, I would argue for the limitation of the universal provisions under Medicare and veterans benefits to those who genuinely need support. Persons over sixty-five and veterans who can pay their own way ought to do so. That would release enormous funds for supporting those who genuinely cannot provide for themselves. We should support them at a level commensurate with that enjoyed by middle-class citizens and in a way that does not visibly identify them as "needy," insofar as that is possible.

Further, we should include in the common good the protection of all citizens from the unbearable costs of catastrophic illness. Only the very wealthy need be excluded from such a provision. As medical technology has become more effective in saving and prolonging life, and more expensive, it is important to protect people from having their accumulated assets reduced to nothing through health disasters.

Perhaps there will be other goods that will need to be included in the common good. In the next section I shall argue that moral, aesthetic and cultural goods should be more directly encompassed in the common good. But I suspect it would be a disaster of major proportions if shelter, employment, and food became universal entitlements. The opportunity to claim them by anyone would likely lead to a dependent populous as well as an administrative monstrosity.

A Deeper Notion of Development

If the norms of solidarity and the common good help us to resist the reduction of democratic capitalist civilization to economic exchange and rationality, the Pope develops other strong themes to help us *elevate* it. Under the general rubric of "Authentic Human Development" (*OSC*, Chapter Four), he criticizes "superdevelopment," which

> consists in an excessive availability of every kind of material goods for the benefit of certain social groups which easily makes people slaves of "possession" and of immediate gratification, with no other horizon than the multiplication or continual replacement of the things already owned with others still better. (*OSC*, pp. 48–49)

This consumerism, he adds, leads to "radical dissatisfaction," because it leaves deeper aspirations unsatisfied and perhaps stifled. (*OSC*, p. 49) Thus, a culture devoted to consumerism thwarts true human development even though it supplies most of its people with material prosperity. As Hannah Arendt has noted, "We can be imprisoned by chains of silk as well as of iron." (Arendt, *On Revolution*, p. 135)

The Pope does not abjure worldly values. Having possessions in itself is not evil. But one should regard "the *quality* and *ordered hierarchy* of the goods one has." (*OSC*, 50) These two considerations enable persons to shape the possession and use of material goods according to one's true vocation. All humans are called to realize their divine likeness. Created in the image of God we are called to have dominion over the creation, and to "tend the garden." The divine likeness also means we are created for communion with others, even as the Trinity involves a communion internal to itself. Further, we have an immortal destiny that qualifies all worldly connections and devotions. (*OSC*, 52) What does it profit a person to gain the world but lose his soul? Thus, the health of our soul, our relation to Christ, is part of our true development.

Here, it seems to me, is a wonderful opportunity for the Pope in particular and Catholic social thought in general to contribute to the enrichment of modern life. We need persons at all levels of society who possess an interior confidence in a plausible hierarchy of values. The classical philosophical and religious traditions of the West have maintained an objective ordering of values that was thought to be necessary for a truly free and fulfilled life. One was nurtured to maintain a certain detachment from the drive for possessions. They were a necessary condition for the higher pursuits of friendship, public life, study and the appreciation of truth and beauty. Christianity affirmed that tradition and added the transcendent calling to faith, love and hope.

There is rich potential in the Catholic tradition for helping moderns achieve an *ordered* liberty. And that is one of the most important needs of contemporary society. In a context of liberty and affluence, our people are sorely tempted to pursue the chaotic, short-term impulses of desire. There are serious signs that the capacities for self-government are eroding. The "little platoons" of life—marriage, family, near-at-hand associations—are threatened by the "sensate" demands of the imperial self.

Goethe remarked at the beginning of the modern era that "Everything that liberates the spirit without a corresponding growth in self-mastery is pernicious." The great liberals of the Enlightenment believed that reason would supply such disciplined guidance after the dead hand of tradition was thrown off. To some extent they were right, of course, but the creative impulses of the Enlightenment were guided more than they were aware of by the freer expression of accumulated Christian moral capital. We are now less confident of the guidance and motivational capacities of reason standing apart from living historical traditions. Reason proceeds on the basis of the premises provided by communities moving through time.

The Catholic community has the first opportunity to take seriously the Pope's challenge to develop the whole human being. Its churches, schools, colleges, universities and related associations should be in the forefront of this richer notion of human development.

There are heartening signs in the world of private higher education that such a "Catholic" notion of the purposes of learning is being taken seriously. Colleges are reconnecting with a classical core of learning. Moral education is entering the required curriculum. Many schools either strongly encourage or require community service as a part of the college experience. These movements are particularly active among private, church-related institutions which have an easier time reaching consensus on a value-laden education that has some chance of helping students achieve an ordered liberty for their lives.

It is extremely important these schools do not forget their calling and that they continue to find support for their mission. Unfortunately, there is a disturbing trend toward public institutions garnering an increasing share of private contributions. With the huge subsidies already enjoyed by the public sector, it is hard to see the fairness in this lamentable trend.

Is this papal notion of the development of the whole human being relevant to the public sector? Should the states become involved in soul-craft? Is education toward an ordered liberty a part of the common good? To some extent it must be. Public education, particularly at the elementary and secondary levels, inevitably must teach values. The state promotes values by modeling them in its leaders and honoring them in its policies.

In view of the widespread vulgarization of popular culture, perhaps it is time for the state to subsidize more generously high quality music, theater, film, radio and TV. A strengthened public effort in these areas might well elevate the general state of culture.

Finally, John Paul II reminds us that development can proceed properly only with due regard to the natural world in which we live. He elaborates this dimension of authentic development in three points: (1) we must respect the nature of each being and connections within an ordered system; (2) we must be frugal with nonrenewable resources; and (3) we must limit the pollution of the environment. (*OSC*, 64-65) These ecological concerns combine with earlier reflections to help us envision a higher stage of development than we have reached. It is a stage where we realize that development cannot be reduced to economic considerations but that it *is* characterized by qualitative development of the human project within the limits and possibilities of the natural environment.

The Moral Duty toward the Development of Others

The first two themes have dealt with the quality or substance of civilization. John Paul II has addressed democratic capitalism's propensity to undermine itself by its very successes. *In this third theme, he urges us to distribute authentic development to all, but especially to the poor and vulnerable in our own country and in the world.*

Again, the religiously and humanly grounded notion of solidarity is the fundamental principle. Solidarity is expressed when humans recognize one another as persons, i.e., they are subjects created in the likeness of God and ransomed by the blood of Christ. All have equal claim to authentic development. This "all" includes those within one's own society and those abroad. (*OSC*, 75–76)

The Pope cites the parable of the talents to emphasize that we are all to use the full measure of our talents for the "development of the whole human being and of all people." (*OSC*, 55) Resisting this call and duty "would be betraying the will of God the Creator, who wills the improving the lot of man in his totality and of all people." (*OSC*, 55)

The strong and wealthy have a special duty because of their gifts. "Those who are more influential, because they have a greater share of goods and common services, should feel *responsible* for the weaker and be ready to share with them all they possess." (*OSC*, 75) The weak are not left off the hook. "Those who are weaker, for their part, in the same spirit of *solidarity*, should not adopt a purely *passive* attitude or one that is *destructive* of the social fabric, but, while claiming their legitimate rights, should do what they can for the good of all." (*OSC*, 75)

Obviously this has direct relevance for Americans. We have major problems domestically with a large under-class as well as with many among the temporarily poor. The widespread presence of the homeless in major U. S. cities is a serious symptom of those deeper problems. Abroad, the number of the poor is staggering. And to ignore them, John Paul II rightly says, "would mean becoming like the rich man who pretended not to know the beggar Lazarus lying at his gate." (*OSC*, 85)

This is not the time or place for an elaboration of my ideas of how we might address underdevelopment both at home and abroad. I have written at some length about this. ("The Preferential Option for the Poor and Public Policy" in *The Preferential Option for the Poor*, ed. Richard Neuhaus, and *The Ethic of Democratic Capitalism*, p. 181 ff). I wish only to offer several reflections in response to the Pope's challenge.

First, it is one of the essential duties of the Church to point out and lift up the plight of the poor. It can do this best when it is actually *involved* with the poor, both at home and abroad. Without such involvements, its words are hollow. Thus, the Church must aim at being truly catholic in the sense that it embraces within its community all sorts and conditions of people.

Second, the Church must communicate the values of human service to its people. As the Pope puts it, the Church, and others in responsible positions, must address "the urgent need to *change* the *spiritual attitudes* which define each individual's relation with self, with neighbor, with even the remotest human communities and with nature itself." (*OSC*, 73) This is done by teaching and practice.

Third, the Church must be open to and yet critical of the variety of options proposed by persons of goodwill with regard to the *means* of attacking the problem of underdevelopment. I have found such critical openness lacking in the Church. It generally does not listen carefully to the full spectrum of its own laity who are involved in the practical aspects of economic and political decision-making. It tips consistently toward those on the liberal or radical side of the ledger, who generally view the poor as helpless victims of active oppression. Thus, it turns away from analyses and prescriptions that insist, through the use of economic incentives and disincentives, on the social obligations of the poor. It then is left with a sentimental interpretation of the poor and their plight.

The root of this sentimentality lies in a faulty, gnostic notion of agape love. In this notion, agape love is always and only outgoing, sacrificial love and, as such, it demands nothing in return. It becomes blind to the legitimate self-interest in both its own and its recipients' agency. In this view, relations, even on an economic level, ought to be characterized by free, self-giving love.

Such a misunderstanding fails to perceive that true love for the other aims at contributing to the strength of being of the other so that he/she might strongly and independently join in mutual relations, not be kept in a dependent status. Gnostic love shuns notions of self-interest, profit, competition, incentives and disincentives because it demands "pure" motives. As such it is unworldly and not very helpful to the task of policy making. This gnostic quality partly explains why Christian religious intellectuals have so much trouble with capitalism and Jewish ones do not. For too many Christian leaders, the process of becoming prosperous is suspect in itself.

This attitude gives an aura of soft-utopianism to the Churches' vision of development. The Church supports only cooperatives, never agencies for training individual entrepreneurs, for example. They cannot bring themselves often to discipline the participants in development efforts. They are embarrassed if their organizations make a profit.

The Pope has some traces of soft utopianism in his thought. He hopes for a "civilization of love." (*OSC*, 64) Profit seems always to be "selfish." (61) He thinks world peace is inconceivable without nations abandoning the politics of blocs and the "sacrifice of *all* forms of economic, military or political imperialism." (77) He quotes favorably Pope Paul's dictum that "development is the new name for peace." (77) This is not exactly in the tradition of St. Augustine.

But the Pope is basically right in his challenge to us. The West does have tendencies to abandon itself to "growing and selfish isolation." (*OSC*, 39) Development at home and abroad will take far more passionate commitment and far more money than we have thus far devoted to the struggle. We need to be reminded again and again.

The Moral Dimension of Economic Interdependence

One of the breath-taking transitions we have experienced in the past few decades is the movement from national economies to an integrated world economy. This transition has been interpreted in two starkly opposed ways. The mainline business and economics view has tended to see this sharp increase in economic interdependence as being to everyone's advantage. Trading in open world markets will make everyone better off and, to some extent, this view is correct. For example, the countries of the Pacific Rim, very poor not too long ago, have benefited greatly from trading their manufactured goods on the world market. This has corroborated the conventional economic wisdom that all participants will find themselves better off in this newly interdependent world. If they would not, why would they want to trade? In this perspective, multinational enterprises are important in transferring capital, skills and technology to lesser developed lands.

The opposing interpretation has been anchored among those who take liberation theology seriously, among Marxists and among liberal Christians in general, specifically among the ecumenical agencies supported by them. This perspective turns on its head the premise held by the first school. Interdependence has meant the exploitation of the poor and the weak. The theory of dependent capitalism asserts that the wealth of the North is sustained by the same process of exchange that pauperizes the South. Multinationals are the vehicles of expropriation. Some in this camp, Ulrich Duchrow, for example, are even arguing that being employed by a multinational is incompatible with being a Christian. It is a matter of "status confessions." (Duchrow, *The Global Economy*)

Pope John Paul II offers a position that challenges the complacency of the former model and the exaggeration of the latter. He raises the question of distributive justice to challenge the pervasive utilitarianism of the former while he insists on heightened responsibility on the part of the "dependent" countries with a regard to the latter. He insists that both have a moral and practical duty to make economic interdependence fairer for all, but particularly for the weak.

To the strong he says:

When this interdependence (among the First, Second, Third and Fourth Worlds) is separated from its ethical requirements, it has *disastrous consequences* for the weakest. Indeed, as a result of a sort of internal dynamism and under the impulse of mechanisms which can only be called perverse, this *interdependence* triggers *negative effects* even in the rich countries. It is precisely within these countries that one encounters, though on a lesser scale, the more *specific manifestations* of under-development. Thus, it should be obvious that development either becomes shared in common by every part of the world or it undergoes a *process of regression* even in zones marked by constant progress. (*OSC*, 27–28)

Perhaps the "perverse mechanism" the Pope is talking about is the process of "creative destruction" that accompanies the increasing economic interdependence of the world. Enterprises are forced to innovate or die in the increasingly competitive world market. In the long run and in general, creative destruction is beneficial but, in the short run for some parties, it certainly is not. It is most often the weakest members of the community of nations or of a specific country who bear the brunt of creative destruction. The strongest often can bend the process to their advantage, as the large banks seem to have done in the debt crisis.

Therefore, the Pope argues, we are called to cushion the effects of this process on the weaker participants, even if it means some sacrifice of economic efficiency for the stronger. That might mean we insist the banks absorb more of the losses connected with bad loans to the South, rather than make the poor suffer abroad or tax the U. S. middle-class at home.

On the other hand, John Paul II advises the poorer countries to allow for economic initiatives, to respect the negative rights of persons, to adopt democratic processes, to take major responsibility for their own political and economic fate, to wean themselves from inordinate concern for military strength, to respect their own cultural integrity and to cooperate with each other.

Interdependence *will* be helpful to all people in the long run but, in the meanwhile, many of the weak will suffer and die. Both wealthy and poor countries must work together to reach a fairer quality of economic interdependence in the shorter run.

Conclusion

Pope John Paul II's encyclicals, especially *On Social Concern*, reveal an openness to historical reality. It is fair to say that, in the past, Catholic papal social thought has not been friendly to the Western liberal traditions of democracy, market economics and social pluralism. In fact, it would be fair to say also that the Catholic religious and ethical tradition has played a part in the underdevelopment of "Catholic" countries.

But slowly and surely, Catholic social thought is coming to terms with the positive contributions of liberal politics, economics and society. The "Protestant principle" is being taken seriously. The present is being appropriated with honesty and integrity; one would wish a bit more of these virtues with regard to the past. Be that as it may, it is clear that the Pope, as well as the U. S. bishops, have developed an "economic counterculture" that has helpful points of contact with contemporary Western political and economic practice. There are enough affirmations and continuities to carry on a helpful dialogue.

This contrasts sharply with the real economic countercultures constructed by much of the social ethics of the World and National Council of Churches. In many of their social statements there simply is not enough common ground for serious conversation. There are only "prophetic" denunciations spoken from high moral ground.

On Social Concern is refreshingly different. The fact that it both affirms and criticizes a variety of contending perspectives suggests that it emerges from an independent, genuinely religious tradition. It sounds notes that the modern world needs to hear. *On Social Concern* brings the insights of "Catholic substance" to bear on the failures and perversities of our fallen world.

Bibliography

Arendt, Hannah. *On Revolution*, New York: Viking, 1963.

Baum, Gregory. *The Priority of Labor*, New York: Paulist Press, 1982.

Becker, Gary. *The Economic Approach to Human Behavior*, Chicago: University of Chicago Press, 1976.

Benne, Robert. *The Ethic of Democratic Capitalism—A Moral Reassessment*, Philadelphia: Fortress Press, 1981.

Berger, Peter. *The Capitalist Revolution*, New York: Basic Books, 1986.

Berger, Peter and Hsiao, Michael, ed. *In Search of An East Asian Development Model*, New Brunswick: Transaction Books, 1988.

Canadian Bishops. *On Unemployment*, 1980.

Cooper, John. "'Pope's Economics Lean Toward Reformed Capitalism,'" Ethics and Public Policy Center, 1988.

Duchrow, Ulrich. *Global Economy*, Geneva: World Council of Churches, 1987.

Etzioni, Amitai. *The Moral Dimension—Toward a New Economics*, New York: The Free Press, 1988.

Heilbroner, Robert. "Reflections—The Triumph of Capitalism," *The New Yorker*, January 23, 1989.

Hollenbach, David. "Liberalism, Communitarianism and the Bishops' Pastoral Letter on the Economy" in *The Annual of the Society of Christian Ethics*, Georgetown University Press, 1987.

John Paul II, *On Human Work*, Washington, D.C.: United States Catholic Conference, 1981.

John Paul II, *On Social Concern*, Washington, D.C.: United States Catholic Conference, 1987.

Novak, Michael. *Free Persons and the Common Good*, Lanham, MD: Madison Books, 1989.

Novak, Michael. *The Spirit of Democratic Capitalism*, New York: Simon and Schuster, 1982.

Neuhaus, Richard, ed. *The Preferential Option for the Poor*, Grand Rapids, MI: Eerdmans, 1988.

Posner, Richard. *The Economic Analysis of Law*, New York: Little and Company, 1973.

Schumpeter, Joseph. *Capitalism, Socialism and Democracy*, New York: Harper and Row (Colophon), 1975.

Seven

The Unconstrained Vision of John Paul II or How to Resist the Temptation of an Economic Counterculture

Dennis P. McCann

The focus of this essay is on the theological assumptions governing John Paul II's understanding of human rights, specifically economic rights, within the tradition of Catholic social teaching. I hope to show that the Pope's view of economic rights is grounded in the theology of Creation which, as many have pointed out, is a characteristic theme of his social encyclicals. That a Papal theory of economic rights should rest upon explicitly theological grounds is hardly a surprise; what is surprising, to me at least, is how certain problems in the Pope's view of economic rights cast suspicion upon the adequacy of this theology. I will argue that the abstract character of John Paul II's claims for economic rights, that is, the difficulties of implementing them in a manner consistent with the limits of human nature and the constraints of current and foreseeable modes of economic and social organization, tends to undermine their credibility. In short, my diagnosis is that John Paul II's Creationist theology succumbs to the temptation of an "Unconstrained Vision" of human possibility, and that Catholic social teaching will not advance the cause of economic rights unless it learns how to resist that temptation.

The appropriate response to this diagnosis, however, is not to abandon either the tradition's commitment to economic rights or the Pope's own emphasis upon the Biblical myths of Creation. Instead, I hope to reinforce both by posing a theological question, namely, whether what economists call "scarcity" must be conceived as part of

139

the Divinely instituted order of Creation or as a consequence of the Fall, the pervasive disorder experienced in faith as a result of Original Sin? I believe this is an important question because what economists analyze under the rubric of "scarcity," theologians traditionally have understood as finitude. Theologically, the question posed to John Paul II is: Where in the Biblical cosmogony does he locate finitude, that is, the common human experience of the constraints of both nature and culture, within which each of us must come to terms with our aspirations toward freedom and transcendence? Having examined the social encyclicals in which the Pope develops his theology of Creation, I am unable to discern an unequivocal answer, especially as it relates to matters of economic and social development.

Whatever the Pope's own inclinations, I will propose that the basic fact of scarcity ought to be interpreted, first, within the Divinely created order of things. Consistent with the insights of Reinhold Niebuhr's Christian realism, I will insist upon a distinction between finitude and sin, and then show how such a distinction, when applied to the problem of scarcity, provides the basis for a sounder understanding of the context in which economic rights may be implemented than the one offered so far by John Paul II.

Before beginning this cross-examination of the Pope's social encyclical, let me explain two things, one theoretical, the other practical. The one has to do with the title of this paper, "The Unconstrained Vision of John Paul II"; the other, with why I think it is wrong to consider Catholic social teaching as a basis for a possible "economic counterculture." The title is inspired by Thomas Sowell's analysis of the unconstrained vision in his recent book, *A Conflict of Visions: Ideological Origins of Political Struggles* (1987). Sowell develops contrasting models of "constrained and unconstrained visions," by which various participants process the complexities of political choice. The contrast between the two is roughly parallel to what Niebuhr argued was the difference between realism and utopianism in politics. Though Sowell shared Niebuhr's basic distrust of the utopian or unconstrained vision, his analysis goes beyond Niebuhr's in developing more systematically both the epistemological assumptions and the typical understandings of social processes in each of the two models. Furthermore, Sowell's models, unlike Niebuhr's, are not developed theologically, which may be an advantage in applying them to articulated theological perspectives such as the one operative in the Pope's encyclicals.

At any rate, Sowell's exercise in model theory encouraged me to think that the issues raised in these encyclicals could be conceptualized along such lines. Despite the realistic intentions generally informing the tradition of Catholic social teaching, my own thought experiments led me to confirm the presence of the unconstrained vision in the thought of John Paul II because, on a variety of questions, the Pope's opinions seemed to conform to the expectations built into that model. Two tendencies in particular struck me as worth pursuing, namely, the Pope's apparent refusal to recognize any trade-offs among the various economic rights that he is advocating, and his penchant for moralizing on the question of their implementation and the possible explanations for our obvious lack of sufficient progress in that direction. I would have found these tendencies disturbing in any case, but Sowell's exercise in model theory provided me with a way of understanding them.

The other preliminary point concerns the appropriateness of considering Catholic social teaching as the basis for an economic counterculture. I wish to oppose this, not only for the sake of Catholic social teaching, but also out of respect and admiration for genuine countercultures. To be an authentically economic counterculture is no simple task, as far as I am concerned. Merely wishing it will not make it so. To qualify as such, a community (not an individual) would have to withdraw from participation in the dominant economic system, and try to organize its common life on a systematically different set of economic principles. The only examples I would consider would be, perhaps, the Cistercian reform movement within Benedictine monasticism during the High Middle Ages, or the utopian communities that dotted Midwestern frontier America before the advent of the railroads, or perhaps the *kibbutzim* in the early stages of the formation of the contemporary state of Israel. What these have in common, possibly along with some of the communes of the 1960s, are forms of internal organization for both the production and distribution of goods, radically and intentionally at odds with the dominant society. Such authentic countercultures do not merely live by certain values selectively in tension with the values of the dominant culture, nor does their activity aspire to reform or transform the dominant culture. They have separated themselves from it to practice a different way of life.

I hope it is clear from the way that I have described them that I hold genuine countercultures in high esteem. It is precisely because I respect their integrity that I resist the confusion likely to arise from identifying

Catholic social teaching with them. This tradition from its beginning in Leo XIII's encyclical, *Rerum Novarum* (1891), has been selectively critical of the dominant society, and reformist in its intentions toward it. It has never advocated anything as non-Catholic as withdrawal from the dominant society, possibly because it cannot ignore the extent of Catholicism's own historic contribution to establishing and maintaining the social *status quo* even in the modern period of Western civilization. The tradition's posture has been one of engaged criticism, a posture toward the dominant culture that recognizes a certain consensus regarding shared values even as it challenges others, or one that within a deep and broad theoretical consensus challenges the dominant culture for its failures to live up to those shared commitments. Needless to say, I also deeply respect this posture, for it is the tradition in which I was formed.

Catholic social teaching, finally, can only be mistaken as countercultural, in the sense previously indicated, when its teachers abandon this tradition's basic realism in favor of some utopian vision. I have reluctantly concluded that, whatever its intent, the effect of John Paul II's social encyclicals is to further this utopian tendency, ironically so non-Catholic and nontraditional. However emotionally satisfying for some may be his moralizing denunciations of the economic constraints dominating the world economy today, I believe they only serve to sow a confusion in which Catholic social teaching will succeed in becoming neither effectively reformist nor authentically countercultural. The danger is that in trying somehow to be both, it will end up condemning itself to irrelevancy. Thus, the polemical stance to the analysis that follows is meant to assist Catholic social teaching to become what at its best it already is, an authentically reformist position. The distinctive integrity of a reformist position will not be enhanced by pretending to be countercultural.

*

It may seem inopportune to criticize John Paul II's doctrine of economic rights for his latest encyclical, *On Social Concern: Sollicitudo Rei Socialis* (1987), seems to make a "right of economic initiative" the keystone for his perspective as a whole. This right, which in at least one instance the Pope places on the same "fundamental" level with "the right to religious freedom" (Par. 42), specifically is asserted to protest the dehumanizing effects of statist economies such as those he has experienced in Poland and in the Soviet bloc. American Catholics committed to the principle of free enterprise can only be heartened by the Pope's recognition ''that the denial of this right or its limitation in the name of an alleged 'equality' of everyone in society, diminishes, or in practice absolutely destroys the spirit of initiative, that is to say *the creative subjectivity of the citizen''* (Par. 15). In defending the right to economic initiative, he specifically notes the destructive spiritual consequences of bureaucratic domination of the economy.

What makes this teaching so welcome is that it represents an advance beyond the doctrine of economic rights outlined in *On Human Work: Laborem Exercens* (1981). In that encyclical commemorating the ninetieth anniversary of Pope Leo XIII's *Rerum Novarum*, John Paul II elaborated systematically on a set of rights specifically entailed by his understanding of work in the context of his theology of Creation, and humanity's role within it. The rights specified follow roughly the same pattern as that set out in Pope John XXIII's *Pacem in Terris* (1963). *Laborem Exercens* thus affirms a right to employment, a right to a ''just wage,'' a single salary sufficient for maintaining a family, a right to adequate health care, a ''right to rest,'' not just at regular intervals every Sunday but also an annual vacation, a right to a pension and to ''insurance for old age in case of accidents at work'' (Pars. 18–19). Finally, the Pope also reasserts laborers' ''right of association'' and the right to strike (Par. 20). In the absence of clear teaching regarding a ''right of economic initiative,'' however, the rights defended in this earlier encyclical might lead to the inference, as it did for Gregory Baum, that John Paul II is advocating socialism: ''In the Western capitalist countries,'' Baum concluded, ''. . . Catholics are asked to support the movements that change the existing order for the better—in other words, that move in the double direction of democracy in the industries and central planning of employment and production'' (Baum, 1982: 85). Thanks to *Sollicitudo Rei Socialis*, and its insistence upon the fundamental character of the right of economic initiative, the inference of papal support for socialism is now a lot harder to sustain.

However comforting or disconcerting we may find this outcome, it is not crucial to the analysis that I wish to pursue. My focus is not governed by the interminable and largely sterile debate over the relative merits of capitalism and socialism, for I believe that the disclaimer attached to *Sollicitudo Rei Socialis* renouncing any attempt to read Catholic social teaching as a " 'third way' between *liberal capitalism* and *Marxist collectivism*, nor even [as] a possible alternative to other solutions less radically opposed to one another" (Par. 41) must be taken seriously. As the Pope says, the "main aim . . . [of Catholic social teaching] . . . is to *interpret* these realities, determining their conformity with or divergence from the lines of the Gospel teaching on man and his vocation. . . . It therefore belongs to the field . . . of *moral theology*" (Par. 41). Following up on the leads the Pope has provided, I thus wish to focus on the adequacy of the Pope's moral theology, for I have doubts about the validity of his interpretation of these realities. His perspective must be criticized, not because we may fear that it favors either socialism or capitalism, but because what he says and does not say about the contexts in which economic rights are to be implemented is so dubious that it ought to lead us to question the Creationist theology that underlies his reading of them.

This line of inquiry cannot be avoided by emphasizing certain characteristics of the drafting process for *Sollicitudo Rei Socialis*, as Richard John Neuhaus appears to do (Myers, ed., 1988: 134). For even if it is true that the latest encyclical, in contrast to *Laborem Exercens*, reads like the work of a committee rather than the considered thought of a single author, I find the continuities between the latest encyclical and John Paul II's previous efforts, including his inaugural letter, *The Redeemer of Man: Redemptor Hominis* (1979), to be very striking, especially at the points upon which I must focus. The interpretation of the economic and social realities, in which the economic rights advocated by Catholic social teaching are to be implemented, has not differed substantially from the beginning of this Pontificate, nor has the basic thrust of the Pope's view of Creation as the theological basis for understanding the dignity of the human person. If the latest encyclical's reading of the situation is troubling, I doubt it can be written off as representing merely the opinions of certain constituencies within the Vatican bureaucracy.

The interpretation of the current status of economic and social development offered in *Sollicitudo Rei Socialis* is a somber one. The fact that this encyclical, in turn, is commemorative of the twentieth anniversary of Pope Paul VI's *On the Development of Peoples: Populorum Progressio* (1967), helps to explain this tone. For *Populorum Progressio* is remembered not just as a ground-breaking attempt to expand the scope of Catholic social teaching, but also as representative of the excessive optimism, perhaps even euphoria, characteristic of Roman Catholicism in the immediate aftermath of Vatican Council II (1962–1965). In commemorating the work of his predecessor, John Paul II, therefore, appears to be striving for a certain balance by emphasizing a pessimistic picture of disappointed hopes. This may help account for distorted generalizations such as the statement that ''in the years since the publication of Pope Paul's Encyclical there has been no development—or very little, irregular, or even contradictory development'' (Par. 35).

Unfortunately, there are other tendencies in the current Pope's reading of the situation that cannot be explained simply as a corrective to the excesses of the 1960s. The problem is that in virtually all the concrete problems the Pope cites as indications of failure, namely, the alleged ''widening of the gap between the areas of the so-called developed North and the developing South'' (Par. 14), including, besides a poverty gap, a gap in the recognition and implementation of human rights (Par. 15), as well as specific indicators such as the housing crisis (Par. 17), the chronically high levels of unemployment and underemployment (Par. 18), and the international debt crisis (Par. 19)—in virtually all of these—the Pope tends to overestimate the moral or political nature of the problem and to discount radically the economic constraints upon any significant progress toward a solution, constraints which are usually denounced as inhibiting and occasionally sinful ''mechanisms.''

This tendency, of course, is what leads him to assert that the Cold War, which has dominated relations between the U.S. and the U.S.S.R. for most of the past forty-five years, is ''an important cause of the retardation of stagnation of the South,'' that among other things ''deadens the impulse towards united cooperation by all for the common good of the human race, to the detriment especially of peaceful peoples who are impeded from their rightful access to the goods meant for all'' (Par. 22). This and similar statements have triggered criticism of *Sollicitudo Rei Socialis* for asserting a moral equivalence between the U.S. and the U.S.S.R. My point here, however, is not simply to join in such criticism but to try to explain how the Pope could have made such an error. For I believe that his opinion here is an exigency of his perspective as a whole, and is not readily subject to modification on an empirical basis.

In the mind of John Paul II, Catholic social teaching may not be " 'a third way' between *liberal capitalism* and *Marxist collectivism*," but its power to influence public opinion in the direction of "authentic development" depends upon its remaining evenhandedly critical of both. I am tempted to add that the role the Vatican would assign to itself in the formation of a new international order also depends upon maintaining Catholic social teaching in this posture, regardless of whatever evidence might be gathered for a more benign view of the activities of either the U.S. or the U.S.S.R., or both. Furthermore, I cannot repress the suspicion that the Pope's view is colored more than a little by the impossibly Messianic aspirations of Polish nationalism, a lost cause, like that of the Irish, that more often than not gets sublimated into the higher passions of ecclesiastical politics. Be that as it may, even if the Pope could be induced to modify his view of the Superpower stalemate, such a change in moral or political perspective would not necessarily involve a different attitude toward the economic "mechanisms" inhibiting our efforts to seek authentic development, for his memorable and innovative denunciation of the error of "economism" in *Laborem Exercens* (Par. 13) may yet block the path toward any serious revision of his overall perspective.

The issue, in short, is not an empirical but a methodological one, involving the relationship between morality and the logic of modern economics in the current Pope's understanding of Catholic social teaching. In his interpretation of the world's failure to move more conspicuously in the direction of "authentic development" as I have been arguing, John Paul II consistently underestimates the constraints upon progress, especially economic constraints, and consistently overestimates the efficacy of moralistic explanations of our current predicament and exhortations to change it. In these passages typical of *Sollicitudo Rei Socialis*, economic constraints are discounted as "mechanisms," at once both open to manipulation by the rich and powerful and yet seemingly operative in a deterministic manner:

> Moreover, one must denounce the existence of economic, financial and social *mechanisms* which, although they are manipulated by people, often function almost automatically, thus accentuating the situation of wealth for some and poverty for the rest. These mechanisms, which are manoeuvred directly or indirectly by the more developed countries, by

their very function favor the interests of the people manipulating them. But in the end they suffocate or condition the economies of the less developed countries. Later on these mechanisms will have to be subjected to a careful analysis under the ethical-moral aspect. (Par. 16)

Such generalities may not, of themselves, suggest what difference this notion of economic "mechanisms" makes in his analysis of specific problems of development. Here is one indication, taken from the Pope's comments on the international debt crisis:

Circumstances having changed, both within the debtor nations and in the international financial market, the instrument chosen to make a contribution to development has turned into a *counter-productive mechanism*. This is because the debtor nations, in order to service their debt, find themselves obliged to export the capital needed for improving or at least maintaining their standard of living. It is also because, for the same reason, they are unable to obtain new and equally essential financing.

Through this mechanism, the means intended for the development of peoples has turned into a *brake* upon development instead, and indeed in some cases has even *aggravated underdevelopment* (Par. 19).

When later on *Sollicitudo Rei Socialis* does offer a moral evaluation of these "mechanisms," they are equated with "structures of sin":

It is important to note therefore that a world which is divided into blocs, sustained by rigid ideologies, and in which instead of interdependence and solidarity different forms of imperialism hold sway, can only be a world subject to structures of sin. The sum total of the negative factors working against a true awareness of the universal *common good*, and the need to further it, gives the impression of creating in persons and institutions, an obstacle which is difficult to overcome (Par. 36).

This *general analysis*, which is religious in nature, can be supplemented by *a number of particular considerations* to demonstrate that among the actions and attitudes opposed to the will of God, the good of neighbor and the "structures" created by them, two are very typical: on the one hand, the *all-consuming desire for profit*, and on the other, *the thirst for power*, with the intention of imposing one's will upon others. In order to characterize better each of these attitudes, one can add the expression: "at any price." In other words, we are faced with the *abso-lutizing* of human attitudes with all its possible consequences. . . . Obviously, not only individuals fall victim to this double attitude of sin; nations and blocs can do so too. And this favors even more the introduction of the "structures of sin" of which I have spoken. If certain forms of modern "imperialism" were considered in the light of these moral criteria, we would see that hidden behind certain decisions, apparently inspired only by economics or politics, are real forms of idolatry: of money, ideology, class, technology (Par. 37).

Granted, in these passages the Pope does not explicitly refer to economic "mechanisms" as such, but three paragraphs later in exhorting us to the virtue of "solidarity" he does equate "evil mechanisms" with "structures of sin" (Par. 40). Furthermore, at no point in the encyclical does he describe any economic "mechanisms" that are not evil in their consequences. His analysis, for example, tellingly lacks any mention of "structures of grace" outside the institutional confines of the Church itself.

When one turns from this pattern of denunciation to the more systematic analysis of the error of "economism" in *Laborem Exercens* (Par. 13), one can begin to see how this tendency to equate economic constraints with "structures of sin" may have occurred. What the Pope denounces as "economism" is "the threat to the right order of values" implicit in the way economists typically define labor for analytic purposes as a factor of production. Marxists, of course, led the way in denouncing the existential consequences of this perspective, with their accusation that capitalism, both in theory and in practice, must regard labor as indistinguishable from any other commodity available in the marketplace. John Paul II, however, goes on to explain this allegedly capitalist distortion as a consequence of "the fundamental . . . error of materialism": ". . . [E]conomism directly or indirectly includes a conviction of the primacy and superiority of the material, and directly or indirectly places the spiritual and the personal (man's activity, moral values and such matters) in a position of subordination to material reality." In the Pope's own view, this error forms the theoretical core of resistance to his own Creationist interpretation of the priority of labor over capital, the priority of persons over things, and thus the theological underpinnings of his notion of economic rights.

My purpose in questioning the Pope's diagnosis of the error of economism is not to deny that the dehumanization of labor is a serious problem for any modern industrial society. It is, however, to determine whether the Papal teaching itself is not involved in systematic distortion, to the extent that its polemic against "economism" lacks the qualifications that might prevent it from becoming an attack upon economics as such. It is as if in repudiating the errors of those who allegedly would subordinate the dignity of a person to the forces of impersonal necessity, the Pope has fallen into the opposite error of assuming that the constraints imposed by both nature and history can simply be set aside in a pure act of moral aspiration. John Paul II's unqualified or, if you will, undialectical denial of materialism yields a metaphysical basis for Catholic social teaching that is as misleading as it is idealistically utopian. The priority of labor over capital that he understandably advocates thus rings rather hollow, for it is compromised by a misunderstanding of the nature of human work that is ultimately theological in character.

The theological problem will emerge from the Pope's unprecedented emphasis upon the Creator's first command to our first parents, as given in the first chapter of Genesis: "Be fruitful and multiply, and fill the earth and subdue it" (Genesis 1:28). But before we ponder the difficulties presented by the Biblical text, it is useful to review *Laborem Exercens'* systematic description of human work in both its objective and its subjective senses. For it is precisely in struggling with the meaning of human work that the significance of the contrast between his own position and that of "materialistic economism" becomes apparent. In the Pope's view, the process of industrialization, understood in the broadest possible sense as coextensive with the history of civilization, defines the meaning of work in the objective sense, The systematic application of technology to the problem of production provides the *means* by which the Creator's first commandment is fulfilled. The meaning of work in the subjective sense, however, is the realization of the *end* for which humanity is working:

> Man has to subdue the earth and dominate it, because as the "image of God" he is a person, that is to say, a subjective being capable of acting in a planned and rational way, capable of deciding about himself and with a tendency to self-realization. As a person, man is therefore the subject of work. As a person works, he performs various actions belong-

ing to the work process; independently of their objective content, these actions must all serve to realize his humanity, to fulfill the calling to be a person that is his by reason of his very humanity (Par. 6).

Just as any *means* must ethically be subordinated to *ends*, so the objective meaning of work must be subordinated to the subjective. Inasmuch as capital may be defined as "the whole collection of the means of production," the priority of labor over capital, in the Pope's view, is directly entailed by the proper ordering of the objective and subjective meanings of human work. A materialist, by contrast, is one who reverses this priority, by collapsing the distinction between the objective and the subjective to the point where the subjective meaning of work becomes epiphenomenal, if not superfluous (Par. 13).

However ingenious this set of logical priorities, I find myself doubting their descriptive adequacy. It is curious, for example, that although John Paul II clearly intends to make a distinction between the objective and subjective dimensions of work, in discussing technology within the objective dimension he slips all too quickly into an analysis of its subjective meanings:

> Understood in this case not as a capacity or aptitude for work, but rather as a whole set of instruments which man uses in his work, technology is undoubtedly man's ally. . . . However, it is also a fact that in some instances technology can cease to be man's ally and become almost his enemy, as when the mechanization of work "supplants" him, taking away all personal satisfaction and the incentive to creativity and responsibility, when it deprives many workers of their previous employment or when, through exalting the machine, it reduces man to the status of its slave (Par. 5).

Instead of enlightening us about the objective relationship between technology and the constraints imposed by both nature and culture, here the Pope moves directly to defining technology as an "ally" or "enemy," based exclusively on its relationship to the subjective meaning of work. As a result, far from having reasserted a properly balanced ordering of the objective and subjective dimensions, the Pope seems merely to have reversed the materialistic error by substituting an empty "moralism" in place of an equally futile "economism."

My argument so far should suggest that there is a consistent pattern here. If my diagnosis of the weakness in John Paul II's perspective on Catholic social teaching is correct, then there exists a methodological problem of relating ethics and economics or, more precisely, our moral aspirations and the constraints explored by economics. This problem, as I must still show, is theologically grounded, but it appears most plainly in the Pope's failure to achieve an adequate understanding of the interrelationship between the objective and subjective dimensions of human work. This methodological problem, I believe, explains the distortion detected in his inability to discern the constraints upon economic and social development imposed by both nature and culture as anything other than "evil mechanisms," subject to moral denunciation and, presumably, new forms of papally inspired political mobilization. Unfortunately, this same problem undermines the Pope's welcome attempt to assert and defend a global agenda for economic rights because this tendency to condemn the obstacles to economic and social development, rather than understand them, robs his teachings of their credibility. What is needed, according to this diagnosis, is a way of discerning the difference between those obstacles to development that are amenable to moral suasion and those that are not. I am convinced that the Pope will remain unable to accept such a distinction unless there are further advances in his theology of Creation. How, then, does John Paul II's interpretation of the myth of Creation orient his thinking about economic and social development? How ought it do so?

A good place to begin is with the Pope's reading of the Creator's command to our first parents: "Be fruitful and multiply, and fill the earth and subdue it" (Genesis 1:28). As indicated in *Laborem Exercens*, he believes that the mythical narrative surrounding this command expresses in an archaic way "the fundamental truths about man. . . . These truths are decisive for man from the very beginning, and at the same time, they trace out the main lines of his earthly existence, both in the state of original justice and also after the breaking, caused by sin, of the creator's original covenant with creation in man" (Par. 4). Specifically, the command to "fill the earth and subdue it" seems to provide the point of departure for John Paul II's view of economics:

The expression "subdue the earth" has an immense range. It means all the resources that the earth (and indirectly the visible world) contains and which, through the conscious activity of man, can be discovered and used for his ends. And so these words, placed at the beginning of the Bible, never cease to be relevant. They embrace equally the past ages of civilization and economy, as also the whole of modern reality and future phases of development. . . . As man, through his work becomes more and more the master of the earth, and as he confirms his dominion over the visible world, again through his work, he nevertheless remains in every case and at every phase of this process within the creator's original ordering (Par. 4).

Clearly the Pope means to use the Creator's original command to place the whole of economic and social development within the sphere of theological concern. But he does not explain precisely how "the creator's original ordering" should actually shape our understanding of economic realities. As I stated at the beginning of this paper, the theological discussion can be advanced only by asking where the apparently perennial problem of scarcity fits in the original ordering of Creation, for apart from the problem of scarcity, specifically economic realities strike me as inconceivable.

The only significant clue given in *Laborem Exercens* toward an answer to this question points us in the direction of John Paul II's inaugural encyclical, *Redemptor Hominis*. This clue comes in a meditation on the "toil" inevitably involved in our experience of human work. Toil is explained as a consequence of the Fall, as confirming evidence of the impact of the original sin of our first parents. The "original blessing of work" has been transformed through the "curse" of the Fall into "an announcement of death." Nevertheless, such is not the final word in this meditation, for the Pope insists that the experience of toil provides us with an opportunity to unite ourselves with "the paschal mystery of Jesus Christ":

By enduring the toil of work in union with Christ crucified for us, man in a way collaborates with the son of God for the redemption of humanity. He shows himself a true disciple of Christ by carrying the cross in his turn everyday in the activity that he is called upon to perform. (Par. 27).

The clue, in short, serves to remind us that John Paul II's Creationist theology is always a theology of Redemption. Nothing, the Pope seems to insist, can be known about the existential meaning of Creation without taking into account both the event of the Fall and the ongoing process of Redemption by which the Fall is overcome.

When one turns to *Redemptor Hominis* for further illumination, it becomes clear that John Paul II is interpreting the Genesis myths of Creation, not on their own terms but, ultimately, in terms of the perspective opened up by the Apostle Paul's Letter to the Romans. Not only is Redemption conceived of as a "New Creation," but our experience of the economic and social environment in which we must work is identified with Paul's description of the "travail" of Creation (Romans 8:18-25):

> Are we of the twentieth century not convinced of the overpoweringly eloquent words of the Apostle of the Gentiles concerning the "creation (that) has been groaning in travail together until now" and "waits with eager longing for the revelation of the sons of God," the creation that "was subjected to futility"? Does not the previously unknown immense progress—which has taken place especially in the course of this century--in the field of man's dominion over the world itself reveal—to a previously unknown degree—that manifold subjection to "futility"? It is enough to recall certain phenomena, such as the threat of pollution of the natural environment in areas of rapid industrialization, or the armed conflicts continually breaking out over and over again, or the prospectives of self-destruction through the use of atomic, hydrogen, neutron, and similar weapons, or the lack of respect for the life of the unborn. The world of the new age, the world of space flights, the world of the previously unattained conquests of science and technology—is it not also the world "groaning in travail" that "waits with eager longing for the revealing of the sons of God"? (Par. 8)

The "futility" to which earth is subject, of course, suggests that the Fall of our first parents has had catastrophic consequences for the whole of Creation, and will continue to threaten every achievement in the direction of economic and social development until Jesus Christ perfects the work of Redemption on us.

In light of this Pauline perspective, we can search once again for the meaning of scarcity: Is scarcity itself a sign of Creation's being subject to the disordering "futility" that results from Fall, or is it an inevitable sign of the ordering of Creation, within which the Creator's will that we should "fill the earth and subdue it" is originally revealed and faithfully accepted? Strangely, there is still no unequivocal answer to this question. Even though John Paul II throughout these encyclicals looks to the myths of Genesis to form the basis for a systematically theological anthropology and despite the fact that these myths are regarded as containing truth about the human condition both before the Fall and after, he does not consider whether this distinction might have any bearing on the problem of scarcity. Is scarcity, that is, "the basic fact of life that there exists only in finite amount of human and nonhuman resources, which the best technical knowledge is capable of using to produce only *limited* maximum amounts of each economic good" (Samuelson, 1980: 20), in theological terms, a blessing or a curse? Is it part of the original ordering of Creation or a result of the Fall? The master metaphor of "travail," which understandably captures the Pope's imagination in the Letter to the Romans, does not help to answer this question, for the situation of "travail" is already the one recognized in our ordinary experience, that is, one in which the original blessings and curses are inextricably mingled. In the absence of any evidence to the contrary, as we have already seen in the social analyses provided in *Sollicitudo Rei Socialis* and as we might confirm in a reading of *Redemptor Hominis* on "What Modern Man is Afraid of" (Par. 15), the clear tendency of the thought of John Paul II is to assume the fact of scarcity under the theological category of "structures of sin" that can be transformed spiritually and politically.

*

Having followed patiently this rather close interrogation of the encyclicals of John Paul II, you may be wondering what difference it might make? So what if the Pope makes a category mistake about the theological meaning of economic scarcity. Were this mistake to be corrected, would it have any impact upon the way in which Catholic social teaching approaches the question of international development? Would it have any bearing on the tradition's understanding of economic rights? Obviously, I think it would, or I would not have focused on this aspect of Catholic social teaching. To see the difference, let us conduct a thought experiment with both alternatives. The first one, namely, that scarcity is a consequence of the Fall, can be dealt with fairly easily, for we will simply construct an abstract model from what apparently is the Pope's own perspective. The second, which affirms scarcity as part of God's original ordering of Creation, will require a little more imagination. Even so, at the end of the experiment, I will argue that only if the second is adopted can Catholic social teaching hope to achieve a concept of "authentic human development" upon which reasonable progress can be made toward implementing economic rights.

If scarcity is a result of the Fall, then underdevelopment is a moral evil, pure and simple. In this model, scarcity is evidence of the pervasive historical impact of "structures of sin," that is, of the formation of evil human institutions ultimately intended to further the revolt of humanity against the sovereignty of God. The lack of symmetry in economic and social development from one region of the globe to another, from one culture to another, and from one socioeconomic class to another, therefore, must be understood as resulting primarily from moral causes. Exegetically, this interpretation of the basic fact of scarcity reaffirms a traditional reading of the myths of Genesis, according to which the cosmos was originally perfect in its Creation, and humanity's own state before the Fall was one of corporeal perfection. This tradition holds that before the Fall, there was no struggle for survival among the various species of plants and animals; there was no death, no disease, and no lack of sufficiency in any spiritual or material goods to trouble the relations of one human being with another. Before the Fall, in short, the cosmos and humanity's role within it unfolded in terms of an unconstrained economy of abundance. The fact that the earth's inhabitants experience themselves as constrained by an economy of scarcity, and not as enjoying the unconstrained opportunities of an economy of abundance, is purely and simply a result of the Fall. It is a catastrophe that we have brought upon ourselves, for which we are exclusively to blame.

If the cause of the scarcity we experience is moral and spiritual, then the resources for overcoming our predicament must also be moral and spiritual. Consistent with the tradition, those resources have already been made available in the Redemption, which it is the Church's mission to disseminate among the inhabitants of the earth. First of all, the ultimate facts regarding the human predicament must be clarified and then, to those who are willing to cease their resistance to God's sovereignty, the offer of participation in the work of Redemption, which is always the work of "authentic human development," must be made.

Though the economy of abundance may not be restored prior to God's final perfection of the work of Redemption, those who cease their resistance must not unwittingly revert to it by allowing their aspirations and achievements to be constrained by the vain—because self-defeating—assumptions of an economy of scarcity. The crisis of "economism" is precisely the crisis of economics as such, to the extent that economics as such is incapable of transcending, even in theory, the constraints of an economy of scarcity. To the extent that we continue to think about "authentic human development" within such constraints, we demonstrate that we are still under the curse of the Fall, and still unable to enter into the work of Redemption.

Thinking about development in terms consistent with this model predictably will yield the following results. The manifest lack of symmetry in the world's economic and social development will be interpreted, first of all, in moral categories. This lack of symmetry will tend to be regarded as a moral evil, a sign of our active resistance to the work of Redemption. Furthermore, within this model, the tendency will be to believe, despite considerable empirical evidence to the contrary, that the "underdevelopment" of the majority of the earth's inhabitants is a direct consequence of the "superdevelopment" of the minority, that is, that the world's poor are poor because the world's rich are rich. Similarly, this model will tend on theological grounds to support the belief that the basic necessities could be provided to all the world's destitute if only the arms race could be stopped. Finally, it will tend to justify advocating a full agenda of economic rights, without taking into account the constraints implicit in the technological and organizational capacities of the nations of the earth, whether considered individually or collectively. The intractable nature of so many of the problems of economic and social development, and the trade-offs implicit in virtually any progress toward a solution to them, cannot be recognized if the assumptions built into an economy of scarcity can be set aside on theological grounds.

What happens, on the other hand, when scarcity is interpreted as part of the original ordering of Creation? Within this second model, scarcity exists prior to the Fall and, like all other such things, is affected by the Fall. But neither it nor underdevelopment as such can be regarded as a moral evil, pure and simple. The problem of scarcity may be exacerbated by the Fall, but it is still part of the original blessing of a sovereign Creator who, in willing to create an order, any order at all, necessarily had to differentiate and set boundaries which entailed fixing limits even to those things humanity would find useful as resources. Such a basic fact of life is, in this model, a blessing rather than a curse for, apart from the order that it represents, the exercise of our capacities for transcendence would be meaningless. Not all gaps in economic and social development can be accepted reverently as indications of this original blessing, but scarcity so interpreted does provide a baseline structure of "common grace" against which to evaluate which of our problems of economic and social development are fairly attributed to "structures of sin" and which are not.

Exegetically, if the basic fact of scarcity were a blessing rather than a curse, then obedience to the Creator's command to our first parents, "Be fruitful and multiply, and fill the earth and subdue it," would seem less arbitrarily self-serving. Scarcity, within this second model, becomes a gift and a task, a structure of opportunity without which there would be no plausible motive for economic and social development in the first place. If the ordering of Creation necessarily were to entail this structure of opportunity, then even before the Fall the cosmos was originally imperfect, not in the sense of being morally flawed in some fundamental way, but in the sense of being radically incomplete. If the Creation were originally imperfect, then some struggle for survival would be expected throughout the entire order of living things. Even death, disease, and the pervasive insufficiency of resources are not necessarily a curse, but the grace-filled opportunity to achieve a degree of moral seriousness in our responses to the Creator's blessing and in our relations with one another. The Fall, then, would be primarily a refusal to develop ourselves in a manner consistent with the limitations inherent in Creation, an anxious rebellion against the original ordering of things within which we are to seek our "authentic human development." The blessing, in short, becomes the occasion of the curse: we bring the curse upon ourselves by refusing the blessing.

This model, of course, does not make the work of Redemption meaningless. On the contrary, the moral and spiritual resources made available through the work of Redemption are still necessary to overcome the consequences of the Fall and to assist in bringing the original ordering of Creation to its ultimate perfection. But the New Creation latent in the work of Redemption need not be conceived as antithetical to the original Creation, as if it were reasonable to hope that the boundaries inherent in the original Creation—including those operative in the problem of scarcity—may all be set aside as the work progresses. Furthermore, the difficulties involved in making progress toward "authentic human development" in and of themselves do not warrant interpreting such difficulties only as "structures of sin." The institutions through which development proceeds are just as likely to be structures of grace as they are structures of sin; indeed, to the extent that they contribute anything at all to the triumph of order over chaos, they must be regarded as contributing to the work of perfecting Creation. The fact that the problem of scarcity persists even through the best of their efforts is no justification for denouncing the constraints imposed upon and by these structures as "evil mechanisms." In such a model, faithful participation in the work of Redemption may require a critique of the error of "economism," but it cannot allow such a critique to become a generalized attack upon economics as such without betraying the "authentic human development" to which it is dedicated.

The following results may be predicted, if one tries to think about the problems of development in these terms. First of all, the moral temperature of the discussion will be considerably lower than that sponsored by the first model, not because the second model concedes the irrelevance of moral and spiritual concerns, but because it recognizes that these concerns are cheapened by empty moralisms. Moreover, social analyses done within this second model will tend to feature a moral discernment that respects the complexity, and often intractability of the problems of development, and will tend to resort to unqualified moral exhortation only under exceptional circumstances. It will tend to be skeptical of neologisms like "superdevelopment," which have little going for them apart from their dubious theological assumptions, and it will demand that seemingly radical schemes for advancing development—such as the hope that ending the arms race between the superpowers might be the key to significant economic progress in the Third World—be backed up by radically plausible arguments. Though there is no reason to think a full agenda for economic rights cannot be honored here too, the tendency in this second model will be to pay careful attention to the possible trade-offs among the various rights advocated, against a baseline for implementing them that takes into account the material capacities of each of the nations in question. These tendencies, of course, follow directly from the second model's recognition of the basic fact of scarcity, not as an excuse for compromising with the moral exigencies of human rights, but as a moral and spiritual constraint partly constitutive of the context in which such rights are to be taken seriously.

*

For reasons that are implicit in the very effort to contrast the two models for interpreting the basic fact of scarcity, I am recommending that Catholic social teaching, as presented by John Paul II, be modified in a manner consistent with the second model. There is no hidden political agenda lurking behind this conclusion, at least none of which I am aware. Ideologically, I remain what I have been more or less consistently throughout my adult life, a Catholic liberal who is unsympathetic to countercultural pretensions, whether Left or Right in their political orientation. While I recognize that, were my proposal to be taken seriously, and in an odd way it does have some promise of overcoming the split between liberal and neoconservative Catholics, that is not what motivates my effort in making it. Rather, my hope is to have engaged the thought of John Paul II at the level of theological seriousness that it rightly claims for itself.

In a sense, what I am proposing is not that the Pope should abandon his Creationist theological perspective in Catholic social teaching but, instead, should develop it in the area of societal reproduction with the same degree of rigor he has applied to questions of sexual reproduction. For, as the series of General Audiences devoted to the *Original Unity of Man and Woman* (1981) suggests, the theological meaning of human sexuality, including the ethics of marriage, ought to be considered in light of the original set of constraints and possibilities, the "ontological structure" in the Pope's words, disclosed in the myths of Creation. An equally rigorous search of these same Scriptures for clues regarding the ontological structure of economic and social development, I contend, ought to disclose a similarly profound theological interpretation of the basic fact of scarcity along the lines I have indicated. At least, it is a possibility worth pursuing, if I am right about the practical consequences that follow from recognizing or failing to recognize it. I make this proposal, not because I seek any substantial revision of Catholic social teaching's commitment to a full agenda of economic rights, but because I would like to change the moral tone of their typical discussion. That tone of moralistic condemnation reminds me of what I am told is an old Irish proverb: "No good deed goes unpunished." As I read them, John Paul II's encyclicals, culminating in *Sollicitudo Rei Socialis* tend to cast suspicion on precisely those Western economic and social institutions that, arguably, have done as much as anyone to promote real progress toward development. Not that these institutions are beyond criticism, but I would hope that such criticism would proceed without prejudice in a climate of genuine understanding.

The model for interpreting the problem of scarcity I have offered is hardly a fully explicated theological perspective. What I have done here is merely to set the stage for such work by clearing some space for it in contemporary discussions of Catholic social teaching. Those familiar with my earliest writings may discern the continuing influence of Reinhold Niebuhr's Christian realism. In particular, the problem of scarcity as discussed by economists would be appropriated by Christian realism, in terms laid out by Niebuhr's discussion of "finitude" in *The Nature and Destiny of Man*. What I have suggested about the original ordering of Creation, including the ways in which even death, disease, and the perennial discrepancy between our aspirations and the material resources available to fulfill them, is already apparent in Niebuhr's category of finitude. Like Niebuhr, I would insist upon a categorical distinction between finitude and sin. In his view, though a person is a paradoxical mix of finitude and freedom, sin occurs only when we humans anxiously act to overturn this paradox which is the Creator's first and greatest gift to us. Sin, in Niebuhr's view, is the refusal to accept in faith the possibilities as well as the constraints implicit in our paradoxical nature, even though that nature is the Creator's will for us and the only possible basis for our faithful participation in the work of Redemption. Similarly, I would argue that the basic fact of scarcity is *prima facie* evidence of finitude, but not necessarily of sin. Consistent with Niebuhr's view, our responses to scarcity inevitably may become sinful, especially given the pervasiveness of economic anxiety among the rich as well as the poor. But in itself scarcity need not be sinful, but a grace-filled opportunity to extend ourselves toward the common good.

Niebuhr's theology, however, is not the end of this inquiry, as far as I am concerned. The Catholic in me is uneasy with his overly austere interpretation of the work of Redemption, for in his hands Christian realism tends to become so single-mindedly vigilant against idolatry that an authentically Incarnational, robustly Trinitarian perspective seems to be ruled out in advance. Besides, Niebuhr's view of the relationship between finitude and freedom, not to mention sin and grace, now strikes me as too anthropocentric to allow the ultimately cosmic dimensions of the problem of scarcity to be developed. Though his own perspective does yield many eloquent passages on the necessity of understanding the vicissitudes of development, what he referred to as "the nicely calculated less and more" of moral and political choices, it is focused too narrowly on human concerns to allow economics to be integrated fully and usefully into it. Lately, I have discovered a way of overcoming these defects in Christian realism by appropriating the philosophy of Charles Sanders Peirce, the founder of American pragmatism. Because Peirce's philosophy moves from investigations of the logic of science toward an ontology capable of comprehending the basic pattern of physical, biological and social evolution, it promises to provide theoretical resources for placing a Creationist theology of "authentic human development" on a proper footing, one in which the methodological relationship between ethics and economics can be pursued usefully. I cannot go into Peirce's work here, but even its initial impact on my own way of thinking about economics ensures that the end of this inquiry may really be only a beginning.

Bibliography

Gregory Baum, *The Priority of Labor: A Commentary on Laborem Exercens.* Ramsey, New Jersey: The Paulist Press, 1982.

Justus Buchler, ed., *Philosophical Writings of Peirce.* New York: Dover Publications, 1955.

David Hollenbach, *Claims in Conflict: Retrieving and Renewing the Catholic Human Rights Tradition.* Ramsey, New Jersey: The Paulist Press, 1979.

Hollenbach; *Justice, Peace, and Human Rights: American Catholic Social Ethics in a Pluralistic Context.* New York: Crossroads, 1988.

John W. Houck and Oliver F. Williams, eds., *Co-Creation and Capitalism: John Paul II's Laborem Exercens.* Washington, D.C.: University Press of America, 1983.

John Paul II, *On Social Concern: Sollicitudo Rei Socialis.* Washington, D.C.: United States Catholic Conference, 1987.

_____, On Human Work: Laborem Exercens. Washington, D.C.: United States Catholic Conference, 1981.

_____, Original Unity of Man and Woman: Catechesis on the Book of Genesis. Preface by Donald W. Wuerl. Boston, Massachusetts: St. Paul Editions, 1981.

_____, Toward a Philosophy of Praxis. Edited by Alfred Block and George T. Czuczka. New York: Crossroads, 1981.

_____, The Redeemer of Man: Redemptor Hominis. Boston, Massachusetts: St. Paul Editions, 1979.

Kenneth L. Ketner and Christian J. W. Kloesel, eds., Peirce, Semeiotic, and Pragmatism: Essays by Max H. Fisch. Bloomington, Indiana: Indiana University Press, 1986.

Dennis P. McCann, Christian Realism and Liberation Theology: Practical Theologies in Creative Conflict. Maryknoll, New York: Orbis Books, 1981.

_____, New Experiment in Democracy: The Challenge for American Catholicism. Kansas City, Missouri: Sheed and Ward, 1987.

Kenneth A. Myers, ed., Aspiring to Freedom: Commentaries on John Paul II's Encyclical "The Social Concerns of the Church." Grand Rapids, Michigan: William B. Eerdmans, 1988.

Reinhold Niebuhr, The Nature and Destiny of Man. Two Volumes. New York: Charles Scribner's Sons, 1964.

Paul Samuelson, Economics. Eleventh Edition. New York: McGraw-Hill, 1980.

Thomas Sowell, A Conflict of Visions: Ideological Origins of Political Struggles. New York: William Morrow, 1987.

Max Stackhouse, Creeds, Society, and Human Rights: A Study in Three Cultures. Grand Rapids, Michigan: William B. Eerdmans, 1984.

Eight

The Catholic Challenge to the United States Culture: The Social Teachings of John Paul II

Ricardo Ramirez, C.S.B.

Each age of the Church seems to have its unique gifts. One of these gifts we have received in the latter days of the twentieth century is a rapid development accompanied by a steady unfolding of greater clarity of the Church's teaching on matters regarding social justice. We are truly in an exciting time in the study and analysis of Catholic social thought. This gathering at Notre Dame is indicative of this gift. The recent U.S. Bishops' pastorals on peace and economic justice, and the writings, speeches and actions of John Paul II point to one thing: The Church, no doubt through the actions of the Holy Spirit, is serious about translating the Gospel's social teachings to the modern world— speaking in fairly understandable terms and to those issues that are real and pressing.

I would agree with those who say these times that devote so much attention to Catholic social thought are creating a "heightened sense of possibility and commitment perhaps unequaled since Vatican II burst on the scene almost a generation ago."[1] What contributes to the excitement is not only the rich, profound and sometimes eminently practical ideas, but the captured attention given by the mass media to papal pronouncements and episcopal processes of pastoral letter writing and bishops' letters themselves. "Pastoral letter" has become a household word, or at least one used at racquetball clubs and maybe on the golf course.

What is at issue in speaking of the dialogical posture between U.S. culture and the social teachings of John Paul II is the Gospel's clear and unequivocal challenge to conversion. It is the age-old tension because culture tends to consume religion as much as religion, particularly one with clear radical purposes, wants to transform the cultural world in which it finds itself. Once more Vatican II in *Gaudium et Spes* repeats the tension between the prophets and the Jewish kings, the early Mediterranean Church and the Roman Empire, the Latin American missionaries of the sixteenth and seventeenth centuries and the colonial powers of Europe: it is Jesus in one corner and Caesar in the other.

Jesus did not solve the church-state problem by his comment on the coin, "Give to Caesar what is Caesar's and to God what is God's." Popular thinking naively sees the phrase as prophetic of the American resolution of the problem. What Jesus really meant was that Caesar should not be given what pertains only to God. Caesar should receive only what is his due and no more. He cannot demand worship nor treatment as a deity. Seen in this way, Jesus was being critical of the Empire's political understanding of itself, and critical as well of the way the people whose land was occupied by the Romans might be accommodating to the imposed rule.

But getting back to the topic under consideration, John Paul II has from the beginning of his pontificate challenged the Church, and indeed the world, with the application of Gospel principle to the contemporary sign of injustice. He specifically challenges the United States' Church and people at large in the *ad limina* visits with the U.S. bishops and in his visits to the United States. During his last visit in 1987, meeting with the bishops in Los Angeles, he responded to the presentation of Archbishop Weakland on "The Role of the Laity in Society and the Church in the U.S.A.," by asking some questions: ". . . how is the American culture evolving? Is this evolution being influenced by the Gospel? Does it clearly reflect Christian inspiration?"[2] He made Paul VI's *ad limina* talk of 1978 his own:

> Your efforts have been directed to the eradication of hunger, the elimination of subhuman living conditions and the promotion of programs on behalf of the poor, the elderly and minorities. You have worked with the improvement of the social order itself. At the same time, we know that you have held up to your people the goal to which God calls them: the life above, in Christ Jesus. (cf. Phil. 3,14).[3]

Without a doubt, Pope John Paul II sees himself as the classical missionary, sent to preach the good news of salvation, affirming what is good and challenging to continued conversion of the individual and of social structures.

Let me offer at this point a working understanding of the term "culture." For our purposes here, I see culture as a unique system whereby people organize, relate and perceive themselves, others and the universe. Culture seen as a human achievement apart from the fine arts appears to be a twentieth century concept. The concept as used in the social sciences was introduced into English in the latter part of the nineteenth century.[4] It would be interesting to trace the concept in theology and in church documents. The most notable attention given culture is in *Gaudium et Spec*, Chapter 2, Nos. 53-62. In that section the council fathers point out the function of the good news of Christ in relation to culture:

> The good news of Christ continually renews the life and culture of fallen men: it combats and removes the error and evil which flow from the ever-present attraction of sin. It never ceases to purify and elevate the morality of peoples. It takes the spiritual qualities and endowments of every age and nation, and with supernatural riches it causes them to blossom as it were from within; it fortifies, completes and restores them in Christ. (No. 58).[5]

The general impression that is held regarding U.S. culture, and I would not disagree with this, is that we are marked by high degrees of materialism, individualism and a spirit of competition. On the plus side, we are seen as people who are industrious, generous and innovative. These characteristics, of course, are extremely general and could be considered stereotypes, yet in every stereotype there is some degree of truth. (Having worked at the Mexican American Cultural Center for several years and struggled with the identification of the Mexican American culture, I can assure you that it is almost impossible to do a good job in identifying the culture of any group. As soon as an adjective pops up, it is just as quickly shot down as a stereotype.) But back to the point, none of us would disagree with the Pope when he challenges the U.S. bishops, and anyone else in a position of leadership in the Church in the United States, in responding to Archbishop John

Quinn's description of American morality, "It would be altogether out of place to try to model this act of religion (the act of faith) on attitudes drawn from secular culture."[6]

We are here because we have the conviction that the Church indeed has something to say to the American cultural scene. John Paul II expresses what is rooted deeply in our Catholic tradition, and he does it in a powerful and persistent way. I am convinced, and this is from observation in my own diocese, that there lies a strong intuitive inclination among our Catholic people toward alleviating the plight of the poor. Unfortunately, this intuition usually stops with charity and does not make the crucial leap toward the structural justice question.

There is no doubt in my mind that Catholicism has a profoundly unique element which is absolutely essential to its teaching, and that is its consistent challenge of social justice in the world. The Synod of 1971 called it the "constitutive element." It is interesting to note that one of the first post-Vatican II synods captured in *Gaudium et Spec* the new focus given social justice. This is why I lament with the deepest sorrow the departure of Roman Catholics to fundamentalist sects who see the world as intrinsically evil, to be shunned, and that one must simply await for the *heavenly* kingdom. Being "born again" in that context means absolving one's responsibilities to our sisters and brothers in reducing salvation to a privatized and highly individualistic approach to God. It goes without saying that this attitude exists among many Roman Catholics in this country and elsewhere. The Church of Vatican II and the papal teachings following it, teach that to be Church, we must be the *Gaudium et Spes*, the joy and hope of the people of our day and the *Lumen Gentium*, the light of all nations.

In what areas of our culture might we especially apply the teaching of John Paul II? I would like to suggest six areas for our consideration. These are not the only ones that exist, but I offer them as examples of Pope John Paul II's challenge to our U.S. culture.

1. The Present Situation of the U.S. Worker

These are hard times for American workers. Unemployment is high, real wages have declined, wage cuts and kickbacks are the order of the day and unions are under assault. The rights of workers are eroding in a manner unprecedented in recent history.'" In *Laborem Exercens*, John Paul II affirms the dignity of work and places work at the center of the social question. The encyclical states that human beings are the proper subjects of work. Work expresses and increases human dignity. He emphatically stresses the priority of labor over things and criticizes systems which do not embody these principles. He supports the rights of workers and labor organizations and concludes by outlining a challenging ''spirituality of work.'' In a society where the worker has become a disposable commodity, the words of John Paul II are most timely and challenging.

2. The United States Family

In the United States 70 percent of all mothers with school-age children work outside the home. This is the greatest single shift in family life in this century, perhaps since the founding of our Republic. For an increasing number of families the second income has become a necessity for economic survival, especially since average weekly earnings for families have declined 14.3 percent since 1973, after accounting for inflation. More than 25 percent of today's families are single-parent families and more than 95 percent of these families are headed by women. Adequate day care and after-school care for children has become truly a national emergency . . . we have not adjusted our consciousness to face the changed reality of the American family. John Paul II presents a wide array of issues in his own responses regarding the present plight of the human family in his apostolic exhortation, *Familaris Consortio*, among other places. In our country we cannot ignore his ''Charter of the Rights of the Family'' wherein the Holy Father speaks of the families' rights to rely on adequate policies on the part of public authorities in the juridical, economic, social and fiscal domains, without discrimination. Families have rights to social and economic order in which the organization of work permits the members to live together and which does not hinder the unity, well-being, health and stability of the family. He goes on to enumerate the families' rights to housing, protection from harmful drugs, pornography, alcoholism, the right of the elderly to have a dignified life and death, and the rights of families to emigrate in their search for a better life (*Familaris Consortio*, No. 46). In our society we need to evaluate laws and evolving patterns of family life and judge them in the light of Gospel values. The teachings of John Paul II are a good place to start.

3. Racism in the United States

We, the U.S. bishops, have spoken of the seemingly inextricable evil of racism in our midst. In our letter on economic justice, we pointed out that despite the gains which have been made toward racial equality, prejudice and discrimination in our time as well as the effects of past discrimination continue to exclude many members of racial minorities from the mainstream of American life. We go on to say in our pastoral letter that discriminatory practices in labor markets, in educational systems, and in electoral politics create major obstacles for Blacks, Hispanics, Native Americans and other racial minorities in their struggle to improve the economic status (*Economic Justice for All*, No. 182). In the pastoral letter, "Brother and Sisters to Us," we described this racism as a sin, "a sin that divides the human family, blots out the image of God among specific members of that family and violates the fundamental human dignity of those called to be children of the same father" (No. 9).

Pope John Paul II, very mindful of racism in U.S. culture, at various times during his last visit to the United States addressed the issue of racism, particularly in his message to Black Catholics in New Orleans. "The Church," he said, "must continue to join her efforts with the efforts of others who are working to correct all imbalances and disorders of a social nature. Indeed, the Church can never remain silent in the face of injustice wherever it is clearly present."[9] Even after a century plus of the freedom of the slaves in our country, we continue to be seriously bothered by racial prejudice. No sooner do we think we have made great strides than the horrible phenomenon of the human indignity of racism reappears.

4. The Growing Disparity between the Rich and the Poor

The situation of poverty in the United States is as follows: The working poor are a significant and rising proportion of the poor. In 1986, 41.5 percent of all poor people over the age of fourteen worked. This is equal to the highest percentage of poor who worked since 1968. Furthermore, in recent years, the fastest growing group among the poor is the working poor, not the welfare poor whose ranks have remained level during that period. In 1979, the incomes of 6.5 million working people fell below the poverty line; by 1983, the number had risen to 9.4 million. In 1986, after four consecutive years of economic recovery, the number of working poor had fallen only slightly to 8.9 million. Another alarming statistic is that children constitute the poorest age group in the United States. In 1986, 20.5 percent of all children lived below the poverty line; 22.1 percent of all children under the age of six were poor. Among the Black and Hispanic children approximately 40 percent were poor, more than three times the rate for all Americans.[10] We are also faced with the contemporary phenomenon of the "feminization of poverty." Since 1965, the annual earnings of full-time year-round working women have hovered at about 60 percent of the earnings of men.[11]

John Paul II in 1979 delivered one of his most significant contributions to the understanding of social justice regarding the poor. He addressed the Indian peasant farmers of Oaxaca and Chiapas. It is well known he rewrote the text the night before he delivered it, to do justice to the poverty he had seen first-hand. He said that he, the Pope, chose to be their voice, the voice of those who cannot speak or who have been silenced. He expressed his wish to be the "conscience of consciences, an invitation to action, to make up for lost time, which has frequently been a time of prolonged sufferings and unsatisfied hopes."[12] In his *Sollicitudo Rei Socialis*, the Holy Father writes of the unequal distribution of the benefits of the world economy. This, he points out, happens not through the *fault* of the needy people and even less through a sort of *inevitability* dependent on natural conditions or circumstances as a whole.[13]

In the light of these statements, John Paul II reminds us that we have an unfinished agenda and that we have not responded to the Third World needs within our own U.S. boundaries.

5. The Arms Race and the U.S. Military Industrial Complex

The facts are these: In 1978, the greatest peacetime military buildup in U.S. history began. All categories of military spending grew, but expenditures on personnel, operations, and maintenance shrank relative to the military budget as a whole. These expenditures are, of course, a boon to large corporations in military-related industries. In 1984 the top ten military contractors won over 34 percent of all military contracts. But the lack of competitive bidding, as well as other problems, led to widely publicized embarrassments, such as the three $7,600 coffee pots purchased by the Air Force.[14] Further statistics show that in 1981, military spending was 24 percent of the total U.S. government budget; by 1985 defense spending had risen to 29.4 percent. Right now the U.S. military budget is around 300 billion dollars.

In his address to the United Nations in 1979, John Paul II repeated the same impassioned plea for peace as did Paul VI. He expressed his concern over the increasing number and size of the means of war and how this increases the risk that sometime, somewhere, somehow, someone can set the war machinery in motion, bringing with it general destruction.[15] Pope Paul II approaches the nuclear arms race in his first encyclical, *Redemptor Hominis*, and in his address at Hiroshima. "Modern technology," he says, "can move beyond both moral and political guidance, thus submitting the human person to an impersonal power. New improvements in weaponry seem to be always one step ahead of any attempts to control them. We are challenged as the human community to reestablish the primacy of ethics and politics over technology."[16]

6. Consumerism

Consumerism is a symptom of greed. Greed is a drive for the attainment not only of basic human needs but for status, power and material goods in excess of what we actually need. When we succumb to the enticement of greed, we lose our perspective as citizens of the world with the responsibilities that this entails. Consumerism, someone has said, is a "bloated late twentieth century version of the American dream" that divides the rich from the poor. In this scenario, prosperity is maintained and advanced at the expense of the marginalized. Bonds of solidarity are destroyed and indifference and even a sense of moral and political powerlessness afflict consumers.[17]

In *Sollicitudo Rei Socialis*, John Paul II describes the "side-by-side miseries of underdevelopment, themselves unacceptable, and we find ourselves up against a form of *super development*, equally inadmissible, because like the former it is contrary to what is good and to true happiness" (No. 28). He goes on to say that this super development which consists of an excessive availability of every kind of material goods for the benefit of certain social groups, easily makes people slaves of "possession" and of immediate gratification, with no other horizon than the multiplication of continual replacement of the things already owned with others still better. The Holy Father describes what happens to the person caught up in the web of consumerism, how empty it is and that it merely leads to radical dissatisfaction because, he says, "one quickly learns that the more one possesses the more one wants, while deeper aspirations remain unsatisfied and perhaps even stifled."[18]

The person's vocation implies, John Paul II goes on to explain, that while being called to use other creatures, we must always remain subject to God's will and He imposes limits upon the use and dominion over things.[19]

This is indeed an important challenge to our American culture which is obsessed with the drive to possess, to have and to hold more and more of the beautiful, and sometimes not so beautiful, things that are produced.

Conclusion

I have no insight on the practical side as to how we in the U.S. are to approach the myriad problems in our back and front yards. I do have questions and challenges, some for the practical-minded, others for those who do the all-important critical reflection of the social justice principle *vis-à-vis* the U.S. problems I have attempted to describe.

What are the implications, for example, of the "option for the poor" we—John Paul II for the universal Church and ourselves the U.S. bishops—have made? Is this option to be taken seriously or are we just trying to match the sometimes heroic Latin American Church in its own "preferential option"? My own diocesan budget does not reflect this option, neither do I personally expend more of my energy in direct service to the poor.

Regarding the question being discussed here of the possible making of an economic counterculture, in our own U.S. Southwest, given the limited natural resources, the scarcity of jobs, the need for better working conditions, the demands for an educated work force, the need for affordable housing, the overdependence on the military industrial complex, the challenge by the sacred teachings of the Church takes on prophetic proportions. The quality of justice in our part of the world will be measured by the treatment given those most vulnerable and marginalized in our society. The Church is lonely out there in the desert, we oftentimes feel we are the only ones speaking of the possibilities of what *can* and *should* be; our voices fall on ears of people who jeer more than cheer, on ears that are not used to hearing this language.

The U.S. is a good testing ground for the social teachings of the Church. We are in many ways the epitome of contemporary culture; our cultural ways and patterns of behavior are seen and emulated around the world. What the Church leadership may be able to do to influence the restructuring of society in this country would be seen as real possibilities elsewhere. There are several reasons to think that the Church in this country has the potential to lead the way in social justice in the world. We have, as was pointed out in the Los Angeles dialogue between the Holy Father and the U.S. bishops, the most educated Catholic laity. We are one of the two largest episcopal conferences, and we have the means to communicate to the world in ways unequalled anywhere.

Meetings such as this bring together the best theological and social minds. Your interest in the topics being discussed is indicative of your own strong convictions, I dare presume, for social justice. You share with the U.S. bishops the function of being links, connections between Church teaching and its application to our cultural and societal milieu. In this conference, I notice you are going beyond the critique of Catholic social teaching to the analysis, to the creative synthesis needed between the American dream and the ideals set forth in Church documents. Your work is crucial, for from a bishop's perspective, it reinforces what we as official teachers have to offer.

Finally, I like to hear that we are in a new era of appreciating Church teaching on social matters. We U.S. bishops are trying to echo the papal focus on justice issues and want nothing less than to be a prime factor in influencing social change. The American church *has* come of age, we are "insiders" in that we have left forever a ghetto existence in this country. The hostility, unease and suspicion experienced by our immigrant ancestors are now things of the past. But we are still "outsiders" in the sense that, as American Catholics, we have a distinct identity, an identity not at all un-American, but certainly *pro-American* in that we feel we have—out of our accumulated Catholic wisdom—something extraneous but sacred nonetheless, to offer the debate in public issues.

We American Catholics have an acute interest in the commonweal that carries with it the dream of the founders of this Republic. I agree with Charles R. Strain that the ideals of Catholic social teaching and the vision of the American Republic in the imaginative design of the founding fathers are not far from each other.[20] Indeed, they are both rooted in the deepest of human aspirations for a community of citizens driven by the same yearnings for liberation, democracy and justice for all.

Notes

1. Charles R. Strain, ed., *Prophetic Visions and Economic Realities*, p. 186.

2. Pope John Paul II, *Unity in the Work of Service, on the Occasion of His Second Visit to the United States*, p. 150.

3. *Ibid.*, p. 152.

4. G.O. Lang, "Culture," *New Catholic Encyclopedia*, Vol. IV, p. 522.

5. Austin Flannery, ed., *Vatican Council II: The Conciliar and Post Conciliar Documents*, No. 58, p. 963.

6. Pope John Paul II, *Unity in the Work of Service*, p. 144.

7. Helen Ginsburg, "Teachings of John Paul II on Work and the Rights of Workers," *The Social Teachings of John Paul II*, p. 46.

8. May Rose Oaker, "Pope John Paul II and Family Policy," *Social Teachings of John Paul II*, p. 134.

9. Pope John Paul II, *Unity in the Work of Service, on the Occasion of His Second Visit to the United States*, p. 54.

10. Michael Harrington, *Who Are the Poor? A Profile on the Changing Faces of Poverty in the United States in 1987*, p. 3.

11. *Ibid.*, p. 16.

12. Pope John Paul II, *Puebla and Beyond*, p. 81.

13. Pope John Paul II, *On Social Concern, Sollicitudo Rei Socialis*, No. 9.
14. Nancy Folbre, *A Field Guide to the U.S. Economy, The Center for Popular Economics*, p. 65.
15. Pope John Paul II, *Pilgrim of Peace*, p. 22 ff.
16. J. Bryan Hehir, "John Paul II: Continuity and Change in the Social Teaching of the Church," *Co-Creation and Capitalism: John Paul II's Laborem Exercens*, p. 138-139.
17. Drew Christiansen, "Social Justice and Consumerism in the Thought of Pope John Paul II, *The Social Teachings of Pope John Paul II*, p. 67.
18. Pope John Paul II, *Sollicitudo Rei Socialis*, No. 28.
19. *Ibid.*, No. 29.
20. Strain, *op. cit.*, p. 188.

Bibliography

Campaign for Human Development, *Poverty Profile USA: In the 'Eighties;* Washington, D.C.: Campaign for Human Development, 1985.

Catholic Charities USA, *The Social Teachings of Pope John Paul II*; Washington, D.C.: Catholic Charities USA, 1987.

Clarke, Thomas E., "Option for the Poor: A Reflection," *America*, 30 Jan., 1988, pp. 95-99.

Flannery, Austin, ed., *Vatican Council II: The Conciliar and Post Conciliar Documents*; New York: Costello, 1981.

Folbre, Nancy, *A Field Guide to the U.S. Economy, The Center for Popular Economics*; New York: Patheon, 1987.

Harrington, Michael, Robert Greenstein, Eleanor Holmes-Norton, *Who Are the Poor? A Profile of the Changing Faces of Poverty in the United States in 1987*; Washington, D.C.: Campaign for Human Development, 1987.

Houck, John W., Oliver F. Williams, eds., *Co-Creation and Capitalism: John Paul's Laborem Exercens*; Lanham, Md.: University Press of America, 1983.

Lang, G.O., "Culture," *New Catholic Encyclopedia*, Vol. 4; Washington, D.C.: The Catholic University of America, 1967.

Malone, Bishop James, "Questions for Social Action Ministers," *Origins*, 16, March 1989, pp. 674-675.

National Conference of Catholic Bishops, *Economic Justice for All: Pastoral Letter on Catholic Social Teaching and the U.S. Economy*; Washington, D.C.: United States Catholic Conference, 1986.

Pope John Paul II, *Ad Limina Addresses—The Addresses of His Holiness Pope John Paul II to the Bishops of the United States during Their Ad*

Limina Visits; Washington, D.C.: United States Catholic Conference, 1989.

Pope John Paul II, "On Human Work," *Third Encyclical Letter*, September 14, 1981; Washington, D.C.: United States Catholic Conference, 1981.

Pope John Paul II, "On Social Concern," *Encyclical Letter*, December 30, 1987; Washington, D.C.: United States Catholic Conference, 1987.

Pope John Paul II, *Pilgrim of Peace: The Homilies and Addresses of His Holiness Pope John Paul II on the Occasion of His Visit to the United States of America, October 1979*. Baltimore, Md.: Garmond/Pridemark Press, Inc., 1979.

Pope John Paul II, *Puebla and Beyond*, Trans. John Eagleson, Philip Scharper; New York: Orbis Books, 1979.

Pope John Paul II, *Unity in the Work of Service, on the Occasion of His Second Visit to the United States*; Washington, D.C.: United States Catholic Conference, 1987.

Schultheis, Michael J., Edward P. DeBerri, Peter J. Henriot, *Our Best Kept Secret: The Rich Heritage of Catholic Social Teaching*; Washington, D.C.: Center of Concern.

Strain, Charles R., ed., *Prophetic Visions and Economic Realities*; Grand Rapids, Mi.: Wm. B. Eerdmans Publishing Co., 1989.

Nine

African-American Perspectives
on the Social Teachings
of John Paul II

Preston Williams

This essay may to some appear not to fit closely with the other essays in this collection on Pope John Paul II's social teachings. If so, it is for a very good reason. The author was asked to make some remarks about the present state of affairs among African Americans as well as reflect on the social teaching of John Paul II. Both tasks are formidable. Comment upon the racial policies and attitudes of the nation is precarious because we have come to a place of great uncertainty. The gains made since the executive order of President Harry Truman desegregating the armed forces, the Brown Decision of 1954, and the Voting Rights Acts seem relatively secure, but the affirmative action programs have been gravely weakened recently, if not destroyed, by a set of Supreme Court decisions in which conservative Roman Catholics played an important part.[1] Although the historic pattern of legal segregation has been broken up, society has, as a result of the presidency of Ronald Reagan, reaffirmed a strong, harmful racism as a value permissible in every aspect of U.S. society. As before, the burden of eradicating this racism falls upon the black minority citizens of the nation. The present Supreme Court seems determined to diffuse and weaken every effort to fight racism. While some relief will come from Congress, its coming will no doubt be long delayed and its nature is unpredictable. The administration of President Bush will undoubtedly be more even-handed in the area of racial justice, but his presidential campaign and actions since entering the office do not suggest any desire to challenge the unnecessarily harsh and narrow recent court decisions.

Developments in the African-American community are as volatile as they are in the larger society. The black middle class has been enlarged somewhat, and black participation in politics has grown sufficiently to

176

assure the community that it will always have a voice, even though it may be unable to persuade Republicans and Democrats to compete for the black vote. On the other hand, deterioration has continued apace in several areas of the black community, especially the family and the school, and for many the work place as well. What this mixture of small blessings and serious troubles portend is hard to say. It does seem clear that there is little sympathy to be found among white Americans for the plight of the African American, and no federal initiative that will go beyond the rhetoric of moral uplift and self help.

Interpretations and commentaries upon the social encyclicals of John Paul II could be as difficult as that of unravelling the racial situation in the U.S. and the outcome without any illumination for the American scene. In an effort to say something about race relations in America and John Paul II's social teaching, my essay will deal with the perspectives of some African-American Roman Catholics on the Pope's social teachings. In this way we can shed at least a small light upon African Americans' thoughts and actions at this juncture in history and view the encyclical letters of the Pope from a vantage point that will provide a new vision for many readers. The reporting happens to be done by a black Protestant. I have chosen this way of meeting the request to write about African Americans and John Paul II's social teaching because I have discovered in my association with black Roman Catholics that John Paul II is highly visible and well liked. I shall attempt to indicate why this is so and why it is important for race relations in the U.S. and in the social teaching of the Roman Catholic Church.

For many, the Second Vatican Ecumenical Council which ended on December 8, 1965, marked the time when the Roman Catholic Church began the effort to become a world church, setting aside its position as the old line depository of Western European high culture. In this context, what should be most stressed is the Church's increased recognition of the Third World and the coming dominance of Africans, Asians, and Latin American and Caribbean people in its membership. The cultural diversity within its unified fellowship set it apart from the Western European and American blocs of nationalistic churches assembled under the rubric of the World Council of Churches. For non-Western peoples, the Vatican was beginning to resemble a church government in which the peoples' voice could be heard and their vote counted.

For African-American Catholics the most significant moment in this new phase of the Church's life occurred on September 12, 1987, when Pope John Paul II had a special meeting with their leadership and told them the Church was concerned for black Americans who had suffered so much—a word not frequently heard from their fellow white Catholics in the United States. In addition, the Pope said the church was neither black, white, nor American, but the one Church of Jesus Christ in which there was a home for blacks, whites, Americans, every culture and race.[2] The Pope's concluding paragraph began with a sentence that found its way into the hearts of the black Catholic leadership and is constantly repeated by them. "Dear brothers and sisters: Your black cultural heritage enriches the Church and makes her witness of universality more complete."[3]

John Paul II's letters are well received by black Catholics because he has recognized their presence in the U.S. Church and has responded to them in a manner that lends credibility to his remarks concerning oppressed people. In May 1987 black Catholics had held a National Black Catholic Congress and had devised a pastoral plan for black American parishes.[4] The Pope's remarks in New Orleans exhibited a familiarity with that plan and gave a warm reception, if not full endorsement, to it. In February 1990 the American Conference of Bishops will vote on its proposals. The plan of the black Catholics is foundational and, except for its stress upon the necessity of recognizing a distinct African-American tradition and community within the world-wide Catholic Church, does not at any point threaten orthodoxy. African-American Catholics are not to be seen as persons dissatisfied with what some would style the more conservative position of the Pope on matters of doctrine and personal morality. Yet the more liberal social morality of the Pope would resemble that of the black American Catholics, their awareness of their rights and their position on issues such as apartheid in South Africa.

Further strengthening of the African American's positive attitude toward the Pope's social teaching would result from shared descriptions of the issues of development and of the theological dimensions of the problem. The African-American Catholics, like members of the developing world, have experienced unfulfilled dreams during the last twenty years and an increase in the gap between themselves and the developed peoples. Their status as a minority in a super-developed nation with a predominantly white church has made them one with people in the Third World. For them, the problems of unemployment, housing, the severe restriction of the right of economic initiative, the allocation of scarce resources to national security issues rather than to human welfare needs, and violence have diminished development. They are willing to acknowledge that some fault lies within themselves, but they also see the larger cause to be the avarice of the rich and the injustices embedded in the social, economic, political, and cultural systems. They share both John Paul II's negative description of the world and his hope that the Church and the Christian faith will be a source of liberation.

Theological Themes

John Paul II's usage of biblical materials in addition to the usual language of natural law philosophy is particularly appealing to the African-American Catholic as the basis for authentic development. Such language is deeply rooted in their own religiosity and was employed extensively in their own civil rights revolution to ground their conception of human rights. The conception of the *imago dei* especially was employed to understand the nature and destiny of the individual self and its relationship to other selves, God, the world, and nature. Like John Paul II, they too thought in terms wider than the economic, and terms which encompassed the total person and community. They stressed achievement both as an obligation to fulfill their total human potential and as a basis for full political and economic equality. While they sought for themselves more than the basic needs, they acted to avoid the adoption of the values of consumerism and super-development. ''Being'' was more important than ''having,'' but actualization of ''being'' did entail the ''having'' of certain concrete social, political, and economic rights. Although African-American Catholic statements on development are not as aware as those of the Pope regarding issues of ecology and peace, nonetheless, they do share a broad general understanding of the foundation and content of authentic human development.

The ''structures of sin''[5] of which the Pope speaks in his encyclical letter, *On Social Concern*, is a general concept but one which carries what seems to African Americans and Third World people a very obvious and true meaning, namely, that the winners in the world economic and political systems have achieved and maintained their position by means less than moral. Order, peace, and development are not to be equated with justice, right, and good. While development specialists might want to replace the concept of "sin" and "structures of sin" with more specific and secular terms, those oppressed are more aware of the structurally systematic manner in which their existence is restricted by the operation of conceptions of merit, trade, or the disproportional rewards bestowed upon the owners, managers, and marketers of business, industry, commerce, and entertainment. The judgment distinguishes between the nature of the system and the doer of evil but, like the Pope, it does conclude that evil is present in both socialism and liberal capitalism. As sufferers in the latter type of system, African Americans are not satisfied with the statements that things would be worse if they had not been brought from the old country or that the government is not able to provide basic welfare needs for all its citizens. The notion of "structures of sin" does tend to bond Third World people and oppressed people in the First World by pointing to the larger evil, the camel, that is swallowed by Western nations, while they struggle to find the source of the world's ills in the behavior and practices of the developing nations. The Pope's analysis is more right than that of many of his critics. "Structures of sin" does not claim that collectivities, bureaucracies, or nations are inherently evil, but it does indicate that many of those who exist in the developed world are organized to injure and harm many because of the interest of the few.

The Pope, in spite of his realism concerning the deeply ingrained nature of sin in individuals and societies, is more optimistic than African Americans about the ability of developed nations and superpowers to overcome the impediments to authentic development. This may be due to his belief in the possibility of the conversion of persons and thereby the creation of the political will that is needed to transform social, political, economic, and cultural institutions. John Paul II looks forward to interdependence and solidarity among humankind. African Americans cherish presently no such hope. They have come to know the recalcitrant heart of white America, its liberal capitalism and democracy, and its unwillingness to dismantle racial, sexual, and class oppression. A little more than twenty years ago African Americans had called for a weak form of solidarity: integration. Their demands were rejected. The dominant white majority and liberal white capitalists placed upon the oppressed blacks the responsibility for evil and injustice in society as well as the discovery of a remedy for it. The nation turned away from interdependence and solidarity, and increased the gaps between white and black, white and white, and black and black. The people elected leaders who sought not solidarity but the triumph of the strong over the weak and the destruction of the communal aid provided to the weak. Moreover, the policies and programs of many religious bodies and persons who professed to be motivated by the religious values held by the Pope took the lead in forwarding alienation and discrimination among persons and groups. African Americans see the path to interdependence and solidarity to be even longer and more complex than does the Pope. This greater pessimism of African Americans is exhibited also with respect to South Africa, the one foreign nation about which the black Catholics passed a resolution. Although their document does not disclose any difference with the views of the Pope, as a body they are very skeptical of a victory in South Africa that is the result of nonviolence alone.

It is in respect to some of the Pope's remarks about Africa that his positions came into clearest disagreement with the feelings of African Americans. While one might expect his convictions about the family or abortion to stir up some controversy, this has not yet happened. Umbrage has been taken, however, about the manner in which John Paul, on occasion, has communicated his views about polygamy on the African continent. His manner of utterance has been seen as being insensitive to the cultural traditions of the African people. African Americans are also more able than the Pope to see the ambiguous nature of terrorism.

Social Injustices

More can be said about the African-American understanding of and response to the social teaching of John Paul II. Whatever is said, however, does not lead to the conclusion that they are a third way between socialism and capitalism or the creation of a counterculture. The teachings are a corrective for liberal, capitalist, Western democracy and the Western Christian Church. John Paul II is a leader, a white Jesse Jackson, who, because of love and conviction, is giving voice to the cry of non-white and oppressed people for cultural and economic justice. John Paul II has kept alive the hope of these people for an expanded life in society by his advocacy of housing, employment, participatory government, fair distribution of technology and scientific knowledge, and more equitable tax and trade policies as well as more equitable life in the Church by the appointment of more Third World cardinals and bishops and by transforming a European church into a world church. John Paul II seems to have supplied not so much specific answers but the stimulus the people need to find their own answers. Given his message, the people will generate the power and acquire the space in the world and in the Church for further empowerment of themselves.

As a consequence, there is more energy and initiative present among black Catholics; the Sixth National Black Congress and the National Black Catholic Pastoral Plan are but two indications of such activity. Not all of this can be attributed to John Paul II. The African-American protest tradition and white American Catholics who have participated in and remained loyal to the civil rights revolution have contributed as well as black Catholics who have come to the U.S. recently from Haiti, Cuba, the Americas and Africa. Mutual cooperation and consensus building with Hispanics also have been important. For African Americans and, they believe, the Pope, the end result of these efforts is not a third way or a counterculture but a bettering of society and the Church.

Until the recent past, most black Catholics were more middle-class oriented than the majority of the American black community. Cultural isolation and the dominant Protestant nature of the African-American community led them to believe that being Roman Catholic meant to cease being black. This was not true for black Catholics from Louisiana, Maryland or some foreign Catholic societies. Most American Catholics who had chosen Catholicism were upwardly mobile people who wanted to escape the stigma of being black or total identification with black life and people or both. When some dioceses conducted mission work in ghetto projects in the fifties, the orientation was toward making blacks Europeans. The blacks who sent their children to parochial schools discovered these children were not only better educated but that they were also educated away from their cultural heritage. The effort was made to make them scions of the high culture of Europe. Paternalism was everywhere and some blacks wanted it to flourish. They needed the *imprimatur* of a white person or white culture to be able to accept themselves. The civil rights revolution and the black power movement as well as the world-wide process of decolonization brought an end to most of these efforts to escape blackness. Many black Catholics were persuaded to reconceptualize themselves and to restore their relationship to the black cultural community. Moreover, they came to see the basis for a reinterpretation of black culture and religion in their Catholic tradition. They began to emphasize the fact that the first six hundred years of Christianity were related to Africa and that men and women of Africa, including Cyprian and Augustine, played prominent roles in the life of the Church. Unlike their Protestant brothers and sisters, they felt themselves to be the possessors of an African-Christian past upon which they could build. This past provided a cultural, racial, and religious continuity. Even some of the slaves brought to the U.S. were baptized Roman Catholics. In his letters, John Paul II supports this idea of an African past and, through it, participates in empowering African Americans to discover their roots and to see themselves as both African and Catholic. This is neither a third way nor a counterculture. It is a reinforcement of a people's reimagining of their past, a reimagining that will result in their becoming more adapted to their present American and Catholic communities.

This reconstruction of the past, if it does succeed, will not leave either the U.S. or the Church untouched. John Paul's letters encourage change by calling for new distribution formulas for allocating the benefits and rewards generated within society and the Church. His details may not always be correct or attainable, but what is more important is his ability to make individuals and societies aware of the injustices in the present economic, political and cultural systems and his ability to encourage them to struggle for more adequate and just societal institutions. For African Americans this is particularly pleasing because it comes at the moment when they have been abandoned by many of their former white friends and when some of the most prominent supporters of oppression against blacks happen to be Roman Catholic lay persons. In addition, at this point in America's history, some of the most racist communities are centered in large Catholic populations. Rightly or wrongly, when one thinks of racism today one thinks of Boston, Chicago, New York, Los Angeles and Washington, D.C., not Atlanta or Birmingham. Just as a few years ago white southern European ethnics longed for the attention the nation seemed to shower upon blacks in the South, today, many black Catholics long for the attention the U.S. Catholic Church seems to shower upon the peoples of Central and South America. John Paul's letters are welcome as a sign that the Catholic Church is larger than any expression of racism in the U.S., including that of Catholic people.

Just as international affairs made for change in patterns of race relations in the U.S. during the fifties and sixties, so today the Vatican may contribute to constructive change in U.S. race relations. The Pope's social teachings are not a third way or counterculture, but they may stimulate a group of bishops and cardinals who have distinguished themselves on policy questions in relation to abortion, the economy, and peace to similarly mobilize their resources to address the issues of racism in society and in the Church. The strategy for reform could well be an agenda item for the Bishops' Conference's subcommittee on black and Hispanic affairs and of the entire conference. Such a program, if carried out at the archdiocesan and diocesan levels with the full participation of black and Hispanic clergymen and lay persons, could transform the nature of U.S. society and make its Roman Catholic Church a truly plural Roman Catholic Church.

What Pope John Paul II's letters bring to light is the recognition that the North-South split and the encounters between the First and Third World is a fact of domestic life in the U.S. The dominant elite has a double debt to pay, one to Third World people abroad and one to Third World people at home. How one is to pay this double debt when the nation is preoccupied with maintaining an affluent standard of living for a few will be exceedingly difficult. Perhaps in this the domestic Third World people can play a more active part, sensitizing the nation and themselves to its overseas responsibilities and, at the same time, helping the Church and the nation to include all the poor in its option for the poor, and true authentic development for all in its quest for peace. In *On Social Concern*, John Paul II has written:

> In the context of the sad experiences of recent years and the mainly negative pictures of the present moment, the Church must strongly affirm the possibility of overcoming the obstacles which by excess or by defect, stand in the way of development. And she must affirm her confidence in a true liberation. Ultimately this confidence and this possibility are based on the Church's awareness of the divine promise guaranteeing

that our present history does not remain closed in upon itself but is open to the Kingdom of God.[6]

An African-American Catholic bishop has said, "He identifies with our struggle. He understands us. He is one of us." Would that these words could be said about a majority of the American hierarchy of the Roman Catholic Church.

As a consequence of his person and his social teachings, Pope John Paul II has energized an important segment of the African-American Catholic community and these people are eager to take up the task of evangelization and of transforming society. With thought and concern they could be enlisted also for the task of helping others to full authentic development. The mainstream U.S. Roman Catholic Church needs to make itself aware of how these African-American Catholics have heard and appropriated John Paul's teaching, and it must find a way to make use of their resolve as it seeks critically and constructively to implement the Pope's teaching.

Notes

1. United States Supreme Court decisions: Richmond v. Croson; Martin v. Wilks; Ward Cove Packing Co. v. Atonio; Patterson v. McLean Credit Union.
2. Vatican Holy See Press Office, U.S.A. New Orleans, 12.IX.19 Meeting with Black Catholic Leadership, p. 9.
3. *Ibid.*
4. The National Black Catholic Pastoral Plan, the National Black Catholic Congress.
5. Encyclical Letter of John Paul II, *On Social Concern,* Chapter V, "A Theological Reading of Modern Problems," paragraph 36.
6. *Ibid.*, Chapter VII, "Conclusion," paragraph 47.

Part III

Moral Thinking about Economic Matters—The Assessment of On Social Concern

The aim of the present *reflection* is to emphasize, through a theological investigation of the present world, the need for a fuller and more nuanced concept of development . . .

On Social Concern, Par. 4

The encyclical derives fundamental—although not final—dimensions of vocation from the Genesis story of creation, and finds in that vocational setting the principles of dominion, hierarchy and obedience. What I find there is stewardship. The process of politicization in the context of reconciliation that calls the international community into being turns away from dominion, hierachy and obedience, and issues a call to membership, participation and mutuality.

Theodore R. Weber

. . . to reaffirm the *continuity* of the social doctrine as well as its constant *renewal*. In effect, continuity and renewal are a proof of the *perennial value* of the teaching of the Church.

On Social Concern, Par. 3

. . . John Paul II may well be playing the role of wise pastor by simply laying out and reaffirming basic principles of Christian faith that have social relevance as a source of hope and challenge, especially for his own flock, as they struggle to make their contribution to a common quest for authentic human development in a pluralistic world.

Ernest J. Bartell, C.S.C.

The *condemnation* of evils and injustices is also part of that *ministry of evangelization* in the social field which is an aspect of the Church's *prophetic role*. But it should be made clear that *proclamation* is always more important than *condemnation* . . .

On Social Concern, Par. 41

John Paul's emphasis on criticism and on personal conversion marks a new level of response and of adaptation to changing political circumstances in the 1980s. Its outlook of moral criticism offers great assets in an era where the failures of political activity are innumerable . . .

Leslie Griffin

It is appropriate to emphasize the *preeminent* role that belongs to the *laity*, both men and women. . . . It is their task to animate temporal realities with Christian commitment, by which they show that they are witnesses and agents of peace and justice.

On Social Concern, Par. 47

. . . we ought properly to ask whether Catholic social teaching is maintaining or developing a capacity to speak to the contemporary moral agenda in some other way than just ratifying or blessing what the present rulers of the system are already doing . . .

John Howard Yoder

It is important to note therefore that a world which is divided into blocs, sustained by rigid ideologies, and in which instead of interdependence and solidarity different forms of imperialism hold sway, can only be a world subject to structures of sin.

On Social Concern, Par. 36

. . . one has reason to suspect that the underlying tendency of this Pope's thought is a utopian and ahistorical moralism.

John Langan, S.J.

Ten

Thinking Theologically about International Development

Theodore R. Weber

Theological thinking about international development usually is prompted by projects or needs for development that are guided conceptually by one or more of the social sciences and practically by the exigencies of political situations. The advantage of such conditions and relationships is that they afford theological thinking the opportunity to connect with historical realities and to be in conversation with various perspectives on the same topic of reference. The disadvantage is that theology works with an agenda that is not its own and with terminology that is not its native language, and allows non-theological authorities to develop the meanings of development that theology will use in its own reflections. Under those circumstances it should not surprise us that theologians experience some difficulty in using theological language confidently and without embarrassment, and feel the urge to match social scientists on their own turf and with their own weapons. Nor should it surprise us that the results of theological thinking about international development often are rather thin.

If we are going to think theologically about development, it will not do to begin with economic, social, or psychological concepts of development and then more reflectively—or reflexively—to theological meanings, hoping thereby to establish some significance for theology in the developmental process. First we must ask what Christian theology *on its own terms* understands development to mean, and then use the answer as a conceptual framework to interpret and test the economic, social, and psychological meanings. In this regard, it is to the credit of Pope John Paul II that he declares the encyclical *Sollicitudo Rei Socialis* to be a *theological* investigation of the present world, leading (theologically) to a fuller concept of development.[1] It is true, of course, that he moves from development as an economic concept to a representation that is theologically and morally integrated, but he does so with prior theological awareness of where he is going. His treatment of international development must be understood primarily, therefore, as a reflection of his theology, and not as a religious gloss on social scientific interpretations.

In what follows I want to develop a way of thinking about international development that is theological from the outset, and interprets and uses within its own theological framework information drawn from other sources. I shall do so to some extent in conversation with *Sollicitudo Rei Socialis*; however, this essay should not be understood primarily as a commentary on the encyclical. I would call the approach "evangelical" if I could separate that term from its contemporary conservative religious, cultural, and political connotations, and use it in its proper sense of a reference to the good news of the gracious love of God in Jesus Christ as the sole foundation of our salvation, calling, and daily life. In any event I shall call it "contextual," referring thereby to the theological method of attempting to understand all things—all life processes, all relationships, all problems, all pasts, presents and futures—in the context of the reconciling work of God in Jesus Christ. This approach is not extended from or closely correlated with any single Christian tradition, but it clearly owes more to St. Paul, Augustine, the Reformers and John Wesley than to Thomas Aquinas and to the theological heritage of the Enlightenment.

There will be resistance, of course, to the effort to apply to international reality a theological framework associated usually with individual salvation and the individual Christian life. A quick response to any such resistance would be to argue that the separation of individual and social reality is a false one, because the self is social, and relationality is built into the concept of selfhood. That is true, of course, but the more pertinent response would be that the understanding of redemption used here is neither simply individual nor social but cosmic and is, therefore, both individual and social in a larger framework. The foundation of the argument I am making is that the reconciling action of God in Christ is the context in which the entire fallen creation is addressed with words of hope and love. It is the objective presupposition of the meaning and future of all being and experience. The notion of cosmic redemption, with institutional as well as individual implications, is a very old one, and any reduction of redemption to individual subjective experience constitutes a theological aberration.

Nevertheless, one must acknowledge that there are practical if not ontological differences between persons and groups, and that these differences became especially obnoxious when one attempts to apply to the life of groups theological concepts usually associated with individual salvation. One may have to speak analogically at times, but with the reassurance that analogies are translations of reality, and often may have great explanatory and even revelatory power.

Development in the Context of Reconciliation

Development, in its precise theological meaning, is the process whereby God brings the broken, sinful, and suffering world to its intended wholeness. Using one set of theological symbols, we speak of the process as the *ordo salutis*, the order of salvation. Using another set, we speak of it as the work of reconciliation. The merit of the former symbolization is that it identifies the necessary steps or stages in the process. It begins with the prevenient grace that discloses to humankind its desperate condition, and reveals to it both the impossibility of rescuing itself and the resources of salvation available to it as a free and unmerited gift. It moves then to repentance, the forgiveness of sins, restoration to favor with God, and the beginning of new life that grows graciously in love and in faithfulness to the divine calling. The merit of the latter symbolization is that it defines the problematic of development in relational terms of antagonism, hatred, brokenness, defensiveness, egoism, alienation—and interprets it in a cosmic context. God works in Christ to renew and reconcile the *kosmos*, the fallen creation, whose persons, institutions, animate and inanimate elements are prevented by the presence of sin from achieving the fullness of their intended destiny. The two sets of symbols refer, of course, to the same reality, and both presuppose the divine work in Christ as the foundation, context, enabling power, and definitive goal of development, theologically understood.

The methodological starting point for thinking theologically about development is the divine work of salvation in Jesus Christ, understood fundamentally as reconciliation. Genuine development is growth in relationships of love and trust, and in the capacity of will to support them even at great cost to oneself or one's group. It presupposes both the reality of sin and the objective work of deliverance from sin, the former because the cosmos is fallen, and the individual or corporate self with it, the latter because the self has no resources of its own sufficient to overcome the effects of the fall. Development requires a reasoned and willing response, to be sure, but it is a work of grace in the context of grace.

This interpretation of development as a process in the context of reconciliation, having the character of reconciliation and whole-making, differs from those prominent interpretations that understand development as the actualizing of the potential of creation, as the fulfillment of what is naturally given. Development, according to these views, may be understood as entelechic, i.e., as the unfolding of an inner nature toward an actualizing end, or as the emerging of naturally endowed capabilities in response to historically given opportunities. The developmental process may be characterized with biological models that represent it as beginning with the germination of a seed and moving through predetermined stages of birth, growth, maturity, and death. Fulfillment may be self-fulfillment, or a process that moves by means of enablement, assistance, and guidance.

An example of this understanding of development is set forth by Pope Paul VI in *Populorum Progressio*:

> In the design of God, every man is called upon to develop and fulfill himself, for every life is a vocation. At birth, everyone is granted, in germ, a set of aptitudes and qualities for him to bring to fruition. . . .
> He is aided, or sometimes impeded, by those who educate him and those with whom he lives, but each one remains, whatever be these influences affecting him, the principal agent of his own success or failure. By the unaided effort of his own intelligence and his will, each man can grow in humanity, can enhance his personal worth, can become more a person.[2]

In this passage the individual person is represented to be an entelechic seed, brought to flowering and fruitfulness through self-husbandry with some assistance from family and other educators. The assumptions concerning agency are largely Pelagian, and the relational understanding of selfhood is minimal.[3] On some other occasion we may discuss the charges of Pelagianism, but on this one we object to the germinal notion of the self and its development. Granted the reality and power of the genetic code, the self's development nevertheless cannot be explained in terms of entelechy, even with the assistance indicated. It is a reflexive, historical reality, with language, nationality, religion, and status, all of which affect mightily what it is, and none of which is reducible to the germ. The self is individual-social, a remarkable creation within history out of biologically and historically given materials. It is not a seed that sprouts and grows. Therefore, its creation must be understood from the standpoint of its historicity and relationality, and not fundamentally from its inherent potentiality.

To apply the point more broadly, our concerns with development are cultural, social, and historical. Development is a process in human society and of the shaping of human society, more than it is a process of the eliciting of the natural. Much of the discussion of development at the present time is associational or structural talk. We use the language of cooperation, organization, power, dependence/interdependence. If we talk about how to exploit or conserve or distribute the treasures of the earth, we evaluate the respective merits of economic and political systems, or organize alliances or regional associations, or plan the division of labor, or consider the alternatives of reform or revolution. Such talk refers to human beings and groups existing in history, to their national identities, ethnic particularities and rivalries, class associations and consciousness, relativities of poverty, affluence and power. The focus is not fundamentally on creation but on relationship and historicity, past, present and future. Development is, therefore, a matter of the formation, preservation and enhancement of sociality, leading often to authoritative and integral community, and at times to intensification of social antagonisms. It is an encounter with history, and with history even when it is an encounter with non-human creation. It is the continuing development of the products of history, the reshaping of culture in the decision between or among historically offered choices. It is not, in essence, the unfolding of the "natural" nor the linear actualization of potential.

These comments apply to any theological approach to development that is fundamentally creational in method, at least in the sense of engaging the creation in some direct way rather than through the media of society, culture, and history. That is why the theological method for inquiring into development cannot be "creational" without further qualification. But there is another reason that is at least as formidable, if not more so. We know the creation always through the effects of the fall, and never in its pristine purity. The problem may be conceptualized in various ways. One may contend, for example, that the effects of the fall have penetrated the entire creation to such an extent as to redefine its ontology—an argument found, for example, in efforts to explain the pervasive violence of non-human creation without attributing the violence to the intentional design of God. Or one may confess with Helmut Thielicke that the power given in creation to fulfill the divine intention has become a power for disorder, and now must be turned against itself to restrain its chaotic and disruptive tendencies.[4] Or one may contend that human beings always know and engage the non-human creation as fallen persons, thereby projecting their original and actual sin into whatever uses and cultural reconstructions they make of it. Whatever the explanation, the point is that we encounter a creation that must be dealt with developmentally as *fallen* creation, and not as what stood before in the beginning as very good. The implications of fallenness, therefore, are drawn into every theological account of development. A method that begins with creation *before* the fall, or does not regard the fall with radical seriousness, is unsuitable for theological thinking about international development.

Is the method of *Sollicitudo Rei Socialis* primarily creational? Clearly the entry into the issues of development is creational. The encyclical grounds the calling to development responsibility in the Book of Genesis—in the hierarchical order of creation, the understanding of human nature as *imago dei* (male and female), in the commission to exercise dominion over the animals and plants and bring forth the bounty of the earth. In doing so, it fights back—implicitly—against the charge of unsuitability by demonstrating that the creational approach clearly is scriptural, and that it is an essential dimension of any theological understanding of development.

The primacy of this creational approach to development appears to be confirmed by the explicit statement of confidence in human nature:

> The Church has *confidence also in man*, though she knows the evil of which he is capable. For she well knows that—in spite of the heritage of sin, and the sin which each one is capable of committing—there exist in

the human person sufficient qualities and energies, a fundamental "goodness" (cf. *Gen.* 1:31). . . .

This statement of confidence is qualified somewhat by the disclosure of its grounds:

. . . because he is the image of the creator, placed under the redemptive influence of Christ, who "united himself in some fashion with every man" and because the efficacious action of the Holy Spirit "fills the earth" (*Wis.* 1:7).[5]

But the qualification is a statement primarily about prevenient grace, and how it assists the created order in coming to fulfillment. It is not a claim that creation has lost, by reason of sin, its capacity to develop and be developed. Creational understanding and empowerment have been damaged by sin, but not radically, and not radically in the human creature as such. The theological focus of integration has not changed to fall or redemption. Development proceeds theologically from creation.

Subsequently, however, the encyclical moves to a Christological orientation, calling on Colossians 1:15-20 for the confession that all things are created in Christ, hold together in Him, and are restored to peace in Him through the reconciling work of God.[6] This maneuver is not explained, however, and a Protestant theologian may read too much into it (thinking of Karl Barth), or not enough. It seems to suggest that John Paul II does not want to encourage thinking of creation apart from redemption and, therefore, acknowledges a larger role for sin in the problem of development than a primary focus on creation would allow. Also, there is much in the encyclical to suggest the necessity of Christian faith, not only for the salvation of souls, but also for a proper understanding of development. That is implied, for example, in his claim that development is understood rightly only in the context of "the divine plan which is meant to order all things to the fullness which dwells in Christ (cf. *Col.* 1:19) and which he communicated to his body."[7] Although the creational thrust is powerfully at work in this encyclical, it is quite apparent that it does not work alone, and that the method cannot be designated "creational" without reservation.

In fact, the theological method for understanding development integrally seems to be the language of "divine plan," and not the primacy of either creation or Christology. In the architectonics of this vision, creation leads to Christ, follows from Christ, and is accompanied by Christ. Creation is through Christ, but is not to be understood only as a work of the second person of the Trinity. Christ as the end of creation neither simply "completes" creation, nor overshadows its unique significance. Creation must be fulfilled in salvation, but salvation does not annul or devalue what is drawn by human effort out of creation. People find their vocations in the context of the divine plan. Looking in one direction, it is the divine plan that they should govern the earth, respect, conserve and protect it, and elicit its plenitude for the benefit of all. Looking in another direction, it is the divine plan that they and all the rest of creation should be reconciled to God in the fullness of Christ. These views from the context of the divine plan are aspects of the same vocation.

This theological method, assuming I have identified it correctly, establishes both the intermediary character and the authority of the principle of solidarity which is central to the encyclical's message concerning the integral character of development. Solidarity can be read as a necessity arising out of the sociality of human nature. There can be no sustainable development without solidarity. But solidarity is not confirmed in its authority over human action unless and until it is seen and accepted as an expression of evangelical love. Up to that point the case for it is prudential and pragmatic: it is a disciplining condition of the fulfillment of self-interest. When seen from the perspective of reconciliation in Christ, solidarity draws on a willingness to sacrifice that transcends both self-interest and simple mutuality, and sets development in the course of the divine plan leading from creation to salvation.

This "higher plan" concept of the encyclical is quite similar to my conviction that the human enterprise, indeed the cosmic enterprise, must find its significance in the framework of the history of God's relationship to the world. Moreover, the Christological witness of the encyclical is welcome with its contention that the fullness of development is the fullness of Christ, and that the solidarity of interdependence must be confirmed ultimately by evangelical love. I remain troubled, however, by the "confidence in man" statement, and its optimistic outworkings in suppositions that leaders will fulfill their responsibilities to the poor of the world and to international society when they "come to realize" the necessity of solidarity to historically present interdependence, and in the real limitations of the "structures of sin" argument (to be discussed later). John Paul II apparently does not, after all, regard the creation as we know it as fallen creation only and, therefore, does not acknowledge the fundamental and persistent limits to international development, whatever the concept of development and whatever the structures that bear it.

Development in the context of reconciliation has an historical and social reference that is integral to its way of knowing and approaching reality. That is always so, because the focus is on the concreteness of existence. In that concreteness the material and moral realities of the creation come to expression. Because it is fallen creation, the expression always bears some resistance to solidarity and some tendencies toward disintegration, and the disordering powers must be turned against themselves to preserve the creation for the fulfillment of God's purposes. Because the fallen creation is caught up in the reconciling work of God in Christ, it draws on powers of renewal that transcend its self-imposed limitations and move through history to shape an international society that draws the fabric of community increasingly over the agents of disintegration and restraint.

International Development and International Community

What is it that is to be developed in the process of international development? In the most literal sense of the term it should be the relationships among the nations, or at least among the states in international society. In the development discussions of recent years, however, the concern has been less with international relations in the political sense than with the contrast between developed and underdeveloped, or less developed, societies. When this contrast is discussed in economic terms, "underdeveloped" refers variously to a role of dependency in the international economic system; to lack of possession of, or access to, adequate resources to provide for the minimum needs of the people of a society; to occupation of a primitive stage in the establishment and maturation of capitalism; to inadequate industrial capacity and infrastructure; to failure or inability to approximate autarchy. When discussed in political terms, it refers to endemic instability of administration and / or arbitrariness of power; to insufficiency of bureaucratic rationalization; to systemic disregard of the rights of individuals and groups; to lack or weakness of representative political institutions and other constitutional controls on power; to absence of a middle class of sufficient size, quality and economic clout to require and sustain such institutions and controls.

Each of these concerns is important, and each of them—by reason of the interconnectedness of domestic and international situations—is an aspect of international development. But their variety evades focus, and persons meeting to discuss international development may have quite different agendas, to say nothing of quite different priorities and perspectives.

The advantage—and at times disadvantage—of attempting to understand international development in the theological context of reconciliation is that it provides a perspective on the whole, that at the same time is a call to wholeness. In this context one attempts to think of world relationships and conflicts as a *polis* in the process of becoming, an integral community whose participants are members but who are not yet aware of and committed to their membership. The implications of this orientation are several. One is that it identifies international development as essentially a political and not an economic process. Its primary and continuing work is that of creating political community. A second implication is that it internalizes the various aspects and agents of development in a comprehensive political community where they are perceived as having systemic relationships of considerable importance but which may not yet have a history or empirical visibility. A third is that it identifies certain central features or problems of international community as a community coming into being, and makes them the primary agenda for international development.

Some of the major agenda items of the third implication are the following:

Protection and preservation of the emergent community and its components
Development of institutions of cooperation and control
Formation of a common consciousness and ethos
Relating power to authority
Assuring equitable participation in the community of all its members.

I shall deal with these items in the course of subsequent theological discussion and, therefore, shall only list them here. What they point to sociologically is the formation of an international community at what Luigi Sturzo called a secondary level of sociality. It is a social form that becomes historically necessary and assumes a character of primary importance, but it is on a secondary level "because it cannot be considered original and is not irresolvable into other forms of sociality, from which it draws the elements for its constitution and development."[8] Theologically, however, what they point to are the relationships and expectations of common humanity coming to expression in social formations that transcend human particularity without discarding it. It is the vocation of international development to work primarily on these issues, whatever else it does. And whatever else it does is to be done within this political framework, if it is rightly to be called international development.

I use the term "international community" rather than "international society" even though the latter more accurately characterizes present empirical reality. Most of what is international is associated loosely, and not fastened with the intimate bonds of community. But the notion of community characterizes the process of politicization, whereas association suggests nothing more secure and comprehensive than contractual relationships.

Of course, "international" also is misleading, given the inclusiveness of the social reality with which we are dealing. The state system certainly is a central aspect, if not *the* central aspect, of the community in the process of becoming. But the social reality, understood in its whole-making context, is much more than the state system. It includes families, churches, economic institutions, educational associations, friendships, etc. Moreover, these multiform relationships penetrate the borders and legal barriers of states, domesticating their sovereignty within the comprehensive community. Nevertheless, "international" signals the points at which the most significant power relations are established. In the absence of a symbol that is more comprehensive of the social reality and descriptive of the problems of the agenda, it is the one we must use.

The absence of any mention of justice as a component of the community coming into being is not an oversight, nor does it imply anything concerning the relative importance of justice, either morally or prudentially. Justice certainly is of central importance on both counts, but it is expressed in and through all items on the agenda, and is not a separate consideration. Justice is fundamentally at issue, for example, in the distribution and control of power and in the affirmation of human rights.

Transformation of the Order of Preservation

Earlier I wrote of the theological argument to the effect that the powers of the fallen creation must be turned against themselves to provide an order in which the inhabitants of the creation can live. That argument brings the notion of preservation to the fore, and identifies it as a work of God, God the preserver being one of the modes in which God relates to the world. Institutions of whatever kind, existing for whatever other purposes, serve the preserving work of God in a fallen world, stabilizing the order under their administration and protecting those in their care. The state exists primarily, although not exclusively, for that purpose and is known in one of its dimensions as an order of preservation.

The fallenness of creation does not change in principle, sin does not go out of style (although styles of sinning change), and chaos lurks always at the heart of even the most tranquil order. Therefore, preservation remains a need at the heart of every social order and every social process.

To this perennial condition we add the effects of human ingenuity in the developmental process, and come up with problems that would dazzle the most imaginative portrayers of the effects of original sin. In the latter part of the twentieth century the enhancement of technological and scientific capabilities of warfare, assisted by political and ideological contributions to the nature of war, have raised the prospects of global destruction and misery to a level unimaginable even as recently as the early part of this century. These apocalyptic war threats have been joined recently by a number of other types of ''preservation'' issues, also global in reach, some of which may prove to be deadlier than war because already they are working their destructive effects on the human race and no longer come simply under the heading of ''risk.'' I refer to such problems as the destruction of the ozone layer, the pollution of land, air and water, the elimination of rain forests, international terrorism, AIDS, the permanent loss of arable land, famine, and others that could be added to a growing list.

Do not these issues put the question of preservation at the center of international development, and especially of theoretical thinking about international development? Some of these problems are themselves the products of development of a particular kind, such as technological or economic, that proceeded along a line of considerable success without asking serious questions of the impact of its ''progress'' on the conditions of planetary life. And some proposals for specifically international development risk making the same mistakes in the effort to open the riches of the world to the benefit of its inhabitants. But whatever may be said on these points, the fact is that these problems are international in character; they are not the bad luck or retribution of any particular society, even though some may feel the effects more than others, or may be more responsible for them than others. They require controls on action, and the controls must be international, the products of common consent. They demand sacrifices of value, and the values lost must be compensated. But as unrelenting issues of preservation they stand athwart every other path to international development.

The theological orientation to this type of problem most likely to see it as a problem presumably would be the traditional theology of the order of preservation. It would take with complete seriousness both the threats to disorder and destruction which the type of problem poses, and the need to impose freedom-limiting order in the interests of protection and preservation. To that point it would make an indispensable contribution, but it would not likely go beyond that point to carry out the developmental functions necessary to effective control, namely, those that constitute the other agenda items of politicization listed in the previous section. The central difficulty is that preservation is a limiting concept, not a developmental concept, and is not equipped on its own terms to go beyond the imposition of limits to a fuller understanding of the political necessities of the process.

On the other hand, theological approaches that diminish the radical effects of the fall are less equipped theologically to speak to ordering requirements, even if they have a better understanding of other aspects of development. They are more likely to place too much trust in persons and processes, including the processes of democratization, socialization, or international capitalism. And a liberationist approach is not prepared on its own fundamental terms to project these ordering requirements because its principal message is one of freedom from re-straining order.

Putting the matter in the context of divine reconciliation covers the theological requisites, however, because it acknowledges the problem of sin forthrightly and continuously, and submits the restraining and controlling mechanisms to a process of the creation of authorizing community and ethos. Reconciliation, let us remember, is not limited to the patching up of quarrels, and it is not a form of conflict avoid-ance. It is a renewal of the cosmos, of a divinely given order plunged continually toward chaos through rebellion against its source. Fallen cosmos requires preservation to stem its bent towards chaos. Preserva-tion, therefore, is an instrument of reconciliation, and its instrumen-tality requires that its force be authorized by the consent of a commu-nity which begins to emerge around a problem that cries out for a work of preservation.

Other aspects of the process of politicization will be dealt with more fully in the following section. In this section it has been my intention to focus the process of international development on fundamental is-sues of preservation, and to show how preservation is included—necessarily—in the work of reconciliation.

International Development in the *Ordo Salutis*

The process of international development, as I stated earlier, can be symbolized and examined theologically in terms of stages of the order of salvation. To do so is the work of most of the remainder of this pa-per. I shall give particular attention to ways in which the stages illumi-nate the so-called "agenda items" of the process of creating an inter-national community as a political community.

Prevenient grace. In the order of salvation there is a point at which a person is brought to awareness of his or her sinful condition and its seriousness, and is offered the possibilities of repentance and a new life. The work of God in preparing this opening is known as prevenient grace, literally the grace that "comes before," because it is not contin-gent on human will or seeking, or even on recognition that the condi-tion in which one stands imperils the soul.

If we use the concept of prevenient grace to explore analogically the process of international development, we become aware of moments of history that are revelatory in the dual sense of disclosing a common peril and pointing to the necessity of international cooperation to cope with it. The most notable of such moments in recent memory surely was the dropping of the atomic bomb on Hiroshima in August 1945. In that event the world was able to see the combination of war and radically new technology and, in the light of the explosion, to read its own future. The early prospects for international control of the technology never were as strong as the hopes that supported them, and they slid rather quickly into the bilateralism of arms build-up and deterrence. Nevertheless, the revelation was sufficiently sobering to stay the military use of nuclear weapons to the present time, to deter war between the world's principal military powers, and to stimulate sporadic bilateral and multilateral efforts in weapons control and war prevention.

Other events of similar function might be mentioned. Most of the states of the world opposed the takeover of the U.S. embassy in Tehran by Irani militants, even though some of them detested the United States, and many others were content to see the United States embarrassed. The explanation for near-unanimity in opposition was that all of them recognized the sanctity of embassies as the basis of international diplomacy, and what they saw in the Iran case was a surge of barbarism that threatened the order at its foundations. The list of ''problems of preservation'' set forth in the preceding section also is a set of illuminating warnings concerning increasingly dangerous dimensions of the human condition.

However, the point is not to develop a catalog of such events but to call attention to their significance for international development. They are occasions of awareness of the linkage of national survival interests with international survival interests. As such they are more than simply moments of new awareness with matching opportunities. Rather, they are *kairos* moments in which to shape policies, enact treaties and establish institutions. If the *kairos* is not grasped as the fullness of time, the chances for conserving the conditions of temporal existence may be missed. The grace that forces awareness upon us may be irresistible, but the grace that enables our response is not.

Moreover, the *kairos* character pertains only to the possibilities for action. The threatening conditions do not pass. They endure and grow worse, inasmuch as they have been built technologically into the common consciousness, the value systems and the institutional structures, not only of particular societies but increasingly of the world as a whole. Persons of vision and commitment will recognize these events as global necessities and opportunities, not simply as considerations of national interest, and will attempt to evoke a global response. It is the proper and necessary work of the process of international development to recognize the *kairos* and move dialectically to translate threats and responses into corporate and cooperative instruments, thereby institutionalizing elements of emergent international community.

Justification. The phenomenon just discussed involves cooperative response to a common threat, but primarily from the standpoint of self-interest. Any qualifications of autonomy and self-regard arise in the course of formulating and authorizing the means for coping with the threat, and not from any principle or norm that calls them into question from some standpoint other than that of the interested self. However, a qualitative step beyond self-interest is indicated by the context of reconciliation. It is the recognition of a common humanity that transcends and relativizes particular historic identities, including national, tribal, religious and racial identities, yet without destroying or dismissing them.

In the context of reconciliation, the common humanity is the new humanity in Jesus Christ. It is a reality that breaks down dividing walls of hostility, inviting individuals and groups in their socially constructed identities to share in the creation of emergent community beyond and above their differences. We must note with emphasis that this common humanity is not something we have naturally, as coming from original creation. The common nature we have naturally is sinful nature. It is precisely that nature which reinforces egoism with moral and religious rationalizations, and prevents the formation of community on grounds other than those that give primacy to self-interest. By contrast, the new humanity that we have in Christ is a redeemed nature, one that stands objectively before us as a gift and a possibility.

In its presence as possibility, the new nature is the work of *sanctification*, a process I shall discuss later. In its presence as gift, the new nature is the status of *justification*, i.e., of the forgiveness of sins, of the gracious restoration to favor with God without qualifying merit of our own. Justification is the condition of humankind before God in the objectivity of the reconciling work in Christ.

Justification in political reference implies a denial of all pretensions to establish a particular historic identity as the norm for humanity as such. Conversely, it is the rejection of all demeaning stereotypes that imply or state a less than fully human status for persons or groups with a different historic identity. The former tendency is idolatry; the latter is a denial of the cross and resurrection of Christ. Both are expressions of the fallen nature, and those who manifest them in their own thought and action know the new humanity in Jesus Christ only as a law that condemns them, and to which they cannot conform.

Justification in moral-juridical reference is the source and final norm of all claims and expectations and, therefore, of the reciprocity of rights and duties. To put the matter that way is not to suggest there is a catalog of expectations that can be sought and discovered through faithful inquiry and then applied to legislation and moral practice. It is to suggest, however, that all morals, laws and policies that exhibit the tendencies identified above have the character only of the fallen world and not of the gift and possibility offered in Jesus Christ. Those that have the character of gift and possibility express an understanding of humanity and human responsibility that transcends the particular historic identities which routinely serve as norm and limit for political and legal action. They register the status of justification.

Up to this point I have written mainly of the objectivity of justification. That is a necessary emphasis to avoid reducing the gift to pure subjectivity of individual feeling. But one must deal nonetheless with the *experience* of justification, because it is through experience that the new humanity becomes intentional in action. Here again we must make rough translations, and speak analogically, because we need to apply the concept to the actions of groups in the process of international development, and groups do not have consciousness, reasoning power and will of the same kind and to the same degree that individuals have.

The individual person's experience of justification is the assurance, witnessed by the holy spirit, that he or she is forgiven by and restored to favor with God. Justification is attended by repentance, which is sorrow over the sin which one has committed and of which one has been a part, and the turning toward Christ for the beginning of a new life. We should not attempt to force all those implications on the life and actions of groups in international relations, but should speak analogically of the experience of justification as the awakening to an authentically political form of participation in international politics. What I mean is that the group, usually the state, experiencing the political counterpart of justification, will act in international politics with a sense of membership, and with the will to encourage and facilitate the coming into existence of an international community that would internalize the relationships of states and provide the criteria and context of their authorization. That does not necessarily imply intending the formation of a world government and the transfer to it of state power and authority. It implies rather that, by reason of membership in the process of international politicization, the state's policies and implementation efforts will be disciplined by its recognition of the rights and needs of others, its desire to shape relationships of reciprocity grounded in trust and commonality of interest, and its intention to act as a member of the society of states and not as dominator or outlaw. That may be as close as we can come to translating the experience of justification into the processes of international society, but the reorientation of national interest thinking to political thinking, thusly defined, would be a major step in the process of international development, and it would not imply a principled renunciation of national interests.

The political self-definition of the state in international relations is the reverse of the military definition. In the latter, the concept of international society is that of the war of all against all. The preoccupation of the state is with national security, and the face it turns toward the world (as well as toward its own people) is primarily a military face.[9] In the former, the concept of international society is that of an incipient order of self- and mutual limitation which strives to civilize the instruments of force by subordinating them to instruments of political control and, in consequence, reducing their importance as means and symbols of security. A state that attempts to find security through massive organization for war has a radically different concept of identity and authorization of power from one that seeks security in some combination of political construction and modest military preparedness. The latter has a taste of what the theologians mean by justification; the former knows only the fears and boasts of self-hypnotic vulnerability and belligerency.

Additional evidences of participation in justification include the following: commitment to human rights as an integral and credible dimension of foreign policy; renunciation of violent, chauvinistic, stereotyping rhetoric ("the Great Satan," "the Evil Empire," etc.);

rejection of military spectaculars designed and timed to build domestic political support; encouragement of regional governments to deal with regional conflicts, avoiding great power intervention; the overcoming of memories of intergroup hostilities, especially those that have long histories and are culturally pervasive. It is clear from this list that national self-righteousness and the experience of justification are contradictory. With common humanity all the members of international society are under judgment, and all must receive the gift of new possibilities from one another.

Sanctification. Sanctification, literally, is the process of becoming holy. Applied to international relations, the characterization seems strange if not bizarre, and hardly credible. Also, it carries some risk of religious imperialism as well as of the sacralizing of power. However, if we translate sanctification as the process of becoming whole, we have a characterization of international development that is congruent with its nature and possibilities, and that also is theologically sound. Wholeness is the biblical *shalom*, the Hebrew word for peace. It is the integral vision of John Paul II, in *Sollicitudo Rei Socialis*. It is the understanding of development that arises in the context of reconciliation. Sanctification as wholeness is, therefore, an appropriate symbol for understanding the possibilities of international development.

There are two principal aspects of sanctification. One is "breaking the power of cancelled sin," to use the words of Charles Wesley's hymn. It is the destroying of the residual power of sin that remains to constrain and threaten the quality of new life in Christ even after the guilt of sin has been removed through justification. The other is growth in grace and love, acquiring the mind of Christ, "going on to perfection." When we adjust these two aspects of sanctification for social application, they raise basic questions for the process of international development.

The persisting "power of cancelled sin" prompts fundamental inquiries about the hindrances to development, and whether and how these hindrances could be removed. *Sollicitudo Rei Socialis* offers several explanations of the hindrance question. None of the explanations, so far as I can see, is examined thoroughly, and they are not brought into systematic relationship with each other. One proposal, fundamental to the encyclical as a whole, is that the process is limited and distorted by the intellectual error of misunderstanding the nature of development itself. Policies are guided by partial understandings of development, not by an integral one, and practice omits the most necessary element, namely, the moral principle of solidarity. Another set of proposals pertains to patterns and systems of organization, interaction, and control. There is a "politics of blocs" that divides the world, prompts militarism and imperialism, diverts the resources of human need to arms production, and turns leaders from their cooperative world responsibilities. Also, there are social, economic, and financial mechanisms, referred to sometimes as "evil mechanisms," that operate almost automatically, always to the advantage of the wealthy and powerful who control them, and exacerbate the patterns of wealth and poverty. Another proposal, one of theological and moral character, is that "structures of sin" underlie these other forms of hindrance and prompt their negative response to the logic of interdependence and solidarity, or perhaps are to be equated with them.

Although I cannot comment on each of these explanations independently, I must offer observations on some of their relationships and implications. One of the most striking aspects of this view of the pathology of development is the paucity of serious structural analysis. One would expect that an argument for integral understanding of development would give careful attention to political and economic analysis, while emphasizing, of course, the otherwise neglected dimensions of moral and religious analysis. The "systems" and "mechanisms" are not named, although apparently they refer to international capitalism. Nor are they subjected to serious economic analysis, an inquiry which presumably would disclose their functions, possibilities, and limitations. When the encyclical asks "in what way and to what extent" liberal capitalism and Marxist collectivism are "capable of changes and updatings such as to favour or promote a true and integral development of individuals and peoples in modern society," it does not answer the question, but conveys the implication that the changes and updatings could be made by their adopting the Pope's idea of integral development. What one needs to know—by way of social scientific analysis—is whether they are inherently capable of such "changes and updatings," or inherently incapable and, therefore, to be cast aside.

The division of the world into two blocs is problematical enough, because the world, including the "blocs" themselves, is more diverse and complex than that model suggests. What may be even more problematical is the suggestion of the encyclical that the division derives from ideological differences which, when corrected by an integral understanding of development, presumably would disappear, allowing the principle of solidarity to claim its universalizing and harmonizing role. The encyclical suggests that the bloc-pattern is geopolitical, but makes no geopolitical analysis of whether international conflicts and patterns of power relationships may be rooted in enduring factors—especially geographical factors—not reducible to ideological differences. Also, it complains about excessive concern with security, but offers no clue as to what a proper concern for security would be on the basis of geopolitical analysis.

The references to "structures of sin" sound promising, until one discovers that the Pope is referring to accumulations of individual sins that lie behind these mechanisms and divisions and prompt their recalcitrance and wickedness. He is not referring to what is *structurally* problematical, that is, to what is characteristic of the structures that requires them in their normal way of operating to sin against the integral understanding of development. The problem of international structures and systems is not that they are constitutionally incapable of affirming solidarity and promoting the common good, but that they provide occasion for and bring to expression the two most typical sins—the "all-consuming desire for profit" and the "thirst for power."[10] It is not surprising, therefore, that the Pope should see the problem confronting the poor as "the inefficiency or corruption of the public authorities,"[11] and not their domination by repressive and unjust structures that may be neither inefficient nor corrupt. Nor is it surprising that the fundamental correctives to the hindrances to international development should be intellectual correction—holding an integral, not a partial view of development—and conversion.[12]

Such failures of analysis make the liberationist treatments of development more plausible. Liberation theologians, especially the Latin Americans, challenge the term "development" itself. In their view, the contemporary discussions of development presuppose the continuation of the world economic structure of capitalist investment with its military and political support systems.[13] They see that as a fundamental error. Reforming the present system simply reinforces its inequalities and oppressiveness and confirms its materialist conception of human good. To serve justice and the common good the system must be replaced, not improved. The controlling concept, therefore, should be neither development nor conversion, but liberation.

On the other hand, liberation is not a simple substitute for development. Even if liberation movements were to succeed in seizing and holding power, they would face development issues on the terms they have established, and with the human nature and domestic and international political implications that attend any approach to development. Moreover, their hypotheses concerning socialization as the way to authentic wholeness are compromised by the enthusiasm which most socialist governments now are showing for the market system. What we can and must say with the liberationists, however, is that conflict is a more serious problem than the gradualists make it out to be, and that in some situations the prospects for integral development, or something approximating it, rest on radical changes in the political, economic, and social structures of societies. There may be theological and moral grounds for declaring a deontological ban on revolutionary and violent means, but when doing so—in those situations—one must acknowledge the probable surrender of the possibilities of authentic or integral development.

Also, we must resist the temptation to see the development process as an entity manageable in its entirety, and to view it primarily from the side of the system that is weighted with power and money. There is no single prescription for removing the hindrances to development, because the process is multi-faceted and because it will be seen differently from different perspectives. All the more reason why it is necessary to see the system from the underside, as free as we can be of the rationalizations with which we protect particular interested approaches to development. All the more reason why it is necessary for those who are not on the underside to be prodded and provoked by those who are, because those who view and control from the topside may be the principal hindrances to integral development.

In this connection, I must report that I see the encyclical addressing the problem of development more from the topside than the underside. I have seen the statement to the effect that the Church stands with the poor, but I read most of the recommendations as being addressed primarily to persons and groups with extensive power, admonishing them to fulfill their responsibilities to the poor, thereby enabling them to make their own special contributions.

Regrettably, the hindrances to international development cannot be removed in any final and fundamental sense, even though significant changes occur in domestic and international society. Sin is present as original sin in all humankind, and it pervades all structures despite—and at times because of—all efforts to perfect them. The world is bounteous but finite, and human needs are great, and the human imagination to fabricate desires is greater still. The leaders of states may be persons of good will, but they will feel morally bound to secure the needs of their own states before attending to the good of others, and especially in conflict with others they will find some transcendent justification for their commitments.

In international society, therefore, it may not be possible to break the power of cancelled sin, certainly with any finality, but it is possible to control sin as power, and it is necessary to control power even when it appears to be benign and not sinful. On the one hand, the problem of hindrances to development points to the limitation of power, always with the assistance of some balancing mechanisms, even though the balance of power seldom is enough to provide stable order. On the other hand, it points to equity (not necessarily equality) in the distribution of power, for power that is radically out of balance with respect to its distribution almost certainly will be the occasion of injustice and, therefore, almost certainly a threat both to the order of distribution and to the prospects for development.

At this point we see even more clearly than before that the development of international society involves a reordering of the power of the society. In this respect the development is conflictual and unstable. Much of the reordering must be accomplished from below, as the people of the underside attempt to establish the concreteness of their justification. It cannot and will not be handed out by the people of the topside, nor can nor should they control the redistribution. The order of power that supports the future of international development must be a common creation. If not, what reaches out into the coming years will be stagnation or chaos or retrogression, but not development.

The second aspect of sanctification, and the one that bears the quality and substance of wholeness, is growth in grace and love. In international society, grace is mutual acceptance and respect, a temporal fruition of the common humanity established in justification. Love is mutual, not sacrificial. To the degree that these qualities are present in international society, there is freedom to be vulnerable, to live with lessened dependence on weapons, to enjoy, express and explore cultural and religious differences; Lazarus sits at the banquet table, not only as a guest but also as a host and, optimally, as a member of the family. Solidarity moves processively to confirm interdependence, and is confirmed itself by reconciliation.

In the context of reconciliation, however, one looks at the process and not only at the desired outcome. This allows one to have a sense of possibility, while retaining awareness of the eschatological struggle that qualifies every gain. The process in large part is a processing of power. As we have seen in discussing the side of sanctification that deals with the hindrances to wholeness, the ever-pressing power of the fallen creation must be turned against itself and used for developmental ends, partly through control and restraint, and partly through equity of distribution. The other side of the sanctification process recognizes that power is not simply force but a combination of force and consent. Growth of the consent dimension of power decreases the arbitrariness of both its possession and its exercise. It makes power increasingly an expression of community and, as power becomes coterminous with the community and serves and integrates it, its authority increases. Therefore, the primary form which sanctification takes in international society is the commitment of power to authority, which is simply another way of looking at the growing solidarity of the community itself.

The development of authority in international society has several manifestations, each of which reflects the wholeness that follows from and anticipates reconciliation. The first is the growing authority of international institutions to handle tasks appropriate to their status in the international system at any given point in time. One anticipates that their authority will expand more in times of peace than in times of tension because, where conflict is actual or threatened, the states—especially the strongest ones—normally will be less willing to yield their freedom of action to the control of some other body. However, the effectiveness with which the international institutions perform their tasks in times either of peace or of conflict will enhance their authority and, thereby, their ability to deflect, limit, and mediate the occasions of conflict.

A second manifestation is the growing authority of human rights in the common consciousness of the peoples of the world. Rights may have authority in the minds of philosophers, but they have no influence over power until they are confirmed in an ethos that power must respect. They achieve agenda status by way of proclamation and advocacy, and some degree of juridical status by way of formulation in international codes, and serious political status when governments are compelled by internal and external pressures to lift them to a level that limits governmental power and makes their enforcement an enduring policy objective. These statuses are layers of authorization that shape the consciousness of peoples and confirm human rights in their particularity as both aspects of power and objects of power by reason of the authority of their moral claims.

A third manifestation is the practice of governments to seek authorization from the international community for their exercises of force in international politics, rather than acting simply on their own judgment of interest and then hoping to collect the authorization that accrues to a winner. Authority from the international community is sought in various ways: in the forums and courts of international organizations, through prior consultation with friends and allies, by inducing others to join the action, by eliciting invitations to act, by attempting or at least alleging conformity with international law. Many such efforts are nothing more than dishonest public relations ploys, but the fact that states reach for them testifies that international authorization is an element of power. It is a sign, however weak, of the growth of the consciousness of international community. It is evidence of a tendency to locate compliance with the just war criterion of competent authority in the context of international community.

Authorization as evidence of sanctification may seem remote from the theological meaning of the term, but it is not when we place the process of international development in the context of the reconciliation of the fallen cosmos. The growth of community toward wholeness, reflected in and requiring the maturation of authority, is a sign of peace and justice and, therefore, of the whole-making work of God.

But does the process of sanctification go on to perfection in the form of a world public authority, presiding over a fully integrated world community? Interestingly, that is not the apparent vision of *Sollicitudo Rei Socialis* and, in that respect, the encyclical differs from other recent documents of the magisterium. John Paul II's picture of solidaristic international society is that of a society of autonomous, democratic states, living at peace with and respecting one another, and using certain international institutions to serve the common good. If he anticipates and hopes for an even more integrated world community, he does not write of it in the encyclical. Although common-good language is used throughout, the concepts of perfect society and subsidiarity do not arise to project the process to a higher and more comprehensive level of international organization.[14]

I agree. Humankind is capable of something more than an unstable balance of power. It can work out relationships of reciprocity based on a degree of trust grounded in past performance, and it can draw truth into political rhetoric processively to replace hypocrisy, cynical lying, and righteous self-deception. It can fashion institutions of cooperation and mutual restraint that reflect those capacities. But it will do all these things in and through the persistent sinfulness of the fallen creation that qualifies all efforts to fashion community, even though it cannot fully defeat them.

Integral Thinking about International Development

Sollicitudo Rei Socialis acknowledges that the term ''development'' comes from the social and economic sciences, but insists that an understanding of development limited to those dimensions will be truncated and defective. An authentic and workable concept of development is an integral one. An integral understanding of development includes at least the following aspects: It acknowledges the cultural and political dimensions of development along with the economic ones; it recognizes the developmental implications of humankind's vocation to salvation, as well as of its temporal existence and material necessities; it correlates human developmental concerns with care of and respect for the non-human elements of creation; and it insists on moral criteria, not only economic criteria, for evaluating the course and results of development.

With no reservations, I subscribe to that integral understanding of development. Yet my way of integral thinking about development is different from that of the encyclical. John Paul II's method is one of completing and correcting. To what is offered by others in the way of concepts of development, he adds what is missing, namely, the moral principle of solidarity and the religious commitments of reconciliation and conversion. My method is a contextual one. Theologically integral thinking is done in the context of reconciliation, where one considers the concreteness of person, group, and process within the whole-making work of God. There one cannot miss the disintegration of the fallen cosmos that penetrates and permeates all human works and associations, nor can one postpone a work of renewal already in effect with the cross and resurrection. With regard to international development, the context discloses the points of disorder and destruction that require works of preservation, and the relationships of power that require authority. Preservation is for the sake of the emerging community, and authorization is coeval with the emerging community. Providing for both is the proper work of international development in the context of reconciliation.

One other thing: The encyclical derives fundamental—although not final—dimensions of vocation from the Genesis story of creation, and finds in that vocational setting the principles of dominion, hierarchy and obedience. What I find there is stewardship. The process of politicization in the context of reconciliation that calls the international community into being turns away from dominion, hierarchy and obedience, and issues a call to membership, participation and mutuality. It presents us with the common care of creation, and of one another, entrusted to us by God.

Notes

1. Pope John Paul II, *On Social Concern: Sollicitudo Rei Socialis* (Washington, D.C.: U. S. Catholic Conference, 1987), Sec. 4, p. 7, footnoted henceforth as *SRS*.

2. Pope Paul VI, *On the Development of Peoples: Populorum Progressio* (Boston: St. Paul's Editions, 1967), Sec. 15, p. 11. This entelechic understanding of development does not appear in *SRS*, so far as I know.

3. In *Populorum Progressio* the "actualizing of potential" argument is not applied directly to groups. One finds such an application, for example, in Oswald Spengler's theory of the history of cultures, in which the course of development is plotted in predictable stages arising out of a monadic cell. See his *The Decline of the West* (New York: A. A. Knopf, 1962). One finds the application also in racial arguments where capabilities for or limits to development are attributable to natural endowments. In the discussion following the presentation of the basic elements of this paper, Dennis McCann raises the question as to whether there are not historical entelechies in the life of groups that could be traced in such processes as routinization and bureaucratization. I agree that such patterns are present, and that their emergence often can be anticipated, but the certainty that they are entelechies derives from observing

them after they have taken historical form. The "stages of economic growth" paradigm is a case in point. In retrospect the stages seem to represent a deterministic pattern, but once the pattern is known, particular societies may be able to alter it to serve their own desires, perhaps by leaping over one or more "stages." I have observed, moreover, that what appear to be historical entelechies are ambiguous in effect. The idea of Messianism, derived from Judaism and transmitted through Christianity, continues to work powerfully in human history, but its effects are both good and evil.

4. See Helmut Thielicke, *Theological Ethics*, II: *Politics* (Philadelphia: Fortress Press, 1969), especially Chapter 14, "The Biblical Concept of the State," pp. 235-255.

5. *SRS*, Sec. 47, pp. 94-95.

6. *SRS*, Sec. 31, p. 56.

7. *SRS*, Sec. 31, p. 57.

8. Luigi Sturzo, *The Inner Laws of Society* (New York: P. J. Kennedy & Sons, 1944), p. 129. Sturzo was an Italian priest, sociologist, and political leader who founded the Italian Popular Party, forerunner of the Christian Democratic Party of Italy.

9. José Comblin, *The Church and the National Security State* (Maryknoll, N.Y.: Orbis Press, 1979).

10. *SRS*, Sec. 37, p. 71.

11. *SRS*, Sec. 39, p. 75.

12. *SRS*, Sec. 38, p. 73. See also Sec. 37, pp. 71-72.

13. See the authoritative statement on this topic by Gustavo Gutierrez, in *A Theology of Liberation* (Maryknoll, N.Y.: Orbis Press, 1973, Chapter Two, "Liberation and Development," pp. 21-42.

14. For a discussion of recent Roman Catholic views on international order see Theodore R. Weber, "Theological Symbols of International Order," *A Journal of Church and State*, 29 (Winter 1987), pp. 79-99.

Eleven

John Paul II and International Development

Ernest J. Bartell, C.S.C.

In his most recent social encyclical, *Sollicitudo Rei Socialis*, Pope John Paul II uses the twentieth anniversary of the landmark international encyclical of Paul VI, *Populorum Progressio*, to extend and update his own teaching on international development, some of which is already apparent in his earlier social encyclicals, *Redemptor Hominis* and *Laborem Exercens*. Since the time of John XXIII's *Mater et Magistra* and *Pacem in Terris*, Catholic social teaching has increasingly been directed at the issues of international development, especially as it affects the welfare of the less developed countries of the world and, in so doing, has addressed itself increasingly beyond the borders of the Catholic Church to the world at large. John Paul II's earlier social encyclicals included international references, but put less emphasis on international issues, especially those affecting Third World development, than the social encyclicals of John XXIII and Paul VI. What John Paul II has done in *Sollicitudo Rei Socialis* is to extend more explicitly the distinctive features of the social thought in his earlier encyclicals to the issues of contemporary international development, at the same time incorporating much of the analysis of Paul VI's *Populorum Progressio*, the anniversary of which *Sollicitudo Rei Socialis* commemorates.

The results suggest a perceptible shift in the social thought of John Paul II from that of Paul VI, especially in three areas to be considered here: the relationship of faith to social justice, the specification of policy changes for authentic international development, and the role of the Church as social actor in the resolution of issues affecting the moral and ethical quality of international development.

Not surprisingly, John Paul II follows papal tradition by affirming the continuity of his own thought with that of his predecessors to demonstrate the "perennial value" of Catholic social teaching.[1] He is clear in affirming that he wishes to extend the "appeal to conscience" that characterizes the teaching of his predecessors and that, like them, he wishes to emphasize the "ethical and cultural character" of development issues.[2]

Papal tradition downplays change in its teaching, so John Paul typically understates the force of changes in his social teaching by, for example, subsuming those changes within his affirmation of "renewal" as a major motive behind his latest social encyclical. Rather than calling attention to differences between his social thought and that of his predecessors, John Paul II puts forth his intention to "extend the impact" of the teaching of Paul VI to the "present historical moment." In so doing he retains, but modifies, the links between Catholic social teaching and contemporary analytic methodology and literature on international development that distinguished the social teaching of Paul VI in *Populorum Progressio* from that of his predecessors, especially Leo XIII and Pius XII. These links helped Catholic social teaching to address a larger world on development issues, rather than to set down a system of beliefs for Catholics. At the same time, these links have exposed Catholic social teaching to comparative analysis, critical evaluation, and intellectual and political controversy.

Faith and Social Justice

Like Paul VI, John Paul II has drawn upon contemporary development literature to elaborate his arguments, and in *Sollicitudo Rei Socialis* he is even more explicit than Paul VI in acknowledging that the terminology of development originates within "the social and economic sciences."[3] Nevertheless, in *Laborem Exercens* and in *Sollicitudo Rei Socialis* there is a difference in the way he draws upon the concepts and methodological formulations of the social sciences to reach his moral conclusions.

On one hand, in *Laborem Exercens*, the major labor encyclical of John Paul II, the analysis is based much more on social observation and less on deduction from natural law than was either of the two major labor encyclicals of his predecessors, *Rerum Novarum* of Leo XIII and *Quadragesimo Anno* of Pius XII. In this respect he follows the lead of Paul VI who broke with the tradition of natural law reasoning that dominated earlier social encyclicals to utilize a much more inductive analysis of the problems of international development.

John XXIII previously had begun to emphasize analysis of social structures in an international context, but his evaluations still rested heavily on principles deduced from natural law reasoning.[4] Paul VI, following the lead of the Second Vatican Council, especially the Council document *Gaudium et Spes*, introduced into papal social encyclicals an explicit pluralism of sources for his moral judgments. His analysis of the economic relations between the less and more developed nations, for example, draws heavily on the dependency literature that was burgeoning in the fields of economics, political science and sociology at the time.[5] Moreover, he refrains from basing his ethical analysis on a single philosophic or theological tradition and never refers to a social *doctrine* of the Church as his predecessor did but, instead, speaks of Catholic social *teaching*. Although Paul VI is perhaps less tolerant of socialism than was John XXIII, especially in *Octogesima Adveniens*, his criticisms of socialism include descriptive critical analysis of the history of socialist regimes along with the philosophical objections repeated by his predecessors back to Leo XIII.[6]

The methodological pluralism of Paul VI allowed him to identify a wide variety of sources of social injustice, especially in the form of market imperfections and structural biases that affect the distribution of income and wealth. At the same time, the link between social justice and religious faith in *Populorum Progressio* is an analytically indirect one, often mediated by the positive analysis of the social sciences. Of course Paul VI uses theological sources, including biblical interpretation, to ground his analysis. Nevertheless, the fact that he also depends heavily upon the conclusions of economic analysis, and that of other social sciences, to define the sources of social injustice and to propose macroeconomic and structural remedies reconfigures the link between theological sources and moral conclusions.

The continuity with his predecessor that John Paul II stresses includes acknowledgment of the social sciences as a source, and some common elements in the critical descriptive analysis of the functioning of both capitalism and socialism that were already evident in *Laborem Exercens*.[7] In *Sollicitudo Rei Socialis* John Paul II offers a descriptive analysis of the history of international development since the publication of *Populorum Progressio*, and he finds that history morally deficient. He repeats Paul VI's criticism of international economic markets and institutions which favor the interests of the developed countries that created them and that widen the gap between rich and poor within societies and between North and South; he decries the clash of cultural and value systems throughout the world with the imperatives of modernization; and he ticks off a list of disturbing indices, including the spread of poverty, unemployment and underemployment, illiteracy, discrimination, lack of housing and of higher educational opportunities, lack of political participation, "various forms of exploitation and of economic, social, political and religious oppression," and the denial of human and civil rights.[8]

In addition, John Paul addresses contemporary international issues that dampen the prospects for development, including demographic pressures, the proliferation of arms production and trade, the international debt burden and the ecological degradation of the global environment.[9] All these are familiar themes in contemporary development literature.

A quick reading of *Sollicitudo Rei Socialis*, therefore, would suggest that John Paul II has accomplished a faithful and straightforward update of the progressive social analysis initiated in papal documentation by Paul VI. On the other hand, a closer comparison of the two documents suggests shifts in the teaching of John Paul II that subordinate the social analysis to theological reflection, thereby strengthening the analytical links between social justice and religious faith but, at the same time, circumscribing the policy implications that flowed more directly from Paul VI's social analysis in his social teaching. While the link between Christian faith and social justice in *Populorum Progressio* was consequential and affected by Paul VI's use of social science for analysis, the link in the social encyclicals of John Paul II is a theologically integral one.[10]

Although John Paul II repeats and extends the social analysis of Paul VI, his own moral and ethical responses for action are based more on a theological analysis of humankind that was already apparent in *Laborem Exercens* and is developed further in *Sollicitudo Rei Socialis*. Furthermore, his analysis of humankind is grounded much more in biblical interpretation than in philosophical or experiential reasoning. If Leo XIII relied on scholastic natural law in *Rerum Novarum* to define the rights of workers, and if Paul VI depended on structural analyses from the social sciences to identify international socioeconomic injustices, John Paul II puts forward an exposition of scripture to articulate a comprehensive vision of people as individuals and social participants.

In *Laborem Exercens* John Paul II adopts an interpretation of the creation account in the Book of Genesis that elevates humankind by creation in the image of God to the level of collaborator in the creative work of God. It is the biblical call to ''subdue the earth'' and attain ''dominion'' over the earth that confers upon each person the status of co-creator.[11] It is this status as co-creator as much as any other quality or characteristic that establishes the dignity of people in a society based heavily on economic relationships. And it is this aspect of human dignity, rather than the principles of commutative justice derived from natural law, that defines the rights of workers as ''subjects'' of their work instead of inputs with commercial value or even as human agents with legal bargaining rights.[12] For John Paul II this principle of human dignity is verified for the Christian in the ''gospel of work'' that is affirmed by the years that Jesus spent ''devoted . . . to manual work at the carpenter's bench.''[13]

Policy Issues

Although there are international references and implications of this logic in *Laborem Exercens*,[14] it is in *Sollicitudo Rei Socialis* that John Paul II explicitly applies his theology of work to the issues of international development. ''To achieve true development,'' he says, ''we must never lose sight of that *dimension* which is the *specific nature* of man, who has been created by God in His image and likeness.''[15] Whereas in *Laborem Exercens* the emphasis on human domination of the earth was treated positively as a source of human dignity, in *Sollicitudo Rei Socialis* the emphasis is placed on the moral limits of that domination as the source for a social ethic of economic distribution. Dominion and possession of created things ''are subordinated to the *transcendent reality* of the human being,'' which for John Paul II is ''fundamentally social'' because of the creation of humankind, in Genesis, as ''a couple, a man and a woman.''[16] Paul VI had approached distributional issues by emphasizing the injustice of structures of the international economy that permitted some countries and peoples to dominate others in an unequal dependency relationship. John Paul acknowledged the existence of unjust international economic structures in *Redemptor Hominis* and *Sollicitudo Rei Socialis*, where he speaks of

> . . . economic, financial and social *mechanisms* which, although they are manipulated by people, often function almost automatically, thus accentuating the situation of wealth for some and poverty for the rest. . . . In the end they suffocate or condition the economies of the less developed countries.[17]

Despite acknowledgments such as these, the focus of John Paul II remains on the social responsibilities of the individual.

This shift of emphasis to the individual is apparent in the treatment of international economic dependency among nations. Following the lead of Paul VI, John Paul II acknowledges the biases in international markets against the industrial and primary products of poor nations. However, unlike his predecessor he cryptically appears to tilt in the direction of international *laissez faire* when he allows that the international trade system is "mortgaged to protectionism and increasing bilateralism."[18] There is, for example, no reference to the protectionist policies of developing countries, which, although they have not proven to be universally successful, were central to many policy proposals advocated for developing countries in the dependency literature of the 1960s and 1970s. Nor is there any note of the fact that many developing countries that are former colonies depend upon bilateral economic agreements with their previous colonizers to escape dependence upon the vagaries of international markets, especially for exports of sugar and other primary products. Elimination of these arrangements might well benefit the poor exporter nations that happen not to have a patron, but would hurt those that do, while elimination of the bilateral arrangements could result in a transfer of resources from poor nations to the rich ones via lower prices set by supply and demand in international markets.

In addition, John Paul II moves away from the dependency theories that influenced his predecessor's writings when he stresses the responsibilities of the developing countries themselves for their own development:

> Development demands above all a spirit of initiative on the part of the countries which need it. Each of them must act in accordance with its own responsibilities, *not expecting everything* from the more favored countries. . . . The development of peoples begins and is most appropriately accomplished in the dedication of each people to its own development, in collaboration with others.[19]

Although this shift of emphasis may appear to be academic and without practical relevance, it does have implications for behavior and policy that set John Paul II apart from his predecessor no matter how much he incorporates Paul VI's descriptive analyses of social reality. The emphasis in *Laborem Exercens* on the responsibility of the individual to share in creation by subduing and dominating the earth calls attention to the tension between each person or nation and the good of the larger society. This emphasis tends to shift the direction of the search for solutions in Catholic social discourse away from the public sphere to personal response. John Paul II's theology of work as co-creation has been used to defend "democratic capitalism" as the system that best supports the creative initiatives implied in the theology of co-creation.[20] In *Sollicitudo Rei Socialis* John Paul II himself seems to support some of the argument of this literature when he includes in his list of rights that are often suppressed "*the right of economic initiative . . .* which is important not only for the individual but also for the common good."[21]

It is worth noting that the relationship in papal social thought between the biblical creation narrative and themes of human dignity and social responsibility has its roots as far back as the teaching of Pius XII.[22] Moreover, it was Paul VI, in *Populorum Progressio*, who anticipated John Paul by clearly articulating a theology of co-creation:

> When God endowed man with intellect, power to reason, and sensitivity he gave him the means with which to complete and perfect, as it were, the work begun by himself, for whoever engages in work, be he artist, artisan manager, laborer, farmer, in a certain sense creates.[23]

However, for Paul VI there was no contradiction between creative initiative and the responsibility of individuals and the state to subordinate private interests to the common good. From the time of *Rerum Novarum* through the publication of *Populorum Progressio*, there had been fairly consistent growth in emphasis on the collective dimension of social responsibility in response to issues like the right of private property, employment and the legitimacy of state intervention in the economy, especially to ensure a socially just distribution of wealth and income. So, while still opposing socialism as a comprehensive economic system, Paul VI was able to affirm the right of the state to intervene in the economy to promote development, to expropriate property and to initiate economic planning, and he was able to leave an opening for public ownership of productive resources, under certain circumstances, for the common good.[24]

He challenged individuals also to support government policies to promote development, even if these restricted individual liberty: "Is [each citizen] ready to pay more taxes so that the public authorities can more vigorously promote development? Is he ready to pay a higher price for imported goods so that the producers get a fairer return?"[25]

For John Paul II, however, there appears to be a higher probability of conflict between the right of economic initiative and government intervention in the economy for egalitarian social goals:

> Experience shows us that the denial of this right, or its limitation in the name of an alleged "equality" of everyone in society, diminishes, or in practice absolutely destroys the spirit of initiative, that is to say *the creative subjectivity of the citizen*. As a consequence, there arises, not so much a true equality as a "leveling down." In the place of creative initiative there appears passivity, dependence and submission to the bureaucratic apparatus. . . .[26]

Admittedly, the context of these words, in which John Paul II refers to the bureaucratic apparatus as the *only* "ordering" and "decision making" body, indicates that his reference is to the stereotypical socialist system. Nevertheless, since there are virtually no pure applications of the stereotype in the contemporary world, the principles enunciated at the very least offer space for continuation of the debate about the proper mix of individual liberty and government intervention in the economy of a developing economy that was fueled by John Paul's use of the theology of co-creation in *Laborem Exercens*.

The authors of papal social documents are not immune from the prevailing intellectual currents of their time. Consequently, it should not be surprising if there is a tendency for the documents to reflect the influence of contemporary social thought, especially when the explicit incorporation of positive analysis from the social sciences has been accepted in the articulation of papal social thought. Paul VI wrote his international social encyclical when there was confidence in the ability of macroeconomic policies to achieve social goals such as full employment and equitable income distribution. Moreover, that was the time of great optimism that structural changes in the economies of developing countries, initiated by their respective governments, could accelerate development by altering traditional patterns of ownership, dependency, participation and decision-making. The degree of public intervention considered desirable, of course, varied with the nature of the regime, reaching very high levels in the emerging socialist regimes of the Third World.

At the same time, emphasis on the necessity of public policies to effect structural changes for more equitable distribution, as used by Paul VI and much of the development literature of his time, may be understood to imply acceptance of equity criteria that postulate equality of results, e.g., equal incomes, as the preferred objective. Domestic social policies to transfer income to the poor and autarkic national development policies of structural changes in ownership and composition of production to respond to dependency analyses of international economic inequalities have, as their explicit or implicit aim, the reduction of inequalities in resulting incomes, personal in one case and national in the other. The greater the resulting equality, the greater the success of the structural change of policy. The move toward public intervention in economic life to realize objectives of economic equality in incomes or benefits, allows Paul VI to justify economic policies for structural change, including agrarian reform, expropriation and nationalization of some production, while remaining opposed to the principles of socialism based on atheistic materialism and adversarial class-consciousness.

In this respect he differs from his predecessors but, also, he set a pattern that heavily influenced subsequent Catholic social thought. In developing areas, structural analysis of economic life and policies favoring government intervention for greater equality in the distribution of economic goods and services played a central role in the discourse of liberation theology and in the documents of the synods of Latin American bishops at Medellin in 1968 and at Puebla in 1978.[27] The same was true in major social documents of the Church in the First World, especially in the pastoral letters on their respective national economies by the bishops of Canada and the United States.[28] It was the words of Paul VI, ''In teaching us charity, the Gospel instructs us in the preferential respect due to the poor,''[29] that inspired the development of the distinctive preferential option for the poor in the Puebla documents and in the pastoral letters of the bishops of Canada and the United States on the economies of their countries.

At the same time, criticism of Catholic social teaching in the tradition of *Populorum Progressio*, particularly from a neoclassical economic perspective, has been directed especially sharply to its emphasis on equality of results, e.g., in the distribution of income.[30] The implication of distributional equality as a practical outcome of socially just economic policies raises criticisms because of its lack of regard for differences in productive abilities and for inefficient allocation of economic resources, as well as criticisms of the high social and economic costs of bureaucratic intervention in economic life and of the biased limitation it places on the menu of options and strategies to achieve high rates of economic growth.

Since the time of *Populorum Progressio* there has been a resurgence of economic policies favoring free markets and minimal government intervention in the marketplace, beginning in countries such as the United States and Britain and spreading to the Third World. During the same period the development record of the more socialistic economies of the Third World has been generally unimpressive in comparison to the economic performance of a few market-oriented economies guided, in large measure, by neoclassical economic trade policies, namely, the Asian NIC's (newly industrialized countries) of South Korea, Taiwan, Hong Kong, Thailand and Singapore along with Chile during the 1980s and those like India that have supported market-oriented policies in major domestic sectors, e.g., agriculture. Even some of the chronically depressed African economies that have begun to pursue more market-oriented economic policies in trade and production have experienced above average growth rates recently.[31]

Consequently, it should not be surprising that the writings of John Paul II reflect some of the current argumentation underlying the shift toward neoclassical economic policies, favoring free markets and private enterprise, that has swept the world in the past decade. John Paul II, as indicated above, repeats many of the structural issues of international development from *Populorum Progressio*, and even updates them. He updates international economic dependence also so that it becomes the *"interdependence* [that] triggers *negative effects* even in the rich countries."[32] Structural interdependence is made current by John Paul's addition of the present international debt crisis to the list of economic issues that structurally link rich and poor nations, and he rightly notes the foresight of Paul VI in anticipating this problem.[33]

Nevertheless, the grounding of social responsibility and ethical evaluation of social reality and economic activity, e.g., work in *Laborem Exercens*, in a biblically interpreted definition of people as creative subjects with dignity, along with the addition of explicit regard for individual economic initiative, reduces the significance of structural issues in the social thought of John Paul II. This shift of emphasis is evident in the relative scarcity of structural and macroeconomic policy recommendations in the social teaching of John Paul II. Paul VI was willing to break new ground by his approval, albeit sometimes qualified, of policies for structural change, as well as by explicitly defining space for monetary, fiscal and regulatory economic policies of governments to achieve social objectives such as employment in the economies of their respective countries,[34] even while criticizing elements of socialist ideology contrary to Catholic faith.

John Paul II does not contradict his predecessor's policy recommendations but, rather than update them, he is very careful to avoid policy recommendations specific enough to risk identification with the recommendations of specific schools of thought in the literature of the social sciences. The last chapter of *Sollicitudo Rei Socialis*, for example, entitled "Some Particular Guidelines," mentions several structural issues that call for reforms, including an international trade system that discriminates against developing countries, an inadequate world monetary and financial system, questions of technology transfer to developing countries and the effectiveness of "International Organizations" (which are nowhere identified).

However, except for general calls for reforms, there are precious few hints of policies that address the structural deficiencies and inequities of the international economy brought forward from the writing of Paul VI and which preserve the individual liberty that, for John Paul II, assures full flowering of the potential for creative work and economic initiative. Although John Paul II does not explicitly reject public initiatives to effect structural changes in developing countries, neither does he offer a papal stamp of approval. In fact, his criticism of the suppression of "the right of economic initiative" that results in "passivity, dependence and submission to the bureaucratic apparatus" in *Sollicitudo Rei Socialis* suggests quite the opposite. Even then, he does not advert to the need for a policy position to address the worsening of income distribution that tends to accompany development in countries like Chile which have emphasized individual economic initiative in free markets as the engine of growth, while de-emphasizing redistributive policies.

At the international level, John Paul II does retain in his general calls for reform an awareness of structural deficiencies and inequities in international markets. As evidence of these defects he cites the behavior of international prices for many primary products, barriers to market access for the industrial and primary product exports of the developing countries, obstacles to technology transfer, and the effects of changes in international interest rates on the debt burden of poor countries.[35] However, there are no suggestions of, or references to, policy proposals that can address these structural issues of social justice without interfering with individual liberty in the marketplace and without ethical trade-offs among sectors and generations of the world population.

Neither are there references to the ethical trade-offs. Proposals to raise and stabilize prices of primary products in world markets, for example, involve distributional and allocative trade-offs with ethical implications. In the typical proposals, exporting nations are expected to accept production or sales quotas which may require their internal regulatory control over the economic initiative of their own domestic producers, thereby suppressing economic initiative and risking inefficient allocation of natural resources. On the other hand, proposals to increase access of industrial producers in developing countries to export markets in developed countries raise questions of curtailment of production of those products, with resulting unemployment and displacement of workers in the developed countries whose firms cannot compete with the low labor costs of the Third World exporters, but whose consumers will benefit from the low prices of imports from the Third

World. The determination of the international common good and social justice for workers, entrepreneurs and consumers in such situations
has thus far defied unambiguous solutions. The social teaching of John
Paul II fails to indicate an awareness of these obvious trade-offs and so
offers limited moral guidance to policy makers or those looking for ethical criteria to evaluate policy proposals.

There is a similar lack of clarity about ethical trade-offs in the comments of John Paul II in *Sollicitudo Rei Socialis* on population questions. On the one hand he acknowledges "a demographic problem
which creates difficulties for development."[36] This statement, however, is immediately followed only by a reference to the potentially
negative effects on development of the drop in birth rates in developed
countries. His criticisms include familiar ones from the social science
literature of the 1960s and 1970s that called attention to the frequent
failure of such campaigns to respect indigenous cultural and religious
values and their tendencies toward racism and suppression of free
choice among the poor in developing countries.[37]

Elsewhere in *Sollicitudo Rei Socialis* John Paul II discusses causes
and effects of poverty as well as the issues raised by increasingly serious
ecological and environmental concerns. Nowhere, however, are the
links between population growth, poverty and environmental degradation acknowledged despite the fact that the relationship between
pollution and the quality of life is mentioned among the considerations affecting the moral character of development.[38] One need not
subscribe to old theories of optimal rates of population growth and
control for economic development[39] to acknowledge the link between
population growth, poverty and environmental degradation in countries lacking adequate capital, natural resources and human skills to
meet basic needs and to improve the quality of life. Even allowing for
the failures of development strategies in Third World countries, it is
difficult to deny that their rural stagnation and inhuman quality of life
in urban slums have often been worsened by population growth that
exceeds the current capacity for economic growth with environmental
protection.

Although the worldwide food shortages predicted decades ago have
failed to materialize, the threat remains a real one in the face of an
annual increase in the world population of 86 million people. Between
1950 and 1984 there was a sharp increase in worldwide grain production which allowed for a 40 percent increase in per capita consumption.

However, it is argued that this surge in production was achieved by cultivating erodible land that should not have been plowed and by excessive pumping for irrigation, which lowered water tables.[40]

These expansionary strategies have diminished now, and grain production is falling. In the past two years world grain reserves have dropped from the highest levels to the lowest level since World War II, partly because of the drought in the United States in the summer of 1988. With an annual worldwide loss of 24 billion tons of topsoil due to soil erosion, many of the major urban areas of the developed and less developed countries of the world depend heavily on grain imports from the United States. At the same time there is the possibility of a long-term warming trend in the United States and other major grain producers in the northern hemisphere due to increases in ozone and other gases, i.e., the so-called greenhouse effect, that could produce more droughts and other climatic changes unfavorable to grain production.[41] So questions of demographic pressures on international development once again are surfacing in a complex context of soil erosion, scarcity of new cropland and water plus the possibility of adverse climatic changes.

The link between population growth, poverty and the environment shows in the migration of populations in search of a livelihood into forested areas like the Brazilian Amazon and rural Haiti, with resulting degradation of the domestic and global environment. In Haiti the simple search of the poor for charcoal for cooking has deforested the country to the point where the resulting soil erosion has blocked rivers, destroyed fishing grounds, clogged hydroelectric dams and led to the annual destruction of several thousand acres of farmland.

Nor is there in the social teaching of John Paul II any serious guidance for ethical evaluation of migration as a challenging remedy to unbalanced population densities in the less developed countries. If indeed "the goods of this world are *originally meant for all*" and that "private property . . . is under a 'social mortgage,' " as John Paul II states in *Sollicitudo Rei Socialis*[42] then there is great need for moral criteria to evaluate the economically rational initiative of migrants from the densely populated countries of Central America and the Caribbean seeking access to the opportunities which the more abundant resources of the less densely populated United States offer. Although the causes of economic deprivation that motivate the migration are many, including internal political and economic injustices in the homelands of the migrants, steadily increasing population is a significant contributing factor to the magnitude of the migration and its potential effects on the economy of the United States and on the quality of life of its citizens.

So John Paul II is correct in acknowledging the demographic problems in international development. Moreover, criticism of his failure to offer more clearly defined moral guidance on the related policy issues of poverty, environment and migration that are influenced by demographic problems need not imply a denial of his teaching on artificial birth control. Rather, the concern is that the impact of his social teaching may well be diminished by the absence of more comprehensive definitions of contemporary development problems and of clearer moral guidance in developing, evaluating and choosing solutions.

Papal social teaching at the turn of the century, despite its principled defense of the rights of workers and its unwillingness to endorse capitalism, can be criticized for being a bit too little too late to avoid losing the loyalty of many of Europe's workers to the Church.[43] Today, campaigns for population control are already well established in many less developed nations and their recommended methods have won acceptance in many countries with a Catholic cultural tradition. So, in the absence of a more fully developed analysis, with conclusions that help direct moral guidance for dealing with contemporary demographic problems, papal social teaching runs the risk of weakening its impact on the solution of development problems despite the significance of its basic principles for development of the individual and human society.

The relative de-emphasis in the social teaching of John Paul II on economic policies for international development is partially offset by a political emphasis that perhaps is clearer in his teaching than in that of his predecessors. For example, after listing the many phenomena that characterize the lag that has delayed achievement of the goals of international development enunciated by Paul VI, John Paul II chooses to bypass many possible "undoubtedly complex" explanations and, instead, chooses to concentrate on the "*political picture* since the Second World War."[44] Lest there be any doubt about the geopolitical subject of that picture, he explicitly says, "I am referring to the existence of two opposing blocs, commonly known as East and West."[45] This opposition, which John Paul II calls "first of all *political*," originates for him in the opposition between "*liberal capitalism* and *Marxist collec-*

tivism," a traditional theme in papal social teaching to emphasize differences in economic systems and policies, but one which is labeled *"ideological* in nature"[46] in *Sollicitudo Rei Socialis*.

Moreover, John Paul II offers more specific endorsement of democracy in *Sollicitudo Rei Socialis* than in his previous social encyclicals or those of his predecessors:

> [Some] nations need to reform certain unjust structures, and in particular their *political institutions*, in order to replace corrupt dictatorial and authoritarian forms of government by *democratic* and *participatory* ones. This is a process which we hope will spread and grow stronger. For the "health" of a political community—as expressed in the free and responsible participation of all citizens in public affairs, in the rule of law and in respect for and promotion of human rights—is the necessary *condition and sure guarantee* of the development of "the whole individual and of all people."[47]

The significance of this stirring endorsement of democracy is heightened by the fact that in *Sollicitudo Rei Socialis* John Paul II, for the first time, explicitly states that "the Church's social doctrine *is not* a 'third way' between *liberal capitalism* and *Marxist collectivism*."[48] His endorsement of democratic participation by all citizens is consistent with his support for conventional vehicles for democratic participation, such as unions and political parties. However, there is no mention of the grass roots social movements and organizations that have been so much a part of the democratic political process in many developing countries, especially among the poor in Catholic Latin America, despite the fact that a case could be made on grounds of a noncorporatist, democratic interpretation of the traditional principle of subsidiarity in papal social teaching.

Moreover, the exclusive focus of John Paul II on the geopolitical conflict between East and West as the source of the failure of international economic development to realize the hopes expressed in *Populorum Progressio* renders the social teaching of the present pontiff somewhat inadequate if *glasnost* leads to a reduction of East-West conflicts, while Third World countries remain exposed to the vagaries of international free markets for goods, services and finance. Economic as well as political factors determine the behavior of the markets that play a determining role in the successful development of most poor countries, especially those currently pursuing policies of freedom of market entry and export promotion.

A reduction in geopolitical conflicts certainly can open the way for cooperation between the superpowers on many of the issues raised in papal social teaching, e.g., reduction of the arms race and protection of the global environment. Nevertheless, despite the economic resources liberated by a diminution of the arms race and other East-West conflicts, it cannot even be assumed that subsequent greater economic cooperation between East and West through mutual trade and investment will automatically further the development of Third World countries. The Soviet bloc may, after all, simply become one more competitor with Third World exporters for access to markets in OECD (Organization for Economic Cooperation and Development) countries, while the U.S. and its allies compete as well for emerging markets in the Soviet bloc.

The Church as Social Actor

The shifts in the social thought of John Paul II from that of his immediate predecessors, with respect to the relationship of religious faith to social justice and the specification of morally acceptable policies discussed here, have implications for the social role of the Church itself in international development. In his social teaching Paul VI acknowledged and used a pluralistic approach to sources that included secular as well as theological analyses. So it is not surprising he also stimulated social action by the Church and its members that reflected this pluralistic approach. He encouraged the bishops of Latin America to take on the issues of development in the synod at Medellin, and journeyed to Colombia to open the synod. The bishops responded by introducing into the documents of Medellin some of the same structural social analyses that characterized *Populorum Progressio* and this spirit endured through the synod at Puebla a decade later. In the interim, liberation theology developed and incorporated social analysis, including some from Marxist and dependency literature, into its own reasoning. Moreover, this action-oriented teaching drew Catholics, clerical and lay, into ecumenical collaboration with others to promote structural changes for the achievement of social justice in development.

John Paul II does not disown the teaching of his predecessor and has reaffirmed much of it in his three social encyclicals. However, while acknowledging a pluralism of sources for description of development problems, his own moral argument was based much more integrally on a definition of humankind founded on faith, that is, as revealed in theological analysis of the Bible. Policies for social change tended to give way in emphasis and clarity to calls for personal conversion and the social responsibility of individuals (though these were not lacking in the teaching of Paul VI). Policies for public intervention in development made way for the exercise of individual liberties. These shifts in social teaching were accompanied by instructions and disciplinary actions restricting the involvement of clerics in public life, by condemnation of overtones of adversarial class-consciousness and secular utopianism in the writings of liberation theologians and by the widespread appointments throughout the world of bishops much less involved in the promotion of specific social policies and structural changes in economy and society. John Paul II has been critical of corporate social agendas undertaken and supported by religious orders such as the Jesuits, while encouraging lay institutes like Opus Dei that place heavy emphasis on the personal behavior of their members within their chosen professions and occupations.

The collective actions of grass roots ecclesial communities founded under the inspiration of *Populorum Progressio* and the documents of Medellin that were endorsed in the documents of Puebla receive virtually no direct attention in *Sollicitudo Rei Socialis* despite the latter's endorsement of the preferential option for the poor and of democratic participation. This absence, of course, is consistent with the lack of reference to any grass roots organizational initiatives mentioned above. The reference to the preferential option for the poor in *Sollicitudo Rei Socialis* is used instead not to endorse collective action by the poor on their own behalf, but to inspire others through a concern for the poor in ''the life of each Christian,'' including ''daily life as well as our decisions in the political and economic fields.''[49]

The institutional changes, along with the shifts in emphasis within the social teaching of John Paul II toward personal behavior inspired by religious faith and away from institutional involvement in issues of social policy, imply a shift in the social role of the Church. That shift is away from institutional leadership by the Church to influence social policy for structural change and toward the exercise of personal responsibility by individual Church members under the inspiration of faith in their professional and occupational lives.

Conclusion

The social teaching of Paul VI was distinctive for its embrace of a pluralism of sources, including the social sciences, to support ethical evaluation and policy recommendations, including profound structural changes in economic life, to achieve social justice. John Paul II in his first social encyclical, *Redemptor Hominis*, while accepting the use of social science and the principles of structural change, emphasizes the importance of "a true conversion of mind, will and heart," to move ahead on the "difficult road of indispensable transformation of the structures of economic life."[50] In *Laborem Exercens* he goes further by grounding the norms for social justice more heavily in a biblical and theological interpretation of humankind, which has the effect of creating more space for elaborating the role of the individual in economic life. Finally, in *Sollicitudo Rei Socialis* John Paul II draws upon his previous teaching to emphasize the personal responsibility of the person of faith in both economic and political life.

These contributions of John Paul II are done without fully abandoning the more pluralistic methodology of Paul VI and without dropping a concern for global transformation of economic and political structures. Still, the attempt to graft a social teaching that is more personal and reflective of individual liberties, faith and personal responsibilities onto the more structuralist teaching of Paul VI may not be satisfying to those looking for clear policy directions for international development.

In *Sollicitudo Rei Socialis* John Paul II recognizes the need for clarity if Catholic social teaching is to be helpful "in promoting both the correct definition of the problems being faced and the best solution to them."[51] Nevertheless, in the absence of greater specification of policy proposals, the teaching of *Sollicitudo Rei Socialis* itself may well be vulnerable to the criticism of inconsistency or wishful thinking for its laudable but undefined calls for the best of all worlds in which the claims of social justice in international distribution are happily reconciled with conditions of personal liberty for the exercise of economic initiative.

Ideally, a greater balance in the relative importance of individual and collective solutions to the problems of international development may be a goal in the social teaching of John Paul II. Indeed, some of the more "collectivist" elements of earlier social teaching such as Paul VI's tolerance for nationalization and expropriation as well as John Paul II's own earlier criticisms of multinational firms, are omitted or muted in *Sollicitudo Rei Socialis*. On the other hand, any perceived tilt toward individualism in his international encyclical is challenged by strong reaffirmations of the social dimension of private property and by his strong criticism of the gap in income and wealth that has continued to grow between the underdevelopment of poor nations and the "superdevelopment" of rich ones.[52] Add to this tension the absence of a set of exemplary and consistent policy recommendations, especially for structural transformation, plus a disavowal of any attempt by papal social teaching to discover or promote a "third way" and it is easy to anticipate frustration on the part of those seeking ethical guidance for resolving complex public policy issues of international development.

The evolution of thought in the social encyclicals of John Paul II may thus be interpreted as an effort to bring his social teaching closer in spirit to early papal social encyclicals which were addressed more directly to believers than to the world at large when compared to the social encyclicals of John XXIII and Paul VI. The social teaching of John Paul II may also be a tacit but honest admission that socially just solutions for the complex problems of the international economy are beyond immediate discovery. In this respect John Paul II may well be playing the role of wise pastor by simply laying out and reaffirming basic principles of Christian faith that have social relevance as a source of hope and challenge, especially for his own flock, as they struggle to make their contribution to a common quest for authentic human development in a pluralistic world.

Notes

1. John Paul II, *On Social Concern: Sollicitudo Rei Socialis*, (Washington: United States Catholic Conference, Publication No. 205-5), p. 5.

2. *Ibid.*, pp. 6, 12.

3. *Ibid.*, p. 12.

4. John XXIII, *Mater et Magistra*, Pars. 200-211, National Council of Catholic Bishops (NCCB), *Justice in the Marketplace* (Washington: United States Catholic Conference, 1985), pp. 141-143.

5. Paul VI, *Populorum Progressio*, NCCB, *op. cit.*, Pars. 56-61, pp. 215-217.

6. Paul VI, *Octagesima Adveniens*, NCCB, *op. cit.*, esp. Par. 31, p.237.

7. John Paul II, *Laborem Exercens* (Washington: United States Catholic Conference, 1981), Par. 13, pp. 27-30.

8. John Paul II, *Sollicitudo Rei Socialis, loc. cit.*, Pars. 13-15, pp. 20-26.

9. *Ibid.*, Par. 19, pp. 30-32, Pars. 23-25, pp. 38-43 and Par. 26, p. 45.

10. Rev. John T. Pawlikowski, O.S.M., Ph.D., "Introduction to Redemptor Hominis and Laborem Exercens," NCCB, *Justice in the Marketplace* (Washington: United States Catholic Conference, 1985), p. 277.

11. John Paul II, *Laborem Exercens, loc. cit.*, Par. 6, pp. 13-15.

12. *Ibid.*, Par. 9, pp. 19-21.

13. *Ibid.*, Par. 6, p. 14.

14. *Vd.* Ernest Bartell, C.S.C., "*Laborem Exercens*: A Third World Perspective, John W. Houck and Oliver F. Williams (eds.), *Co-Creation and Capitalism* (Washington: University Press of America, 1983), pp. 174-198.

15. John Paul II, *Sollicitudo Rei Socialis, loc. cit.*, Par. 29, p.52.

16. *Ibid.*, Par. 29, pp. 51-53.

17. *Ibid.*, Par. 16, p. 26.

18. *Ibid.*, Par. 43, p. 87.

19. *Ibid.*, Par. 44, pp. 88-89.

20. See, for example, Michael Novak, "Creation Theology," John W. Houck and Oliver F. Williams (eds.), *Co-Creation and Capitalism* (Washington: University Press of America, 1983), pp. 17-41.

21. John Paul II, *Sollicitudo Rei Socialis, loc. cit.*, Par. 15, p. 24.

22. Piux XII, *Christmas Message*, December 1942, NCCB, *op. cit.*, pp. 103-104.

23. *Ibid.*, Par. 27, p. 208.

24. Paul VI, *Populorum Progressio*, NCCB, *op. cit.*, Pars. 24, 33, 50, pp. 207, 210, 213.

25. *Ibid.*, Par. 47, p. 212.

26. John Paul II, *Sollicitudo Rei Socialis, loc. cit.*, Par. 15, p. 24.

27. See, for example, Gustavo Gutierrez, *The Theology of Liberation* (Maryknoll: Orbis Books, 1973), Ch. 6; Second General Conference of the Latin American Bishops, "The Medellin Conference Documents," David J. O'Brien and Thomas A. Shannon (eds.), *Renewing the Earth: Catholic Docu-*

ments on Peace, Justice and Liberation (New York: Image Books, 1977), pp. 549-564; Third General Conference of Latin American Bishops, *Puebla: Evangelization at Present and in the Future of Latin America* (Washington: National Conference of Catholic Bishops, 1979), Part I, Ch. 2.

28. See Canadian Conference of Catholic Bishops, *Ethical Reflections on the Economic Crisis* (Catholic New Times, 1983) and United States Catholic Bishops, *Economic Justice for All: Catholic Social Teaching and the U.S. Economy*, NC Documentary Service, *Origins*, Vol. 16, No. 24, November 27, 1986.

29. Paul VI, *Octagesima Adveniens*, NCCB, *op. cit.*, Par. 23, p. 235.

30. See, for example, Joseph Ramos, "Reflections on Gustavo Gutierrez's Theology of Liberation," and "Dependency and Development: An Attempt to Clarify the Issues," Michael Novak (ed.), *Liberation South, Liberation North* (Washington: American Enterprise Institute for Public Policy Research, 1981), pp. 50-67.

31. The World Bank and United Nations Development Programme joint report, *Africa's Adjustment and Growth in the 1980's* (Washington and New York, 1989) cit. *The Economist*, 4-10 March, 1989, pp. 13-14, 63.

32. *Ibid.*, Par. 17, p. 27.

33. According to Paul VI "[aid should be] equitably apportioned . . . according to the real need for assistance and the ability of using the aid on the part of the recipients. There will consequently then be no danger that developing nations be overwhelmed with a debt in the payment of which they spend their chief gains. Both parties will be able to reach an agreement . . . satisfactory to both sides, namely, by balancing free gifts, interest-free or low-interest loans, and the years for gradually repaying the loan." *Populorum Progressio*, Par. 54, pp. 214-215.

34. Paul VI, *Populorum Progressio*, NCCB, *op. cit.*, Par. 37, p. 233.

35. John Paul II, *Sollicitudo Rei Socialis*, *loc. cit.*, Par. 43, p. 87.

36. *Ibid.*, Par. 25, pp. 41-42.

37. See, for example, Terry L. McCoy (ed.), *The Dynamics of Population Policy in Latin America* (Cambridge: Ballinger Publishing Co., 1974), esp. Chs. 1, 2, 9.

38. John Paul II, *Sollicitudo Rei Socialis*, *loc. cit.*, Par. 34, p. 65.

39. See, for example, Michael C. Keeley (ed.), *Population, Public Policy, and Economic Development* (New York: Praeger Publishers, 1976), esp. Ch. 1, "Economic-Demographic Modeling." *Cf.* Working Group on Population Growth and Economic Development, *et al.*, *Population Growth and Economic Development: Policy Questions* (Washington: National Academy Press, 1986).

40. Lester R. Brown, *et al.*, *State of the World 1989* (New York: W. W. Norton & Co., 1989), Ch. 1, esp. pp. 12-13.

41. *Ibid.*
42. John Paul II, *Sollicitudo Rei Socialis, loc. cit.*, Par. 42, p. 86.
43. For a brief historical discussion see Rev. John T. Pawlikowski, O.S.M., Ph.D., "Introduction to *Rerum Novarum*," NCCB, *op. cit.*, pp. 9-12.
44. John Paul II, *Sollicitudo Rei Socialis, loc. cit.*, Par. 20, p. 33.
45. *Ibid.*
46. *Ibid.*
47. *Ibid.*, Par. 44, p. 90.
48. *Ibid.*, Par. 41, p. 83.
49. *Ibid.*, Par. 42, p. 84-85.
50. John Paul II, *Redemptor Hominis*, NCCB, *op. cit.*, p. 288.
51. John Paul II, *Sollicitudo Rei Socialis, loc. cit.*, Par. 41, p. 82.
52. John Paul II, *Sollicitudo Rei Socialis, loc. cit.*, Pars. 15-16, pp. 23-27; Par. 31, p. 57.

Twelve

Moral Criticism as Moral Teaching: Pope John Paul II's *Sollicitudo Rei Socialis*

Leslie Griffin

This essay explores the recent social teaching of Pope John Paul II as a resource for political ethics and focuses on his latest social encyclical, *Sollicitudo Rei Socialis*. In the realm of political ethics, my interest is in the guidance John Paul's teachings offer to political institutions as well as to individuals who participate in politics. My argument is that *Sollicitudo Rei Socialis* proposes a theological assessment of political activity and is skeptical of the accomplishments of the political arena. Despite the encyclical's claim to provide a moral theology, *Sollicitudo* supplies a limited institutional and individual political ethic. Moreover, the encyclical's ambivalence about politics at least suggests a new direction in Catholic social teaching for the state and politics.

The Background: Catholic Social Teaching on Politics

In the near centenary of modern Roman Catholic social thought, popes from Leo XIII to John Paul II have identified an appropriate magisterial role in political questions. The justification for their intervention in politics, as well as the limits to that intervention, are rooted in a claim to moral authority. Magisterial competence in politics does not extend to technical political knowledge, but does reach to moral questions about people, their dignity and well-being. The magisterium calls upon political institutions and individuals active in politics to operate according to the demands of the natural moral law.

A central question about the magisterium's moral teaching about politics has been the relationship between moral principles and the application of those principles. Part of magisterial teaching has been the annunciation of general principles of Christian morality. Yet Leo XIII and his successors have also reserved the right to apply those principles to concrete situations. For example, they could argue that societies should be regulated by principles of justice, or should respect religious freedom; they could also condemn a specific nation which fails to act in accordance with those fundamental principles. The magisterium refuses to limit itself to the identification of general principles because it recognizes that such an enterprise could become vague, empty of content and meaning. On the other hand, it realizes as well that too much specificity in its teaching oversteps its natural law competence and encroaches on the expertise of political scientists or politicians. While the pontiffs defend their right to apply the principles of natural law teaching, it is difficult to discern in the tradition consistent criteria or procedures by which the popes undertake this activity.[1]

A significant development in the magisterium's delineation of the natural law occurs in the pontificate of John XXIII, and is reinforced in the writings of the Second Vatican Council and of Pope Paul VI. The new approach fosters respect for the ''signs of the times,'' and favors an inductive rather than a deductive approach to natural law. In addition, biblical and theological language receives a new emphasis and complements the strict philosophical readings of natural law of the past.[2] In many ways, the 1971 apostolic letter of Paul VI, *Octogesima Adveniens*, marks the culmination of this movement. In a widely-cited text from that letter, Paul admits that:

> In the face of such widely varying situations it is difficult for us to utter a unified message and to put forward a solution which has universal validity. Such is not our ambition, nor is it our mission. It is up to the Christian communities to analyze with objectivity the situation which is proper to their own country, to shed on it the light of the Gospel's unutterable words and to draw principles of reflection, norms of judgment and directives for action from the social teaching of the Church.[3]

Marie-Dominique Chenu analyzes the shift from a deductive to an inductive approach to social problems in a 1979 book, entitled *La "Doctrine Sociale" de l'Eglise comme Ideologie*.[4] In the earlier era of papal teaching (i.e., especially under Leo XIII and Pius XI), Chenu argues that there was a Catholic social doctrine, a set teaching which should be applied in the concrete circumstances of social life. This Catholic social doctrine was defined by the hierarchy and applied by the laity. It encouraged the development of Catholic Action groups, as well as the formation of distinctive Catholic political parties. Chenu asserts that Catholic social doctrine was an "ideology" whose fundamental principles were determined (and limited) by the social environment in which it was written. When (after the papacy of Pius XII) the magisterium shifts from a deductive to an inductive approach, the language of social doctrine disappears. The text cited above from *Octogesima Adveniens*, with its call for the laity to discern rather than apply norms for political engagement, is representative of this change.

At the same time the tradition accentuates the individual's discernment in politics, there is growing recognition of the importance of political institutions. In the papacies of John XXIII and Paul VI, the need for appropriate state intervention to protect the dignity of individuals is underlined. This is evident, for example, in John XXIII's recognition in *Mater et Magistra* of the importance of a principle of socialization (allowing state intervention) as well as the traditional principle of subsidiarity (limiting such intervention). It is also present in Paul's assertion in *Octogesima Adveniens* that, due to the predominance of politics in contemporary life, it is time for Christians to "pass from economics to politics" to promote integral development.[5]

John Paul II

In an essay on John Paul's social teaching, Peter Hebblethwaite examines whether or not the encyclicals and other writings of John Paul II have resurrected the notion of Catholic social doctrine. Hebblethwaite finds the evidence ambiguous. John Paul does employ the "social doctrine" terminology (e.g., at Puebla), and yet at times uses it interchangeably with other expressions such as social teaching, social concerns, etc., which lack the connotations of social doctrine.[6]

Hebblethwaite's question is substantial and not merely terminological. For behind the label "Catholic Social Doctrine" is the fundamental topic of the range of the magisterium's competence in social questions. The "doctrine vs. teaching" debate, for example, demands a reexamination of the deductive and inductive approaches of earlier magisterial teaching. It forces renewed attention also to the roles of hierarchy and laity in politics. Hebblethwaite's description of Catholic social doctrine (CSD) defines the issue which is at stake:

> The difficulty of CSD was this: it could fly so high in the stratosphere of principles that, from above, the whole landscape was flattened out and no details could be perceived; or—more rarely—it could hew so close to the ground that a particular statement was too localized to be applicable elsewhere.[7]

The two poles which Hebblethwaite describes are extremes the magisterium consistently seeks to avoid, at times with greater or lesser degrees of success. The balance official Catholic social teaching attains between general principles and concrete situations has profound implications for the institutional and individual political ethics it can offer. If *Sollicitudo* is to be used as a resource for political ethics, it is important to see how the most recent papal social encyclical handles this difficult question.

Sollicitudo Rei Socialis

The ambivalence which Hebblethwaite notes toward social doctrine in John Paul's earlier writings is present also in *Sollicitudo*. The social doctrine language is employed, yet is often used synonymously with the language of social concerns or social teaching. More significant is the terminology's correspondence to an ambivalence about moral teaching which is at the heart of the document itself.

Catholic Social Doctrine?

John Paul begins his encyclical by noting that ''continuity'' as well as ''renewal'' characterize Catholic social teaching; this is what contributes to its ''perennial value.''[8] One early indicator of support for Hebblethwaite's analysis of a new Catholic social doctrine is John Paul's definition of what is continuous. He argues that social teaching ''is constant, for it remains identical in its fundamental inspiration, in its 'principles of reflection,' in its 'criteria of judgment,' in its basic 'directives for action,' and, above all, in its vital link with the Gospel of the Lord.''[9] Here John Paul's footnote is to *Octogesima Adveniens*, number four. Yet Paul's admission of the lack of solutions of universal validity to social problems is not noted. Indeed, John Paul appears to take something of universal validity from the text. In another section, John Paul identifies the social doctrine as an *''application* of the word of God to people's lives and the life of society. . . .''[10] Both citations at least suggest a deductive rather than an inductive approach to social problems.

On the other hand, and in opposition to the social doctrine of Pius XI, John Paul is emphatic that

> The Church's social doctrine is not a ''third way'' between *liberal capitalism* and *Marxist collectivism*, nor even a possible alternative to other solutions less radically opposed to one another: rather, it constitutes a *category of its own*. Nor is it an *ideology*, but rather the *accurate formulation* of the results of a careful reflection on the complex realities of human existence, in society and in the international order, in the light of faith and of the Church's tradition. Its main aim is to *interpret* these realities, determining their conformity with or divergence from the lines of the Gospel teaching on man and his vocation.[11]

John Paul himself, then, refuses a return to an earlier era of Catholic social doctrine which offers a third way of its own to Catholic followers.

At first glance, then, the moral teaching of *Sollicitudo* appears to be somewhere between the inductive approach of Paul VI and the third way of Pius XI. Further analysis of *Sollicitudo* will clarify this role of moral teaching in John Paul's social thought. My interpretation of the encyclical is that John Paul's style of moral teaching lends itself more easily to moral criticism than to constructive social discourse. In the sections that follow, I will argue that John Paul's vision of people and of political institutions contributes to a theory of moral teaching as moral criticism. The implications of this for political activity will become apparent below.

The Fundamental Way for the Church: Moral Criticism?

In *Sollicitudo*, John Paul bases his moral teaching upon the concept of the dignity of a person, a concept central to Roman Catholic social teaching. John Paul's personalist philosophy causes him to place special emphasis on the individual, and to urge throughout *Sollicitudo* the protection and promotion of the dignity of each person. In his first encyclical letter, *Redemptor Hominis*, John Paul proclaimed that "man is the primary route that the Church must travel in fulfilling her mission: he is the *primary and fundamental way for the Church*."[12] This theme remains a cornerstone of John Paul's pontificate and is reaffirmed in John Paul's constant attention to the individual in *Sollicitudo*.

These strong claims for human dignity propel John Paul to defend the rights already identified by his predecessors. Throughout the encyclical he defends the basic rights enunciated in *Pacem in Terris*, although his treatment of them is not systematic. He mentions the right to life, family rights, rights inherent in the political community, justice in employment relationships, religious freedom, the right to be "seated at the table of the common banquet," the right of peoples to identity, independence, security, and to a share in the goods of all. He also appears to single out a right not fully explicated in the tradition to this point, the right to economic initiative.[13]

John Paul's emphasis on the dignity of the individual is evident in his appropriation of Paul VI's term "integral development" as well as in his repetition of the fundamental rights of *Pacem in Terris*. A constant refrain of the encyclical is that economic development is not sufficient for people. Instead, respect for human dignity demands the development of all aspects of a person, spiritual and intellectual as well as political and economic. Limiting development to economic well-being "easily subjects the human person and his deepest needs to the demands of economic planning and selfish profit."[4]

This vision of human rights and of integral development leaves John Paul with some positive goals and standards of human society. He commits himself to the preferential option for the poor (or to love of preference for the poor) and reminds readers of the social mortgage on all property. A just nation will protect all the fundamental rights of the individual and promote the full development of all aspects of each person. Near the end of *Sollicitudo*, John Paul is clear about the importance of positive goals for Catholic social teaching:

> The *condemnation* of evils and injustices is also part of that *ministry of evangelization* in the social field which is an aspect of the Church's *prophetic role*. But it should be made clear that *proclamation* is always more important than *condemnation*, and the latter cannot ignore the former, which gives it true solidarity and the force of higher motivation.[15]

John Paul follows this text with a lengthy list of activities which should be undertaken to bring about the attainment of these rights, including the reform of international trade, of world monetary and financial systems, and the control of the forms and transfer of technology.[16]

However, this wide-ranging defense of human rights and integral development presents difficulties at the level of John Paul's moral teaching. That is, as John Paul defends such a full theory of the individual, he fails to provide a hierarchy of rights or values. The result is that John Paul's theory appears unable to deal with the conflicts of values or conflicts of rights which arise in the concrete circumstances of human social life. His offering of positive social goals may be endangered by its inability to provide a social program capable of resolution of conflict. This becomes especially true when, as we shall see below, his theory also lacks a positive assessment of political institutions. The implication of this aspect of John Paul's social ethic is that, despite his insistence that the Church must proclaim as well as condemn, his ethic lends itself more readily to condemnation of what is imperfect than to positive norms for human society.

Throughout *Sollicitudo*, John Paul has no recourse but to criticize all those systems, all those societies, which fail to accord with Catholic social teaching. It is clear in *Sollicitudo* that there is much to criticize in contemporary society—the poverty of innumerable multitudes, the gap between North and South, illiteracy, exploitation and religious oppression, unemployment and underemployment, the suppression of the right to economic initiative, and international debt, among other social ills. But the level of criticism runs deeper than that. For example, John Paul sides with the tradition's preferential option for the poor, which "embrace[s] the immense multitudes of the hungry, the needy, the homeless, those without medical care and, above all, those without hope of a better future."[17] Two paragraphs later, John Paul adds that "one must not overlook that *special form of poverty* which consists of being deprived of fundamental human rights, in particular the right to religious freedom and also the right to freedom of economic initiative."[18] If poverty has a broad meaning, it may become difficult to make the elimination of certain forms of poverty a priority.

The lack of a hierarchy of goods, and the propensity of John Paul's teaching to be critical rather than constructive, is especially evident in the parts of the encyclical which attracted immediate attention upon publication, namely, those sections which propose the so-called "moral equivalence" theory.[19] John Paul is critical of both liberal capitalism and Marxist collectivism, without distinction. It is significant that it is not levels of development in the two systems, but rather concepts of development, that he assesses. Both concepts are at fault, and there is no gradation of fault, because neither supports the full theory of the individual proposed in Catholic thought. Neither system supports the duties of human solidarity, since the West advocates "selfish isolation" while the East avoids "its duty to cooperate in the task of alleviating human misery."[20] Both the "desire for profit" and the "thirst for power" are morally culpable.[21] The same approach of undifferentiated moral criticism is evident in John Paul's treatment of underdevelopment (the lack of material goods) and superdevelopment (possession of too many consumer goods). Because integral development respects all aspects of a person, both underdevelopment and superdevelopment are "equally inadmissible."[22]

There is some justification, then, in charges that John Paul allows a theory of "moral equivalence." The reason is rooted in a style of moral teaching which makes levels of criticism difficult to distinguish.

Institutions and Individuals

The encyclical's failure to resolve conflicts of rights, and its corresponding critical approach to moral teaching, is also connected to John Paul's treatment of political institutions. *Sollicitudo* appears to offer little hope of effective political agency. John Paul's response to political institutions is to be critical of them for their shortcomings, rather than impressed by their accomplishments. Once again, such an approach leaves him little room to distinguish between levels of abuse or levels of accomplishment in specific human societies.

In *Sollicitudo*, John Paul's dismay at the failures of societies to protect the fundamental dignity of people, added to his strong personalist philosophy, causes him to focus more on individuals as agents of change than on institutions. I do not wish to overstate this claim, since John Paul's is not an either/or approach. He does not abandon institutional action and reform. He does require both individual and institutional change. Having said that, however, his emphasis on the personal conversion of the individual remains striking.[23]

Some comparison of John Paul's treatment of individuals and of institutions may help to elucidate this point. For example, while John Paul's list of complaints about contemporary society includes condemnations of governments, nations, and political and economic systems, individual strengths are preponderant in his analysis of the positive aspects of the world.[24] Among these commendable features are men and women's awareness of their own dignity, their realization of a common destiny, their recognition of the need for commitment from every single individual, the respect for life and for peace, the growing ecological concern, and the commitment of "statesmen, politicians, economists, trade unionists, people of science and international officials . . . who at no small personal sacrifice try to resolve the world's ills."[25] John Paul does mention international organizations (especially private ones) and the growing awareness of nations, yet the individual appears preeminent.

John Paul's treatment of development reinforces this focus on individual conversion and character. Underdevelopment and superdevelopment are assessed, not just in their institutional aspects, but as problems rooted in the nature of each person, particularly in a distinction between "having" and "being."[26] John Paul's concern fastens on the individual and while he speaks of hierarchy, he offers few criteria for appropriate and inappropriate "having."

> The evil does not consist in "having" as such, but in possessing without regard for the *quality* and the *ordered hierarchy* of the good one has. *Quality* and *hierarchy* arise from the subordination of goods and their availability to man's "being" and his true vocation.[27]

Finally, in Section V of *Sollicitudo*, John Paul notes the political problems that have beset society and he asserts that political will has been insufficient to solve them. Yet he turns immediately to moral attitudes as the solution to these evils. He employs the language of "structures of sin" as an explanation of society's ills. Yet even his analysis of structural sin turns not primarily to the institution but to the individual: structures of sin "are rooted in personal sin, and thus always linked to the *concrete* acts of individuals who introduce these structures, consolidate them and make them difficult to remove."[28] In the footnote to this text, John Paul cites his own *Reconciliatio et Paenitentia*, adding that: "The real responsibility, then, lies with individuals. A situation—or likewise an institution, a structure, society itself—is not in itself the subject of moral acts. Hence a situation cannot in itself be good or bad."[29] Later, he describes the structures of sin as giving way before personal solidarity, and names saints as exemplars of the approach to overcoming social evils.[30] The evaluation of structural sin, then, is not undertaken in terms of characteristics of institutions or of social analysis, but reverts to the personal moral agent.

John Paul's emphasis on the person clearly is not individualistic. He places solidarity at the center of the encyclical. In number 32, he urges Catholics not to see development as just a personal or individualistic obligation, and calls attention to the responsibilities of nations and peoples. Nonetheless, he appears to downplay the capacities of political and social institutions to resolve the problems confronting persons in the late twentieth century.

Laborem Exercens

While I will not pursue the analysis of Laborem Exercens here (in part because it does not provide a full discussion of political ethics), there are elements of John Paul's treatment of work in this encyclical which reinforce the view of moral teaching present in *Sollicitudo*. In an essay prepared for an earlier conference at Notre Dame on *Laborem Exercens*, David Hollenbach notes that John Paul's theology (especially his theological interpretation of Genesis) deemphasizes the elements of conflict in human life.

> John Paul, in other words, gives primacy to a style of theology which is more metaphysical and ontological over theological approaches which are more historical and social. This approach is quite capable of denouncing all situations which do not conform to the structure of human personhood as this structure is discerned through ontological analysis. Its danger, however, is that it will lack the categories which are necessary to guide action in non-ideal circumstances.[31]

Drew Christiansen points to an "ambivalence" in *Laborem Exercens*. The encyclical offers a radical principle of the priority of labor over capital, yet "his rights program lacks details for implementation in an overall social program.[32] Both the theology of creation propounded in Genesis as well as the implementation of rights theory, therefore, provoke questions similar to those about *Sollicitudo*.

In his assessment of John Paul's social doctrine, Hebblethwaite questions John Paul's treatment of the indirect employer in number seventeen.[33] John Paul warns unions against becoming too closely entangled with politics. Hebblethwaite challenges this analysis of unions, and argues that it may be an appropriate approach for Polish labor unions, but not for British ones. In this instance, he argues, Catholic social teaching has been too narrow, rather than too broad.

All three commentators, then, suggest that some difficulty in the definition of appropriate moral teaching is not new to *Sollicitudo*.

Developments from Paul VI

Students of Roman Catholic social teaching are familiar with the nuanced process of interpretation to which new encyclicals are subjected. Recent documents are assessed in light of the past tradition; minor changes in terminology can convey major departures from past arguments. Only over time does the significance of certain wording become apparent. Until that point is reached, one can but identify ostensible changes and question their importance. John Paul honors and celebrates *Populorum Progressio* in *Sollicitudo*, and often cites *Octogesima Adveniens*. Yet there are noteworthy changes from Paul VI that must be signaled here, while their possible importance for Roman Catholic social teaching is explored.

Populorum Progressio and Octogesima Adveniens

I have noted already that John Paul quotes the famous passage from *Octogesima Adveniens*, number four. He cites it three times, and each time he refers to the "principles of reflection," "criteria of judgment" and "directives for action" without remarking on Paul's humility about universal solutions to social problems. In the first citation, these three factors are recognized as "constant."[34] In the second reference, they are viewed as an "*application* of the word of God to people's lives" and possessed of a "practical orientation . . . towards *moral conduct*."[35] In the third quotation, John Paul employs the term "social doctrine" and calls for more "awareness" and greater "diffusion" of these three elements of social doctrine.[36] There is good reason to believe that the inductive method described by Paul VI is in some disfavor with John Paul II.

Second, in *Populorum Progressio*, Paul VI places an important accent on political institutions. Paul, like John Paul, describes dire circumstances in the world, but insists[37] that local and individual undertakings are not sufficient to resolve the complex, world-wide problems of the modern era. Public authorities are important agents in the resolution of conflicts of rights and in the attainment of social objectives. They should not usurp authority, and their role mandates that they include involved groups and individuals in decision-making. The role of political authorities, thus, is clearly limited by the demands of individual participation and intermediary bodies. Nonetheless, Paul opposes "scattered" or "isolated" approaches to social problems, preferring a "planned programme" over "occasional aid left to individual good will."[38] Paul VI also appears more optimistic than John Paul II about the possibility of international organizations and institutions.

He speaks of "world-wide collaboration," both political and economic. At the end of *Populorum Progressio*, he argues: "This international collaboration on a world-wide scale requires institutions that
will prepare, coordinate, and direct it, until finally there is established
an order of justice which is universally recognized."[39] Echoing his
United Nations address, he calls for a world authority, and he urges
active participation by Catholics in the institutions which will guide
humanity through these troubling times.

Paul's emphasis on political institutions appears even more pronounced in *Octogesima Adveniens*.[40] He recognizes that no model of
government is perfect, yet reminds Christians that their vocation is to
commit themselves to the quest for the best institutions possible.
While he acknowledges the limitations of political institutions, Paul
continues to promote the positive role of politics in serving the well-
being of people.

There may be some deep significance, then, in the summary slogan
of *Sollicitudo*. While Paul VI asserted that "development is the new
name for peace," John Paul II affirms that "peace is the fruit of solidarity." Without attempting to overstate the significance of the
phrases, it is plausible to suggest that Paul and John Paul offer different theories of political institutions. In some contrast to Paul VI, then,
in *Sollicitudo* a new weight is attached to personal conversion and to
individual endeavor, while a pronounced skepticism attaches to the
possibilities of political activism.[41]

Interpretations of Paul VI and Politics

Some sense of the possible impact of John Paul's analysis of political
institutions can be gleaned from an overview of two interpretations of
Paul VI, those of David Hollenbach and Drew Christiansen. Hollenbach's book, *Claims in Conflict*,[42] focuses on the problem already
treated in John Paul's social teaching, namely the resolution of conflicts of rights in people's social and political experiences. Hollenbach
acknowledges the historical difficulty which Roman Catholic rights
theory has had in resolving conflicts; he attributes this in part to the
organic (and non-conflictual) model of society favored by the early
pontiffs. In addition, as we have seen in *Sollicitudo*, resolving conflicts

is also complicated by the tradition's desire to defend a broad array of rights, social and economic as well as political. Hollenbach's analysis emphasizes the necessary interconnection of personal, social and instrumental rights in Roman Catholic social teaching.

In *Claims in Conflict*, Hollenbach argues that Roman Catholic social teaching must not restrict its task to the criticism of views of human rights which do not accord with its own. He states: "Unless the relations between the transcendental worth of the person and the particular material, interpersonal, social and political structures of human existence can be specified, human dignity will become an empty notion."[43] In his own normative treatment of Catholic human rights theory, Hollenbach asserts that the magisterium has shifted from an organic to a conflictual vision of society. Moreover, he discovers three resources within the tradition that provide some guidance for conflict resolution. The first is its theory of justice, which specifies human rights and which "is a practical guideline for the use of the instruments of power, especially governmental power."[44] The second resource is social and political theory. A conflictual model of political life can accept pluralism while still struggling for the establishment of justice. Hollenbach proposes a model of political solidarity which refuses "detailed, normative models of social organization"[45] but calls for political decision-making and discernment. Love is the third resource. In love, Christians respond to the actual dignity of a person. If there are no longer set answers to social problems, it is imperative for Christians to discern solutions by responding to individuals in concrete circumstances. From the demands of love, Hollenbach develops certain priority principles that can guide Catholic rights theory in situations of conflict.

Hollenbach argues that *Populorum Progressio* does acknowledge the conflictual notion of political society. It and *Octogesima Adveniens* provide as well some "norms of discernment" for conflict resolution. Moreover, political institutions play an important role in this discernment process.

Drew Christiansen proposes a norm of relative equality to interpret *Populorum Progressio*.[46] Christiansen argues that Paul VI's recognition of the primacy of evils of inequality allows him to specify some of the requirements of justice for individuals and institutions. Overcoming inequality, then, offers some concretization of magisterial teaching. In an essay on John Paul's (pre-*Sollicitudo*) social thought, Christiansen argues that John Paul lacks a corresponding theory of inequality: "Unlike his predecessors, however, John Paul does not make explicit the connection between human fulfillment and equality. His social ethics is expressed almost entirely in terms of human rights and it lacks a theory of justice for adjudicating between conflicting rights claims."[47] In another essay, Christiansen asserts that "John Paul's conception of justice is an empty one."[48]

According to Hollenbach, a theory of justice, a proper role for social and political institutions, and Christian love help prevent Catholic rights theory from becoming empty teaching. Christiansen finds a specific theory of justice to be lacking in John Paul's thought. My analysis of *Sollicitudo* suggests that John Paul's vision of social and political institutions is a limited one. Moreover, while love—especially the language of solidarity—is present throughout the encyclical, it is unclear if it fulfills the function suggested by Hollenbach. For Hollenbach, love insures an attention to the concrete dignity of humanity that will enable moral insight and discernment. It suggests, I think, an inductive approach to ethics not present in *Sollicitudo*.

Those elements which assist Roman Catholic social teaching to avoid empty proclamation of rights appear to be less present in the social thought of John Paul II than in that of his predecessor. What remains is a social theory that can be critical but not constructive, and which may not help guide political activity. The task that remains is an assessment of the strengths and weaknesses of John Paul's moral theory.

Theological and Ethical Implications

In part because of H. Richard Niebuhr's classic work, it is by now standard fare for theologians to assert that a Christian author's reflections on nature and grace influence her or his perception of the relationship between Christian faith and political activity. John Paul's theological presuppositions serve as important bases for his claims about political ethics, and warrant some attention before the analysis of his political ethic can be completed.

One of the key theological themes which undergirds the magisterium's assessment of political institutions is the relationship it envisions between the spiritual and the temporal dimensions of human life. In twentieth century magisterial documents, there has been a growing recognition of the importance of human temporal activity to spirituality. Early in the tradition (in Leo XIII, Pius XI and Pius XII) a subordination of temporal to spiritual was more apparent, and temporal duties were often treated as means to the higher life with God. But the documents of the Second Vatican Council call into question the language of subordination. The most forceful statement of a new relationship between spiritual and temporal occurs in *Justice in the World*, from the 1971 Synod of Bishops. This document affirms that "action on behalf of justice and participation in the transformation of the world fully appear to us as a constitutive dimension of the preaching of the Gospel."[49] Paul's treatment of evangelization and of integral development appear in continuity with the synod's statement.

In John Paul's theology, there is more room to be suspicious of the temporal, and to assess it in terms of its sinfulness and limitations. This may explain why, in *Sollicitudo*, the work of development is identified as a "duty of her [the Church's] pastoral ministry."[50] It may help to clarify the new emphasis on personal sin as opposed to structural sin. It may elucidate John Paul's call to "*subordinate* the possession, dominion and use [of created things] to man's divine likeness and to his vocation to immortality. This is the *transcendent reality* of the human being."[51] It may also illuminate the "ontological," "metaphysical" approach to people noted by Hollenbach in *Laborem Exercens* and present throughout *Sollicitudo*.

A theological perspective which is suspicious of the actual temporal experience of individuals is more likely to emphasize the spiritual and salvific works of the Church. It may also question an inductive, experiential approach to ethics, and turn instead to metaphysical definitions of personhood. If suspicion of the temporal extends to politics, political institutions may be viewed as provisional and finite, and as incapable of accomplishing much promotion of the common good.

At least one commentator has called attention to John Paul's "Augustinian" theology.[52] John Paul's emphasis on human sinfulness and his skepticism about human institutions certainly leave him closer to an Augustinian vision of humanness than to a Thomistic account. In an essay on Augustine's vision of the two cities, Eugene TeSelle[53] argues that the legacy of Augustinian thought leads in different directions. First (and most authentic) is a dualistic interpretation. The earthly city has limited importance, and Christians will not change its ways. TeSelle admits that, in some environments, Christians might recognize, with justification, that they will have no impact on political power. In the second approach, an earthly presence of Christians does exist. It may be the strong medieval church, giving orders to emperors. Or, more importantly for our purposes, TeSelle argues that a community could offer so powerful a vision that it could change society. He states that ''. . . a theology of world-defying election and world-transcending pilgrimage can, under the right combination of circumstances, become world-transforming.''[54] Third, Augustinian theology at times affirms ''the limited but genuine value of the earthly city, precisely as earthly.''[55] In John Paul's theology, and in his treatment of political institutions in *Sollicitudo*, there are clear overtones of these Augustinian approaches to the earthly city. John Paul proclaims a message that calls into question the worth of earthly institutions, yet which also speaks of their transformation by moral and religious attitudes. However, the connection of John Paul's theology to theories one and two appears clearer than its connection to theme three. In other words, John Paul's social thought appears more able to capture the insight of those whose political experience is unsuccessful, or of those who find themselves far from political power, especially if their response is to form a community of solidarity.

As a resource for political ethics, therefore, John Paul's encyclical is heavily prophetic or, to use the language of this conference, counter-cultural. It is clearly not just that, since John Paul's social thought leads (as does Augustine's) in a number of directions. However, in its emphasis on moral criticism and in its suspicion of political institutions, it offers a focus and approach somewhat different from its predecessors.

In the North American context, however, such an approach may have its limitations. A critical teaching that is suspicious of political institutions and of political activity may be weak in providing norms to politicians or to others active in the public sphere. A theory which is primarily critical in nature may have trouble, for example, appreciating the virtues of democratic capitalism.[56] Or, instead of respecting—or providing criteria for—compromises in the political arena, it may regard them as inappropriate rather than appropriate cooperation with evil.[57]

In the late nineteenth and early twentieth centuries, praise for the theological virtue of charity and identification of individual obligations toward the neighbor formed a solid foundation for Catholic social teaching. In the 1960s and 1970s, the focus of Catholic social teaching shifted to institutional analysis, including increased respect for political activism and the virtue of justice. John Paul's emphasis on criticism and on personal conversion marks a new level of response and of adaptation to changing political circumstances in the 1980s. Its outlook of moral criticism offers great assets in an era where the failures of political activity are innumerable, yet it presents some liabilities at a time when political accomplishments are still possible. The problem, of course, is that if John Paul's teaching about politics is not meaningful in a variety of social and political settings, then renewed concerns about a revival of Catholic social doctrine may be justified. That concern calls the Church to a new enterprise—one in which Catholics in political institutions assess their activity in light of *Sollicitudo*, and evaluate *Sollicitudo* in light of their political experience.

Notes

1. I treat these themes in detail in ''The Integration of Spiritual and Temporal: Contemporary Roman Catholic Church-State Theory,'' *Theological Studies* 48, 1987, pp. 225-57. For discussions of the principles/application of principles issue, see Bryan Hehir, ''Church-State and Church-World: The Ecclesiological Implications,'' *Proceedings*, Catholic Theological Society of America 41 (1986), pp. 54-74; Avery Dulles, ''The Gospel, The Church and Politics,'' *Origins* 16 (1987), pp. 637-646; Richard McCormick, ''Catholic Moral Theology: Is Pluralism Pathogenic?'' unpublished manuscript, Inaugural Address, University of Notre Dame, January 28, 1988.

2. For treatment of these themes, see, e.g., M. D. Chenu, *La ''Doctrine Sociale'' de l'Eglise comme Ideologie* (Paris: Cerf., 1979); David Hollenbach, ''Modern Catholic Teachings Concerning Justice,'' John C. Haughey, ed., *The Faith That Does Justice* (New York: Paulist, 1977), pp. 216-24; Charles E. Curran, ''Dialogue With Social Ethics—Past, Present and Future,'' *Catholic Moral Theology in Dialogue* (Notre Dame: University of Notre Dame Press, 1976), pp. 116-17, 128.

3. Henceforth *OA*, in Joseph Gremillion, ed., *The Gospel of Peace and Justice* (Maryknoll: Orbis, 1976), no. 4, p. 487. For an analysis of this text, see Philip S. Land, ''The Social Theology of Pope Paul VI,'' *America* 140, no. 18 (12 May 1979), pp. 394; Charles Curran, ''The Changing Anthropological Bases of Catholic Social Ethics,'' in *Moral Theology: A Continuing Journey* (Notre Dame: University of Notre Dame Press, 1982), pp. 189-91; Donald

Dorr, *Option for the Poor: A Hundred Years of Vatican Social Teaching* (Maryknoll: Orbis, 1983), pp. 168-69.

4. (Paris: Cerf., 1979).

5. *OA*, no. 46, p. 507. See also Land, "Social Theology," p. 392, and Dorr, *Option*, pp. 162-76. For a discussion of socialization, see Donald R. Campion, "*Mater et Magistra* and It's Commentators," *Theological Studies* 24, 1963, pp. 8-15.

6. "The Popes and Politics: Shifting Patterns in Catholic Social Doctrine," Charles Curran and Richard McCormick, eds., *Readings in Moral Theology Number Five: Official Catholic Social Teaching* (New York: Paulist, 1986), pp. 264-84.

7. *Ibid.*, p. 268.

8. John Paul II, *On Social Concern: Sollicitudo Rei Socialis* (henceforth *SRS*) (Washington, D.C.: United States Catholic Conference, 1987), no. 3, pp. 5-6.

9. *SRS*, no. 3, p. 6.

10. *SRS*, no. 8, p. 12.

11. *SRS*, no. 41, p. 83.

12. Claudia Carlen, ed., *The Papal Encyclicals 1958-1981* (Raleigh: McGrath Publishing Co., 1981), no. 40, p. 255.

13. See, e.g., *SRS*, no. 21, p. 36; no. 33, p. 62; no. 44, pp. 89-90; no. 15, p. 24.

14. *SRS*, no. 33, p. 61.

15. *SRS*, no. 41, pp. 83-84.

16. *SRS*, no. 43, pp. 87-88.

17. *SRS*, no. 42, p. 85.

18. *SRS*, no. 42, p. 86.

19. William Safire, "Structures of Sin," *The New York Times*, February 22, 1988, p. A19.

20. *SRS*, no. 23, p. 39. See also nos. 20-23, pp. 32-39.

21. *SRS*, no. 37, p. 71.

22. *SRS*, no. 28, p. 48.

23. The theme of personal conversion is important in John Paul's earlier writings as well. See, e.g., "Chegado a esta," *The Pope Speaks* 25 (1980), pp. 78-81; "Na alegre," *The Pope Speaks* 26 (1981), p. 71.

24. *SRS*, no. 26.

25. *SRS*, no. 26, p. 45.

26. *SRS*, no. 28, p. 49.

27. *SRS*, no. 28, p. 51.

28. *SRS*, no. 36, p. 69.

29. *SRS*, p. 69, footnote 65.

30. *SRS*, nos. 38 and 40.

31. "Human Work and the Story of Creation: Theology and Ethics in *Laborem Exercens*," John W. Houck and Oliver F. Williams, *Co-Creation and Capitalism* (Lanham, MD: University Press of America, 1983), p. 75.

32. "Americanizing Catholic Social Teaching," *Quarterly Review* 7 (Winter, 1987), pp. 15-32.

33. "Popes and Politics," pp. 274-80.

34. *SRS*, no. 3, p. 6.

35. *SRS*, no. 8, pp. 12-13.

36. *SRS*, no. 41, p. 82.

37. Henceforth *PP*, in Gremillion, *The Gospel*, no. 13, p. 391.

38. *PP*, no. 50, p. 402; see also no. 33.

39. *PP*, no. 78, p. 410.

40. See, e.g., *OA*, no. 24.

41. For a different interpretation of the thought of John Paul and Paul VI, see Michael Novak, "The Development of Nations," *Aspiring to Freedom: Commentaries on John Paul II's Encyclical 'The Social Concerns of the Church,'* Kenneth A. Myers, ed. (Grand Rapids: Eerdmans Publishing Co., 1988), pp. 67-109.

42. *Claims in Conflict: Retrieving and Renewing the Catholic Human Rights Tradition* (New York: Paulist Press, 1977).

43. *Ibid.*, p. 91.

44. *Ibid.*, p. 155.

45. *Ibid.*, p. 166.

46. "On Relative Equality: Catholic Egalitarianism After Vatican II," *Theological Studies* 45 (1984), pp. 651-75.

47. Draft of "Americanizing Catholic Social Teaching," unpublished manuscript, pp. 11-12.

48. "Social Justice and Consumerism in the Thought of Pope John Paul II," *Social Thought* 13 (1987), p. 70.

49. Vincent P. Mainelli, ed., *Social Justice* (Wilmington, NC: McGrath, 1978), p. 285.

50. *SRS*, no. 31, p. 57.

51. *SRS*, no. 29, pp. 52-53.

52. Christiansen, "Social Justice," p. 69; see also Paul Johnson, *Pope John Paul II and the Catholic Restoration* (New York: St. Martin's Press, 1981), pp. 191-92.

53. "The Civic Vision in Augustine's *City of God*," *Thought* 62 (1987), pp. 268-80.

54. *Ibid.*, p. 279.

55. *Ibid.*

56. For treatment of democratic capitalism, see Michael Novak, *The Spirit of Democratic Capitalism* (New York: Simon & Schuster, 1982). Novak's response to John Paul II differs from my own.

57. For treatment of politics and compromise, see, e.g., Barry Jay Seltser, *The Principles and Practice of Political Compromise: A Case Study of the United States Senate*, Studies in American Religion, volume 12 (New York: The Edwin Mellen Press, 1984); John Langan, "Politics—Good, Bad, or Indifferent? A Philosophical Assessment," in Madonna Kolbenschlag, ed., *Between God and Caesar: Priests, Sisters and Political Office in the United States*, (New York: Paulist, 1985), pp. 127-48. For an illustration of the principle of cooperation in a contemporary discussion, see Richard McCormick, "Medicaid and Abortion," *Theological Studies* 45 (1984), pp. 715-21.

Thirteen

The Conditions of Countercultural Credibility

John Howard Yoder

The interpretation of encyclicals like *Sollicitudo* is a science *sui generis*. The recurrent self-quotations, designed to indicate at the same time (paragraph 3) "continuity" and "renewal," enough permanence to be reassuring and enough innovation to justify a new text, make it especially difficult for the non-initiated to discern what it is that is being said that matters. This is not a problem of careful reading, but of esoteric semantics. The proliferation of quotation marks and italicizations signals a special density of meaning not transparent to the ordinary reader.

Some readers select out of the text the passages they like as most important, some those they do not like, without the ordinary readers being helped to see why it is those sentences which should be selected. Having observed for a while how others practice that special discipline[1] does not move me to try either to correct or to emulate them.

What I can best undertake, within the complementarity of perspectives and competences already richly represented in the case of this event, is a meditation on the pertinence of the subtitle of our program: "The Making of an Economic Counterculture?" That phrase appears on our program as an interrogation, without any statement about what it might mean. I shall attempt to define what should make that a proper question, and what ought to count toward an answer.

Dennis McCann has made my task both easier and more immediately imperative by introducing his pejorative understanding of the term "counterculture," which he calls a "temptation." McCann accords a certain esteem to the moral integrity of what he calls a "counterculture," most typically represented by the utopian communities on the American frontier or by the fringe movements of the Protestant

Reformation which Ernst Troeltsch called "sectarian." Yet what he esteems in them is their having the courage of irrelevance. When forced by the nature of things to choose between moral faithfulness and social responsibility, these people dare to choose the former and, thereby, have a witness which contributes long-range to authentic moral insight.

This is by no means what I mean in picking up as my topic the phrase from the title chosen by the planners of our event. I am not sure that McCann is fair to Ephrata, New Harmony, Oneida and Amana, or the *kibbutzim*, but that is not my concern. Nor is this the place to try to correct for the reading of "sectarianism" by Troeltsch and his pupils.[2] My concern in approaching a definition is that none of McCann's characterizations—utopian, "unconstrained," "no tradeoffs," "withdrawing from participation in the dominant system"— describes what I am looking for. Nor would any of them help to describe either what *Sollicitudo* does or what it should have done. An alternative community (i.e., one like the Shakers, the Holy Cross, or the Amish) has certain values, but that is certainly not a pertinent yardstick here.

What is appropriately meant by "counter" is simply that we ought properly to ask whether Catholic social teaching is maintaining or developing a capacity to speak to the contemporary moral agenda in some other way than just ratifying or blessing what the present rulers of the system are already doing, and to do that speaking in a way that is theologically accountable. By attaching that adjective to the noun "culture," we mean that we shall be looking for the critique to take shape, not only in terms of spirituality or a set of general theological affirmations, from which it might be held that evaluations and behavior ought to be derived, but in substantive cultural terms, able to be so formulated that no special insider hermeneutics is needed to know what social and economic strategies are specifically rejected or required.

The Roman Catholic community has in the past unashamedly implemented such a countercultural commitment. In fact, the phrase "Catholic Social Teachings" meant, until recently, a set of guidelines with just such substantive precision. A good example was the notion of a living wage, reaching from *Rerum Novarum* through decades of the ministry of John A. Ryan. What the head of a family has a right to earn is determined not by the market value of his or her labor but by the basic needs of the family. Similarly, Catholic teachings on abortion and on divorce refuse any cognitive bargaining with the surrounding mores. Our question then is whether *Sollicitudo* provides clarity as to the points where Christian faithfulness will continue concretely to critique the trends of our culture.

The Dominant, Normative Culture

Catholic Christendom has for a millennium and a half assumed with a good conscience the role of being, or seeking to be, the dominant, normative culture, interpreting and imposing the vision of what a human community properly ought to be. The Church claims to be in herself a "perfect society,"[3] but in that quality she could also guide normatively the state, the economy, the family, the schools. . . . In recent years a complex experience of disestablishment, migration and secularization has replaced that foundational claim with another, more modest but also potentially more true vision. Now the vision is one of presence in the world as *diaspora*. That might make a difference in what it means to care about social reality.

There may be components of how to be ethical in societies which do not depend much on the macro-social setting. The difference between establishment and its alternatives may not matter much for some moral questions. I am to look at the ones where it does. There are components of social ethics that an encyclopedic view would cover but about which the encyclical does not ask; I shall attend to the questions raised by those it does treat.

"Preferential Option for the Poor"

From a posture of domination or establishment it is possible, and it was possible in Catholic thought for a millennium, for ecclesiastical moral instruction to claim as taken-for-granted a relative homogeneity of value insights throughout the population. No other values than ours have standing. The claim is made that the moral values of the faith are the same as those of "nature," known to everyone else, or at least to everyone else "of good will." If anyone differs deeply, this heresy should be decried and, if possible, repressed by "the secular arm." There need be no countercultural witnessing, no beleaguered minority advocacy. Those assumptions now no longer hold.

A prerequisite for a Christian countercultural economic vision in our day then will be the ability and the readiness to account for value commitments that differ from those which dominate a society. For example, let us begin where *Sollicitudo* ends, with a recently introduced slogan. The last scriptural reference in the encyclical is a verse from the Magnificat. It undergirds the notion, quite new at least in this verbal form, of a "preferential option for the poor." This line of argument exemplifies how easily moral thought about society becomes the hostage of stereotypical abstractions. A large sector of the conversation has been taken over by this phrase borrowed from the Spanish, "preferential option for the poor." When filtered through the Polish or the Italian, this becomes in paragraph 42 of *Sollicitudo* the odd formulation, "love of preference for the poor." Some of the grumpier commentators, accustomed to the rule of "If you cannot say it in standard English it must be wrong," point out that in standard English the word "option" means keeping your choices open, not taking sides. In Spanish it means having taken sides. So the phrase "preferential option" in English is both a barbarism[4] and an oxymoron. "Love of preference," on the other hand, is neither. Taken literally it is nonsense. Yet "people who know" go on using it as if the meaning from Spanish were clear.

That kind of linguistic finesse is, however, not my concern. What we need to ask is: What would it take to move the notion of a divine bias in favor of the poor from the status of a social-theory slogan, or a liturgical poem, to that of an institutional rule of thumb? The *Sollicitudo* text is characteristic of its genre in not giving reasons for what it holds to be self-evident, nor definitions of the familiar. In what sense, to use the hallowed phrase, is casting the mighty down from their thrones papal policy? By what means does the encyclical propose that the rich should be sent away empty?

As a theme of poetry and prophecy, the bias of God in favor of the poor is at least as old as the Exodus. It was two centuries old when it was celebrated in the Song of Hannah, and nearly a millennium older when it was sung in the Magnificat. There it meant radical structural change. Since then, however, the liturgical recitation of that language has been found compatible, by the Roman Catholic episcopal magisterium, with every possible social arrangement with which the Church has collaborated, most of them nondemocratic, most of them violent, sexist, most of them ethnocentric, most of them economically stratified, and most of them not generous to the poor. We must, therefore, ask now just what is changing.

To make of the platitudinous poetry a moral management maxim, capable of providing structure to an accountable, verifiable, dialogical process of discernment, I suggest would call for certain formal requirements to be met. I do not find these requisites explicitly present in *Sollicitudo* or in *Laborem Exercens*. This may not mean that they are not there, it may only mean that reading this genre of literature calls for special insider hermeneutics which I am the last to claim to master.

"Having" and "Being"

But the bias in favor of the poor is only one criterion; there would have to be others. There would have to be a whole system, at least a skeletal one, of social-ethical vocabulary and insight. The language would have to be precise enough to give real guidance and ordinary enough to be understandable to non-technicians. The latter requisite, ordinary language, can be found in the encyclical, but the former, the systemic understanding, is elusive. Taken straight, one sentence at a time, *Sollicitudo* says very little to which anyone could take exception. Careful readers, therefore, have to look between the lines, or "behind" the text for some of its stylistic signals.

One key we might reach for would seem (at first) to be the disjunction between "having" and "being" (paragraph 28). It is introduced as if it were foundational and of some help. Originally, it would seem that this contrast was developed as a criticism of consumerist materialism, perhaps also of socialist materialism. What it contributes to defining true development is not spelled out. It hardly helps to explain just why or how to meet the needs of the poor. That "having" and "being" are "not necessarily contradictory" is reassuring, but *Sollicitudo* does not provide substantial criteria for discerning when and how they are compatible, or which kinds of "having" are supportive of the right kind of "being."

The encyclical frequently uses pointed, undefined value adjectives. It speaks of "true" development (paragraphs 24 and 26) or "full" development (paragraph 28). The adjectives seem to mean "properly so-called," as if to signal a contrast between correct and unauthentic uses of the concept in question. Yet the way to make those distinctions between properly and improperly so-called is not clearly laid out or argued. A potential for discernment is hinted at, or presupposed, without being expressed. If I were a militant in Catholic Action, or a Christian Democratic parliamentarian, this text would not make it clear to me what I should do next, or which side to take.

The above two paragraphs have made two stabs at bringing to the surface something like a latent social value analysis beneath the surface of the text. I conclude that it is not there, at least not with the precision which would suffice to provide concrete guidelines.

Test for Compatibility

Any concrete social vision with regard to economic and cultural development will need to be linked intrinsically to the rest of the value priorities of Christians. If, instead of speaking of a "posture" (which might be only interior, or only intellectual, or only individual), we are discussing a "counterculture" with criteria authentically its own, the cross-references to all the rest of the texture of life together will be especially essential. Is there a correlation between "true development" and truth-telling, between "true development" and gender roles and sexism, between "true development" and legislation to diminish acid rain?

High priority in this setting belongs to the most primitive level of "being," i.e., to questions of the sacredness of life: war, capital punishment, abortion. . . . It is striking how little attention this crossover gets in *Sollicitudo*. The text denounces war as bad economics (paragraphs 10 and 24) but not as morally wrong, thereby maintaining the present Pope's posture of being less critical of nuclear war than were his three predecessors. The occasional references to "structures of sin" do not identify nationalism as one of them. Military rule as a bad form of civil government bears more blame for misdevelopment than the text indicates. There is no reference to the phenomenon of the anticommunist National Security State, one of the major reasons for misallocation of resources and for the abuse of the poor. I find no reference to corrections and prison. I find none to abortion; the closest he comes to it is an unclear allusion (paragraph 25) to public pressure in favor of contraception or sterilization. My point is not that every encyclical should cover every subject, but that caring for the social process, accentuating the difference between authentic and unauthentic development, should on intrinsic grounds, not bypass most of the other standard considerations of the sacredness of life.

Social/Ethical Analysis

What is the document's understanding of historical causation? The song of Miriam at the Red Sea, the Song of Deborah at the River Kishon, the Song of Hannah and the Magnificat have in common that the God whose saving deeds they proclaim is not a mere code word for the course of events as they naturally go. God is the savior of lost causes, not the inherent logic of history. God's siding with the poor is not the same as Marx's inherent and ineluctable dialectic of history, nor as social Darwinism's equally ineluctable selection of the fittest. It is a commitment against the natural course of events.

Informed social concern demands a theologically informed vision of what or who makes history happen. From Eusebius until the age of Revolution, the answer of the Roman magisterium was clear: God uses the pious sovereign, working hand-in-hand with the hierarchy, to rule the world. Social causative connections were transparent because the good guys had the power. From the eighteenth century on, the adjustment to the world of democracy was difficult for Rome, but with *Rerum Novarum* it began in earnest and by Vatican II it seemed to be settled.

Yet that shift with regard to the preferred forms of government, including a newly reaffirmed ability to survive under unacceptable regimes, especially in Eastern Europe, did not reconstitute a full alternative understanding of the nature of the historical process, or of how God works in it.

No system of social/ethical analysis can proceed without facing at this point, whether overtly or not, a method question which ecclesiastical documents generally skim past. Do we assume, with ancient cultures, that human events are the product of the arbitrary interventions of the gods, with JHWH the strongest but not the only intervenor among them? Then the link between our good deeds and desirable social outcomes is not a discernible causal connection but a god or God whom our piety has caused to be well-disposed toward us, or who perhaps will also send us chastisement or cause us to suffer.

Do we assume, with modern scientific determinism, that the social system is a cause-effect nexus, without gaps or surprises? Then to implement God's biases would call for manipulating well-known causal linkages toward those good ends. It would call for using the obvious kinds of power of which people of good will dispose, against the other obvious kinds of power possessed by the "structures of sin." Or is there some other option? Is there some way—I state it naively—to affirm both enough determinism to make sense of social systems and enough divine intervention to give hope to lost causes?

Two elements of the biblical language on the subject could be made pertinent to this question. I designated them above as participating in the genres of "poetry or prophecy." I thereby recognized the prevalent uncertainty as to whether they describe the real world or something else.

Discerning the Signs. First, it is clear that the cause of the poor, of which JHWH of Hosts is the defender, is a hopeless cause. The oldest song in the canon, that of Miriam, praises events which could not have happened; lay language would call it "miracle." God's salvific intrusions are unpredictable, His detailed design inscrutable, yet for our good. The Song of Hannah in the beginning of the Samuel story and the Magnificat at the beginning of the Gospel (and at the end of the encyclical) make the same assumptions, so did Saint Francis and Dorothy Day. There is no transparent causal continuity between people of goodwill doing wise and good deeds, and the saving mighty acts of JHWH of hosts. He saves those for whom there is no help. This world view would have to make some difference in thinking about social strategies.

I have no interest in intervening in the professional precincts of either scripture scholars or the philosophers of science. Some people in both categories are my esteemed colleagues here at Notre Dame. Both kinds can abundantly demonstrate that the word "miracle" is not univocal. It is, however, my duty here to ask whether the encyclicals do or do not claim to be making sense in terms of secular social science, politics and economics.

The introduction (paragraph 7) of the rare biblical phrase "to discern the signs of the times," a usage first made current by Vatican II, makes the problem a little more visible and a lot more difficult. Does "discerning the signs" mean trend-watching? Is it baptized futurology? Does it mean finding a logic which is inherent in the events themselves and which becomes transparent to everyone when they are sensitively watched? And, if so, are those trends to be taken as good, or must some of them be judged evil? Or does it mean that events pose us a question to which the answer is derived from elsewhere, from beyond the causal nexus, e.g., from salvation history or from revelation?[5]

One cannot tell from the text of *Sollicitudo* whether the Pope and all the people of goodwill whom he seeks to mobilize will or will not claim to converse on an even terrain with social science realists who claim to know what really makes things happen. One cannot tell for sure whether the detailed criteria of economic righteousness which should be followed are known to everyone.

On the one hand, *Sollicitudo* reaffirms recourse to prayer. Adherents of other faiths are invited to give witness together to the humane values which religion (presumably all kinds of religion)[6] supports. Catholics are invited to implore Mary (paragraph 49) for her intercession. But the connection—disjunctive, complementary, or otherwise—between prayer and whatever else people ought to be doing is opaque.

On the other hand, the encyclical is full of descriptive statements about specified cases of social evils and their specifiable causes. Thus, the interpretive tools of social science determinism are used, in a commonsense lay way, diagnostically, yet without entering into the intradisciplinary debates which that opens up.

Sinful Structures. A second component of the biblical vision is the perception that evil is not purely personal but structured. In the Hebrew scriptures the evil rulers and the gods they serve are named. In the apostolic witness we read of "principalities and powers," i.e., created structures, linked with but not reducible to social institutions, linked with but not reducible to human individuals.[7]

The encyclical does open the door to the concept of "sinful structures." This concept is introduced in paragraph 36 (again in paragraphs 39 and 40) with some indication that it is a new usage. It could be exploited to enable serious grappling with the nature of evil institutions. It could appropriate the just-mentioned apostolic vision of the cosmos under the control of rebellious powers. It could help to come to grips with the way in which violence, materialism, falsehood, or nationalism, are more than the sum of the distinct decisions of specific individuals made at particular points in time. It could help to integrate in a deeper way the dimensions of causation and responsibility. But then the text sweeps those promising possibilities aside by a rapid argument which explicitly reduces all "evil structures" to nothing but the evil decisions and actions of individuals. Thus, at one blow, one of the most promising components of a biblical cosmology and one of the most illuminating method contributions of liberation theology are shrugged off without a real hearing.

Central Planning and Management

Any system of social-ethical guidance must come to terms with the debate about the value and possibility of central planning and management as the means toward social goals. Most of *Sollicitudo* is content to name the evils we all face, without risking prescriptive guidance about what to do about them. "Each local situation will show what reforms are most urgent and how they can be achieved" (paragraph 43). How does a "local situation" go about doing that? Does it mean that there is some naturally self-evident, morally right givenness in the mechanisms of the political economy? Why then is it going so badly for the poor? Does it mean there is a providential "invisible hand" which will make things work out for the best if only the right market mechanisms are left alone?

Does it mean that expert local administrators, wisely taking responsibility for leadership as pious sovereigns used to do, will find reasonable solutions to manageable problems? Overtly, *Sollicitudo* seems to avow no specifiable understanding of social process. Though it describes the worsening situation of the poor, names specific proximated causes of some kinds of suffering, and calls on the moral motivations of solidarity and the common good, it does not provide concrete guidance. In the absence thereof, everyone will assume a papal mandate to do what seems good in his or her own eyes.

Is the state, as for the New Testament and for Hobbes, basically the sword, or, as for Aquinas, basically the natural creaturely structure of sociality? Failure to come to grips explicitly with the specific problem of the state as agent of development correlates with the low visibility, in *Sollicitudo*, of the problems of military authoritarianism and the arms race, in both the poor countries and the rich ones, as obstacles to "true development." It also weakens the closer-in discussions of whether the order needed in the economy and the rest of society needs to be, or can be, imposed by the state.[8]

Occasional juxtaposition of "liberal capitalism and Marxist collectivism" (paragraphs 20, 21 and 41), serves to set aside the more extreme doctrinaire answers which some might give to the above question. But "a plague on both your houses" is not a policy. We are assured (paragraph 41) that the right answer is not a mere midpoint between the two, not a mediating "third way," but "a category of its own," not ideology but theology.

The more presumptuously that claim is made explicit, namely that there is a distinct, epistemologically autonomous view, the less adequate for guidance is an inventory of evils which does not provide the criteria for their resolution. Paragraph 43, for instance, lays certain injustices at the door of the international economic institutions, calling for "a greater degree of ordering." Who is to do that ordering? States? Banks? Bishops? *Opus Dei?* Parliamentary party politics? Mass movements of civil disobedience? The Trilateral Commission? Intergovernmental agencies? Should such "greater ordering" mean more or less regulation of market mechanisms?

Who Will Do Our Thinking?

Any coherent countercultural vision of social concern will need to identify the privileged bearer of social awareness. If neither the state nor the private powers centrally managed from Wall Street are to do our thinking, who will? I noted the statement that "each local situation will show. . . ." Who has that knowing?

The first powerful response of Catholic social thought after *Rerum Novarum* was that an intellectual elite of the style of Maritain and Mounier will think for the Church and the people in the light of a renewed Christian humanist vision. Their insights will be implemented by lay Catholic Action movements. Something similar was done in the United States between the world wars by John A. Ryan; its most concrete component, which I noted above as a specimen of "countercultural" courage, was the notion of a "fair wage" calculated on the basis of need, not the market.

A third response would be the confrontational experience of the Polish Catholics, where the Pope's own habits were formed. A yet younger vision, like the Pope's in ways he does not discern, would be what some Latin American theologians call "the epistemological privilege of the poor." The encyclical does not seem to me to have its own answer to this question; that probably leaves us with a tacit commitment to something between the Polish and the elitist visions.

Conclusion

By the nature of the case, it has turned out that the kinds of questions I have been seeking to formulate cannot be answered from within this encyclical. *Pacem in Terris* or *Populorum Progressio* might have yielded more concrete answers. I have excluded from the study any suggestion of what my own answer might be, since the questions properly were those which arise from within the text.

The act of asking must suffice, at this place in the conversation, to identify part of what it might take for social concern to find a shape which would be more definable, more accountable, and thereby more capable of unifying and guiding a community whose moral/cultural vision would be more efficaciously critical of the way things are than that of its world's rulers.

Sollicitudo ends with words from the Magnificat, used liturgically.

He has put down the mighty from their thrones and exalted those of low degree; he has filled the hungry with good things, and the rich he has sent empty away.[9]

What if the encyclical had begun with those words, and used them programmatically?

Notes

1. At the end of paragraph 42, concluding a passage on the limits of the moral autonomy of private property, there is a throwaway reference to a right to "freedom of economic initiative," intended perhaps to welcome contemporary changes in the Communist world. Numerous commentators have sought to make of it a whole new doctrinal chapter.

2. In terms of moral theology the question posed by the Troeltschian interpretation of "sectarian" relevance is whether faithfulness and responsibility in fact must stand in a zero-sum relationship. In terms of systematic theology the question is one of the authority of incarnation (cf. in my *The Original Revolution*, paragraph 132 ff the discussion of Christ and "other lights"). In terms of history it has to do with whether the post-Constantinian situation is the norm or the exception (cf. in my *The Priestly Kingdom*, pp. 135 ff).

In challenging the adequacy of McCann's Troeltschian-Niebuhrian categories for illuminating Catholic social thinking, I do not cast doubt on his intentions. The liberal Protestant historiographical line from Troeltsch and Weber to McCann is more objective and generous than others were or are in ascribing at least some values to the stance it calls "sectarian."

3. This phrase did not claim moral perfection or infallibility. It meant merely that the Church possesses all of what it takes to be what it ought to be. But the use of "society" as the noun for that "what it ought to be" did presume a normative vision relevant to all other uses of "society."

4. "Barbarism" is a term neither of taste nor of morals but of linguistics. It designates with technical precision a word ostensibly in one language used according to the rules of another.

5. The modern use of the phrase from Matthew 16:4 is credited to John XXIII, in *Peace on Earth*, paragraph 39 ff, developed after that in *Gaudium et Spec*, 10 f, 42 ff. Despite the optimistic evaluation by Cardinal Maurice Roy (in Joseph Gremillion, *The Gospel of Peace and Justice*, 1976; Maryknoll: Orbis, p. 542), there seems to be no clarity intended about how the watching and evaluating of trends is to be validated. Which trends are real and which deceptive? Which to be welcomed and which to be denounced?

6. Not all forms of religion do. Resurgent Christianity as articulated by Pat Robertson or Margaret Thatcher, resurgent Islam as articulated by the Ayatollah do not, nor did most religious establishments of history.

7. I capsuled the then current consensus of NT scholarship on the theme of "Principalities and Powers" in my *Politics of Jesus* (Grand Rapids: Eerdmans, 1972) pp. 135 ff. The theme has been pursued since, especially by Walter Wink; *Naming the Powers*, 1984; Philadelphia: Fortress.

8. Chewing away at the capitalism/socialism debate is a perennial undercurrent of conferences at Notre Dame on economic ethics. I am less sure than my perennial friends Benne, Wogaman and Novak of the utility of pursuing that debate in principle; but if I were Pope I would recognize a duty to speak to it more clearly. Setting the two forms of materialism back-to-back is no help. Replacing both with a whole new alternative vision, theologically mandated, would be most worthy of attention, but the mere assertion that such a different way exists will not do.

9. Luke 1:52-53.

Fourteen

Solidarity, Sin, Common Good, and Responsibility for Change in Contemporary Society

John Langan, S.J.

This paper bears a weighty title which may strike people as being more appropriate to a dissertation than to a conference paper or reflective essay. But I want to make two observations about the title. The first is that I am attempting to situate a point of intersection of ideas or themes. The second is that a certain ponderousness is consistent with the teaching style of John Paul II in his universal moral pedagogy. What follows on my part is much less ambitious than either an encyclical or a dissertation. This is a preliminary work of analysis and exploration and, in personal terms, it is my effort to explain to myself why I am simultaneously attracted and disconcerted by this Pope's two major social encyclicals, *Laborem Exercens* (*LE*) and *Sollicitudo Rei Socialis* (*SRS*). Trying to answer this question is not a matter of purely autobiographical interest, since it seems clear that these documents have puzzled many people in English-speaking cultures in the academic, public policy, and business arenas. They have appeared as signs of encouragement to many on the left who are often out of sympathy with much that the present Pope says on moral and religious issues, and as signs of contradiction to many on the right who applaud his opposition to Marxism and liberal permissiveness.

I propose that we focus on paragraphs 36-40 of *SRS*, which begins with a remarkable conclusion: "It is important to note therefore that a world which is divided into blocs, sustained by rigid ideologies, and in which instead of interdependence and solidarity different forms of imperialism hold sway, can only be a world subject to structures of sin."

Here is the East-West conflict with its negative consequences for the development of the South which John Paul has laid out in Section III, "Survey of the Contemporary World." Already he has made it clear

275

that he regards the ideological bases of this conflict as temporally and historically conditioned and, indeed, as somewhat archaic. He observes that both the fundamental intellectual conceptions of shaping the present conflict, liberal capitalism and Marxist collectivism, are "imperfect and in need of radical correction" and that the Church takes a critical attitude to both these competing world systems. He proceeds to raise a very interesting and fundamental question about both systems: "In what way and to what extent are these two systems capable of changes and updatings such as *to favor or promote a true and integral development of individuals and peoples in modern society?"*

All of this is reasonably familiar to students of Catholic social teaching which has, over the last century, striven to offer itself as an alternative to both Marxist socialism and liberal capitalism. But he goes beyond the range of customary platitudes on this subject in characterizing the bipolar world of East-West relations as necessarily a world "subject to structures of sin," as he does in *SRS*. Here, as the argument of this paragraph makes plain, he is making a double move. On the one hand, there is the move from personal sin to structures of sin, a move that he had made already in the Apostolic Exhortation, *Reconciliatio et Paenitentia,* of 1984. There he had insisted that institutions, structures and societies are not the subjects of moral acts, and that social sins are "the result of the accumulation and concentration of many personal sins." In *SRS* he maintains that structures of sin are "always linked to the concrete acts of individuals who introduce these structures, consolidate them and make them difficult to remove." The earlier treatment of this theme in *Reconciliatio et Paenitentia,* quoted in the footnote, makes it clear that the Pope wishes to accuse of personal sin not merely those who introduce, promote, or defend evil structures, but also those

> . . . who are in a position to avoid, eliminate or at least limit certain social evils but who fail to do so out of laziness, fear, or the conspiracy of silence, through secret complicity or indifference, of those who take refuge in the supposed impossibility of changing the world and also of those who sidestep the effort and sacrifice required, producing specious reasons of a high order.

This listing of the factors that lead us to passivity and to sins of omission in the face of grave evils is sufficiently pointed and comprehensive to make most of us at least consider the possibility that our own passivity may lack not merely justification but even excuse. At any rate, it is important to see that the Pope's affirmation of personal responsibility and personal sin is not intended to restrict the scope of socially significant sin to a relatively small number of "movers and shakers" who initiate harmful practices or who derive substantial benefits from them. Rather, it seems to apply to almost all who are citizens or agents. John Paul II's approach does not allow us to draw a comforting line between a sinful social realm of powerful institutions and a private realm of passive innocents whose lives are occasionally marred by personal vices. Rather, the point is that many of us are guilty of personal sins which help to establish or maintain structures of sin. The Pope does admit, however, that the situation confronting ordinary moral agents working in contemporary society is not an easy one when he observes: "The sum total of negative factors working against a true awareness of the universal common good, and the need to further it, gives the impression of creating, in persons and institutions, an obstacle which is difficult to overcome." This implies that many people are functioning with a diminished awareness of the social moral demands of their situation. It is clear that for John Paul II personal sin remains the fundamental category, and the notion of structures of sin is secondary and derivative both in terms of our thinking and our actions.

The other move the Pope is making in this paragraph is that he defends the appropriateness of speaking of social and political problems in terms of sin. This is a move which puts him at odds with those who on empiricist or naturalistic grounds would reject the application of theological categories to social phenomena. But it puts him also at odds with the much larger number of those who, because of a variety of intellectual and nonintellectual factors, prefer to think about social realities in more neutral, value-free, impartial ways. These ways have become the *lingua franca* for political and social reporting and analysis, but even in a secularized *milieu* it is not easy to eliminate all moral implications and resonances from our language in these areas. As John Paul II observes:

> One can certainly speak of "selfishness" and of "shortsightedness," of "mistaken political calculations" and "imprudent economic decisions." And in each of these evaluations one hears an echo of a moral

and ethical nature. Man's condition is such that a more profound analysis of individuals' actions and omissions cannot be achieved without implying, in one way or another, judgments or references of an ethical nature.

In the Pope's view, sociopolitical analysis contains an evaluative element which may or may not be based on "faith in God and on his law."

Analysis from the theological viewpoint takes the further step of considering social phenomena in terms of "the will of the Triune God" who "requires from people clearcut attitudes which express themselves also in actions or omissions towards one's neighbor." The failure to observe the commandments of the "second tablet," (those that deal with our treatment of our fellow human beings) is both an offense against God and a source of harm to the neighbor. It introduces "into the world influences and obstacles which go far beyond the actions and the brief lifespan of an individual" and also "involves interference in the process of the development of peoples." What we should notice here is not merely the affirmation of the close connection of our attitudes to God and to the neighbor, which is a standard theme in contemporary Catholic moral theology, but also the very strong emphasis on the causal interconnectedness of our actions and the enduring and irretrievable character of their consequences. The emphasis on consequences, especially as these affect the social context, is, interestingly enough, a theme that is common to this Pope and to utilitarian moralists.

But the moral atmosphere, the climate of concern which the Pope deems appropriate for the making of moral decisions is clearly more intense, more charged, even more anxious than the neutral and secular climate usually favored by utilitarians. Rather, it seems closer to the more strenuous approaches to the moral life propounded by Augustine and Kierkegaard in which sin and guilt are inescapable and in which freedom, if not exercised in union with God's will, is more burden than benefit. The decisive step forward from the present sinful situation is not for John Paul II the adoption of a new set of policies which will have better consequences. Rather, it is the recognition of "the urgent need to change the spiritual attitudes which define each individual's relationship with self, with neighbor, with even the remotest human communities, and with nature itself, and all of this in view of higher values such as the *common good*, or . . . the full development of the whole individual and of all people. In Christian terms, he observes, this is a matter of "conversion" which "entails a relationship to God, to the sin committed, to its consequences and hence to one's neighbor."

All-Consuming Desire for Profit and Thirst for Power

In the presentation of both the moral problem and its resolution there is a strong emphasis on the movement from attitude through action to consequences, and a profound reluctance to adopt a restricted understanding of the moral life which would concentrate exclusively on either attitudes or consequences. This is not surprising in religious social ethics which is under the double requirement of looking to the relationship of the believer to God and to the effects of actions on other persons. It is quite appropriate, then, for John Paul II to direct our attention specifically to two attitudes that have easily understood social consequences. These are: "the all-consuming desire for profit" and "the thirst for power." The Pope is particularly concerned about these attitudes when they are found in extreme or absolute forms. He recognizes that these attitudes can exist independently of each other; but he resists the temptation to attribute the first of these attitudes to the West and the second to the East in our present bipolar world. Rather, he makes the claim that "in today's world both are indissolubly united with one or the other predominating." He does not offer any specific evidence or arguments for this interesting claim which seems both attractive and vulnerable to counterexamples. What he does insist on is that these sinful attitudes favor the introduction of "structures of sin" and that they serve as the deep explanation of socially significant decisions even when these are not expressed in moral terms. He affirms that "hidden behind certain decisions, apparently inspired only by economics or politics, are real forms of idolatry: of money, ideology, class, technology." For these are not merely the values of individuals, they can be found also in nations and blocs. In John Paul II's view, thinking in terms of the various "forms of idolatry" rather than in terms of "imperialism" enables us to grasp "the true nature of the evil which faces us with respect to the development of peoples: it is a question of moral evil, the fruit of many sins which lead to 'structures of sin.' ''

Analysis of the problem of development in moral and theological terms also enables us to ''identify precisely, on the level of human conduct, the path to be followed in order to overcome it.'' This path involves the recognition of moral value and of the necessity for the transformation of spiritual attitudes. More specifically, the Pope points to ''the positive and moral value of the growing awareness of interdependence among individuals and nations.'' Interdependence is both a social system determining relationships in the contemporary world and a moral category. The virtue that expresses our new moral and social attitude is the virtue of solidarity which John Paul II defines in the following way:

> This [solidarity] then is not a feeling of vague compassion or shallow distress at the misfortunes of so many people, both near and far. On the contrary, it is a firm and persevering determination to commit oneself to the common good; that is to say to the good of all and of each individual, because we are all really responsible for all.

The Pope's language here makes it clear that he sees solidarity as very closely linked to justice; for his definition of it echoes the definition that Aquinas gives of the virtue of justice, that is, justice as present in the agent or subject rather than as a set of norms for social institutions. But instead of the indefinite and potentially individualistic *unicuique* (''each one'') that figures in Thomas's definition, John Paul places ''the common good.'' While the classical definition uses the comparatively objective and restricted notion of rendering to each person what is due (*reddere debitum*), John Paul employs the more personalist notion of self-commitment, a notion which strikes this observer as more open to the future and to the possibility of unspecified demands.

The connection between solidarity and the classical understanding of justice is apparent also if we reflect on the two previously mentioned attitudes that John Paul II sees as most opposed to solidarity: the desire for profit and the thirst for power. For these are both attitudes that lead people to take more than their share, to manifest the *pleonexia*, or graspingness which Aristotle saw as the most fruitful source of injustice in our social lives. To overcome these attitudes that generate sinful structures, John Paul II commends "a diametrically opposed attitude: a commitment to the good of one's neighbor with the readiness, in the Gospel sense, to 'lose oneself' for the sake of the other instead of exploiting him and to 'serve him' instead of oppressing him for one's own advantage." This, of course, is what one might call a top-of-the-line form of solidarity which draws on the heroic altruism of Christ's teaching and example. There can be little doubt that sustained commitment to such a self-surrendering and serving attitude would remove the typical human agent from the possibility of falling under the dominion of the desires for power and profit that the Pope sees as fundamental sources of social evils.

But there seems to be a continuing need also for more mundane and less sacrificial forms of solidarity, which are not simply the polar opposites of our desires for profit and power. In fact, in paragraph 39, John Paul II specifies the exercise of solidarity so that it includes both the responsibility of the more influential for the weaker and the claiming of their legitimate rights by the weaker. Among the positive developments in the contemporary world the former archbishop of Krakow wants to commend are: "the growing awareness of the solidarity of the poor among themselves, their efforts to support one another, and their public demonstrations on the social scene which, without recourse to violence present their own needs and rights in the face of the inefficiency or corruption of the public authorities." In a passage such as this, John Paul II acknowledges the necessity and value of self-assertion by the poor, a self-assertion which takes its ethical shape from the needs and rights of the poor and which brings them from passive subjection through to active citizenship. In this regard John Paul II points in the same direction as do liberation theologians when they call for the empowerment of the poor and the U.S. Catholic bishops when they call for an economy which makes the right to participate effective for all.

We should note that combining the endorsement of an ethic of nonviolent self-assertion for the poor and weak with an ethic of generous self-giving for the rich and strong produces a situation of formal asymmetry and practical convergence, with those above the median being urged to accept less favorable outcomes for themselves and those below it being encouraged to seek more favorable outcomes for themselves. This, I would argue, will make sense only if certain conditions are satisfied. First, there has to be a clear recognition that the goods necessary

for survival and for functioning as a free and equal citizen are sufficiently valuable that their absence can be a legitimate basis for social
criticism and for broad economic and political changes. The value of
these goods is such that it is a serious moral and religious error to urge
others to do without them or to acquiesce in social arrangements that
deprive significant numbers of people of these goods or of the opportunity to achieve them. *A fortiori,* it is morally and religiously unacceptable, indeed, sinful, to deprive people of these goods. At the same
time these goods, some of which we label material (food, clothing,
shelter, health care) and some of which we label civic or cultural (civil
liberties, education, the rule of law), do not have the ultimate and
transcendent worth of moral and religious values. For it is these values
that justify, require and, in some cases, facilitate the redistribution
and reallocation of the instrumental goods we need for living as persons and as citizens. More particularly, the goods we have labeled as
material and the wealth that enables us to obtain them have to be understood as goods not by reason of their correspondence to our ever-
increasing desires or by reason of the possibilities of indefinite multiplication and maximization that they present but because of their
instrumental contribution to comprehensive human well-being. Such
an understanding of these goods provides a middle ground between
the otherwise otherworldly depreciation of the goods of "this world"
that has marked a great deal of traditional Catholicism and those exces-
sively avid commendations of material goods which appeal to naive or
desperate desires for personal happiness through consumption and
which often serve to give a specious legitimation to *pleonexia* in the
lives of individuals and societies.

Second, the moral urgency of rights has to be interpreted so that it
applies to those rights necessary for survival with a decent minimum
and for participation in society as a free and equal citizen. Thus, rights
to private property, rights to goods and services that are not included in
this core take a secondary place and are open to restriction and renunciation for the sake of the common good. This is in accordance with the
traditional recognition in Catholic social teaching that property rights
are not to be absolutized and with the general philosophical view that
human rights, at least in their central instances, take precedence over
rights that arise from particular decisions and historical circumstances.
The point at issue here is whether the strong and the rich are well-off
because all their gains are ill-gotten and originate in violations of moral

norms and of the rights of others. Given the manifest disparities in human talent and willingness to work and venture, and given the enormous diversity of the ways in which circumstances alter human lives and fortunes, this would be a very difficult thesis to sustain. If at least some of the resulting differences in people's economic and social situations are not the result of morally suspect activity, then we have to deal with a situation of inequality in which people have been exercising their rights to make economically significant decisions and in which they have been acting in accordance with legal and ethical norms such as the honoring of contracts. In Nozick's terminology, they have been observing justice in transfers. So it seems that what gains they have made are rightfully theirs. At the same time, these gains have to be restricted and redistributed. This will require a division of rights according to the weight and urgency of considerations which justify their being overridden.

Catholic social teaching has registered its disapproval of increasingly inegalitarian outcomes, even while it has never insisted on a strict or leveling equality. Rather than arguing for confiscation of the property of the wealthy on the grounds it has been acquired unjustly, it has advocated redistribution, both legally required and voluntary, to meet the needs of those who fall below a decent minimum. This advocacy of redistribution goes beyond urging generosity to the poor as a commendable exercise of supererogation and Christian charity. Rather, it involves a claim that as a matter of justice the common good requires redistribution to meet the basic needs of the poor. The common good itself has to be understood in such a way that it is both an integral and necessary part of the good of the rich which they are not free to neglect and that it includes the basic well-being of the poor (as well as of the rich). The obligation to promote the common good falls upon all. But such a formulation tells us little, since the common good is a complex analogical good which cannot be promoted by simple maximization and since the obligation to promote the common good turns out to be a set of more specific obligations to act in ways that will promote the common good, obligations which have to be argued for in more specific ways.

Third, there has to be a network of psychological motives and social considerations that will be effective in causing people and groups above the median to accept a diminishing of their prospects, interests, and even rights so that those who are at or below the decent minimum may fare better. It has been common ground to both liberal and Catholic social thinkers that achieving this convergence of prospects by purely coercive methods would require a dangerous concentration of power in the state and would set administrators and regulators a task of enormous complexity that would quickly surpass their capacities for judgment and decision. It would be quite likely also to produce economic stultification on a grand scale, a phenomenon that has figured prominently in the recent wave of self-criticism within communist regimes. On the other hand, Catholic social thought has been willing to accept and even urge a considerable measure of governmentally imposed redistribution for the sake of those least well-off. So it has not relied simply on calls to conversion and voluntary giving. It has presented the issue clearly as a matter of justice, and so it rules out complacency and passivity in the face of outcomes which diverge systematically or constantly from the norms it proposes. Once these various points are noted, it may not be possible to go much further, since the proper mixture of appeals to compassion and generosity, of reminders of the stern demands of justice, of legal enactments with proportionate penalties, of macroeconomic policy adjustments and tax incentives, of community activism and personal initiatives, will probably vary with different cultures and with different policy problems. But we should not underestimate the difficulties of persuading the rich and the powerful to accept restrictions on their prospects, whether these rich and powerful constitute a small elite or an extensive stratum of an affluent society. I do not mean to suggest that such a task of persuasion is impossible, but that it is normally very difficult and grows comparatively easy only at certain moments of opportunity which, I suspect, will be found only in times of great economic and political crisis (the Great Depression, World War II, the current wave of economic failures in the Second and Third Worlds) or in times of sustained economic expansion.

So far, my remarks on *SRS* have been expository and interpretative. These are functions that cannot be taken lightly in assessing the social teachings of the present Pope whose writings are more abstract and concrete, more expansive and demanding than papal social teachings usually have been in this century. Furthermore, this encyclical manifests a high proportion of assertion to argument and frequently crosses with unwarranted facility from analysis to admonition. These are traits that trouble those of us who have been trained in the more modest and painstaking disciplines of moral and political philosophy as these are practiced currently in the Anglophone world. We lack many of the signposts familiar to us both in the philosophical debates arising from the work of John Rawls and Robert Nozick, and in the broader cultural and policy debates carried on by Daniel Bell, Michael Novak, the U.S. Catholic bishops, Robert Bellah and others. My own conviction is that initially, at least, we should not criticize papal teaching for its failure to speak to American experience in American terms, although we should be sensitive to the real differences in terminology and intellectual outlook that result from this fact.

The first task, as I have seen it, has been to conduct a preliminary reconnaissance to determine what is the general outline of the teaching of this document and what is the structure of the thought and the aspirations that inform it. Still, without feeling any desire to rush to judgment, I want to raise some critical questions. First, there seems to this reader to be a profound tension between the affirmation of the possibilities for conversion and the recognition of the ways in which people are involved with or enmeshed in structures of sin. Second, I sense an underlying impatience with those historical, technical, and institutional ways of explaining how manifest problems came to have the shape they actually have. Such explanations can dull our sense of the moral urgency of change and may cause us too readily to identify the real and the rational, the contingent outcome of historical events and the necessary unfolding of historical process. But without them we are likely to lack historical perspective and a sense of the roots of our problems. Third, alongside the reiterated affirmations of interdependence, there is a refusal to come to terms with the interlocking character of our decisions, with the ways in which the freedom of others complicates and frustrates our efforts to resolve the problems the Pope indicates. Fourth, there is a persistent reluctance to examine the problems presented by the negative and unintended consequences of those actions we perform even with the best of intentions and attitudes, as well as to think through the problem of trade-offs in interdependent systems. If one thinks that something like this set of criticisms is correct, even if it is put in rather cryptic and undiscriminating fashion, then one has reason to suspect that the underlying tendency of this Pope's social thought is a utopian and ahistorical moralism.

Part IV

Business Priorities
in the Economic Vision

. . . at this point we have to ask ourselves if the sad reality of today might not be, at least in part, the result of a *too narrow idea* of development, that is, a mainly economic one.

On Social Concern, Par. 15

The Pope's views on development, the option for the poor, and solidarity are strongly stated, but the translation to specific action remains a question. How does the manager translate this guidance to action?

Lee A. Tavis

The *intrinsic connection* between authentic development and respect for human rights once again reveals the *moral* character of development . . .

On Social Concern, Par. 33

Managers are at the center of this interplay of contending ideas, values, and principles. The ethical dilemmas of managers are acknowledged and understood more widely today than in years past.

James E. Post

It is necessary to state once more the characteristic principle of Christian social doctrine: the goods of this world are *originally meant for all.*
. . . Private property, in fact, is under a "social mortgage," which

means that it has an intrinsically social function, based upon and justified precisely by the principle of the universal destination of goods.

On Social Concern, Par. 42

In capitalist societies, individual genius and effort are compensated through rewards accruing from control and exploitation of one's technology. . . . In capitalism, the legitimacy of a new technology is expressed in terms of market demand, and accountability is contained within legal approval. The Church imposes communitarian criteria. It wants to know what technology does for people and to people.

S. Prakash Sethi and Paul Steidlmeier

As we observe the various parts of the world separated by this widening gap, and note that each of these parts seems to follow its own path with its own achievements, we can understand the current usage which speaks of different worlds within our *one world:* the First World, the Second World, the Third World and at times the Fourth World. . . . The expression ''Fourth World'' is used not just occasionally for the so-called *less advanced* countries, but also and especially for the bands of great or extreme poverty in countries of medium and high income.

On Social Concern, Par. 14

At the end of 1988, 80 percent of families will have experienced an income decline since 1977, but the top 10 percent will gain a 50 percent increase in their incomes. . . . The data help explain the emergence of the Fourth World in the U.S.

Teresa Ghilarducci

Fifteen

Papal Encyclicals and the Multinational Manager

Lee A. Tavis

The encyclicals of Pope John Paul II express a forceful view of how we should shape our environment. He calls each of us as members of the various institutions that influence our world to observe, judge, and act in light of these teachings. The Pope is explicit in his direction of responsibility to the individual,[1] even though the generalities of the encyclicals are a long step from implementation by people in the trenches.

In his latest encyclical, *Sollicitudo Rei Socialis*, John Paul repeatedly refers to global interdependence and the responsibility of the strong for the weak. This teaching uniquely applies to the managers of multinational firms (corporations and banks) since these firms are at the core of global interdependence. Multinational firms provide the critical linkages across which interdependence takes place and thus serve as the conduit for interactions between the strong and the weak. These are the linkages across which the rebalancing called for by the Pope will occur.

This paper focuses on individuals in their professional roles as multinational managers. It examines the issues of the conference from their perspectives. The managers of our concern are those who listen to the papal message; who interpret it in their own decision-making environment; and who attempt to act on it in their allocation of resources within the multinational firm. Daily in their professional lives, managers must act as well as observe and judge. What guidance can they glean from the encyclicals? Given guidance, to what extent does the individual manager have the freedom of action, the flexibility within the constraints of the economic system, and the confines of his or her institution to act on personal convictions to influence the activities of the firm?

This paper will view the encyclicals as they apply to multinational management decisions, and analyze the potential for managerial reaction within the boundaries of their decision environment. At the present time, the constraints imposed on banking managers are different from those that bind the activities of multinational manufacturers, agribusinesses, and resource or service corporations. While the devastation of Third World debt and the associated misallocation of global resources have changed the climate dramatically and fundamentally for corporate and banking decisions, banking managers find themselves more constrained in their potential range of actions than their multinational corporate counterparts.

The Papal Message to Multinational Managers

Based on the Pope's observation of a "radical interdependence," if his call for "authentic development," "the responsibility of the rich for the poor" as well as "liberation" and "solidarity" are to take hold, they will necessarily involve multinational firms.

Interdependence lies at the heart of the papal teaching in *Sollicitudo Rei Socialis* as it did in *Populorum Progressio*. Throughout the encyclical, John Paul stresses the importance of global interdependence and its critical moral dimension.

> However much society worldwide shows signs of fragmentation, expressed in the conventional names First, Second, Third, and even Fourth World, their *interdependence* remains close. When this interdependence is separated from its ethical requirements, it has *disastrous consequences* for the weakest. (*SRS*, p. 27)[2]

> At the same time, in a world divided and beset by every type of conflict, the *conviction* is growing of a radical *interdependence* and consequently of the need for a solidarity which will take up interdependence and transfer it to the moral plane. (*SRS*, p. 44)

Multinational firms provide connectors for this interdependence and, thus, are addressed uniquely by the statements on ethical responsibility. These firms have investments in numerous countries, developed and less-developed. Banks in the developed countries hold massive amounts of Third World debt. Multinational corporations, while investing most of their funds in developed countries, have substantial commitments in the less-developed world, and are often major factors in key sectors of those economies.

The activities of multinational firms are managed on a global basis. For example, multinational manufacturers build components in one country for assembly in a second, to sell across the world. If they manufacture, say, computer components in Mexico for assembly in the United States, the Mexican production will exclude supply from other countries such as Korea. Managers are continually allocating resources among the firm's subsidiaries, between the peoples in one country and another. For banks, loan portfolios are managed on a global basis. Credit flows to one location rather than another. Multinational managers, thus, are critical decision makers in a world the Pope would change.

Earlier, in *Laborem Exercens*, the Pope recognized the role of multinational corporations in global interdependence and leveled a blanket criticism of their actions.

> The concept of indirect employer is applicable to every society and in the first place to the state. . . . These links also create mutual dependence, and as a result it would be difficult to speak in the case of any state, even the economically most powerful, of complete self-sufficiency or autarky. . . . For instance the highly industrialized countries, and even more the businesses that direct on a large scale the means of industrial production (the companies referred to as multinational or transnational), fix the highest possible prices for their products, while trying at the same time to fix the lowest possible prices for raw materials or semi-manufactured goods. This is one of the causes of an ever increasing disproportion between national incomes. (*LE*, pp. 38–39)

The Pope sees the activities of multinationals as part of the persons and institutions which "determine the whole socioeconomic system," a system which he views as unjust. The question is, does the system always work that way? Do managers have freedom within the system to allocate resources to purposes that would be more in line with papal teaching? If managers have this freedom, what should they do—are there helpful guidelines in the encyclicals?

Addressing the last question first, there are a number of themes in *Sollicitudo Rei Socialis* such as the importance of development, the option for the poor, and the call for solidarity that are meaningful for multinational managers.

Development is the central theme of *Sollicitudo Rei Socialis*.[3] The Pope begins with a review of the originality of *Populorum Progressio*.

> . . . finally, on the specific theme of development, which is precisely the theme of the encyclical, the insistence on the "most serious duty" incumbent on the more developed nations "to help the developing countries." The same idea of development proposed by the encyclical flows directly from the approach which the Pastoral Constitution takes to this problem. These and other explicit references to the Pastoral Constitution lead one to conclude that the encyclical presents itself as an *application* of the Council's teaching in social matters to the specific problem of the *development* and the *underdevelopment* of peoples. (*SRS*, p. 11)

In *Sollicitudo Rei Socialis*, the Pope admits to the economic component of development when he states:

> There is no doubt that he [humankind] needs created goods and the products of industry, which are constantly being enriched by scientific and technological progress. And the ever greater availability of material goods not only meets needs but also opens new horizons. The danger of the misuse of material goods and the appearance of artificial needs should in no way hinder the regard we have for the new goods and resources placed at our disposal and the use we make of them. On the contrary, we must see them as a gift from God and as a response to the human vocation, which is fully realized in Christ. (*SRS*, pp. 51–52)

Still, the Pope's version of development goes well beyond economic considerations.

> Although *development* has a *necessary economic dimension*, since it must supply the greatest possible number of the world's inhabitants

with an availability of goods essential for them ''to be,'' it is not limited to that dimension. If it is limited to this, then it turns against those whom it is meant to benefit. (*SRS*, p. 51)

In his bleak summary of the contemporary world he notes:

Hence at this point we have to ask ourselves if the sad reality of today might not be, at least in part, the result of a *too narrow* idea of development, that is, a mainly economic one. (*SRS*, p. 26)

To the extent that multinational firms contribute to production efficiency in the Third World and, thus, the economic component of development, the goal of the multinational manager would fit readily the requirements set forth by the Pope. There are positive economic effects associated with the human and material resources that flow from the developed to the less-developed countries across the multinational corporate and banking linkages. The problem occurs when the power of First World financial and product markets, labor, and governmental interests are transmitted across these same multinational linkages to exploit the less-powerful Third World societies—when the fruits of the enhanced Third World productivity flow back to the First World beyond their reasonable share.

The groups most damaged by the First World power blocs are the poor and marginalized people in Third World societies, those who seldom are represented adequately by their own governments. The Pope articulates the needs of these poor.

Here I would like to indicate one of them: the *option* or *love of preference* for the poor. This is an option, or a *special form* of primacy in the exercise of Christian charity, to which the whole tradition of the Church bears witness. . . . Likewise the *leaders* of nations and the heads of *international bodies*, while they are obliged always to keep in mind the true human dimension as a priority in their development plans, should not forget to give precedence to the phenomenon of growing poverty. (*SRS*, pp. 84–85)

In his focus on the poor, the Pope calls for specific action.

The motivating concern for the poor—who are, in the very meaningful term, "the Lord's poor"—must be translated at all levels into concrete actions, until it decisively attains a series of necessary reforms. . . . In this respect I wish to mention specifically: the *reform of the international trade system*, which is mortgaged to protectionism and increasing bilateralism; the *reform of the world monetary and financial system*, today recognized as inadequate; the *question of technological exchanges* and their proper use; the *need for a review of the structure of the existing international organizations*, in the framework of an international juridical order. (*SRS*, pp. 86–87)

The Pope states our responsibility to work for development, including the option for the poor, in terms of solidarity. His initial definition is, again, based on *Populorum Progressio* and derives from interdependence.

In this framework, the *originality* of the encyclical consists not so much in the affirmation, historical in character, of the universality of the social question, but rather in the *moral evaluation* of this reality. Therefore political leaders, and citizens of rich countries considered as individuals, especially if they are Christians, have the *moral obligation*, according to the degree of each one's responsibility, to *take into consideration*, in personal decisions and decisions of government, this relationship of universality, this interdependence which exists between their conduct and the poverty and underdevelopment of so many millions of people. Pope Paul's encyclical translates more succinctly the moral obligation as the "duty of solidarity"; and this affirmation, even though many situations have changed in the world, has the same force and validity today as when it was written. (*SRS*, p. 15)

In solidarity, the Pope ties the responsibilities for development to the requirement for liberation. Solidarity involves how we go about development—through liberation. Referring to the intimate connection between liberation, development, and solidarity, the Pope states:

Thus the process of *development* and *liberation* takes concrete shape in the exercise of *solidarity*, that is to say in the love and service of neighbor, especially of the poorest. (*SRS*, p. 93)

Given the global connecting role of the multinational firms, the responsibility for solidarity becomes that of the multinational manager. Solidarity is his or her responsibility to manage the corporate linkages between developed and developing countries in a manner that enhances development as broadly defined, including the liberation of the firm's constituents in the Third World.

The Pope's views on development, the option for the poor, and solidarity are strongly stated, but the translation to specific action remains a question. How does the manager translate this guidance to action? Here we need to make a distinction between multinational banking and corporate managers. As noted above, they face fundamentally different decision environments.

Multinational Banking Managers

The credit that spurred Third World economic growth in the 1970s turned on these countries in the 1980s and has led to suffering that is hard to comprehend in our privileged circumstances. The large surpluses that accumulated in OPEC countries with the rise in the price of oil were recycled through commercial banks in the Eurodollar markets to anxious borrowers in the Third World. This credit was readily available and in a form more acceptable to nationalistic governments than giving up ownership of local assets to foreign direct investors. Local companies and governments feasted on short-term hard currency borrowings. Due to a combination of recession in the First World, weak commodity prices, high interest rates, and the frequent use of credit in nonproductive investments, economic enthusiasm in the Third World was cut short as countries were unable to service their debt. Major Third World debtors, particularly those in Latin America, are in much greater economic and political peril than we in the First World, until recently, have been willing to admit.

Through the "ritual" of rescheduling, banks have been able to maintain the fiction that their Third World debt is still a viable credit.[4] Bankers' consortia negotiate with individual governments to extend maturities, reduce debt service, and lend new funds to help the debtor countries pay their interest. As a precondition to these agreements, the International Monetary Fund (IMF) and, on occasion, the World Bank

(WB), imposed conditions on the developing countries to devalue, deflate, and deregulate—to promote exports, reduce imports, cut public deficits, reduce domestic credit, increase domestic interest rates, allow prices to float, and to sell government companies to the private sector.

In this rescheduling process, the banks have done quite well, particularly considering the quality of these loans. Interest paid on outstanding credit has remained close to the London Interbank Offer Rate (LIBOR is the world standard for interest rates) throughout the crisis.[5] With rescheduling, of course, the debt outstanding has increased as new funds have been loaned to pay interest.

There has been a massive transfer of funds from the Third to the First World. In Latin America and the Caribbean for example, the net transfer was $67 billion between 1982 and 1985 as outstanding debt went from $331 to $384 billion.[6] This flow of funds is in the wrong direction.

The debtor developing countries have fared less well than the banks. They have suffered a deep, long recession. Average per capita incomes are back to the levels of the mid-1970s, after the significant progress that was made in the last half of that decade. Within the developing countries, the burden is borne unevenly. Workers have paid dearly. Real wages in Mexico, for example, fell a third in the two years between 1982 and 1984.

The relatively well-to-do individuals in the Third World with savings, access to borrowing, and international connections have taken their money out. Much of the bank lending turned around and came right back as personal deposits in multinational banks. There has been a hemorrhage of capital flight since 1982. For Latin America, estimates vary but are all high—from an admittedly low $19 billion to $100 billion (one-fourth of the outstanding debt) and higher.[7] Many citizens of Third World countries are now creditors, not debtors. Is this the "responsibility of the rich for the poor?"

The people who have been most penalized by the debt crisis to date are the poor. They did not share in the good times of credit-spurred economic growth, but now bear the brunt of the rescheduling-required austerity. As Third World governments cut their expenditures, the one category that remains intact is defense. Other expenditures critical for the poor have been slashed. Health spending has dropped dramatically. Spending on education and infrastructure has been postponed as countries mortgage the future of their children and their long-range prospects for development to meet current interest requirements.[8]

While statistics do not exist for these marginalized groups, the effect of the IMF conditionality can be traced directly to them:

> Currency devaluations increase the cost of imports, such as food, and of imports essential to developmental projects, such as oil. When combined with a reduction of subsidies and with wage controls, the resulting increase in the costs of food and transportation directly reduces the real income. . . . Imposition of wage controls and elimination of price controls cut workers' ability to meet basic human needs as prices rise and purchasing is cut. Increased taxes, when levied on consumption or as value-added taxes, increase the cost of meeting basic human needs. Reduction of governmental spending lowers social services, food subsidies, and public employment—on all of which the poor and working classes are disproportionately dependent.[9]

This is a monstrous, global injustice imposed on those who had no involvement in, and bore no responsibility for, the debt accumulated by First and Third World leaders in conjunction with the international financial system.

The present approach to "solving" the debt crisis goes against everything in Catholic social teaching. In *Sollicitudo Rei Socialis*, the Pope is surprisingly dispassionate about the debt situation. He notes that it is "indicative of the interdependence between developed and less-developed countries." (*SRS*, p. 31) Further he states:

> The instrument chosen to make a contribution to development has turned into a *counter-productive mechanism* . . . through this mechanism the means intended for the development of peoples has turned into a brake upon development instead, and indeed in some cases has even aggravated underdevelopment. (*SRS*, p. 32)

The document, "An Ethical Approach to the International Debt Question," from the Pontifical Justice and Peace Commission, to which the Pope refers in *Sollicitudo Rei Socialis*, calls for a reorganization of the multilateral institutions (IMF, WB, and the regional development banks) to provide greater representation from developing countries and more participation in the economic decisions that affect them.[10] Surprisingly few comments were directed to commercial banks. The Pontifical Justice and Peace Commission recognizes the banks' duties toward depositors, the need to reschedule debt, to provide new credit, and to channel credit to the growth-enhancing projects. Multinational bankers have demonstrated their agreement with these requirements, except for the provision of new credit. The pontifical commission did not suggest debt forgiveness or more fundamental changes. The papal calls for development, option for the poor, and solidarity in *Sollicitudo Rei Socialis* would surely require more dramatic systemic change.

What can the individual multinational banking manager do about this injustice? Unfortunately, not much. The current decision environment has the multinational banks constrained to strategies of reducing existing Third World credit and minimizing new loans.

The nine large money center banks, holding 70 percent of Third World commercial debt owed to banks in the United States, are clearly overextended. Third World debt represents almost one-and-a-half times their total equity when measured at face value—debt that is worth far less.[11] For example, in the fledgling secondary market for Third World debt, Argentinean debt was valued at $.29 per dollar at the beginning of 1988, decreasing to $.21 at its close. Brazilian debt reached its highest price of $.53 in May 1988, decreasing to a low of $.40 by year end. Chilean debt, the most valuable debt in Latin America, ranged from $.66 to $.55 in 1988.[12] Money center banks, on average, carry these loans on their books at about two-thirds of face value after offsetting their reserves. While this may reflect the market value of debt for countries such as Chile, it seriously overdevalues the others.

The U. S. stock market has signaled its judgment on the quality of this debt. As of April 1988, six of the nine money center banks had values in the stock market below their book values. For Manufacturers Hanover, market value was 53 percent of book value; for Bank of America it was 54 percent; Chase Manhattan, 59 percent; others such as First Chicago, Bankers Trust, Irving Bank, or J. P. Morgan were trading close to or above book value. This is not the case for the large regional banks. Regionals, having trimmed their outstanding debt and accumulated larger reserves, enjoy market values substantially higher than book values (187 percent for Suntrust Banks, 182 percent for PNC

Financial, 163 percent for First Wachovia).[14] Regionals are in a position of stalking the money center banks as takeover targets.

Little wonder, then, that banks are working to liquidate their Third World debt through sales in the secondary market, debt-to-debt, or debt-to-equity swaps. Little wonder they minimize the extension of new credit, other than for the repayment of interest. Money center banks are following a survival strategy, and no manager would be able to convince the institution to do otherwise.

The only option available to the multinational banking manager is to work for systemic change, to use his or her influence within the institution to join other banks in pressing the United States government to pursue fundamental change in the treatment of the debt issue and in the international financial system.

The Brady proposal is a welcome attempt to reduce the overall debt burden while simultaneously providing needed new funds for growth. It signals an interest on the part of the Bush Administration to address the debt problem.

The motivation for the United States government is clearly self-interest. Economic depression in the Third World is turning into political upheaval as we knew it would, where the inability to pay is turning into a determination not to pay; Latin American democracies are threatened as their citizens learn that these governments cannot handle the debt problem any better than their military predecessors; U. S. leadership in the IMF and the WB is being challenged, particularly by Japan; there is a significant danger that a Latin American debt repudiation will be viewed globally as a Western Hemisphere problem, rather than one concerning the international monetary system; there is, finally, a growing recognition that the Third World's vulnerability to debt is about to challenge the First World international financial system to its core.

In all the discussion of the Brady plan, there has been no suggestion of our responsibility to the poor in the debtor countries. There is a genuine, although self-interested concern for renewed development and growth, but no concern for the poor who are bearing an unjust burden. Even if the Brady proposal were not too little too late, and even if the Third World governments were to have a better chance to work their way out of the debt overhang, there is no suggestion that the burden on the poor would be lightened during this long process. The core issue of Third World debt is an ethical one, and the burden on the poor in debtor countries must be lightened by more dramatic action at the systemic level.[15]

Multinational Corporate Managers

The decision environment for multinational corporate managers is different from the one faced by bankers. While multinational banks are limited to short-term Third World credit minimization strategies, many multinational corporations have viable alternatives in the Third World and the freedom in which to explore them. In spite of the debt-related economic havoc in the less-developed debtor countries, there are long-term opportunities for the alert multinational manager. Ironically, the most favorable of these are accessed through debt/equity swaps derived from the existence of the debt crisis.

Managing the Internal and External Linkages

As noted earlier, multinational firms are key connectors in our "interdependent" world. The multinational manager is thus in a unique position to bring about the changes for which the Pope calls, within the constraints of his or her decision environment.[16]

To evaluate the decision freedom available to the manager, we need to look at the international economic system to assess the sources of pressure and power. The various groups affected by the activities of the firm at each end of the multinational corporate linkages are diagramed in Figure 1. These are the firm's stakeholders. The direct constituents in the First and Third Worlds include owners, creditors, suppliers, consumers, and workers. Other stakeholders are communities and regions affected by the activities of the firm, governments (developed parent and less-developed host), multilateral institutions (such as the IMF and WB), and activist adoptive stakeholders. Each of these groups makes its own demands of the multinational corporation and has varying degrees of power with which to enforce them.

Assessments vary as to the flexibility available to the multinational manager in balancing the demands of the various stakeholders. Religious activists (identified in Figure 1 as adoptive stakeholders since they purchase shares primarily for the purpose of representing, or

Figure 1
Multinational Corporate Stakeholders

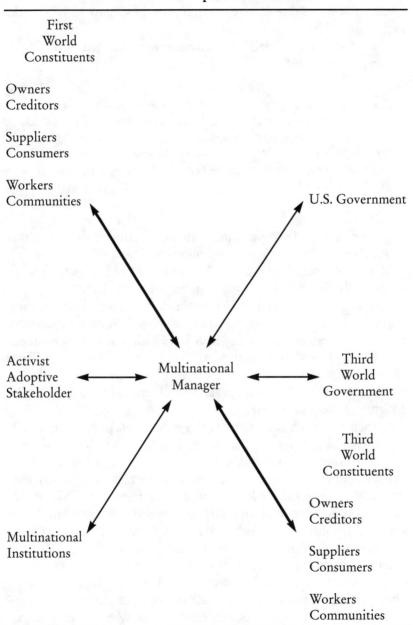

First
World
Constituents

Owners
Creditors

Suppliers
Consumers

Workers
Communities

U.S. Government

Activist
Adoptive
Stakeholder

Multinational
Manager

Third
World
Government

Third
World
Constituents

Owners
Creditors

Multinational
Institutions

Suppliers
Consumers

Workers
Communities

Adopted from Volume II, *Multinational Managers and Host Government Interactions*, Editor, Lee A. Tavis, Notre Dame, Indiana: University of Notre Dame Press, 1988. p. 13.

adopting, Third World groups) understand full well the importance and strength of the multinational linkages as they bring pressure in the United States to create change in other countries. Activists believe the multinational has great freedom of action.

The Pope assumes freedom of action when, as noted earlier in *Laborem Exercens*, he criticizes multinationals:

> For instance the highly industrialized countries, and even more the businesses that direct on a large scale the means of industrial production (the companies referred to as multinational or transnational), fix the highest possible prices for their products, while trying at the same time to fix the lowest possible prices for raw materials or semimanufactured goods. (*LE*, p. 39)

In this statement, the Pope assumes greater pricing freedom than that existing in most active First World industrial markets.

Managers generally argue that they have less freedom in their interaction with First World constituents than others claim. They note there is little pricing freedom in most markets; labor, although granting concessions in recent years, still has the power to enforce reasonable demands; investors react swiftly to any indication of waning competitiveness which might expose the firm to unfriendly takeovers. In Third World countries where governments assume many of the marketing mechanisms, managers view laws and regulations as reflecting the sovereignty of the nation state.

In their actions, however, managers reflect a greater degree of freedom. On the positive side, managers regularly go well beyond what could be considered corporate self-interest in their Third World operations. They pay their taxes (unlike many indigenous companies), they regularly pay wages above local standards, contribute to local communities, contract with local suppliers, and provide meals for employees and their families. They break local laws in deference to a higher code, as in the case of South African apartheid.

On the negative side, multinational managers can take advantage of the inefficient markets and ineffective regulations of the Third World. They can pass the power of First World constituents across the multinational linkages against less powerful Third World stakeholders.

Multinationals can interfere with the activities of legitimate Third World governments.

To the extent that managers have freedom of action in their decision environments, the Pope provides general but forceful guidelines. Managers are called to take responsibility for contributing to development, to provide an option for the poor and, through solidarity, to do so in a way that allows for the people's independence. These responsibilities have to do with the operating decisions of the firm as positive or negative pressures flow across the corporate linkages. To meet these responsibilities, managers must lean against the power of the First World constituents, and stand for the interests of the unrepresented Third World groups.[17]

The first requirement for meeting this "developmental responsibility" is to measure the impact of existing or potential corporate actions on local development as broadly defined by the Pope. Not only the initial influence must be monitored, but also the secondary and later effects of the corporate actions as they spread through the community and touch the poor. Some multinationals have close links to the poor, such as a pharmaceutical company providing critical health-care products, a manufacturer drawing employees from urban slums, or an agribusiness in a remote, poor, rural area. In other cases the connection will be less obvious; still, they are always there.

Information on how other, seemingly unrelated, groups are affected by the firm's activities adds a new dimension and challenge to information networks. Attention to its collection is more than a first step in implementing Catholic social teaching. The collection effort itself will have a massive impact on management across the corporation as it extends the concept and coverage of its decision environment. In this effort, we should remember that multinational corporate information networks are among the best in the world.

Thus, as a result of the central role played by multinational corporations in providing the linkages for the international economic system as well as their ties to development and to the poor within the Third World, multinational managers are uniquely positioned to bring about the changes directed by the encyclicals. Measuring the firm's full impact on that environment, and incorporating that information into its planning and control networks, is a necessary initial condition for an effective response.[18]

Issues Raised by Encyclicals

Underlying the management of developmental responsibility, the encyclicals raise two fundamental issues. What right does a manager have to follow Catholic doctrine in a non-Catholic decision environment and to what extent is solidarity possible in corporate decision models?

Multinational managers work in a pluri-cultural, pluri-religious world. The stakeholders at each end of the multinational linkages in Figure 1 hold to different religions and value systems.

Cultural differences cause major operating problems for the corporation. In addition to communications barriers, differences in value systems, and incongruent objectives, multinationals must balance a sensitivity to local societies against the standardization of policies and procedures upon which their global approach to management is based. This balancing is a delicate application of cultural universalism versus cultural relativism.[19]

John Paul's encyclicals raise a similar issue for the committed Catholic multinational manager. To what extent does he or she have the right to base corporate decisions on Catholic social teaching when the affected stakeholders are predominately non-Catholic, and often non-Christian?

John Paul addresses his encyclical to all Christians, Jews, Muslims, and followers of the "world's great religions."

I wish to address especially those who, through the Sacrament of Baptism and the profession of the same Creed, *share a real*, though imperfect, *communion* with us. I am certain that the concern expressed in this Encyclical as well as the motives inspiring it *will be familiar to them*, for these motives are inspired by the Gospel of Jesus Christ. We can find here a new invitation to *bear witness together* to our *common convictions* concerning the dignity of man [humankind], created by God, redeemed by Christ, made holy by the Spirit, and called upon in this world to live a life in conformity with this dignity.

I likewise address this appeal to the Jewish people, who share with us the inheritance of Abraham, "our father in faith" (Romans 4:11f) and the tradition of the Old Testament, as well as to the Muslims who, like us, believe in the just and merciful God. And I extend it to all the followers of *the world's great religions*. (*SRS*, pp. 97–98)

These comments of course do not suggest that these non-Catholics agree with the Pope.

A critical area of agreement among all major religions is the commitment to the poor. In Buddhism, Karuna is one of four principles of personality development. It calls for efficacious action to remove the cause of another's suffering. For Hindus, to help others is a form of prayer to God. In Islam, the idea to support the poor is one of the five pillars of the religions—the notion of Zakat or "due to the poor." The Catholic emphasis on the option for the poor, thus, is essentially global although the nuances and articulation of the Pope's position may not be.

As for solidarity, the Pope describes it as having a "specifically Christian dimension."

> *Solidarity* is undoubtedly a *Christian virtue*. . . . In the light of faith, solidarity seeks to go beyond itself, to take on the *specifically Christian* dimensions of total gratuity, forgiveness, and reconciliation." (*SRS*, p. 78)

Multinational managers need guidance from religious scholars on the notion of solidarity as it exists in other religions.[20]

Beyond the issue of whether managers have the right to pursue solidarity for the activities of a non-Catholic corporation in a non-Catholic and non-Judeo/Christian environment, solidarity itself can be antithetical to the way decisions are made in economic institutions—indeed, in most institutions across the world. From a corporate decision-modeling standpoint, solidarity means assuring that the stakeholders, particularly the poor, have the freedom to pursue their own interests—the freedom and the power to represent themselves to the corporation and across the corporate linkages to other stakeholders.[21]

In approaching the solidarity requirement, managers should fix their sights on the ideal environment. In an ideal environment, all the firm's stakeholders have the capability (the interest, the ability, and the power) to represent themselves. First and Third World governments, as overarching stakeholders, would accept the responsibility of balancing these interests within and among countries. In this ideal environment, the manager would not be caught in the difficult position of trading off the interests of one group against those of another; of leaning against the power of First World products and financial markets, labor, and governments to represent somehow the relatively less powerful Third World stakeholders. Ideally, managers could focus on what they do best—enhancing productivity.

A proper, practical, long-term objective in corporate stakeholder relations would be to enhance the capabilities of stakeholders to represent themselves. Stakeholders would become effective "consultative mechanisms." A consultative mechanism is

> . . . a structure through which the manager can discover the collective desires of a stakeholder group. An effective consultative mechanism would be one through which the true interests of a particular constituency can be expressed or demanded. These mechanisms can be in the form of efficient markets, effective regulation, or representatives of specific constituencies such as labor organizations or consumer advocacy associations.[22]

Effective consultative mechanisms bring stability to the decision environment, and less risk. Thus, in the very long run, the papal call for solidarity is not that far from the corporate self-interest of optimizing present value through minimizing risk as well as maximizing returns. Unfortunately, in the interim (a long one indeed), these mechanisms are too seldom effective in the Third World and it is up to the manager to make the trade-offs within the freedom of his or her unique decision environment.

The steps toward enhancing the capability of stakeholders to represent themselves call for a good deal of managerial guts. The first step is to stand for those who cannot represent themselves, especially the poor. As many firms have found, however, representing the poor and marginalized groups leads to paternalism and eventually to resentment among those whose interests are being represented. This is a sad lesson learned by agribusinesses in their management of remote plantations. In the long term, the development of consultative mechanisms, and the need to move beyond paternalism is in both the papal and the corporate self-interest.

To enhance consultative mechanisms, multinationals need to share information with stakeholders and enhance their capability of processing that information. In the short term, of course, sharing information is a relinquishment of power. In the long run as groups represent themselves more responsibly, the goals of solidarity are met, and power bargaining is less necessary.[23]

Solidarity remains the most challenging element of John Paul's encyclicals for multinational managers and perhaps for us all. It is demanding in the sense that it requires us to cooperate and respect the freedom of those with whom we interact, as well as being the ones the Pope most explicitly identifies as Christians. Even though building effective consultative mechanisms is an example of solidarity, it is a long-range project and will never reach its ideal.

Summary Observations

There are four dimensions of Catholic social teaching as reflected in *Sollicitudo Rei Socialis* that are of particular importance to multinational managers.

The core concept of the encyclical is interdependence among individuals or groups on a world-wide basis. Economic connectors among different countries, among the First and Third Worlds, among individuals in those developed and less-developed countries, are provided by multinational firms (corporations and banks). This places the managers, like it or not, inextricably at the heart of the global balance the Pope wants to change.

Multinational firms are deeply involved in the development of Third World countries. Across their international linkages, they bring human and material resources that enhance productivity. Across the same linkages, however, can come oppression from powerful First World stakeholders.

The overall conclusion relative to development is that there is a mutuality of interest between the firm and Third World stakeholders for enhanced economic standards of living in these countries, a goal congruence that fits the Pope's direction. There remains, however, open warfare between managers and corporate critics over how firms can and should affect the broader dimensions of development as outlined in *Sollicitudo Rei Socialis*.

To serve the poor, the view of multinational linkages must be extended beyond connectors among countries to stakeholder linkages within developing countries. Managers must look beyond employees, for example, to the families of employees, to the local communities, and to the firm's involvement with the very poor. Attempts to analyze these linkages with the poor will naturally lead the firm to be more responsive to their needs.

Solidarity is involved with how to accomplish development and the option for the poor. Its call for the independence of stakeholder groups poses the most serious challenge to corporate decision makers—indeed, to us all. It is hard to let someone else have a word in a decision that affects us, particularly if, in our view, they are detracting from their own interests as well as our own.

This teaching has meaning for multinational managers in their professional lives only to the extent they have freedom within their decision environment to respond in solidarity with the poor. Freedom to respond involves flexibility within the relative power balance among the firm's stakeholders. This paper argues that individual multinational banking managers do not have this freedom while multinational corporate managers, in many cases, do. It is to be hoped that, in the not too distant future, with credit flowing back to the Third World, individual bankers can concern themselves with development, the poor, and solidarity.

Freedom to respond also involves the right to pursue objectives tied to Catholic social teaching in a non-Catholic, non-Judeo/Christian world. This issue has not been resolved. Overall, an option for the poor is supported in major religions, although the importance of international interdependence and solidarity are probably less so.

The Catholic church must pay more attention to individuals such as corporate managers who attempt to implement the ideals of Catholic social teaching in their imperfect, or worse, decision environments.

Notes

1. John Paul II, *On Social Concern, Sollicitudo Rei Socialis*, encyclical letter, Publication No. 205-5, Washington, D.C.: Office of Publishing and Promotion Services, United States Catholic Conference, December 30, 1987, p. 69.

2. References to the papal encyclicals will be noted as follows:

SRS = *On Social Concern, Sollicitudo Rei Socialis*

LE = *On Human Work, Laborem Exercens*, third encyclical letter, Publication No. 825, Washington, D.C.: Office of Publishing and Promotion Services, United States Catholic Conference, September 14, 1981.

3. Bartell provides a good review of Catholic social teaching on development at the time of *Laborem Exercens*, see Ernest Bartell, C.S.C., *"Laborem Exercens*: A Third World Perspective" in *Co-Creation and Capitalism: John Paul II's Laborem Exercens*, Editors John W. Houck and Oliver F. Williams, University Press of America, 1983, pp. 174–198.

4. For an insightful comparison of rescheduling to ritual, see William P. Glade, "Rescheduling as Ritual," *Rekindling Development: Multinational Firms and World Debt*, Editor, Lee A. Tavis, Notre Dame, Indiana: University of Notre Dame Press, 1988, pp. 244–252.

5. In Latin America and the Caribbean, for example, interest paid on all outstanding debt (commercial banks, multilateral institutions, governments) was 5.6% in 1973 (a comfortable increment over the LIBOR assessed by bankers) to 12.8% in the midst of the crisis compared to a LIBOR of 13.5% and a service of 8.4% in 1986 compared to a LIBOR of 7.0%. The interest and outstanding debt were derived by Kuczynski. Pedro-Pablo Kuczynski, *Latin American Debt*, Baltimore, Maryland: The Johns Hopkins University Press, 1988, p. 33. LIBOR is taken from the International Financial Statistics.

6. *Ibid.*, pp. 33 and 155.

7. Kuczynski measured capital flight from the eight largest Latin American debtors from 1977 to 1983 by bank deposits as $28 billion to $56 billion and by balance of payment figures as $19 billion to $43 billion. Ibid., pp. 48–49. He estimated capital flight from Argentina, Mexico, and Venezuela in the two years 1982 and 1983 as $30 billion to $40 billion. Commenting on the claims that $100 billion in capital flight occurred from mid-1970s to 1983, he states, "Such a number would amount to a third or so of disposable savings for a long period, an unlikely although not impossible proportion. . . ." *Ibid.*, pp. 48–50.

8. Giovanni A. Cornia, Richard Jolly, and Francis Stewart, *Adjustment with a Human Face: A Study by UNICEF*, New York: Oxford, 1987. See also, World Bank, *The World Bank Development Report*, 1988, Washington, D.C.: Oxford, 1988.

9. Peter J. Henriot, S.J., and Kenneth Jameson, "International Debt, Austerity, and the Poor," *Rekindling Development: Multinational Firms and World Debt*, Editor, Lee A. Tavis, Notre Dame, Indiana: University of Notre Dame Press, 1988, pp. 24–25.

10. Pontifical Justice and Peace Commission, "An Ethical Approach to the International Debt Question," *Origins*, February 5, 1987, Vol. 16: No. 34, pp. 602–611.

11. Kuczynski, op. cit., p. 109.

12. The secondary market is thin, and transactions take a long time, although a number of brokers quote bid and offer rates on a regular basis. Prices are low and variable, particularly for Latin American debtors. Solomon Brothers, *International Loan Trading*, various issues.

13. Banks report losses on the income statement when the charge is made to loan loss reserves. A tax loss does not occur until the loan is declared uncollectible. That is the point at which the taxpayers bear part of the burden.

14. Gary Hector, "How Banks Will Shake Out," *Fortune*, April 25, 1988, p. 216.

15. In its projects, the World Bank has recently been focusing more directly on poverty reduction although these efforts need to be pursued on a much broader scale. See World Bank, *Strengthening Efforts to Reduce Poverty*, Washington, D.C.: World Bank Publications, 1989.

16. For a summary of Catholic social teaching and the challenges it poses for the multinational firm from a Latin American viewpoint, see Archbishop Marcos McGrath, C.S.C., and Fernando Bastos de Avila, S.J., "Multinationals and Catholic Social Teaching in Latin America," *Multinational Managers and Host Government Interactions*, Editor, Lee A. Tavis, Notre Dame, Indiana: University of Notre Dame Press, 1988.

17. Operating decisions incur greater responsibilities than is the case with philanthropy. In philanthropy, decisions and responsibilities are passed to someone else. For operating decisions, they are retained within the firm.

18. A model incorporating this kind of information is presented in Lee A. Tavis and Roy L. Crum, "Performance-Based Strategies for MNC Portfolio Balancing," *Columbia Journal of World Business*, Summer 1984, pp. 85–94.

19. For an extended discussion of cultural difficulties and how they can be confronted by multinational managers in their interaction with governmental officials, see *Multinational Managers and Host Government Interactions*, Editor, Lee A. Tavis, Notre Dame, Indiana: University of Notre Dame Press, 1988.

20. For example, the notion of independence would probably not fit the Confucian tradition. To the extent that solidarity is perceived as giving up power, it would not be acceptable. Steinberg argues that in the Confucian tradition, power is considered to be limited and, therefore, seldom delegated. David I. Steinberg, "The Confucian Backdrop: Setting the Stage for Economic Development, *Multinational Managers and Host Government Interactions*, Editor, Lee A. Tavis, Notre Dame, Indiana: University of Notre Dame Press, 1988, pp. 73–102.

21. The Pope's statement, "What is hindering full development is the desire for profit and the thrust for power," and that it must be replaced by a "commitment to the good of one's neighbor" (SRS, p. 74), provides little guidance for the manager.

22. Lee A. Tavis, "Stewardship Across National Borders," *Stewardship: The Corporations and the Individual*, The ITT Key Issues Lecture Series, Editor, T. R. Martin, New York: K.C.G. Productions, Inc., 1984, p. 89.

23. For an extended discussion of information sharing, how it is tied to multinational corporate power and to corporate strategies, see Lee A. Tavis and William P. Glade, "Implications for Corporate Strategy," *Multinational Managers and Host Government Interactions*, Editor, Lee A. Tavis, Notre Dame, Indiana: University of Notre Dame Press, 1988, pp. 287–319.

Sixteen

Managerial Responsibility and Socioeconomic Systems: Assessing the Papal Encyclicals

James E. Post

Introduction

A recent issue of the *New York Times* contained three front page stories that caught my eye as I was finishing this paper. One described the agreement of more than one hundred nations to an international agreement to limit toxic waste dumping. The second announced the release of a recent Congressional study of assistance programs that found the gap between the rich and the poor was widening in the U.S. A third story announced the tenth anniversary of the nuclear plant catastrophe at Three Mile Island. In those three stories—and the current events they reflect—are, I believe, several vital connections between the encyclicals under discussion in this conference and the responsibilities of modern managers.

To speak of social concern in the 1990s is to speak, inevitably, to issues of the relationship between business, government, and society. Similarly, to speak of social concern is to address the relationship between people and the institutions that serve, shape, and influence their daily lives: family, economy, church, and government. And to speak of social concern is to speak of issues, conflicts, and problems arising out of those relationships between people and institutions.

Inevitably, a world of highly developed, complex institutions requires managers or administrators of the highest capability. Today, neither business, government, universities, nor churches can be effective in accomplishing their purpose without the presence of capable administrators and managers. Because these are the people who, in various ways, guide, direct, and plan the activities of the world's great institutions, it is reasonable to claim that to speak of social concern is to speak directly of the relationship between management and society and to the managers who perform those important tasks.

Management, in this conception, is an expression that describes the great work of guiding, directing, and planning organizational activity. It is also a description of those many individuals who actually make decisions affecting the activities of others. Management is, therefore, a special form of human work, with the many characteristics described in John Paul's encyclical, *On Human Work*. There is a value and dignity to managerial work. When it is done well, it serves people. When it fails to serve people, it falls short of the dignity that it deserves.

Managerial decisions are also a real source of social issues, conflicts, and problems. For this reason alone, the encyclicals of John Paul II have importance to the practice of management and to our understanding of the role and relationship of management to society. It is not difficult to see a message of special importance to the practice of management in these encyclicals.

The modern world is a world of institutions. They have made possible the advantages of organized human effort. As a practical matter, the world's population cannot be fed, housed, or given adequate medical care without the involvement of institutions and their managers. In this fact there resides, I believe, the critical weakness in the proposition that an economic counterculture can be created without managerial and administrative guidance and direction. The greater challenge is how to refocus institutional activity toward ends—and with means—that serve human beings more effectively.

This paper has three objectives:

1. To elaborate several basic models (understandings) of the relationship between management and society and to relate the encyclicals to each;

2. To distill from the encyclicals a number of key ideas that are of special importance to the practice and theory of management in the modern context; and

3. To highlight current developments that relate to the themes of these encyclicals.

Economics, Politics, and Culture

Scientists often refer to a living organism, be it human, animal, or plant, as a "system" or an "organic system." For the past several decades, social scientists have attempted to apply "systems thinking" to the analysis of groups, organizations, and societies. Social systems theory thereby has developed and aided our comprehension of the diverse yet predictable ways human affairs are ordered and conducted. Systems thinking has much to offer in understanding the institutions of society—business, government, unions, public action groups—and the ways in which they interact.

Michael Novak discovered the value of systems thinking in the analysis of economic and political matters contained in his book, *The Spirit of Democratic Capitalism* (1982). He argues that democratic capitalism consists of three "systems," one economic, one political, and one cultural in nature. The economic system is organized around the marketplace, in which there is freedom of exchange among buyers and sellers. The political system is organized around citizen voting, and the political institutions of the executive, legislative, and judicial branches of government. The cultural system is less organized than the others, functioning as an open system and allowing innumerable ideas and influences to flourish or fail amidst vigorous intellectual competition. These three systems, in turn, interact and influence one another in myriad ways. They are what sociologist Talcott Parsons termed "interpenetrating social systems," each independent but influencing the others directly and indirectly through the processes of continuing interaction.

It is not only at the broadest level of economic, political, and cultural matters that systems thinking and language is helpful. At a more intermediate level, business, government, and society are also interpenetrating systems, each independent, but also an influence on the others. Each of these systems has goals, resources, and engages in activities which distinguish it from the others. Each also has a "boundary," enabling the observer to know where one system stops and the other begins.

Several examples of this interpenetration illustrate the interaction of social systems at both the macro- and intermediate levels, and highlight the types of issues implied in John Paul II's encyclical letters. For example, society has generally been "technologized" by the advent and spread of the computer. Beginning with business and government use of computers, we have now reached an era of home and personal computers that may very well revolutionize the way we shop, provide entertainment, and work. Similarly, it is rare to find an office in which secretaries use typewriters with carbon paper or Ditto machines for duplication. The rise of Xerox Corporation and the copying process it introduced has revolutionized a major aspect of office work in the global community.

These technological changes have mostly occurred through the mechanism of the marketplace, with the buyers and sellers of computer and copy equipment finding one another. But some ramifications have occurred in the political and cultural arenas as well. Government has institutionalized computer logic in the organization of tax forms, census data, and innumerable regulatory reports. Education at the primary and secondary school level, as well as the collegiate level, has introduced computer language courses, and we are well into an era of computer programmed learning that could replace some human teachers with teaching machines and software programs. Thus, innovation from the corporate sector has penetrated the political and cultural milieus and transformed our world into what genuinely can be termed an age of computers.

Values, as well as technology, revolutionize social systems. Today, the United States still is trying to digest twenty years of important value conflicts and change. The tremendous growth of public entitlements which characterized the Great Society program of the Johnson administration and the successor programs of the Nixon, Ford, and Carter administrations rested heavily on such emerging values as equality, community, and public participation. Many scholars believe that while revolutions in technology are easier to observe, revolutions in values are more profound and lasting in their consequences. Shared values and the willingness of people to fight for gains hard won will prevent a turning back of the cultural and political clock. Amitai Etzioni speaks to a similar point in his book, *The Moral Dimension* (1988), when he argues that self-interested behavior ("I") rests within a broader social collectivity ("we"). Interestingly, the Reagan administration did not take the position that equal employment opportunity for men and women, whites and non-whites, should be completely abandoned. Despite the neoconservative atmosphere of the 1980s, it is unlikely that the country will return to a 1950s style of capitalism. Rather, it is more likely that a new direction will be found to accommodate the values of equal opportunity and entrepreneurship. Moral commitments may even motivate people to behave in ways that oppose narrow self-interest.

Change can be threatening, as well as liberating, and it is not surprising that resistance to it takes political form. New technologies challenge industries based on other technologies; not wishing to be rendered obsolete, companies may fight back by asking government to ban, regulate, or tax the new technology in the name of jobs, markets, and the "public interest." Citizens and organizations who dislike zip codes, universal product codes, and the metric system, or some other change may use the political system to prevent, slow down, or nibble away at the offending scheme. Affirmative action, environmental protection, consumer protection, each has antagonized and injured some interests even while advancing others. Each has economic and cultural effects, and each has provoked political action. They are separable dimensions in the abstract, but not in the real world.

The boundaries of social systems are permeable, and both technology and values influence the structure and behavior of those systems. Business, government, and society have been affected in profound ways by technological and value shifts. Some effects have been structural, as in the way work is organized or the size and configuration of industries. Others have been behavioral, including the way institutions manage relations with one another and toward individuals. Often, even the symbols of these changes have become mythologized in our culture (e.g., computer terminals, fast food restaurants, Theory Z).

Economics, politics, and culture all interact with one another and shape the environment in which human institutions—business, government, churches, unions, public action groups—exist and function. That is the reality of the modern world, capitalist and Marxist ideologies notwithstanding. The development of an economic counterculture turns less on whether capitalism or socialism is superior than on how managers guide and direct institutions. The question is whether current socioeconomic systems are capable of improvement. Can an improved social economy emerge that is consistent with the concerns expressed in the encyclicals?

The Scope of Institutional Responsibility

John Paul's encyclical, *On Social Concern*, speaks to the responsibilities of all people, and by extension, to the institutions they create and direct. He is greatly concerned with the interpenetration of economic and social life that is embedded in the concept of "development." To whom and for what are human beings responsible? To whom and for what are the institutions they create to be held accountable? What is the scope of managerial responsibility in the modern world?

It is to this last question that the Pope and the American Catholic bishops have added their views and perspectives in recent years. Those responses need to be considered in the context of views based on well-established understandings of the management-society relationship.

There are important and distinct points of view on the scope of responsibility. Each derives, in some measure, from fundamentally different assumptions about the nature of the relationship between organizations and the rest of society. These views can be expressed as models of the management-society relationship (Preston and Post, 1975; Rouner and Dickie, 1986). A short synopsis of each view—expressed in systems terms—follows, and the models are illustrated in Figure 1.

Legal Model: The legal view assumes that society, through law, has created a superordinate system of laws, regulations, and standards which govern the creation (e.g., charter) and behavior of public and private sector institutions. Law is, therefore, a "suprasystem."

The scope of any institution's responsibility is defined by law and extends only as far as the law requires. Social responsibility is equivalent to legal responsibility. The system is in balance because institutional failure can be remedied through law, and the law itself can be altered and modified to adjust to new realities and circumstances. Management thereby owes to society only that which society demands and requires through the legal system.

Market-Contract Model: This view holds, as Milton Friedman has so clearly stated, that "the only responsibility of business is to make profits." The assumption underlying this view is that organizations (especially business) and society interact only through exchanges in the marketplace and thereby serve the large public good. They are "collateral systems," separate and distinct from one another. Thus, management is responsible only to deal honestly in those exchange transactions.

Exploitation Model: This model is also a collateral system's view of the world, but one which maintains that managed institutions always extract more from society through exchange than they return to it. This excess is known as "surplus value." In this view, the concept of institutional responsibility is a non sequitur since the very existence of these institutions involves continuous exploitation of other elements of society through the exchange process. In the modern world, where institutions are strong relative to individuals, the only possible refuge for the individual is in an organization of like-minded citizens. But in these circumstances, too, membership organizations such as labor unions, public action groups, and political parties have demonstrated bureaucratic tendencies that further exploit the individual.

Technostructure Model: There is both obvious truth and falsity embedded in the market contract and exploitation views of the world. This had led some to observe that whether collateral or exchange transactions are exploitive or not is a secondary issue in the modern world. More important is the fact that there is a new class—a "managerial class" in James Burnham's terms—which dominates all institutions in society and, hence, sets the "rules of the game." Popularized by John Kenneth Galbraith in *The New Industrial State* (1967) the managerial class becomes the "technostructure," a suprasystems concept in which the technocrats are a dominant shaper of culture (media, fashions, tastes), politics, and markets. The scope of responsibility institutions bear in such a society is defined by the controlling technocrats. They bear the burden of keeping the social system in approximate equilibrium.

Interpenetrating Systems: As discussed above, this view acknowledges the limited validity of each of the aforementioned views, but emphasizes the constant change and flux among actors in the social system. None of the other views prevails, because none of the other views captures all of reality. The law is an imperfect means of social control; the market does not leave parties with equally satisfactory results; exploitation may sometimes occur, but not always when one considers the millions of market transactions that occur each day; the technocrats, even in the heyday of organizational "rationalism" never completely dominated political, economic, and cultural institutions.

However, the influence of managed organizations and society on each other, in direct and indirect ways, and upon the processes of the market, public policy, and value formation is unmistakable. Hence, there is tension, but also equilibrium. Thus, the scope of responsibility must be defined in the context of that which each institution chooses to do or not do, and in the primary and secondary involvements and relationships that flow therefrom.

Stakeholder Model: In recent years, the view has emerged that it is in the process of interaction between the organization and the external environment that the scope of the responsibility question is resolved.

The stakeholder view is that an organization's scope of responsibility is defined, de facto, by the issues brought to it by other elements in society. These are usually in the form of requests, demands, or other pressures. The criteria for responding are found, not in deciding what to do but, rather, by engaging in a process of discussion, dialogue, and stakeholder participation in reaching a mutually acceptable result. Because any external group, however large or small, is capable of imposing some harm on the organization, it must be reckoned with by the organization's leaders. It is a practical managerial necessity and renders moot more abstract issues of the nature of the management-society relationship or the scope of institutional responsibility.

In systems terms, this model emphasizes the interrelationships of groups and organizations in society and the fact that elements in society are always reconfiguring themselves. New public action groups arise as fast as or faster than new corporations and joint ventures are formed. Networks of private and public sector managers, employees, and organizations are constantly in flux. In this milieu, the organization faces the constant need to secure the support, or at least the neutrality, of these many stakeholders.

Of these models, it is the technocratic, interpenetrating systems, and stakeholder models that most clearly dominate current discussion of the relationship between management and society. The technocratic emphasizes the special importance and power of knowledge, information, and "technique" as J. Ellul termed it. Those who possess technocratic power are extraordinarily powerful in the modern economy, whether their abilities are focused on the economy, the financial markets, the political process, or the shaping of modern culture. Production, consumption, and distribution distortions addressed by the

Figure 1
Models of Management and Society

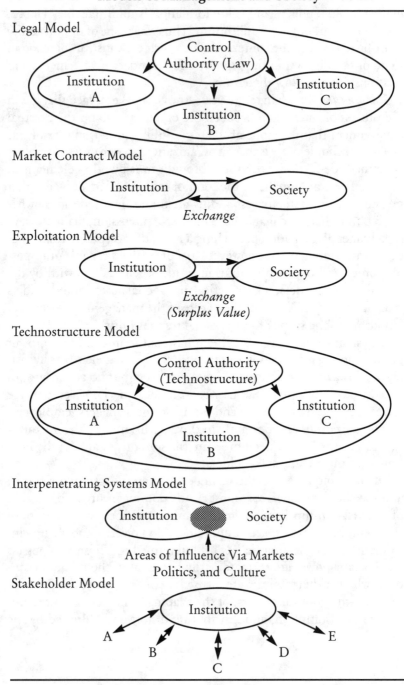

Legal Model

Control
Authority (Law)

Institution
A

Institution
C

Institution
B

Market Contract Model

Institution

Society

Exchange

Exploitation Model

Institution

Society

*Exchange
(Surplus Value)*

Technostructure Model

Control Authority
(Technostructure)

Institution
A

Institution
C

Institution
B

Interpenetrating Systems Model

Institution   Society

Areas of Influence Via Markets
Politics, and Culture

Stakeholder Model

Institution

A   E

B   D

C

encyclicals are clearly traceable in part to the technocratic disparities that exist within populations and among nations.

The interpenetrating systems model recognizes the simultaneous presence of conflict and harmony in society, and the emergence of the processes of the marketplace, political arena, and cultural (value) world to shape and influence the institutions of the market, politics, and culture. Most importantly, this perspective makes clear that management directly and indirectly influences society through decisions about what is done and what is not done; so too, however, does society directly and indirectly influence and affect management through the signals of the market, the political arena, and culture. Values translate into expectations and, ultimately, no organization can ignore the expectations of the public without endangering its own existence.

The stakeholder model of management and society is perhaps the most popular at this time. It is, at one level, a specialized form of interest group theory in which segments of the population have unique or special "stakes" in particular decisions made by an organization and its managers. In one respect, this formulation highlights the technocrat's need to incorporate special knowledge of the affected stakeholder(s) into decision-making and to adjust organizational action to the real economic, political, or cultural implications of those decisions on the affected stakeholders. As an applied concept, stakeholder thinking has gained great popularity with managerial audiences. It is reasonably simple to conceptualize, easy to operationalize, and it helps organizations and their managers avoid the worst conflicts in favor of common ground.

To summarize the three models, then, the technocratic suggests to us that there has emerged in the modern world a cadre of people whose specialized knowledge, information, and skill empower them in the course of conduct in human affairs. For the most part, this power is exercised through institutions—the private sector, public sector, and nonprofit sector—that affect all people. Knowledge is power. Unstated, however, is the issue of accountability: to whom and for what are the members of this technocratic elite responsible?

The interpenetrating systems view answers the latter question by recognizing that managers and organizations are responsible for those primary involvements which are deliberately and knowingly made, and for those secondary effects which flow directly from the primary activities of the organization. Thus, the organizations that choose to interact with a set of several segments of the population through the marketplace cannot avoid the implication of accountability when those people establish new expectations of performance.

The stakeholder model, in turn, extends both of these models by articulating the broad range of direct and indirect stakeholders to be considered in managerial decision-making, and refining the manager's understanding of what must be considered and at what risk if it is not.

A Theory of Institutional Responsibility

John Paul's letters remind us that there is a dignity to each person, whatever his/her social and economic circumstance, that responsibly cannot be ignored in the name of progress, development, or organizational growth. This commitment to personal dignity and interdependence is highly compatible with systems thinking. The principal lesson to be drawn from systems analysis is that of interdependence among all elements of a society. The reality of this interdependence, which is ever more visible in modern society, undermines the narrow responsibility concepts expressed in the legal, market, and exploitation models. The effects and consequences of managerial decisions are not confined to a single process, whether it is the market process or the legal process. This leaves us with the technostructure model's proposition of an omnipotent decision-making class which bears responsibility for preserving social equilibrium. However, this proposition conflicts with our political, social, and moral ideology which emphasizes individual rights and responsibilities. As a society, we remain uncomfortable with the proposition that an elite group of persons, with proper skills, educational credentials, and values will be the architects of a social guidance system. The Pope seems more at ease with that view, however, but sees in it a corresponding responsibility.

If socioeconomic systems are to be improved, institutional change is the critical vehicle for doing so, and an accepted theory of institutional responsibility is a critical need. There are fundamental reasons why definitions of institutional responsibility organized solely around concepts of market and political transactions are doomed to fail. Principally, it is because decisions made in either the economic or political arenas are not static. Employment decisions were once made solely in the market; today there is affirmative action to consider and reconcile. Product decisions and production externalities are now often affected by political (regulatory) considerations. The critical question, therefore, is not where the decision is made but, rather, what is the nature of the decision. Is it central to the running of the organization? Is it a necessary, or avoidable, consequence of primary activities? Is it peripheral or tertiary? These are systems questions.

Conventional theory offers no simple answers to these questions, but the application of systems thinking can help clarify how to proceed. Every organization engages in a set of core activities which are vital to its continuance. These are its primary involvements and include those actions that give the organization its distinctive definition, especially the technical actions which transform resources and inputs into outputs of value.

Every organization must bear responsibility to all other elements in society for the direct consequences of its primary activities. In addition to these primary involvements, every organization or institution engages in activities which support, coordinate, and enhance performance of the core activities. These are secondary involvements and include actions to secure resources (recruitment of personnel, purchasing of supplies), distribute output (marketing, distribution), and provide information to both the resource and product markets (advertising). Because these activities are directly related to the core activities of the organization, it must be responsible for the consequences of these actions as well. After all, they would not exist, or exist in such magnitude, if the organization had not initiated its activities. Thus, responsibility cannot be avoided within the social system.

An organization cannot bear direct responsibility for all social problems of course. Some impacts of doing business are so removed from the direct actions of the organization as to be beyond the reasonable scope of responsibility. We call these effects tertiary impacts. Consider the problem of neighborhood deterioration, a problem afflicting every urban community. If a manufacturing business located in a suburban neighborhood is about to expand its facilities and ignores the inner city location, choosing instead to site a new facility in a more attractive area, it has contributed in a most nondirect way to the plight of the deteriorated neighborhood. But the contribution is neither intentional, in the sense of wanting to harm the neighborhood, nor causal in the sense of producing the original blight. This situation can be contrasted with the actions of a bank which, while receiving deposits from businesses and residents of the area, refuses to lend funds to these same people and organizations for mortgages or improvement loans. The inability to improve the neighborhood would then be directly attributable to the bank's primary involvement (lending), and the bank would have to assume responsibility for the consequences of its policies and actions.

Within the entire social system, such a schema places institutional responsibility on those entities which know or should have known the consequences of their actions and intentionally or negligently allowed those consequences to occur. Moreover, as cultural standards change, and public views change with respect to what is properly private sector versus public sector responsibility, these guidelines continue to apply. Managers are responsible for scanning society to pick up changes in the cultural values, a responsibility which is not unreasonable in a world of rapidly improving communications technology. The barriers to such knowledge are growing smaller steadily, and the propriety of public inputs into organizational decision-making widely accepted.

The encyclicals add several new dimensions to this emergent theory. For convenience, I shall refer to them as "productive justice," "consumption justice," and "distributive justice."

Productive justice refers to John Paul's clear concern for the dependency that can arise between the industrialized and less industrialized nations. One can envision three distinct "states" in which a community might exist relative to productive capability: a state of dependency on others, not unlike historic colonialism; a state of relative independence deriving from self-sufficiency; and a state of dominance, in which the needs of other people are served solely by the focal society. These states correspond roughly to the conditions of underdevelopment, development, and superdevelopment as discussed in the encyclicals.

Consumption justice refers to John Paul's concern for the tendency toward absolute and relative excesses in the use of outputs from the productive processes. Again, three states seem evident: a state of inadequate consumption in which too little is available to permit life to be sustained; a state of balanced consumption, in which each person's minimal needs are met and additional wants can be satisfied without endangering the ability of others to meet their minimal needs; and a state of excessive consumption in which a community's pattern of behavior is imbalanced in absolute and/or relative terms. Inadequate or imbalanced consumption seems a prevalent condition in many underdeveloped nations, while excessive consumption clearly characterizes the superdeveloped nations in John Paul's view. Examples of both balanced and excessive consumption can be found in developed nations. The presence of obvious cultural, economic, and political conflicts are their manifestations.

Distributive justice refers to John Paul's concern for how productive resources and the outputs derived from them are shared among people. There is a clear distaste for a state of imbalance in which the gap between the wealthy and the poor is so extreme as to leave the disadvantaged with inadequate resources to sustain a dignified, secure life. The Pope's concern for such imbalances at the macro level is discussed early in the encyclical (p. 21), and the theme is drawn throughout the letter. A state of balance is approximated when each is able to meet his or her needs and sustain a dignified, secure life. This is rarely achieved in conditions of underdevelopment and often fails to occur in conditions of development or superdevelopment. The pervasive absence of this balanced state of distributive justice in the global community energizes the encyclical, *On Social Concern*. Yet, in the context of development as a fusion of social and economic elements, the Pope resists endorsing completely equal distribution. Perhaps it is the historical evidence that such equity is possible on a large scale only when dignity, freedom, and individualism are suppressed. Such a state imposes on people in ways that diminish other dimensions of human potential.

Managerial Implications

These concepts enrich our understanding of managerial and institutional responsibility in two distinct ways. First, decisions regarding primary activities in which an organization engages requires managerial attention to the productive, consumptive, and distributive effects and to the conditions in which such activities would be conducted. Thus, for example, the decision to locate the new manufacturing facility in a developed or superdeveloped economy when it will produce products

Figure 2
Productive, Consumption, and Distributive Activities in Three States of Development (X indicates dominant condition)

Socioeconomic Conditions in Key Spheres of Activity		States of Development		
		Under-developed	Developed	Super-development
Productive justice	Dependancy	X		
	Self-sufficiency		X	
	Dominance			X
Consumptive justice	Inadequate	X		
	Balanced		X	
	Excessive		X	X
Distributive justice	Extreme Inequality	X	X	X
	Each as to Needs		X	X
	Equalized			

to be sold in less developed nations raises serious productive and distributive justice questions. Conversely, a decision to locate a manufacturing facility in a less developed economy solely to take advantage of low labor rates requires a careful examination of the distributive impact in that nation. As discussed above, the primary and secondary impacts of such decisions are central to managerial responsibility. Second, these concepts help refine the criteria against which managers can assess the effectiveness of their social performance. Is there an unjust production effect? Distribution effect? Consumption effect? What are they? Can they be ameliorated? If so, how? If not, should we proceed?

Current Trends

The concept of organizational interaction with many stakeholders is broadly accepted in the modern management community. Organizations have institutionalized their commitment to such responsiveness through specialized communications mechanisms, offices, and staffs.

In general, these mechanisms are designed to facilitate two-way communication flow: the organization addresses its stakeholders through these devices and it receives messages from them as well.

A well-conceived response process can yield demonstrable positive results. These are the "products" of social performance, and they are the outcomes to which stakeholders look in assessing whether or not expectations have been met adequately. For reasons that are beyond the scope of this paper, the 1980s seem to have been a period of substantial innovation and progress in corporate social performance. Within the framework discussed above, a few examples can usefully highlight some of the ways in which John Paul's concerns are being addressed.

Environmentalism: The concern that productive justice be achieved in ways that do not damage or destroy the world's productive capabilities is highlighted in John Paul's discussion of environmentalism. The growing and increasingly urgent concern for preserving the earth's atmosphere from irreparable damage of ozone destruction is but one of a number of extraordinary examples. The decision of nations to join in the Treaty of Montreal to reduce chloroflurocarbon production and use is a commitment that underscores the global recognition of the need for action. Interestingly, many of the industry actors whose narrow self-interest might have been expected to argue against such action have displayed commendable leadership.

The action of 100 nations to act on toxic waste disposal is another example of the type of international cooperation that seems to be occurring in the environmental arena. Individual managerial action is also happening in some new and noteworthy ways. The impact of fossil fuels on the earth's temperature through carbon dioxide emissions can be offset by increasing the number of trees which absorb CO_2. The Applied Energy Services, Inc., an energy-producing company in Connecticut, recognized that it needed to build a new coal-fired plant but worked with environmental groups to design a "balancing action" through the planting of nearly 52 million trees in Guatemala. The media attention given this response has stimulated many other utilities to examine the approach as a possible way of minimizing their contribution to the greenhouse effect. Similarly, the past decade has seen an enormous growth in voluntary recycling activity in an effort to curb organizational contributions to increasingly critical problems of waste disposal.

Balanced Consumerism: The conspicuous consumption and resource wastefulness that are of such concern to the Pope are being recognized by manufacturers and sellers of products as well. Granted that such recognition is often the result of external pressure, the fact remains that there are some signs of an appreciation for balanced consumerism in even the superdeveloped conditions discussed in *On Social Concern*.

Production of military weapons, for example, has drawn increasing public concern and pressure. Some firms have reconsidered their involvements in this business. The production and sale of hazardous products which threaten life has aroused public and commercial concern. The slaughter of animals for fur coats has drawn angry and extreme protests, including attacks on retail fur shops and their patrons. Overly aggressive marketing to customers who are significantly at risk for product misuse has been targeted, as in the infant formula campaign and actions to restrain consumption of drugs, tobacco, and alcohol. And the pressure for restrained growth in consumption has contributed to restrictions on highly risky investments in nuclear power. No U.S. nuclear power plant has been built and fully operated since the Three Mile Island incident in 1979.

Two additional examples underscore the scope of this new consumerism. The Body Shop International, PLC, is an innovative cosmetics firm that takes a deliberate "non exploitive" approach toward its suppliers. A policy of paying "First World prices for Third World products" helps ensure that the price of its cosmetic products is not artificially understated. This has the positive effect, in turn, of returning to Third World suppliers a larger share of the value added tax created in those nations. The second example of "balanced" thinking is the decision of such consumer product companies as Gillette, Procter and Gamble, and Unilever to alter their product development and testing procedures to de-emphasize animal testing. The growth of the animal rights movement has fueled this trend, but pressure alone cannot move managers who are not ethically sensitive to such concerns.

Creating Economic Opportunities: The human hardships following from economic inequality are being addressed increasingly by the private sector, as well as nonprofit and governmental organizations. The growing domestic phenomenon of public-private partnerships to address social and economic needs is of note. The Hands Across America campaign in 1986 presaged a widespread public involvement in the campaign against hunger. Significant corporate involvement is now an important aspect of national efforts; international pilot projects are under way as well. An effort such as the Partnership for a Drug Free America represents a serious private sector commitment of people, time, and resources to deal with a profound problem threatening all social institutions, including the family itself. To the extent that drug usage creates dependency, forces hard economic decisions on users, and impairs the ability of the person to participate fully in other life activities, it affects all institutions in society.

There has been a growing trend to refocus corporate philanthropy toward partnership creation and expanded socioeconomic opportunity. Some view this as the "new philanthropy," in contrast to established giving patterns. More importantly, the commitments being undertaken tend to address more broadly the distributive imbalances discussed in the encyclicals. These commitments also reflect a refined understanding of management and institutional responsibility to society.

The broad discussion of capital flight and the international debt problems of the developing world is also worth noting. The pressure to develop new approaches that are more sensitive to social costs of strict debt accountability has grown enormously in the 1980s. There runs throughout the debate and dialogue on international debt the twin themes of economic responsibility and social justice. Often in conflict, these themes are increasingly, albeit slowly, being woven into a framework of actions that will respond better to the needs of debtor nations to harmonize their social and economic needs. The problems are too large to expect quick solutions. But the creativity being demonstrated in various new proposals such as "debt for nature" swaps holds the promise of hope that certainly is in spirit with John Paul II's call for "authentic human development."

Conclusion

Issues of institutional responsibility cannot be ignored or avoided in modern society. To do so is to condemn society to injuries that are publicly unacceptable and, in time, destructive.

Americans have needed two centuries to develop reasonably complete concepts of individual responsibility. Less advanced, but more vital in an organizational society, are concepts of institutional responsibility. We can no more tolerate *laissez-faire* institutional behavior than *laissez-faire* personal behavior. Indeed, we can tolerate institutional misbehavior less because institutions generally have greater consequences on more people. The errant institution is often far more dangerous than the lunatic individual.

Just as society consists of economic, political, and cultural systems that interpenetrate and influence one another, so too are our institutions an amalgam of economic, political, and cultural characteristics. A theory of institutional responsibility cannot be worked out in economic and political terms alone, but rather must include both, and absorb the ever-changing play of ideas, values, and moral principles.

Managers are at the center of this interplay of contending ideas, values, and principles. The ethical dilemmas of managers are acknowledged and understood more widely today than in years past, which helps to explain the phenomenal rise in business ethics writing and discussion. But managers at all levels still have relatively few forums in which to discuss their concerns with peers in nonthreatening ways.

A concern for the nature and scope of institutional responsibility to society is vital if socioeconomic systems are to be perfected. The encyclicals advance our understanding of the scope of managerial and organizational responsibility and sharpen the criteria by which we judge performance. John Paul's encyclicals hold the hope that socioeconomic systems can and will be improved. It remains with human beings, including managers, to effect that change. And it remains with human beings to create the means by which the dialogue can proceed.

Bibliography

R. B. Dickie and L. S. Rouner, eds., *Corporation and the Common Good* (Notre Dame, IN: University of Notre Dame Press, 1986).

A. Etzioni, *The Moral Dimension: Toward a New Economics* (New York, NY: The Free Press, 1988).

John Paul II, *On Human Labor* (*Laborem Exercens*), Third Encyclical Letter, September 14, 1981 (Washington, D.C.: U.S. Catholic Conference, 1981).

John Paul II, *On Social Concern* (*Sollicitudo Rei Socialis*), Encyclical Letter, December 30, 1987 (Washington, D.C.: U.S. Catholic Conference, 1987).

M. Novak, *The Spirit of Democratic Capitalism* (New York, NY: American Enterprise Institute/Simon and Schuster, 1982).

L. Preston and J. Post, *Private Management and Public Policy* (Englewood Cliffs, NJ: Prentice-Hall, Inc., 1975).

R. P. Taub, *Community Capitalism: Banking Strategies and Economic Development* (Boston, MA: Harvard Business School Press, 1988).

U. S. Bishops, *Economic Justice for All: Catholic Social Teaching and the U. S. Economy* (Washington, D.C.: U. S. Catholic Conference, 1986).

Seventeen

Radicalization of the Socioeconomic Environment of the Third World— Conflicting and Cooperative Roles for the Catholic Church and Multinational Corporations

S. Prakash Sethi
Paul Steidlmeier

Since 1945 Africa, the Middle East and most of Asia has passed from colonial rule to political independence. Central and Latin America, while still not free from the talons of the Monroe Doctrine, have nonetheless experienced significant increases in autonomy since the halcyon days of "banana republics." In economic terms the gross domestic product of the Third World has risen dramatically over the past 45 years. Notwithstanding this "success," the Third World has become increasingly marked by social strife and the radicalization of the socioeconomic milieu. The issues vary, from political rights in Taiwan and South Korea to more basic survival needs in Zaire and Brazil. Even so, there is a common theme running throughout the protest against "development": the prevalence of poverty and powerlessness. Scores of social indicators are marshalled in the indictment of prevailing development models: the preponderance of corrupt and repressive regimes, systematic violations of human rights, the mounting debt burden, negative terms of trade for primary products, highly skewed resource distribution, population growth far in excess of social resources, militarism, inappropriate technology, the chronic lack of food, health care, habitat, education and other means to meet basic needs. All of these factors have led to social discontent and the radicalization of the political economic environment.

Pope John Paul II has joined the chorus of critics when he says that what has passed for "development" is not authentically human. No wonder the American capitalist press greeted his latest encyclical, *On Social Concern*, with howls of alarm.[1] They find he seriously understates the vast social benefits of private enterprise. However, while the Pope shares with many observers a critique of development, he does not share the ideologies and radical solutions which many have proposed. He is trying to head off the spread of radical ideologies and solutions, notably Marxism, and in this he has some common ground with multinationals.

The Church and multinationals (MNCs) have long played an important role in the Third World. They are both as much a part of the problem as they may be part of any solution. In facing the radicalization of the developing world they share some common characteristics.

1) Neither is the principal source of the radicalization which has built up over the past forty-five years; both, in fact, are reactive.

2) Both have an affinity for social stability and reject the ideology of class struggle and the solutions it portends.

3) Both are being pushed by various constituencies from within and without to change; the church is urged to clearly side with the poor, and the MNCs are asked to assume a more proactive social role in building up justice.

4) Both hope to shape the world to come.

The theme of this conference is that Catholic social teaching, in general, and the writing of Pope John Paul II, in particular, will help to shape a countercultural environment in which multinationals will have to operate. In what follows we examine whether the teaching of the Church really represents a challenging counterculture and, to the degree that it does, what changes it may evoke in the management of multinationals. A conceptual framework is presented to analyze differences between business and church communities on three dimensions: core values; objectives and goals; and organizational structures and policies.[2]

We address in turn 1) the Church as a countercultural prophet in a secular society; 2) the Church and multinationals as prudent social agents; and 3) MNC management strategies which may emerge in developing countries.

The Prophetic Countercultural Church in a Secular Society: The Struggle over the Intellectual Basis of Social Legitimacy

The religious evaluation of society is based upon faith which expresses a view of ultimate reality and meaning. This world view acts as a gyroscope of authentic human development. No matter which way the rings of social, economic and political life may turn, the axis of faith serves to maintain the Church's stability and equilibrium as it carries out its mission in the world.

The Church in society has a mission: to point to the "beyond in our midst" and, in so doing, to foster the harmonious integration of human endeavor and divine purpose. In carrying this out it has three major concerns: to maintain a clear focus on its transcendental mission, to organize itself and behave in such a way that is consistent with and fulfills that mission, and to interact with other groups in society to enhance the fulfillment of the mission.[3]

The first point puts it in a prophetic countercultural relationship with secular society. The legitimacy of the social system, in general, and of MNC policies in particular, is judged on the basis of consistency with the mission of the Catholic Church in the world and the Church's correlative vision of the vocation of humanity.

We have summarized these points of contrast in Figure 1.[4] The Church's transcendental mission sharply contrasts with a secular view of society on two points: 1) the view of ultimate reality and meaning and 2) criteria of legitimacy for development patterns and models.[5]

These considerations form the foundations of an ideal model of a socially just system. Both the social order and individual conduct must be brought into harmony with "the way," which constitutes the Truth above all truths. This orientation is summarized in the belief that Jesus is "the Way, the Truth and the Life."

The first part of the figure outlines the gyroscope of authenticity, uniting as it does a view of human destiny, truth, goodness and fulfillment. The primary source of this vision is the religious tradition which expresses God's gift of self to humanity. This yields a theocentric, not a mere anthropocentric vision of human development. All the marvels of human invention and achievement only have meaning if grounded in this transcendent reality.

In the concrete, this model of human destiny becomes the litmus test of development patterns and models. Any "business ethics" derives from just such assumptions about the ultimate meaning of human existence. This vision of human fulfillment provides the precise rationale why Pope John Paul II has chosen to ground his social ethics and his analysis of economic development on the three virtues which provide the basis of social legitimacy: solidarity, creative liberty of the subject and distribution. It is precisely that normative vision of Church teaching which is countercultural.[6] One may add that it is even countercultural for the Church's own historical institutional forms and practices.

The business community does not proceed from such a vision of universal and objective truth.[7] It takes its cues primarily from 1) public opinion polls and value surveys; 2) the relevant laws, regulations and officials of governments; and 3) the leadership of enterprises. What the Pope says is clearly relevant to the business community for pragmatic reasons if nothing else. The Church is one of the most important sociological institutions in the world, with a "population" of over 800 million and with grass roots organizations in practically every country. If the Pope can influence the three sets of people from whom business takes its cues (as he surely hopes to do), business will listen. At the same time, business hopes to shape what the Church says and does.

The Pope maintains that the Church's identity makes it an expert in humanity (SC #41).[8] His assessment of the market-based corporate world is clearly reformist, yet not hostile as classic Marxist socialism has tended to be. Thus, there is no argument to do away with free enterprise, private property or profits; yet, he calls for changes in present policy.

John Paul II presents a rich and nuanced vision of what he calls the vocation of humanity.[9] The main points of contrast between his vision and the corporate world are the following:

1. *Solidarity* (#38-40): The notion of a common good, based upon religious covenant (rather than the social contract), qualifies the legitimacy of self-interest.

2. *Creative liberty of the subject* (#15): The subjectivity of people in institutions is contrasted with their utility in a particular functional role; notable here are the development of conscience and of effective freedom to participate.

Figure 1
Secular and Transcendental Models of Development

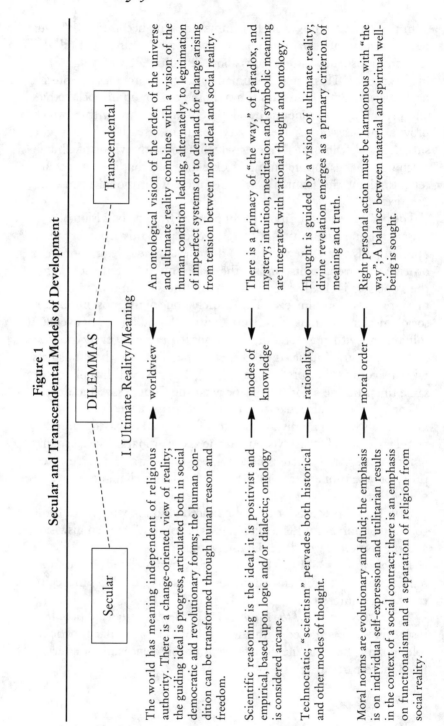

	DILEMMAS	Secular	Transcendental
	I. Ultimate Reality/Meaning		
	worldview	The world has meaning independent of religious authority. There is a change-oriented view of reality; the guiding ideal is progress, articulated both in social democratic and revolutionary forms; the human condition can be transformed through human reason and freedom.	An ontological vision of the order of the universe and ultimate reality combines with a vision of the human condition leading, alternately, to legitimation of imperfect systems or to demand for change arising from tension between moral ideal and social reality.
	modes of knowledge	Scientific reasoning is the ideal; it is positivist and empirical, based upon logic and/or dialectic; ontology is considered arcane.	There is a primacy of "the way," of paradox, and mystery; intuition, meditation and symbolic meaning are integrated with rational thought and ontology.
	rationality	Technocratic; "scientism" pervades both historical and other modes of thought.	Thought is guided by a vision of ultimate reality; divine revelation emerges as a primary criterion of meaning and truth.
	moral order	Moral norms are evolutionary and fluid; the emphasis is on individual self-expression and utilitarian results in the context of a social contract; there is an emphasis on functionalism and a separation of religion from social reality.	Right personal action must be harmonious with "the way"; A balance between material and spiritual well-being is sought.

II. Development Patterns and Models

Primary goals are self-realization and maximization of material well-being; the emphasis is on this world and people having liberty and equal opportunity to pursue their happiness.	→ personal goals ←	Goals of achievement, family, and career are seen within a context of eternal life, calling, and spiritual well-being.
Goals are set as priorities over time; the primary emphasis is upon growth in a utilitarian sense; trade-offs with other goals are seen as necessary.	→ goals ←	Growth must meet the demands of a good moral life, articulated by social justice, community, equity, and participation.
There is a pragmatic choice of strategies to produce growth; trade-offs are practical necessities, leaving policy open for other goals to be realized later; policy is change-oriented in light of immediate goals.	→ strategies ←	There is a simultaneous pursuit of the total goal cluster; pragmatic trade-offs between growth and primary values are rejected; strategy is order-oriented in terms of equitable sharing of benefits and costs in light of transcendental order.
The means employed are pragmatic in terms of technoeconomic efficiency; the emphasis is upon the economic bottom line and providing economic incentives based on self-interest and mutual self-interest.	→ instruments ←	The means employed must be in harmony with ultimate ends; expedient choices of efficiency over primary goals are rejected; equity in bearing social costs and sharing benefits is called for.
The majority rules, whether in institutions of democratic choice or by the masses seen as under the tutelage of a vanguard party; there is no direct role for religious authority as such.	→ nature of social choice ←	Choice is guided by religious authority and those who speak for "ultimate concerns"; human reason and individual choice are limited by religious authority and divine law.

3. *Distribution* (#28): Emphasis upon distributional outcomes as well as on social processes of liberty and opportunity.

People may well wonder what this means in practice for the business world. While the Church in the last century has historically exhibited a preferential option for capitalism, it has been less out of conviction than out of a prudent concern for the interests of its own mission—communists promised annihilation while capitalists afforded social privileges. The Church has never, however, fully accepted liberal ideology.[10]

The business community is not necessarily secular. It is, however, dominated by immediate rather than ultimate concerns and by social relativism rather than by moral absolutes. The heart of the Pope's critique is expressed in Section 3 where he mounts a critique of what might be called "economism"—the reduction of development to mere economic indicators.[11] He maintains there is a higher order by which all human institutions and endeavors are to be judged (#29, 20, 31). What it means to be human is not a relative issue for each to decide by oneself. He clearly has in mind a vision of human community where the "common good" affords a rich array of human developmental possibilities not possible through the pursuit of individual self-interest alone. The day-to-day issues of life and ultimate human fulfillment are essentially interdependent realities. The issue, then, is the *quality of interdependence between people* in the day-to-day occurrences of life. The "quality" of human interdependence is spelled out in terms of *solidarity, liberation with creative subjectivity*, and *fair distribution*. The persistent reality of poverty—the concrete antithesis of these virtues—gives the lie to what has passed as "development." Thus, John Paul II condemns contemporary economic development as "inauthentic."

Solidarity contrasts with self-interest as a social virtue (#38, 39, 40). The lack of it is seen in "consumerism" and the relentless desire of people to *have* more and more rather than *be* more. The lack of solidarity is further manifested in treating "the other" as an instrument (#39), using people as a means to one's own ends. The objective order of the universe (as mirrored in the trinitarian God) is communitarian, and it expresses a notion of *covenant* between people and God and between all people in God. The Church's position is based on the notion of *covenant*. Modern capitalism, however, is *contractual* not covenental in ethos. Aside from mutual respect for individual rights, one only owes others what one chooses to owe them. Duty to others is put negatively (do not...) rather than positively (e.g., the Beatitudes). There is no indissoluble bond of community other than the bonds one chooses.

At this point the faithful divide over the interpretation of the religious significance of capitalism. Some argue that the self-interest rationale of modern capitalism contrasts sharply with the faith even when it is pursued in a way that is mutually beneficial. On the contrary, most Catholic business people find that contemporary capitalism (not to be confused with semi-feudal Third World regimes) represents the closest approximation of the Church's social ideals of any existing social system, that is, while there may be obvious mistakes, the system is, in essence, legitimate.

In addition to solidarity, the Pope sees liberation as the fundamental category and first principle of development (#48). The emphasis, however, does not fall simply upon the freedom of individuals as it does with modern society. Rather, the liberation of the *people* is uppermost. The liberty of some which leaves others enslaved is clearly suspect. To the point, Pope John Paul II argues that "development which is purely economic is incapable of setting man free; on the contrary, it will end up by enslaving him further" (#46). What the Pope is looking for is the "creative subjectivity" of both individuals as well as of peoples (#15, p. 24). The hallmarks of such creative subjectivity are self-determination coupled with participation in co-determination.

More than anything, perhaps, present patterns of distribution shatter the illusion of progress in "development." In commenting on the growing gap between those living in the worlds of "underdevelopment" and superdevelopment," the Pope finds that "the evil . . . consist(s) in . . . possessing without regard for the *quality* and *ordered hierarchy* of the goods one has. *Quality* and *hierarchy* arise from the subordination of goods and their availability to man's 'being' and his true vocation" (#28), p. 50–51).

The trouble with "development," in short, is that it does not add up to a truly common and human good, to a truly flourishing human community. The Pope's rejection of such spurious development is based on his view of the *vocation* of all persons and peoples in God and the kind of world order such a vocation evokes.

The Pope does not condemn capitalism as such; rather, he points out that the operative social virtues of the international economy are tilted toward economism. He rejects the mere economic legitimization of the social system. The guiding ethos of the international economy is (at best) mutual self-interest (not solidarity), individual liberty (not collective liberty), and meritocratic distribution (not distribution based primarily on need or even on effort). The "development" which has been produced (in the non-socialist world) since World War II corresponds to such a business rationale and, for that reason, the Pope finds that it embodies "structures of sin" (#36). "Development" is all the worse when, instead of mutual self-interest it substitutes a zero-sum game, instead of individual liberty it brings coercion and oppression, and instead of fair distribution it affords only subsistence or less.

The Church and MNCs as Prudent Social Agents: Goals and Objectives

Despite its countercultural mission, the Catholic Church has historically been a cautious social agent. In a sociological sense it has manifested amazing survivability skills. Both the Church and the business community have agendas. Our purpose here is to review the general instruments and strategies each employs in its programs. We first examine the general process and focus areas and then comment upon changing institutional priorities and diverse constituencies within the Church and MNC ranks.

Special Processes of Interaction

In their attempts to shape the social environment and patterns of development, both the Church and MNCs face a complex process of interaction between very diverse social groups. The main lines of this process are summarized in Figure 2.

We present the process from the vantage point of MNCs which are at the center of the diagram. Up until the 1970s their life was simpler; they principally interacted with home and host country governments.[12] The radicalized environment which has built up over the past twenty years has changed all that. For want of a better term, what are called "private voluntary organizations" (PVOs) have become participants to be reckoned with. PVOs include any nongovernmental or nonbusi-

Figure 2
International Sociopolitical Environment of Multinational
Corporations—Post-1970s

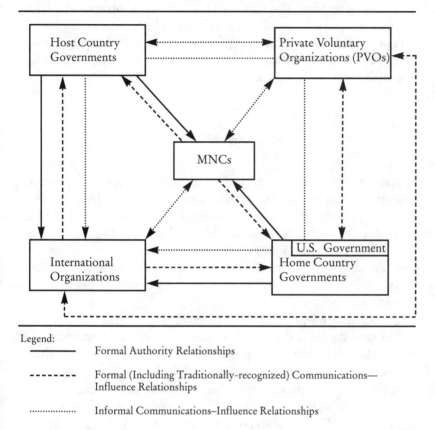

Legend:
———————— Formal Authority Relationships

- - - - - - - Formal (Including Traditionally-recognized) Communications—
Influence Relationships

················ Informal Communications–Influence Relationships

ness organization. They are as varied as the Greenpeace Movement, the National Council of Churches, and Planned Parenthood. In this sort of sociological framework the Catholic Church qualifies primarily as a PVO, notwithstanding that it is also a city-state with a diplomatic corps. The point to note about PVOs is that in the last decades they have become increasingly politically active and astute. Not only have they exerted considerable influence on public opinion (regarding South Africa and armaments, for example) but they have increasing clout with governments and international organizations, particularly U.N. organizations such as WHO, UNESCO and UNCTAD which grant PVOs observer status. The result is that the development policy process is no longer a business/government affair.

The principal agenda of the corporation is to run an economically successful enterprise. The Church's mission is to propagate the faith. Their circles intersect in many ways, two of which are most important for our purposes: 1) responsibility for social justice, and 2) personnel—many church people are also business people. These points yield different focus areas and constituencies.

MNCs and the Church: Focus Areas

The Pope is well aware that the Church has no armies, yet it possesses considerable power to mount strategies in focus areas. In sociological terms its power to effect what it desires lies in the attractiveness of its message, its unprecedented sociological organization and in its strength of persuasion. It uses three general instruments to achieve this: 1) *teaching* its values and orientation, 2) *diplomacy* and political action, and 3) *Catholic action*, which is social action undertaken primarily by lay people.

The teaching of the Church has remarkable powers of diffusion due to its international and grass-roots structure. Its own command of the media is modest, but its deep involvement in education throughout the world guarantees that its message will be heard. Furthermore, the Church mounts a very serious diplomatic offensive, making sure that most governments and the major international organizations and agencies are well aware of its position. In addition, through "Catholic action," the Church hopes that lay men and women will find their way to responsible positions in business and political circles as well as in private voluntary organizations, and will steer those organizations toward the desired ends. Finally, the Church remains very active in international charity and relief works. As a result, the Church is sociologically very able to focus on issues and mount strategies of action. It is a key player that MNCs would only ignore with peril.

The business community is also noteworthy for its ability to focus on issues and mount effective campaigns. Business counters the Church's vision of community with a plea for the emancipation of individuals from countless social institutions which have oppressed them precisely in the name of community. "Community," it is argued, is a beautiful idea. In historical practice, however, it carries with it the onerous burden of coercive and often arbitrary authority; witness the Inquisition or the ayatollahs of Iran. It is precisely this type of coercive and arbitrary authority which shattered the idyllic vision of the commune and other forms of utopia. Furthermore, in a profoundly pluralistic world it is naive to think that one ideal of community will emerge and be spontaneously accepted by all. It is unlikely that Ayatollah Khomeini and Pope John Paul would have signed a "concordant"; rather, each insists on allegiance to his "objective truth." Instead, the business community promises 1) *tolerance* for all viewpoints and 2) *progress* (economic, political and cultural) based on individual liberty.[13]

Secondly, the business community maintains vigorous contacts with governments in terms of lobbying as well as through contributions (notably PACs in the U. S.).[14] A tremendous amount of business resources go to creating what they call a "positive" business environment. In practice, this means that business devotes a good deal of its resources precisely to shape and define the cultural environment in which it operates. It is by no means passive with respect to the proclaimed countercultures of other groups. In fact, business exhibits considerable expertise in co-opting and subverting them.

Along these lines, business increasingly has come to realize that it has made a mistake in dealing exclusively with governments and neglecting the grass roots of private voluntary organizations in society.[15] Its managers are now charged with forging "partnerships" with members of the local community. It is in the long-term interests of the company to convert potential conflicts into areas of mutual self-interest.[16]

The general strategies it employs are, first, to persuade the various constituencies of the legitimacy of its mission. If that is not successful, tactics shift to co-option and then to pressure and power plays. The corporate world aims to shape public opinion about itself and development, and to control those who are opinion makers.

The Church follows similar strategies. In addition to convincing business that it is a stakeholder to be reckoned with, it rallies other stakeholders (especially in ecumenical settings of other religions). The Church also has its own methods of co-option and in bringing pressure to bear from other sources.

At this point the intersection of Church and MNCs in the area of personnel is crucial. The Church sees lay people as bringing the gospel

Figure 3
Focus Areas and Strategies

Focus Area	Strategies	
	Church	Business
Ideology	Vision of community	Progress
Governments	Vatican diplomacy	Lobbying, PACs
Grass roots	Catholic action	Managers
Instruments	Persuade, co-opt	Persuade, co-opt

Figure 4
The Impact of the Religious Counterculture
On Multinational Strategies and Decisions

MNC Functional Decisions	Social Critique	Possible Agenda	
		Political	Economic
Resource ownership	Class	Nationalization	Land reform
Production decisions	Elitist	Fiscal policy price controls	Boycott
Technology choice	Not appropriate	Regulation fiscal policy	Boycott
Technology transfer	Monopoly; brain drain	Lax patent law	Pirating
Salaries & wages	Subsistence level	Minimum wage taxes	Strike
Expatriate personnel	Hinders locals	Visa problems taxes	Boycott
Repatriation of profit	Lacks commitment to people	Regulation	Boycott
Marketing	Exploitive consumerism	Regulation	Boycott
Political action	Corruption	Codes of conduct	

to the workplace; they are also, however, bringing the corporate gospel to the Church. Business has a very strong constituency within the Church and it is trying actively to shape Church social teaching.[17]

Changing Institutional Priorities and Diverse Constituencies

Each side is getting to know how to put the other in play. Historically, the business community and political circles know that the church has been most exercised over itself over 1) its right to worship and evangelize, 2) laws regarding marriage and the family (including divorce, birth control and abortion), 3) education, and 4) various privileges regarding land ownership, taxation and exemptions. Poverty has never really been at the top of the list, and one questions to what extent it really will be now, even though it is the focal point of *On Social Concern*. Business, quite frankly, proceeds from the belief that every person and institution has its priorities and is open to trade-offs. It enters upon the scene ready to deal. Both the Vatican and multinational corporations approach the prospect of social change very cautiously. One point that might make the Church less disposed to "trade-offs" than before, however, is the fact that more than half of the Church population is now in the developing world. Movements of liberation theology within the Church are not inclined to acquiesce, and talk in recent years of a "popular church" and a "church that rises from the people" has sent a message to the traditional institution in the First World.

At the same time, the Church can put governments and corporations on notice that they very much need the good will of the Church. From the United States to Brazil, local bishops have addressed the "structures of sin" in the local economies. However, Church and MNCs share some common ground: their love of social stability and their perception of Marxism as a common enemy.

The corporate world also is showing some signs of changing priorities as it edges away from a kind of free market fundamentalism toward the creation of social partnerships. Over the past thirty years there has been a gradual transformation in the business community from an "absolute ownership" approach to a "stakeholder" approach.[16]

Neither within the Church nor within the business community are people marching at lock step. Each must be analyzed in terms of their respective internal constituencies which try to shape their agendas. The diagram presented in Figure 2 does not capture this diversity as it represents a social aggregate; one needs caution in interpreting it.

The Church has many diverse groups within itself, as is only natural with a culturally diverse body with over 800 million people. For our purpose we consider four: *Opus Dei*, the Konrad Adenauer Institute, Liberation Theology and North American Liberal Catholics. These groups are struggling to define the Church's social teaching.

Liberation theology is most inclined to radical social change, aligned as its methodology is to critical structuralism.[19] Liberal Catholics in North America are reform-minded and exhibit a greater orientation toward change and consensus in social values. The Vatican has viewed both with suspicion, the former because of a seeming tilt toward socialism and the latter for flirting with liberalism—both alien ideologies.

Any follower of the contemporary Vatican scene knows that it is more at home with *Opus Dei* and especially with the Christian Democrats represented by the Konrad Adenauer Institute. *Opus Dei* grew up and ran Franco's Spain. It is widespread in the Hispanic world and is generally pro-establishment. It features a concern for the poor that reflects a harmony among the social classes. The upper classes have a duty toward the poor to be generous in charity, a duty exercised in a paternalistic way. People of this persuasion may be generous and dedicated but are typically little inclined toward institutional change, working things out instead within the *status quo*.

The social stance the Vatican most associates with is clearly that of the Western European Christian Democrats, notably the West Germans as represented by the Konrad Adenauer Institute and its notion of the "social market economy" (sozialmarktwirtschaft). The latter features active government policy, especially fiscal and budgetary measures, to achieve desired social ends.

The reformist business community likewise exhibits a number of configurations, ranging from the Heritage Foundation and Cato Institute to the American Enterprise Institute, the Business Roundtable and entities such as the Brookings Institution, to name a few within the United States. These organizations generally seek to address issues as they arise in terms of the realities of public opinion and relevant law. The latter three would tend toward a "stakeholder" approach to business and society. They are reform-minded but nonetheless leery of what they perceive as the fixed ideology of the Church. The Heritage Foundation and Cato Institute more firmly espouse the values of classic liberalism and, thus, reject social relativism. At the same time they exhibit little tolerance for the letter on the U. S. Economy issued by the Catholic Bishops, precisely because the Bishops criticized the "liberalism" of market fundamentalists. These groups tend to take a "strict property ownership" view of business and society, leaving the relation to be clarified in terms of individual liberty and property rights.

The social teaching of the Church does not suggest precise policies in any of these areas. The impact of the Church's social teaching depends on which constituency is speaking: both Opus Dei and Liberation Theology claim to be in line with Church teaching and they have very different business agendas.

MNC Management Options in Dealing with the New Counterculture: Oppose, Co-Opt, Tactically Adapt, Genuinely Change

The economic counterculture proposed by Pope John Paul II stands on three legs: 1) solidarity, 2) creative subjectivity, and 3) distributive justice. In general, the corporate world has chosen not to fight on normative turf. Indeed, in commenting on the United States' Bishops letter on the economy, business leaders said they applauded the end sought but differed on the means to the end, maintaining that democratic and capitalist institutions would most efficaciously deliver the ends sought.[20]

The Christian scriptures are replete with countercultural orientations. That spirit, which the Pope clearly evokes, would lead to a radical transformation of the items listed in Figure 4 (liberation theologians contend precisely that). Institutions of property, production decision priorities, the rate and use of profits, price levels and wages would all be radically transformed in a measure far beyond what socialists threaten. We discuss these points under three considerations: the agenda for the international economy, technology transfer and the role of government.

Agenda for the International Economy

At the international level, the Church is calling for a new set of rules of the game but it does not spell them out. The main topics of interest are: the terms of trade, debt, the transfer of technology, voting power in international organizations such as the IMF and GATT, and eliminating the support of local elites by outside powers. Other issues such as migration policy and the brain drain, trade in armaments and the quality of international media also figure prominently. Most of these themes are not new and have been sounded by various groups in developing countries for years. Yet in providing a theological underpinning for such concerns the Church confers legitimacy upon them, raising them to the level of received truth and, thereby, not subject to doubt. The general consensus is that in all of these areas the playing field is not level; power wins out over concerns for human dignity.

In practical issues the Church position is more common sense than theoretical.[21] Its experience with "development" has convinced it that its major benefits neither reach the masses nor benefit the poor. The Church argues that the sacred scripture of modernization theory, which invokes the divine plan of "investment-growth-jobs," has not provided its promised trickle down of benefits for all.[22] The Church spells out the social virtues it would like to see put into practice. It has no explicit recipe for doing this. Implicitly, however, it appears to argue for the type of social system one sees in Western Europe and is expressed in the notion of a social market economy. The objection to MNCs is that they play by different rules once they are outside OECD borders. The Vatican's position seems implicitly to call for internationalization of the types of controls one sees within the OECD. All this would imply a new role for government as well as the development of international law.

Multinational corporations face an uncertain future in a changing international sociopolitical environment. However, this is not entirely without its positive aspects. There is growing awareness among many less developed countries of the important role that private capitalism and MNCs can play in the development process. At the same time, behavioral patterns of MNCs have been refashioned. Diverse technology and manufacturing processes have made MNCs less dependent on cheap labor and mineral resources of the Third World. Also, the mix of

MNCs has been changing, with more of them coming from Third World and Asian countries. These MNCs not only bring various time perspectives and risk orientations to their overseas investments—they also carry different institutional baggage about the management of their enterprises.

LDCs are becoming more sophisticated about their economic and social needs and the variety of sources available to them to meet those needs. The challenge for the MNCs would be to find a role for themselves that would take into account these new realities. This would involve an awareness of the increased information and negotiating abilities of the LDCs and the growing power of these countries in the international arena to raise issues and exchange information that would make it all but impossible for the unscrupulous among the MNCs to hide behind legal or technological considerations or raise the flag of defense of free enterprise.

As a starting point, MNCs will have to re-evaluate their operative model of business and society. It is commonplace in Western treatises on strategic management to treat society as an "external environment" and then to assess the factors of that environment that either enhance or threaten the conduct of business. At issue is the philosophy of private property and enterprise itself. Catholic tradition rejects the notion of private property which is absolutist, individualist and, hence, exclusive of others. Rather, property is a relative right conferred by society. Dominion over property carries with it an exercise of stewardship on behalf of the people. Therefore, the notion of property entails a fiduciary duty to society and a responsibility for the common good.

Furthermore, a corporation's mission and line of business also come in for scrutiny. The mere production of wealth and a healthy balance sheet are not sufficient. The rightness of any system must be measured by its impact upon the three social virtues of solidarity, creative subjectivity and distribution. This position introduces a social dimension to the determination of the line of business and provides a prism through which the social value of a corporation's mission statement and choice of business may be judged.

The use of profits is also a major bone of contention. In the view of the Church, many multinationals have mined the Third World of its resources and have given little, if anything, back. Such business behavior only seems to confirm the corporation's lack of commitment to the people of a country and the tendency to treat a country as "external environment." The Church is, therefore, very concerned with what happens to profits. It would vigorously object to financial practices that bleed the country of already scarce capital, and insist on re-investment of those earnings for further development of the country.

A fourth major priority is the provision of jobs. As mentioned below, technological choice must provide for employment. But there is more. The Church is critical of Western personnel management policies which generally favor some sort of worker participation. The emphasis is upon workers as subjects in the workplace rather than mere objects. Their personal dignity must be provided for in terms of participation, just wages, job security and appropriate benefits.

Finally, the Church argues that economic exchange should be based upon the normative notion of just and fair prices, even if just prices are hard to define. In the absence of competitive markets, some sort of public pricing policy may be called for. MNCs must be able to deal with public pricing policy. It is perhaps best to be positive and constructive in its proposed alternatives. For example, they should work for the development of truly competitive markets in the first place. MNCs should see public policy as supplementary to market imperfections. At any rate, economic exchange is to be just that: a transaction for the mutual and fair benefit of the parties concerned, and not a zero-sum game stacked in favor of MNCs.

Role of Technology and Technology Transfer

The suspicion toward MNCs becomes very manifest in discussions of technology. Technology is approached primarily in terms of its "relevance" in the sociological and situational context in which a particular technology will be used in a society. Technology here is defined as not only including new manufacturing processes but also new products and even services. The liberal capitalist context of technology is that of improving efficiency or expanding demand in a manner that enhances the profits and rewards of an enterprise. The benefits to society are dispersed through increased competition, where old and inefficient products are driven out of market; consumers receive higher value for money through better products and lower prices, workers through better wages, and communities through shift of capital to more productive uses. This idealistic model, however, does not provide a "good fit" with the reality of the Third World and, thus, poses one of the most serious challenges to the multinational corporation which, after all, are the major agents for bringing technological change to the Third World countries.

Technologies that are developed within the context of the economic and sociopolitical infrastructures of industrialized economies do not always yield similar results in Third World settings. They may even have quite adverse, albeit unintended, consequences or harmful effects. Laborsaving technologies may reduce employment among unskilled workers while, at the same time, raising wages of skilled workers to levels that are affordable only by large MNCs. In so doing they may shift resources to those industries that are dominated by MNCs. New products may appeal to the small, affluent segments of the population but, through "demonstration effect," may cause poor people to buy those products they can ill afford and do not need. They cause shifts in consumption patterns and thereby adversely affect both the local industry and consumer welfare. For example, Coca-Cola might displace the consumption of local fruit juices and thereby harm farm income, agricultural employment, and consumers' nutrition intake. Moreover, since the new products have their greatest value-added component in processing and not raw materials, they divert a larger proportion of the enterprise of income to owners of technology, e.g., the MNC.[23]

Products and technologies transferred may be inherently safe, but may create undesirable side effects because of poor fit within the context of local culture or work environment. An example of the former is infant formula foods which were alleged to have contributed to infant malnutrition and disease because of illiteracy and unsanitary conditions under which the food was prepared. The example of the second type of technology transfer may be a steel mill or a chemical plant where an otherwise safe technology becomes unsafe because of a lack of local emphasis on preventive maintenance or inadequate worker training.

Technology transfer may take place to avoid stringent environmental laws in an MNC's home country or to take advantage of the lack of technical knowledge on the part of LDCs to develop adequate safeguards. Alternately, MNCs might export products, e.g., pesticides, whose usage had been banned at home. In both these cases one can make rational arguments to defend these decisions. For example, the relatively pristine nature of LDC environment allows for greater capacity to absorb pollution-related side effects of new plants. Also, there may be beneficial trade-offs between pollution, economic growth and employment. Moreover, decisions to introduce and implement complex, and potentially dangerous, technologies and products are based on criteria that are relevant and beneficial primarily to those introducing such technologies. Many stakeholders, including innocent bystanders and hapless victims, are unaware of the dangers to which they are being exposed and are rarely in a position to have an impact on those decisions until it is too late.

In capitalist societies, individual genius and effort are compensated through rewards accruing from control and exploitation of one's technology. However, under the liberation concept of the community, the fruits of research are somehow a common patrimony. In capitalism, the legitimacy of a new technology is expressed in terms of market demand, and accountability is contained within legal approval. The Church imposes communitarian criteria. It wants to know what technology does for people and to people. MNCs will have to become more sensitive to the entire spectrum of technology transfer that will take into account not only the profit-maximizing aspects of the MNC enterprise but, even more important, contribute to the stability of the society and its cultural values on the one hand, and on the other hand, a growth that is accompanied with more equitable distribution of income. It is only when the interests of the MNCs and the countries involved are in harmony, and can stand the test of public scrutiny, that the MNCs will be able to survive and grow in the new international environment.

Government Control and Regulation of Economic Activity

Similar to the pattern followed in most of the Third World countries, many Church people view the role of government in expansive terms. On the face of it, such a position might seem anomalous. From an historical point of view, the quality of governments in developing countries presents a rather sorry picture in terms of democratic ideals. The history of the Third World has been punctuated with authoritarian military rule and oligarchic elites who have manifested little concern for guaranteeing human rights or a decent standard of living for the masses. In such a context, critics of "development" often view private economic institutions as "agents of oppression," and personal economic activity as driven by personal greed.

Government is seen to have a necessary guiding role. State intervention in these countries should not necessarily focus primarily on facilitating the growth of private economic institutions or on improving their productivity. Instead, government intervention should be aimed at improving the distribution of economic benefits through direct control, if necessary, of large segments of economic activity so that they could be used for the benefit of the masses. There is to be redistribution then growth. The quarrel is not with small business but with entrenched oligarchies. Where private enterprise is allowed, it may be subjected to detailed regulation and supervision to ensure that it operates in a manner that enhances social welfare. The goal is first to wrest control of the government from powerful elites and then use it to protect and further the interests of the people. The government is seen to have a crucial role in resource and income distribution.

The Pope's critique of development views the social benefits of private property with a degree of suspicion due to the historical experience of local oligarchies. Often the historical set of property rights is morally repulsive. Such property rights owe their origin to grants by the Crown as well as to the private armies of local elites, not to honest hard work in a fair social setting. However, rather than being against private property, Church advocates would argue that all should have some. The present social "starting point" of gross distributional inequities calls for radical property reform. As an example, the Church in Brazil and in the Philippines has been quite vocal in regard to land reform. The Vatican itself has not been particularly vocal, however.

With respect to their investment and operating climate, Western MNCs tend to view an interventionist government as bad and, therefore, prefer either a minimal government or one that can be co-opted and manipulated to serve the MNCs' own ends. This has been borne out historically in their experience of dealing with authoritarian and generally corrupt governments which the MNCs have been willing to use for their own purposes. As we have stated before, this approach is likely to be counterproductive even in the short run, given the new sociopolitical environment, and will be quite harmful in the long run. MNCs will have to face up to activist governments.

Many Church people seem to favor the option of government control or cooperatives over private enterprise. The problem is not with small landowners, shopkeepers and family businesses; it is with oligopoly and monopoly power. Large-scale private enterprise historically is likely to be exploitive. The only realistic compensating power to such private power would be the government, provided it is in the hands of people who would act on behalf of the poor. The argument for public control of economic activity is presented more in political than economic terms. That is, the argument is not that public enterprise or government intervention is necessarily more efficient but that, given the historical reality, it is likely to be more beneficial to the masses.

Unfortunately, in the case of most Third World countries, there have not been other people-based organizations to provide alternative models of governance. The only other institution of substance, i.e., the Roman Catholic Church, has also historically been hierarchical and authoritative in character. Thus, unlike Western democracies, critics of contemporary development patterns put less faith in "institutions" and more faith in "people" who control those institutions. Government is evil if it is controlled by "evil men," but the same government is "good" if it is governed by "moral men." Thus the power of the state, like that of a gun, becomes good or bad depending on who wields it and the purposes for which it is being wielded. It is, therefore, not surprising that Church people opt for greater state control, or state- (read "community") directed institutions to control economic activities both at the micro and macro level.

MNCs, therefore, must develop a new outlook that provides for the acceptance of a greater role in the management of economy on the part of governments in the Third World. European and Japanese MNCs clearly have more experience in this regard. Such an orientation, however, must be qualified and entered into on an *ad hoc* basis rather than used as a normal state of affairs. As we shall discuss below, an unquestioned acceptance of a local government's directives may lead MNCs into highly dangerous and financially ruinous situations.[24]

A cooperative approach toward host country governments does not mean that MNCs must work with every "people's government" regardless of its commitment to democratic values, human rights and private enterprise. Peoples' governments can be as coercive as right-wing dictatorships, notwithstanding their high moral tone and "halo" effect borne out of their professed representation of the poor and the downtrodden. Centrally planned and controlled societies do not become democratic or market oriented just because they use some elements of a market economy and price mechanisms to improve resource allocations. On the contrary, these relaxations are used to make totalitarianism more tolerable and do not necessarily lighten their grip on society. By the same token, just because a government has an active involvement in the direction of the economy, and important parts or industry are state-controlled, this does not automatically make such a nation to be against private enterprise.

Strategic Options for the MNCs

In the Church's history there have been precise movements to live the ideal: notably in the monastic movement and later forms of "religious life," and in such enduring countercultural figures as Francis of Assisi whose striking life choices have served as models for over seven centuries. At the same time as it maintained the highest social ideals, however, the historical Church has been decidedly prudent and "accommodationist" in practice. Life "in the world" was admittedly not the "way of perfection" associated with monastic or "religious life." the MNCs are well aware of history. They pay lip service to the idealistic traditions expressed by the Church, but they are *counting on* the prudent accommodationist approach. They know full well, for instance, that in the Papal social teaching there is condemnation of poverty and corruption, but not a word about the Swiss banks that are the principal institutions in making it possible.

The accommodationist Vatican does not pose a major challenge to the items listed in Figure 4. It is reformist, however. It is our opinion that the Vatican, in fact, opts for Western European models of economic progress and social justice, particularly as expressed in the notion of the "social market economy." The basic needs and well-being of people are also more securely met. Yet Western Europe is more of a class society and exhibits less social mobility than the United States. Americans will have their liberty and they bridle at coercive authority and the patriarchal role of the upper classes, even if benevolent in intention. In this they not only differ from the Europeans but also from the Asian economic powerhouses, where the upper classes provide workers with lifetime job security and welfare, but not with equality, even of opportunity.

In general, the corporate world has four options: 1) to openly oppose either the ends or the means entailed in the Church's message; 2) to co-opt Church leaders and, in so doing, favorably shape the Church's statements regarding MNCs; 3) to tactically and even cosmetically embrace what is being said and adapt in ways that cost little as a sign of good faith, and 4) to genuinely restructure the corporation so that it reflects the core values of the Church. In our opinion the favored tactics are choices 2 and 3. Furthermore, MNCs have a very good chance of being successful in implementing them.

We think it unlikely that the MNCs will attack the Church's social values head-on, especially at a time when a Pope enjoys high personal popularity. Furthermore, MNCs are well aware of the unique sociological power and "halo effect" of the Church and realize that an open attack would likely raise the question of their own legitimacy in uncomfortable ways, particularly in the Third World. Options 2 and 3 are clearly the most likely and can pay off handsomely: good will at little real cost. That Mother Theresa and works such as Covenant House are so well received by the corporate world is no accident. It enables the MNCs to appear caring and compassionate with minimal structure change. If the ideals proposed by the Pope were taken in dead earnest, particularly equitable distribution, MNCs would be quaking in their boots.

We suspect that Asian and European MNCs can live very easily with the Vatican document. Never mind that Christianity in ideal is radically countercultural; the Vatican in practice is only cautiously so. Asian and European MNCs also are historically habituated to their social role and to working closely with each other and with governments to achieve it. Even though their behavior in the Third World has been predominantly neocolonial, they are more able to see that their future is not bright if they continue to adopt a double standard. They must play by the same rules abroad as they do at home.

American multinationals will have a harder time seeing this point because the ideal of a "social market economy" demands an ideological change among American executives who have been overdosed on positivism and the myth of free, competitive, efficient markets. American executives have a profound sense of liberty and law. This is so true that the law, in effect, has become a proxy of one's duties to others. At the same time, in the Third World they have done all in their power historically to undermine the evolution of a legal system and the types of laws which would make the realization of the Pope's social virtues (solidarity, creative subjectivity and distributive justice) at all possible. American business has a sorry record not only of going to bed with the Marcos', Mobutu's, and Pinochet's of the world, but of lobbying the U. S. government to help them coercively stay in power. For this type of behavior, the Pope's message is indeed countercultural. It will grow increasingly so as the Church, more than 50 percent of whose members come from the Third World, tries effectively to put itself on the side of the poor. Indeed, given the new demographics of the Church, the business world can only view the future with a degree of apprehension and uncertainty. They would most fear a spread of the type of Bishops' Conference that one sees in Brazil. But they can feel at home with a Bishops' Conference such as that of Colombia or Mexico. The latter seems the more likely.

Notes

1. When John Paul II was elected in 1978, the capitalist world generally breathed a sigh of relief. The business community was clearly out of sorts with Paul VI, especially since 1967 when he criticized historical patterns of "development" as unjust and seemingly veered to the left. The issue now as then is world poverty and what causes it. The business community resents being associated with causing or exacerbating poverty. It would much prefer the approach of Pius XII in 1950 when he wrote On Human Misery. Pius XII wrote a clear condemnation of poverty but remained clearly aligned with the political economic institutions of the West prevailing at the time. Since Pius XII the Catholic Church is no longer the steadfast ally of capitalism. The split manifested itself in 1965 (when Vatican II published On Joy And Hope), in 1967 (when Paul VI published On The Development of Peoples) and in 1981 (with John Paul II's publication of On Human Work) and now with On Social Concern. It is clear the Catholic Church cannot be counted on as a staunch ally of Western capitalism. Indeed, Pope Paul II criticizes it for its imperialist tendencies (SC #22).

2. S. Prakash Sethi, "A Strategic Framework for Dealing with Schism between Business and Academe," Public Affairs Review, 1983, pp. 44–59.

3. Paul Steidlmeier, *Social Justice Ministry: Foundations and Concerns*, New York, LeJacq Publishing Co., 1984, ch. 1.

4. This figure has been adapted from an ethical analysis of development proposed by Buddhist scholars in Sri Lanka; G. Gunnatilleke *et al.*, *Ethical Dilemmas In Development*, Lexington, MA: Lexington Books, 1983; presented in Paul Steidlmeier, *The Paradox of Poverty: A Reappraisal of Economic Development Policy*, Cambridge, MA: Ballinger Publishing Co., 1987, ch. 6.

5. We are contrasting "transcendental" with "secular." While models of business and society historically have been highly positivist, this does not mean that corporate persons are secular. Indeed, there is a decidedly religious strain in American business ideology. At the same time major religions find themselves in cultural counterpoint with secular models of development. This is an obvious concern of Judaism and Christianity and also of contemporary Islam.

6. There has been considerable discussion in Catholic circles about whether doctrine can develop or whether it is eternal truth captured once and for all. On the one hand the understanding of faith is not immutable for the stark reality of new experience can shock accepted meanings, forcing a re-articulation of the faith paradigm. At the same time, while historical understanding of a truth may develop, the truth is itself held to be immutable.

7. The Business Roundtable, *Corporate Ethics: A Prime Business Asset*, New York, 1988; Archibald S. Alexander and Robert L. Swinth, *A Value Framework for Assessing the Social Impacts of Multinational Corporations*, The University of South Carolina, Center for International Business Studies, *Essays in International Business*, No. 7, November 1987.

8. In this text we concentrate on the recent encyclical *On Social Concern*; In the following text we refer to this document by paragraph numbers (e.g., #n).

9. In our comments we concentrate on John Paul II's latest encyclical, *On Social Concern*. For a more detailed history of Church social teaching see Joseph Gremillion, *The Gospel of Justice and Peace*, New York, Orbis Books, 1976.

10. At the same time, the Church has not sought refuge in other secular ideologies. It has fought furious ideological battles with the Marxists over what constitutes objective truth as well as over the structure of reality and the course of human history (see #22). It has also addressed the various strains of secular neo-humanism with its own based religious humanism. The church claims to be "an expert in humanity" (#41) and finds secular humanism which is at odds with its avowed universal values and the fundamental order of the universe to be unpalatable.

11. "Economism" (jingjizhuyi) was the phrase used during China's cultural revolution, criticizing those who saw development in primarily economic rather than political/revolutionary terms.

12. S. Prakash Sethi, "Opportunities and Pitfalls for Multinational Corporations in a Changed Political Environment," *Long Range Planning*, 20, 6, 1987, pp. 45–53.

13. Michael Novak, *The Spirit of Democratic Capitalism*, New York, Harper and Row, 1982.

14. S. Prakash Sethi, *Handbook of Advocacy Advertising*, Cambridge, MA: Ballinger Publishing Co. 1987.

15. S. Prakash Sethi, "Operational Pitfalls for Multinational Corporations in a Changed Political Environment," *Long Range Planning*, Vol. 20, 6, 1987, pp. 45–53.

16. The Business Roundtable, *Corporate Ethics: A Prime Asset*. New York, NY: February 1988.

17. A good example of this was provided by *The Lay Letter* which critiqued the U. S. Bishops' draft letter on the economy.

18. R. Edward Freeman, *Strategic Management: A Stakeholder Approach*, Boston, MA: Pittman Publishing Co. 1984.

19. Paul Steidlmeier, *Social Justice Ministry: Foundations and Concerns*, New York, NY: LeJacq Publishing Co. 1984, ch. 7.

20. These reflections were developed in S. Prakash Sethi and Paul Steidlmeier, "A New Paradigm of the Business/Society Relationship in the Third World: The Challenge of Liberation Theology," in Lee Preston, ed., *Research in Corporate Policy and Performance*, Vol. 10, Greenwich, CT: Jai Press Inc., pp. 29–43.

21. There is some question as to whether Church critics of development accept the dependency theory model of economic development and whether they harbor a bias against capitalism. Dependency theory is hard to categorize. It does not fit with orthodox Marxism, yet it shares a focus upon structures and social class. The central focus of the liberation model, however, is the social process of change from the status quo. Most liberationists, therefore, accept dependency as an historical fact, that is, they sense that the terms of their lives are determined by a combination of outside interests and local elites—dependent on an international class structure.

22. Insofar as they are theoretical, they are talking theology and explaining why Christians cannot authentically acquiesce to the *status quo*. They observe that poverty is persistent, if not growing. Furthermore, real power rests with the OECD countries, internationally, and with local oligarchies domestically. They believe that on issues such as the debt, technology transfer, military might and international media, the balance of power is clearly with the

OECD. Their view of dependency means that 1) they are not on an equal footing and 2) are not in command of their own destiny. Since for them this type of dependency is associated with capitalism, it means that MNCs will be viewed with suspicion.

23. Denis Goulet, *The Uncertain Promise: Value Conflicts in Technology Transfer*, New York, DOC/North America, 1977.

24. S. Prakash Sethi, Hamid Etemad and K. A. N. Luther, "New Sociopolitical Forces: The Globalization of Conflict," *Journal of Business Strategy*, Spring, 1986, pp. 24–32.

Eighteen

John Paul II
and American Workers
in the Emerging Fourth World

Teresa Ghilarducci

Both papal encyclicals on labor and society, *Sollicitudo Rei Socialis* and *Laborem Exercens*, teach that human dignity is derived from the distribution of meaningful jobs: work "is a key, probably the essential key to . . . making life more human."[1]

Human enfranchisement[2] requires full employment and the resources (including time) to reproduce (provide upkeep for) family and community.[3] The encyclicals are meant to be not technical documents but a "set of principles for reflection, criteria for judgment and directives for action."[4] This paper examines some of the technical implications of the encyclicals. Two micro changes in U.S. labor relations would have macro effects on the status of U.S. and global labor. Such reforms are supported by the principles in the encyclicals; the reforms are within our reach and they provide the foundations for an economic counterculture.

The two changes are: greater worker participation and ownership, and a shorter work week. Democratized financial investment decisions would, most likely, put greater weight on full employment and stability and less importance on developing cheap supplies of labor for greater short-term profits. A shorter work week would enable a more efficient and human distribution of working hours among family members and work among workers. (*Laborem Exercens* brings forward the meaning and importance of nonmarket work—a shorter work week would help balance the time between the two—market and community/family work.)

Principles of Work and Principled Work

Both encyclicals are extraordinary economic tracts. They traverse history, recognize different meanings in different contexts, and have, most importantly, a world perspective. Few, if any, world leaders today show this range of vision. The encyclical letters are a flexible ring clasping immutable principles, principles that can be used to evaluate the success of an economy at any point in time. In this paper I will concentrate on the principles set forth in one encyclical, *Laborem Exercens*, to evaluate the U. S. economy.

The main principle of the encyclical is that humans are central actors and we are actualized through work (p. 29).[5] This implies capital is subordinate to labor and property ownership should be distributed so that each person is fully entitled to call her or himself "a part owner of the great workbench."[6] State ownership of capital is viewed as inappropriate and an insufficient "socialization of ownership," described as the universality of access to needed goods and the lack of an overbearing power and inequality.[7] The encyclical also defines a duty for governments as an indirect employer to set fair labor standards, pursue full employment standards, and produce and maintain the environment for an economy that gives preference to workers. (The relationship between a preference for the poor and a preference for workers will be discussed later.) Furthermore, worker solidarity, unions and other organizations, including those of intellectual laborers, are needed to affect profound changes in institutions governing labor conditions and to bring about interactions of people as workers.

Therefore, a just and human economy is one in which people live in dignity. Dignity is achieved in two ways: 1) through self-actualization which is ultimately achieved by working, and 2) living in families and households that can reproduce themselves. An economy can be evaluated by a dignity index composed of the following six factors:

a. Workers participate and hold sway over decisions affecting their jobs;
b. There is no unemployment or underemployment—without work no self-actualization can occur;
c. Society honors labor needed to maintain a home and educate children as well as the labor needed to maintain a community;[8]

d. Labor unions and other forms of worker organizations are supported
    for two reasons: unions provide protection against the stronger forces
    of the employer, and unions contribute to worker participation;
e. Government protects workers as an indirect employer;
f. Employers, as owners of property, must make labor a priority.[9]

A dignified economy is one in which workers are enfranchised. The
U. S. economy's dignity index is low and fluctuates widely with business cycles, financial institutional crises, and changes in the popularity
of political economy ideologies because workers are not regarded nor
represented in most economic decisions affecting their lives. In addition, macroeconomic policy relies on unemployment to achieve policy
goals. Moving the U.S. economy to a dignified "neocapitalism," a notion developed in both encyclicals, would bring on an economic counterculture. One change is directly implied by the document and it is a
means and end in itself—more worker control over investment decisions and the pace and organization of work. The other reform is a
means to the goal of stable full employment and more time for repro-
ducing family and community life—the shorter work week. These
changes must, in light of *Sollicitudo Rei Socialis*, work toward greater
equality in the distribution of wealth and income between developing
and developed nations and the developed nations and the Fourth
world[10]—the new band of poverty spreading throughout developed
countries.

Labor and the U.S. Economy

The U. S. evolved from a society of families of self-employed farmers
and craftsmen into a wage-labor economy. At the time of the U. S.
Revolution one-fifth of the workers were slaves but 80 percent of free
persons were self-employed. By 1920, 24 percent of workers were self-
employed and, concomitant with the rise of the twentieth century con-
glomerates and trusts, a new class of worker emerged—the manager.
Managers represented 7 percent of the work force. In 1974, 10 percent
of workers were classified as managers, 83 percent were wage and salary
workers, and 8 percent were self-employed (with fewer than one-half
self-sustaining).[11] Women and teenagers increasingly are entering the

workforce. So as capitalism develops and the largest percentage of workers become wage earners, more of the population are becoming workers—proletarianized.

Another way to examine the relationship Americans have with their work is to categorize jobs by the amount of control workers have over the content, pace, and security of their jobs, and to what extent they supervise others. Among those with ownership and/or control are large employers, small employers, and three kinds of managers, decision makers, executives, advisors, and supervisors. Large employers are proprietors of companies with more than six employees. Small employers employ between one and five persons; self-employed have no employees. Managers are divided into three categories, depending on their role in decision making and supervising. Decision makers make policy decisions and hire and dismiss subordinates. Advisors have considerable input into policy and personnel decisions, while supervisors, semiautonomous workers, and nonautonomous workers have little or no control. Supervisors direct others but have little or no role in major decisions. Semiautonomous workers have some control over the content and pace of work, but do not supervise anyone, nor participate in managerial decisions. Nonautonomous workers have little control over their work. Categorized in these terms, only 28 percent of the U.S. population participate as owners or part owners of the great workbench, leaving 73 percent as disenfranchised (workers, supervisors, one-half of self-employed). Please see Table One.

These figures do not include family members who work inside the home; 37 percent of wives do not work outside the home and, in most couples, the money earner has more choice, influence and power over major economic decisions facing the household. Wives, for the most part, could be classified as nonautonomous, semiautonomous or supervisory workers. Moreover, the labor of children has not been studied enough to be categorized. (At the turn of the century children brought more money to the household than wives.)[12]

Another dimension of the status of the U.S. worker is the fact that the U.S. government is unusual in its lack of protection of workers. In most countries of Europe, social insurance plans—vacations, medical insurance, pensions, etc.—are the right of a citizen; in this country, many of these protections are obtained only through the voluntary act of the employer (except for collectively-bargained social insurance plans which an employer may not unilaterally terminate).[13] The work

Table 1
U.S. Class Structure
1980

Class	Percentage of Population
Large employers (six or more employees)	2%
Small employers (one-five employees)	6%
Self-employed	7%
Managers	
Decision maker	12%
Advisor	5%
Supervisor	13%
Semiautonomous Worker	10%
Nonautonomous Worker	46%

Source: Erik Olin Wright, David Hachen, Cynthia Costello, Joey Sprague, "The American Class Structure" *American Sociological Review*, Vol. 47 (Dec. 1982) p. 709-726.

ethic is not even protected; a person working full time at the minimum wage would still be thousands of dollars below the poverty level.[14] Over ten million children do not have access to medical care and one out of five children live in poverty. To an ever increasing extent this is because their parents work at low-paying jobs unprotected by a minimum standard.

The persistent decline in profit rates for U.S. corporations since 1973 encouraged low-wage strategies, and the Reagan Administration's tax and spending policies based on the supply side tenets (that the poor had too much money and the rich too little) exacerbated the inequality of income and wealth. In 1986, the percentage of all U.S. income going to the poorest 20 percent of the population was lower than the percentage in 1947, despite the improvements made throughout the 1960s and 1970s (when the highest percentage of all income going to the poorest 20 percent was 5.6 percent). The richest 20 percent of families have a greater percentage of total income than they ever had. See Table Two.

Wealth inequality has also grown. The Joint Economic Committee of Congress' 1986 report, "The Concentration of Wealth in the U.S.," showed that the richest households, the top .5 percent, held 25.4 percent of the total wealth in 1963, but, in 1983, held 35.1 percent. In 1963, the bottom 90 percent of the households held 34.9 percent of the wealth, which reduced to 28.2 percent in 1983.[15] The rich

Table Two
Growing Income Inequality
(Percentage of all money income
received by families in each quintile)

Year	Lowest	Second	Middle	Fourth	Top
		Quintile			
1947	5.1	11.8	16.7	23.2	43.2
1950	4.5	11.9	17.4	23.6	42.7
1960	4.8	12.2	17.8	24.0	41.3
1966	5.6	12.4	17.8	23.8	40.5
1969	5.6	12.4	17.7	23.4	40.6
1974	5.5	12.0	17.5	24.0	41.0
1979	5.2	11.6	17.5	24.1	41.7
1980	5.1	11.6	17.5	24.3	41.6
1981	5.0	11.3	17.4	24.4	41.9
1983	4.7	11.1	17.1	24.3	42.8
1985	4.6	10.9	16.9	24.2	43.5
1986	4.6	10.8	16.8	24.0	43.7

Source: Department of the Census

get richer as profitability, productivity, and real incomes to workers fall. According to a Congressional Budget Office the poorest one-tenth of Americans will pay 20 percent more on their 1988 earnings in federal taxes than they did in 1977, and the richest 10 percent will pay 20 percent less. At the end of 1988, 80 percent of families will have experienced an income decline since 1977, but the top 10 percent will gain a 50 percent increase in their incomes.

The data help explain the emergence of the Fourth World in the U.S. Growing poverty rates are a result of the deliberate economic policy of allowing capital more freedom to seek profits and raise profit rates. Poverty analysts quickly discovered in the 1960s and 1970s that they could not study the poor without taking into account the non-poor, and the institutions and policies that determine the distribution of income and jobs. The connection between capitalism and poverty is direct: the reserve army of the poor serves as a warning to middle-income workers and induces them to work in dangerous, menial jobs. The poor also engender animosity within the middle class which sees the poor as usurpers of federal monies. This division prevents coalitions from forming to support more public spending and progressive taxation. Additionally, the nonpoor benefit from the undervaluation of human labor when we buy clothes, eat prepared food, and buy many services produced by undervalued labor.[16] These examples show that poverty in the U.S. is linked to the global labor market.[17]

The U.S. government's role as an indirect employer is feeble, but understandable as an accommodation to the current capitalist profitability crisis partially brought on by a decline in productive investment. The declining competitiveness of the U.S. has been attributed to American corporate strategies of sweating labor, instead of enhancing skills and forging partnerships with workers, and pursuing financial transactions instead of production innovations.[18]

One of the forces of capitalism, as we have noted, is to bring a larger percentage of the population gradually into the work-wage-consumption nexus. Married women and mothers are working in greater numbers than ever before, due to economic necessity and the need for self-actualization. Working-class women have always worked (because of economic necessity) but, in the 1980s, middle-class families have been feeling the pinch because male real income is no higher than it was fifteen years ago. Family income is falling at the same time new income demands on families are developing from the young and older generations. Government aid for education has fallen and older parents are living longer, requiring the support of their married adult children. But the solution often put forward, the return to the ''family wage'' so that the male ''head'' can work and support his wife and children, has outlived its purpose. The working-class employed the family wage concept to resist the efforts of employers to use women and children to drive down the wages of men. The family wage constricted the possibility of men to be fulfilled in a human sense, because the family wage restricts their role to monetary providers and not nurturers. The family wage ideology (some analysts doubt it was ever used to set pay) justified the subordination and undervaluation of women's work, making it possible to drive a wedge between male and female occupations and pay. The family wage was a protection device, not necessarily a goal.[19] *Laborem Exercens* demands that an economic/political system allow for the reproduction of the family, time and resources to educate one's children. How home and market work is divided between family members is irrelevant so long as equity, choice, and cooperation are the ruling criteria.[20] Families lose time not because women are working but because real wages are falling and the

Table 3
Number of Hours of Work when Husband
is a Full-Time Worker

	All work		Housework		Child care & Hsld. repair		Market Work	
	W(ife)	H(usband)	W	H	W	H	W	H
Wife is Part-time Worker	56	64	24	5	13	8	19	51
Wife is Full-time Worker	71	65	20	4	8	5	43	56

(Source: Barbara Bergmann, *The Economic Emergence of Women*, Basic Books, 1986.)

commodity-content of life is increasing. As more women are working, families are using less time for parenting and home production. Please examine the above table and note how many hours of work are being taken up by market work.

Equity between men and women's share of house and market work will be difficult to achieve until women's wages are comparable to men's. Over the past decade women have had to work approximately 20 percent more hours to keep family income the same because men's pay falls. Families are working longer hours for less pay.

Shorter Work Week and Full Employment

If human dignity is achieved through enfranchisement, and in a capitalist society the major form of engagement is employment, then it follows that unemployment is a dangerous attack on human dignity. The post W.W. II period is marked by a government policy guided by a supposed trade-off between unemployment and inflation.

Inflation and unemployment have redistributive effects—some groups win at the expense of others. Knowing these effects helps us understand the policy choices made. Inflation erodes the value of currency; if you have lent money at a fixed interest rate by buying bonds or issuing a mortgage, inflation means you are paid back in less valuable dollars. Inflation hurts creditors, savers, banks and bond holders. Unemployment, on the other hand, holds down wage rates and creates conditions for profitability. Unemployment is used to fight inflation which is regarded by the Federal Reserve and wealth holders as a greater evil than unemployment. In fact, for some sectors—labor intensive industries—unemployment is beneficial.[22] Unemployment could be mitigated by work sharing and a shorter work week, but that would eliminate this source of downward pressure on wages.[23]

A shorter work week would reduce unemployment and place a higher value on time spent away from market work. These outcomes are consistent with the encyclicals' principles, as well as the technical requirement of an efficient economy. For instance, traditional capitalist firms will attempt to raise profits by lowering costs—usually labor is the most flexible—or raising prices. These firms are slow to innovate—that requires start-up costs. They would rather seek cheap labor. Short-term profits are helped, but productivity does not budge. Productivity improves when the same amount of goods is produced with fewer resources, not when one Michigan worker is substituted with ten Guatemalans or two Floridians because they are cheaper. Instead of improving productivity, a low-wage economy produces the reverse: it stymies innovation and causes social unrest.

An enfranchised working-class family needs resources: ownership, time, goods, and security. Despite the tremendous increase in productivity of U.S. workers over the last forty years, and the increase in automation, time has become more scarce, insecurity has increased, the standard of living for families has fallen. At the turn of the century a sixty-hour work week was common. Unions and state governments pushed hard for a forty-hour week—one policy designed to encourage employers to arrange forty-hour schedules was overtime pay. However, the structure of taxes, employee benefits, and a weak commitment to full employment, encouraged employers to employ few workers for long hours, instead of hiring many workers at shorter hours. Employers pay the bulk of hiring and training costs, and because the U.S. lacks national health insurance, employers' health insurance premiums and pension costs for each employee are estimated at 10-15 percent of pay. This raises the fixed costs for each employee, regardless of how many hours she or he works. Obviously, the more the employee works, the more hours she or he pays off the employer's fixed costs. Moreover, during slack times, an employee can collect unemployment insurance only if laid off completely.[24]

During recessions the uneven, inequitable and inefficient distribution of time in a capitalist society is seen easily. When unemployment rates are high the average work week increases. Since businesses pay the fixed cost, it is cheaper to lay off workers and overwork the remaining employees than to reduce the hours of work for everyone. In Germany in 1984 the powerful metal workers union struck for and won the shorter work week, mainly as a means to stem the increasing levels of unemployment.

Long hours of work are also explained by falling incomes. In a local factory in Indiana union workers accepted a 10 percent wage cut and their hours went up by 10 percent. Most workers in the plant work between forty-seven and sixty hours per week.

Indeed, if U.S. workers had been compensated for increases in productivity with time instead of pay, imagine what our culture would be like. Time-intensive activities would have been preferable to money-intensive activities, reading books more valued than watching T.V.,[25] walking in parks more valuable than Bahamian vacations, preparing food rather than microwaving frozen tidbits, parenting rather than day-care.

Phasing in a four-day work week or a six-hour day would require more employment and more pressure for government assistance to pay for training and social insurance. At the same time, more employment would expand the tax base and make it easier to pay for increased government expenditures. Unemployment and welfare costs also would fall. If the progressive income tax were reinstated, some of the new expenditures could be paid for by wealth holders and high-income families. For every 1 percent drop in unemployment the deficit shrinks by $20-30 billion.

More importantly, the reduction in unemployment would alter the strategies of U.S. businesses profoundly. Cutting labor costs and competing with more efficient and innovative competitors would require more ingenuity than using unemployment as a threat to sweat labor. We need a system that brings out the best from employers. Will this lead some employers to seek out low-wage labor in Mexico and other Third World nations—thus widening the gap between the First and Third Worlds? That is the question the next section discusses.

Worker Participation

The extent of worker ownership in the great "workbench" in the United States has a number of dimensions, and firms can be rated by the degree of worker participation—from no enfranchisement to full enfranchisement.[26] There are four levels of worker management: traditional hierarchical firms where workers have no representation; employee ownership (about 20 percent of employees work in firms with some employee stock ownership); union representation (17 percent of workers); employee ownership and management representation (about 4 percent of employees); and worker-owned cooperatives (a few thousand, mostly small firms). There are overlaps in each of these categories.

Unionization and worker cooperatives are the two most serious forms of worker participation. Worker representation through unionization is the most traditional method and is embedded in the U.S. system of industrial relations as a means to bring about economic democracy. The highest percentage of unionization was 35-39 percent in the 1950s and it has been falling ever since. Would reversing this deunionization result in an economic counterculture? How does unionization affect worker enfranchisement, productivity, inequality, protection of workers' rights? Union effectiveness depends on its bargaining power—determined by industry structure (greatly altered by conglomeration), extent of worker solidarity, and economic conditions.

During times of financial crisis companies usually will offer some participation scheme to the union in exchange for fewer work rules and pay cuts. Unions often balk, insisting they want to be represented in financial, marketing and investment decisions to forestall a crises. In 1981, United Automobile Workers made labor relations' history by negotiating a position on the Chrysler Corporation's board of directors for their president, Douglas Fraser. The precedent was not infectious. Unions perceive little gain for being a small minority on a company board of directors. The Eastern Airline machinists were represented on the board at the time of Frank Lorenzo's takeover of the airline in 1986. With hindsight, the union says it should have prevented the sale by buying the airline itself, or choosing a buyer. Representation is often an ineffective substitute for ownership.

The growing numbers of mergers and acquisitions have put jobs and unions in peril (90,000 jobs have been lost due to leveraged buyouts in the 1980s). Charles Craypo and Bennett Harrison, in separate studies, have shown that when firms are bought by an absentee owner the chances of plant closings and relocation rise.[27] This means lost jobs, lost union status and loss of community production. Even when corporate reorganization does not entail terminations, the indebtedness limits flexibility in downturns. A forthcoming General Accounting Office report shows that if a recession comparable to the one in 1981 were to occur in 1990, more than half the Fortune 500 companies would be in danger of bankruptcy because of their unprecedented levels of debt and low levels of productivity. A firm involved in a leveraged buy-out may regard any piece of a company as a candidate for ''milking''—a source of cash for the new parent.

The labor and financial problems caused by leveraged buy-outs and corporate raider management was demonstrated by the 1989 Eastern Airlines strike. Both a unionized workforce employed by a manager, and an owner who is dedicated to the community and the industry, are important dimensions for worker protection. However, hoping for good managers will not be enough of a guarantee that all costs paid by workers are considered and weighed by a firm's owners. Worker and community interests should be represented in investment decisions to achieve what is called, in *Laborem Exercens*, socialized capital.

Since both encyclicals insist on a world-wide perspective on any economic reform, any U.S. reform for a shorter work week or democratized investment must speak to the possible impact on the Third World. In 1983, the Bureau of National Affairs discerned a pattern in plant closings and runaways. The North was losing manufacturing to the southern part of the United States, but that move was only a step in the corporations' eventual move overseas. Capital is becoming more mobile and will seek the lowest labor cost. This mobility directly competes with labor in the U.S. and contributes to the developing Fourth World. The cost of moving a plant is low in the U.S. The tax code will subsidize new investment and the host states will offer land and training for the new workers.

Joe Miltimore[28] has documented the development of a hostile environment for worker-owned cooperatives. Access to financing is limited because banks blackball worker cooperatives and workers lack wealth to capitalize their companies. Legal restrictions regarding partnerships and liability, and the restrictions against unions becoming part-owners (because of the National Labor Relations Act ban against company unions) also discourage worker-owned cooperatives. Government policies to require employee-owned (ESOP's) firms (now a large and growing source of tax savings for corporations) to include worker representation to qualify for the tax savings would be a step in the direction of "socializing ownership." Credit policies and legal changes also could go a long way in nurturing worker-owned cooperatives.

An example of where government policy could have saved a community by encouraging worker ownership is found in the case of Youngstown, Ohio. In the late 1970s, Lykes Steel owned Youngstown Sheet and Tube Steel Mill and declared the mill was not meeting its profit requirements and the company was shutting it down. A union, church, and community coalition petitioned the company to negotiate a purchase by the coalition. A feasibility study was required for a loan and, at the last minute, the Carter administration refused a grant for the study. The last act of the owners reveals their judgment about the potential viability of the mill: they dynamited the blast furnace to prevent the mill from ever becoming a competitor. Clearly, capital might have been used productively by labor, but current property rights contravene goals for full employment and efficiency.

Conclusions

Worker dignity requires enfranchisement which requires worker participation, choice, equity, and full employment. This paper has shown how a shorter work week and greater worker participation in management would enhance the nation's dignity index by reducing unemployment and underemployment, and would place capital subordinate to labor, equalize the value placed on production, reproduction and social ownership. Dignity to U.S. workers must also entail just and equitable development in nonindustrialized nations. Weakening the ability to move capital to seek low-cost labor would prevent bidding global labor costs to the lowest level. Both encyclicals are, indeed, extraordinary economic tracts; would that this range of vision be embraced by world leaders.

Notes

1. John Paul II Encyclical Letter, *On Human Work (Laborem Exercens)*, September 14, 1981, p. 71.

2. I use the term "enfranchisement" to embody the emphasis in the encyclical letters on human need for connection to production and reproduction. To be enfranchised means to be working and engaged in that work, rather than merely attached to the material goods your wages can buy. Nonalienation requires participation in investment and labor process decisions and part-ownership of the means of production—your skills, tools, capital. An enfranchised worker can educate and maintain her or his family and living standards.

3. *Laborem Exercens*, p. 21.

4. John Paul II Encyclical Letter, *On Social Concern (Sollicitudo Rei Socialis)*, December 30, 1987, p. 72 ff.

5. Labor is not a unit of production. The hegemonic paradigm in economic theory in neoclassical economics characterizes labor as an input selling its services or "owners of input services." See Armen A. Alchian and Harold Demsetz, "Production, Information Costs and Economic Organization," *American Economic Review*, Vol. 52 (1972), pp. 777-95, for a classic neoclassical treatment of labor.

6. *Laborem Exercens*, p. 33.

7. The encyclical letter rejects what is called the economist version of history as materialistically based—it rejects the notion that history is explained by class struggle. The ultimate warfare between capitalists and workers is not seen as inevitable, so long as the workers are part owners and work is dignified.

8. John Paul II uses women as an example of home workers who are undervalued. The example's point is still made without the gender roles designated in the example. The letter equates nonmarket labor with remunerative labor. Since the work is given equal value, now men and women could divide the labor of educating children and working for wages, increasing dignity since it increases choice.

9. *Laborem Exercens*, p. 25.

10. *Sollicitudo Rei Socialis*, p. 23.

11. Michael Reich, "The Development of the Wage-Labor Force" in *The Capitalist System*, Richard Edwards, et al., eds., second edition, Englewood Cliffs: Prentice Hall, 1978, p. 179-184.

12. Clair Brown, "Consumption Norms," *Gender in the Workplace*, C. Brown and J. Pechman, eds., Washington, D.C.: Brookings Institution, 1987.

13. For a comprehensive review of federal, state and private forms of worker protection see *Protecting American Workers*, Sar A. Levitan, Peter Carlson and Issac Shapiro, Washington, D.C.: Bureau of National Affairs, 1986.

14. Teresa Ghilarducci, "Women, Jobs and the Minimum Wage" in *Taking Sides*, T. R. Swartz and Frank Bonello, eds., Guilford, Ct.: Dushkin Press, 1988, pp. 155-161.

15. See the *Federal Reserve Bulletin* of March 1986.

16. Howard Wachtel, "Capitalism and Poverty in America: Paradox or Contradiction," *American Economics Review*, Vol. 62, No. 2 (May 1972), p. 187-90.

17. Fred Block, Richard Cloward, Barbara Ehrenreich, Francis Fox Piven, *The Mean Season: Attack on the Welfare State*, NY: Pantheon Press, 1987. Thomas Byrne Edsall, *The New Politics of Inequality*, NY: W. W. Norton, 1984.

18. Samuel Bowles, David Gordon, Thomas Weiskopf, *Beyond the Wasteland: A Democratic Alternative to Economic Decline*, Garden Cliffs, New Jersey: Doubleday, 1983. Ernest Lieberman, *Unfit to Manage: How Mis-Management Endangers America and What Working People Can Do About It*, New York: McGraw Hill, 1988.

19. Jane Humphries, "Class Struggle and the Persistence of the Working Class Family," *Cambridge Journal of Economics*, Sept. 1977.

20. Lisa Sowle Cahill, "Women's Work, Family, Church and Society," Ninth Annual Moreau Lecture, Holy Cross Community of Kings College, Wilkes-Barre, Pa., April 13, 1988.

21. Clair Brown, "Unemployment Theory and Policy," *Industrial Relations*, Spring 1982.

22. C. Shapiro and J. Stiglitz, "Equilibrium Unemployment as a Discipline Device," *American Economic Review*, June 1984. S. Bowles and J. Schor, "Employment Rents and the Incidence of Strikes," *Review of Economics and Statistics*, 1987.

23. Juliet Schor, "The Underproduction of Leisure in Capitalism," paper delivered at the 1986 meetings of the American Economic Association in New York, New York.

24. Ronald Ehrenberg and Paul L. Schuman, *Longer Hours or More Jobs?*, Ithaca, N.Y., Industrial Relations Press, Cornell University, 1982.

25. William O'Rourke, "Morphological Metaphors for the Short Story: Matters of Production, Reproduction and Consumption," in *Short Story Theory at a Crossroads*, Susan Lohafer and Jo Ellyn Clarey, eds., LSU Press, 1990.

26. For a discussion of alternative industrial relations structures see Thomas Kochan, Harry Katz, Richard McKersie, *The Transformation of American Industrial Relations*, New York: Basic Books 1986.

27. Charles Craypo, "The Deindustrialization of a Factory Town in South Bend, Indiana: 1954-1983," in *Labor and Reindustrialization: Workers and Corporate Change*, Donald Kennedy, ed., University Park, Pa: Department of Labor Studies, 1984. Bennett Harrison and Barry Bluestone, *The Deindustrialization of America*, NY: Basic Books, 1982. Bennett Harrison, "Gulf and Western: A Model of Conglomerate Disinvestment" in *Labor Research Review*, Vol. 1, No. 1, Fall 1982.

28. Unpublished dissertation research at the University of Notre Dame.

Contributors

Ernest J. Bartell, C.S.C., executive director, Helen Kellogg Institute for International Studies, University of Notre Dame. Author: *Private Goods, Public Goods, and the Common Good.*

Robert Benne, professor of philosophy and religion, Roanoke College, Virginia. Author: *The Ethic of Democratic Capitalism: A Moral Dilemma.*

Richard T. De George, university distinguished professor of philosophy, University of Kansas. Author: *The New Marxism, The Philosopher's Guide,* and *Business Ethics.*

Teresa Ghilarducci, professor of economics, University of Notre Dame. Author of several articles on labor economics.

Denis Goulet, O'Neill professor of education for justice, University of Notre Dame. Author: *Participation: The Road to Equity in Development.*

Leslie Griffin, professor of theology, University of Notre Dame. Author of several articles on social ethics.

J. Bryan Hehir, counselor for social policy, U.S. Catholic Conference, Washington, D.C. Author: *Challenge of Peacemaking.*

John Langan, S.J., professor of Christian ethics, Woodstock Theological Center, Georgetown University. Author: *Nuclear Dilemma and the Just War Tradition.*

Dennis P. McCann, professor of religious studies, DePaul University, Illinois. Author: *Christian Realism and Liberation Theology* and *New Experiment in Democracy.*

Michael Novak, senior scholar, American Enterprise Institute, Washington, D.C. Author: *The Spirit of Democratic Capitalism* and *Freedom with Justice.*

377

James E. Post, professor of management and public policy, Boston University. Author: *Corporate Behavior and Social Change* and *Private Management and Public Policy*.

Ricardo Ramirez, C.S.B., Bishop of Las Cruces, Las Cruces, New Mexico.

S. Prakash Sethi, professor of business policy, Baruch College, New York. Author: *Up Against the Corporate Wall* and *Business and Society: Dimensions of Conflict*.

Paul Steidlmeier, professor of management, State University of New York. Author: *The Paradox of Poverty: A Reappraisal of Economic Development Policy*.

Lee A. Tavis, C.R. Smith professor of finance, University of Notre Dame. Editor: *Multinational Managers and Host Government Interactions* and *Rekindling Development: Multinational Firms and World Debt*.

Theodore R. Weber, professor of theology, Emory University, Georgia. Author: *Foreign Policy Is Your Business* and *The Pursuit of Peace*.

Preston Williams, professor of theology and contemporary change, Harvard Divinity School. Editor-at-large: *Christian Century*. Author of numerous articles on social ethics.

J. Philip Wogaman, professor of Christian social ethics, Wesley Theological Seminary, Washington, D.C. Author: *Quality of Life in a Global Society* and *The Great Economic Debate: An Analysis*.

John Howard Yoder, professor of theology, University of Notre Dame. Author: *The Fullness of Christ* and *The Politics of Jesus*.